MICROSOFT® PROJECT 98 FOR DUMMIES®

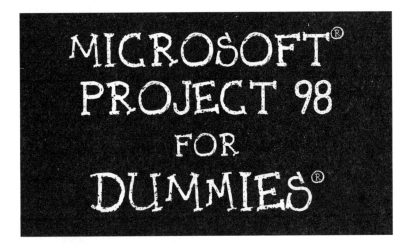

MICROSOFT® PROJECT 98 FOR DUMMIES®

by Martin Doucette

IDG BOOKS WORLDWIDE™

IDG Books Worldwide, Inc.
An International Data Group Company

Foster City, CA ♦ Chicago, IL ♦ Indianapolis, IN ♦ Southlake, TX

Microsoft® Project 98 For Dummies®

Published by
IDG Books Worldwide, Inc.
An International Data Group Company
919 E. Hillsdale Blvd.
Suite 400
Foster City, CA 94404
www.idgbooks.com (IDG Books Worldwide Web site)
www.dummies.com (Dummies Press Web site)

Library of Congress Catalog Card No.: 97-81230

ISBN: 0-7645-0321-9

Printed in the United States of America

10 9 8 7 6 5 4 3

1DD/SU/QT/ZY/IN

Distributed in the United States by IDG Books Worldwide, Inc.

Distributed by Macmillan Canada for Canada; by Transworld Publishers Limited in the United Kingdom; by IDG Norge Books for Norway; by IDG Sweden Books for Sweden; by Woodslane Pty. Ltd. for Australia; by Woodslane Enterprises Ltd. for New Zealand; by Longman Singapore Publishers Ltd. for Singapore, Malaysia, Thailand, and Indonesia; by Simron Pty. Ltd. for South Africa; by Toppan Company Ltd. for Japan; by Distribuidora Cuspide for Argentina; by Livraria Cultura for Brazil; by Ediciencia S.A. for Ecuador; by Addison-Wesley Publishing Company for Korea; by Ediciones ZETA S.C.R. Ltda. for Peru; by WS Computer Publishing Corporation, Inc., for the Philippines; by Unalis Corporation for Taiwan; by Contemporanea de Ediciones for Venezuela; by Computer Book & Magazine Store for Puerto Rico; by Express Computer Distributors for the Caribbean and West Indies. Authorized Sales Agent: Anthony Rudkin Associates for the Middle East and North Africa.

For general information on IDG Books Worldwide's books in the U.S., please call our Consumer Customer Service department at 800-762-2974. For reseller information, including discounts and premium sales, please call our Reseller Customer Service department at 800-434-3422.

For information on where to purchase IDG Books Worldwide's books outside the U.S., please contact our International Sales department at 650-655-3200 or fax 650-655-3295.

For information on foreign language translations, please contact our Foreign & Subsidiary Rights department at 650-655-3021 or fax 650-655-3281.

For sales inquiries and special prices for bulk quantities, please contact our Sales department at 650-655-3200 or write to the address above.

For information on using IDG Books Worldwide's books in the classroom or for ordering examination copies, please contact our Educational Sales department at 800-434-2086 or fax 817-251-8174.

For press review copies, author interviews, or other publicity information, please contact our Public Relations department at 650-655-3000 or fax 650-655-3299.

About the Author

Marty Doucette is a designer and developer of interactive educational and marketing programs. In the past few years, he has produced and managed technical and managerial training programs for and with the State of Indiana, the Department of Justice, FEMA, the American Institute of Architects, Johnson Controls, the International Conference of Building Officials, and other Indianapolis, Indiana, area firms. Marty was introduced to project management in 1991 while producing a series of teleconferences with the Public Broadcasting Service. Marty resides with his beautiful wife Lorita and their four children, Nicole, Ariel, Lindsay, and Eve, in Indianapolis. You can e-mail Marty at `mdoucette@iquest.net`.

ABOUT IDG BOOKS WORLDWIDE

Welcome to the world of IDG Books Worldwide.

IDG Books Worldwide, Inc., is a subsidiary of International Data Group, the world's largest publisher of computer-related information and the leading global provider of information services on information technology. IDG was founded more than 25 years ago and now employs more than 8,500 people worldwide. IDG publishes more than 275 computer publications in over 75 countries (see listing below). More than 60 million people read one or more IDG publications each month.

Launched in 1990, IDG Books Worldwide is today the #1 publisher of best-selling computer books in the United States. We are proud to have received eight awards from the Computer Press Association in recognition of editorial excellence and three from *Computer Currents*' First Annual Readers' Choice Awards. Our best-selling *...For Dummies*® series has more than 30 million copies in print with translations in 30 languages. IDG Books Worldwide, through a joint venture with IDG's Hi-Tech Beijing, became the first U.S. publisher to publish a computer book in the People's Republic of China. In record time, IDG Books Worldwide has become the first choice for millions of readers around the world who want to learn how to better manage their businesses.

Our mission is simple: Every one of our books is designed to bring extra value and skill-building instructions to the reader. Our books are written by experts who understand and care about our readers. The knowledge base of our editorial staff comes from years of experience in publishing, education, and journalism — experience we use to produce books for the '90s. In short, we care about books, so we attract the best people. We devote special attention to details such as audience, interior design, use of icons, and illustrations. And because we use an efficient process of authoring, editing, and desktop publishing our books electronically, we can spend more time ensuring superior content and spend less time on the technicalities of making books.

You can count on our commitment to deliver high-quality books at competitive prices on topics you want to read about. At IDG Books Worldwide, we continue in the IDG tradition of delivering quality for more than 25 years. You'll find no better book on a subject than one from IDG Books Worldwide.

John Kilcullen
CEO
IDG Books Worldwide, Inc.

Steven Berkowitz
President and Publisher
IDG Books Worldwide, Inc.

Eighth Annual Computer Press Awards 1992

Ninth Annual Computer Press Awards 1993

Tenth Annual Computer Press Awards 1994

Eleventh Annual Computer Press Awards 1995

IDG Books Worldwide, Inc., is a subsidiary of International Data Group, the world's largest publisher of computer-related information and the leading global provider of information services on information technology. International Data Group publishes over 275 computer publications in over 75 countries. Sixty million people read one or more International Data Group publications each month. International Data Group's publications include: **ARGENTINA:** Buyer's Guide, Computerworld Argentina, PC World Argentina; **AUSTRALIA:** Australian Macworld, Australian PC World, Australian Reseller News, Computerworld, IT Casebook, Network World, Publish, Webmaster; **AUSTRIA:** Computerwelt Osterreich, Networks Austria, PC Tip Austria; **BANGLADESH:** PC World Bangladesh; **BELARUS:** PC World Belarus; **BELGIUM:** Data News; **BRAZIL:** Annuário de Informática, Computerworld, Connections, Macworld, PC Player, PC World, Publish, Reseller News, Supergamepower; **BULGARIA:** Computerworld Bulgaria, Network World Bulgaria, PC & MacWorld Bulgaria; **CANADA:** CIO Canada, Client/Server World, ComputerWorld Canada, InfoWorld Canada, NetworkWorld Canada, WebWorld; **CHILE:** Computerworld Chile, PC World Chile; **COLOMBIA:** Computerworld Colombia, PC World Colombia; **COSTA RICA:** PC World Centro America; **THE CZECH AND SLOVAK REPUBLICS:** Computerworld Czechoslovakia, Macworld Czech Republic, PC World Czechoslovakia; **DENMARK:** Communications World Danmark, Computerworld Danmark, Macworld Danmark, PC World Danmark, Techworld Denmark; **DOMINICAN REPUBLIC:** PC World Republica Dominicana; **ECUADOR:** PC World Ecuador; **EGYPT:** Computerworld Middle East, PC World Middle East; **EL SALVADOR:** PC World Centro America; **FINLAND:** MikroPC, Tietoverkko, Tietoviikko; **FRANCE:** Distributique, Hebdo, Info PC, Le Monde Informatique, Macworld, Reseaux & Telecoms, WebMaster France; **GERMANY:** Computer Partner, Computerwoche, Computerwoche Extra, Computerwoche FOCUS, Global Online, Macwelt, PC Welt; **GREECE:** Amiga Computing, GamePro Greece, Multimedia World; **GUATEMALA:** PC World Centro America; **HONDURAS:** PC World Centro America; **HONG KONG:** Computerworld Hong Kong, PC World Hong Kong, Publish in Asia; **HUNGARY:** ABCD CD-ROM, Computerworld Szamitastechnika, Internetto online Magazine, PC World Hungary, PC-X Magazin Hungary; **ICELAND:** Tolvuheimur PC World Island; **INDIA:** Information Communications World, Information Systems Computerworld, PC World India, Publish in Asia; **INDONESIA:** InfoKomputer PC World, Komputek Computerworld, Publish in Asia; **IRELAND:** ComputerScope, PC Live!; **ISRAEL:** Macworld Israel, People & Computers/Computerworld; **ITALY:** Computerworld Italia, Macworld Italia, Networking Italia, PC World Italia; **JAPAN:** DTP World, Macworld Japan, Nikkei Personal Computing, OS/2 World Japan, SunWorld Japan, Windows NT World, Windows World Japan; **KENYA:** PC World East African; **KOREA:** Hi-Tech Information, Macworld Korea, PC World Korea; **MACEDONIA:** PC World Macedonia; **MALAYSIA:** Computerworld Malaysia, PC World Malaysia, Publish in Asia; **MALTA:** PC World Malta; **MEXICO:** Computerworld Mexico, PC World Mexico; **MYANMAR:** PC World Myanmar; **NETHERLANDS:** Computer! Totaal, LAN Internetworking Magazine, LAN World Buyers Guide, Macworld Netherlands, Net, WebWereld; **NEW ZEALAND:** Absolute Beginners Guide and Plain & Simple Series, Computer Buyer, Computer Industry Directory, Computerworld New Zealand, MTB, Network World, PC World New Zealand; **NICARAGUA:** PC World Centro America; **NORWAY:** Computerworld Norge, CW Rapport, Datamagasinet, Financial Rapport, Kursguide Norge, Macworld Norge, Multimediaworld Norge, PC World Ekspress Norge, PC World Nettverk, PC World Norge, PC World ProduktGuide Norge; **PAKISTAN:** Computerworld Pakistan; **PANAMA:** PC World Panama; **PEOPLE'S REPUBLIC OF CHINA:** China Computer Users, China Computerworld, China InfoWorld, China Telecom World Weekly, Computer & Communication, Electronic Design China, Electronics Today, Electronics Weekly, Game Software, PC World China, Popular Computer Week, Software Weekly, Software World, Telecom World; **PERU:** Computerworld Peru, PC World Profesional Peru, PC World SoHo Peru; **PHILIPPINES:** Click!, Computerworld Philippines, PC World Philippines, Publish in Asia; **POLAND:** Computerworld Poland, Computerworld Special Report Poland, Cyber, Macworld Poland, Networld Poland, PC World Komputer; **PORTUGAL:** Cerebro/PC World, Computerworld/Correio Informático, Dealer World Portugal, Mac*In/PC*In Portugal, Multimedia World; **PUERTO RICO:** PC World Puerto Rico; **ROMANIA:** Computerworld Romania, PC World Romania, Telecom Romania; **RUSSIA:** Computerworld Russia, Mir PK, Publish, Seti; **SINGAPORE:** Computerworld Singapore, PC World Singapore, Publish in Asia; **SLOVENIA:** Monitor; **SOUTH AFRICA:** Computing SA, Network World SA, Software World SA; **SPAIN:** Communicaciones World España, Computerworld España, Dealer World España, Macworld España, PC World España; **SRI LANKA:** Infolink PC World; **SWEDEN:** CAP&Design, Computer Sweden, Corporate Computing Sweden, Internetworld Sweden, it.branschen, Macworld Sweden, MaxiData Sweden, MikroDatorn, Nätverk & Kommunikation, PC World Sweden, PCaktiv, Windows World Sweden; **SWITZERLAND:** Computerworld Schweiz, Macworld Schweiz, PCtip; **TAIWAN:** Computerworld Taiwan, Macworld Taiwan, NEW ViSiON/Publish, PC World Taiwan, Windows World Taiwan; **THAILAND:** Publish in Asia, Thai Computerworld; **TURKEY:** Computerworld Turkiye, Macworld Turkiye, Network World Turkiye, PC World Turkiye; **UKRAINE:** Computerworld Kiev, Multimedia World Ukraine, PC World Ukraine; **UNITED KINGDOM:** Acorn User UK, Amiga Action UK, Amiga Computing UK, Apple Talk UK, Computing, Macworld, Parents and Computers UK, PC Advisor, PC Home, PSX Pro, The WEB; **UNITED STATES:** Cable in the Classroom, CIO Magazine, Computerworld, DOS World, Federal Computer Week, GamePro Magazine, InfoWorld, I-Way, Macworld, Network World, PC Games, PC World, Publish, Video Event, THE WEB Magazine, and WebMaster; online webzines: JavaWorld, NetscapeWorld, and SunWorld Online; **URUGUAY:** InfoWorld Uruguay; **VENEZUELA:** Computerworld Venezuela, PC World Venezuela; and **VIETNAM:** PC World Vietnam. 3/24/97

Dedication

To Jim Weaver because all environments can be made sacred, and to Jon Bereman because miracles happen when someone extends a hand to a friend.

Author's Acknowledgments

Although this book has a single author, many people have put long hours into its creation. This is an acknowledgement of just a couple of them.

My first acknowledgement is to my project editor, Susan Pink. Susan, thank you for the grace with which you took my midnight grumblings. With that said, I still say you are one of the pickiest, most demanding people I have ever met. In other words, you're great. You care about your work and you care about the reader.

And thank you Lorita. Twenty-nine years (not counting the courting) have come and gone, and you are more beautiful, more kind, more spiritual, and more fun today than on our first date — and that was some first date.
I love you.

Publisher's Acknowledgments

We're proud of this book; please register your comments through our IDG Books Worldwide Online Registration Form located at `http://my2cents.dummies.com`.

Some of the people who helped bring this book to market include the following:

Acquisitions, Development, and Editorial

Project Editor: Susan Pink

Senior Acquisitions Editor: Jill Pisoni

Media Development Manager: Joyce Pepple

Permissions Editor: Heather Heath Dismore

Technical Editor: Colin Banfield

Editorial Manager: Mary C. Corder

Editorial Assistant: Donna Love

Production

Project Coordinator: Sherry Gomoll

Layout and Graphics: Lou Boudreau, Linda M. Boyer, J. Tyler Connor, Angela F. Hunckler, Todd Klemme, Heather Pearson, Brent Savage

Proofreaders: Vickie Broyles, Kathleen Prata, Christine Berman, Kelli Botta, Rachel Garvey, Nancy Price

Indexer: Liz Cunningham

Special Help

Suzanne Thomas, Associate Editor; Joell Smith, Media Development Assistant; Stephanie Koutek, Proof Editor; Tina Sims, Copy Editor; Kathleen Dobie, Copy Editor; Access Technology

General and Administrative

IDG Books Worldwide, Inc.: John Kilcullen, CEO; Steven Berkowitz, President and Publisher

IDG Books Technology Publishing: Brenda McLaughlin, Senior Vice President and Group Publisher

Dummies Technology Press and Dummies Editorial: Diane Graves Steele, Vice President and Associate Publisher; Mary Bednarek, Acquisitions and Product Development Director; Kristin A. Cocks, Editorial Director

Dummies Trade Press: Kathleen A. Welton, Vice President and Publisher; Kevin Thornton, Acquisitions Manager

IDG Books Production for Dummies Press: Beth Jenkins Roberts, Production Director; Cindy L. Phipps, Manager of Project Coordination, Production Proofreading, and Indexing; Kathie S. Schutte, Supervisor of Page Layout; Shelley Lea, Supervisor of Graphics and Design; Debbie J. Gates, Production Systems Specialist; Robert Springer, Supervisor of Proofreading; Debbie Stailey, Special Projects Coordinator; Tony Augsburger, Supervisor of Reprints and Bluelines; Leslie Popplewell, Media Archive Coordinator

Dummies Packaging and Book Design: Patti Crane, Packaging Specialist; Lance Kayser, Packaging Assistant; Kavish + Kavish, Cover Design

♦

The publisher would like to give special thanks to Patrick J. McGovern, without whom this book would not have been possible.

♦

Contents at a Glance

Cartoons at a Glance

By Rich Tennant

The 5th Wave
By Rich Tennant
WHY DOGS DON'T USE LAPTOPS
THERE HE GOES AGAIN. I'LL BET IF I LEANED AGAINST A TREE, I COULD DO IT.

page 323

The 5th Wave
By Rich Tennant

"IT'S NOT THAT IT DOESN'T WORK AS A COMPUTER; IT JUST WORKS BETTER AS A PAPERWEIGHT."

page 219

The 5th Wave
By Rich Tennant
...and so, with a multifunction system like this, whenever you press the DELETE key, you...
OK - this seems like a good time to move on to the UNDO function.

page 305

The 5th Wave
By Rich Tennant

" RIGHT NOW I'M KEEPING A LOW PROFILE. LAST NIGHT, I CRANKED IT ALL UP AND BLEW OUT THREE BLOCKS OF STREETLIGHTS."

page 261

The 5th Wave
By Rich Tennant

"WHAT DO YOU MEAN IT SORT OF IS AND ISN'T COMPATIBLE?"

page 7

The 5th Wave
By Rich Tennant

"NAAAH - HE'S NOT THAT SMART. HE WON'T BACK UP HIS HARD DISK, FORGETS TO CONSISTENTLY NAME HIS FILES, AND DROOLS ALL OVER THE KEYBOARD."

page 285

The 5th Wave
By Rich Tennant
I TOLD you not to build him too close to the monitor.

page 49

The 5th Wave
By Rich Tennant

"HOW'S THAT FOR FAST SCROLLING?"

page 129

Fax: 978-546-7747 • E-mail: the5wave@tiac.net

Table of Contents

Introduction

Here's a scary picture. At this very moment, thousands of people are busily managing projects without knowing anything about the professional discipline of project management. This is a humongous crisis, folks! Well, actually, you know it isn't a crisis at all. You've been doing it for years.

You've probably performed a layperson's version of project management many times and muddled along just fine. You organized the plan, created a schedule, made assignments, and mothered the project to completion, sometimes even on time and under budget.

So why put yourself through all the trouble of figuring out a project management software program? Even more basic, why find out about project management? The answer is self-evident. Because you've managed projects before, you know there has to be a better way. You're ready to discover what all this project management hoopla is about, and you'd like to use Microsoft Project to do the job. You've just made two good management decisions.

Confidentially Speaking

Deep down, the first question you'd like answered is whether or not this is going to hurt. Between us, finding out about Microsoft Project is straightforward and kind of fun. You don't have to know anything special about computers or project management to begin. As you'll see in the upcoming chapters, a simple wisdom is evident throughout the software program. You're going to look very good throwing all those Gantt charts and reports around at the office. And what's really neat is that you can let people assume that it took grueling labor and a steel will to figure out the program. It's our secret.

Using This Book

As this book's title so subtly implies, the following chapters show you how to use Microsoft Project. But what the title doesn't say is that this book also gives you a basic explanation of project management. Two for the price of one. You are some manager!

So how should you read it? You can read this book in three ways. First, if you want to check out the basics of project management and then figure out Microsoft Project step by glorious step, start at the very beginning and read the book to completion.

As a second approach, you can skip the basics of project management. Start in Chapter 3, where the Microsoft Project stuff begins, and progress from there.

Third, if you're like many managers, you don't have the time for a full-course meal. You're lucky to get fast-food carryout. You can use this book strictly as a reference tool. If it's possible, though, Chapters 4 through 7 are best read in sequence. Other than that, smorgasbord to your heart's content.

As you read this book, you may notice that, whenever I specifically tell you to choose a command, button, or dialog box option, certain letters are underlined. You can use these underlined letters, known as *hot keys,* instead of clicking with a mouse. If you press Alt plus the underlined letter, you quickly activate the command, button, or option.

About the CD-ROM

In the book, I assume that you have Microsoft Project 98 and that you can use it as you read the chapters. The book is written in a way that lets you master your project management skills by practice. I've also provided a CD-ROM with a number of project files so that you can read the material and practice. (I tell you exactly when you can use the files from the CD-ROM.) At any time, you can use information in your own project instead of practicing with the sample files.

See Appendix B for instructions about using the sample project files and for information about other valuable tools and information you'll find on the CD-ROM.

How This Book Is Organized

This book has eight parts. Each part is a logical grouping of chapters, with each chapter focusing on a major point about project management or Microsoft Project. The chapters are kept as brief as possible without sacrificing important details.

In each chapter, individual sections describe a specific function. Navigating the chapters' headings, you can easily find an explanation or specific information you need.

Part I: Basic Project Stuff

Starting at the beginning is often the right place for most of us. Quite frankly, there's nothing embarrassing about asking a question like "What's a project?" Most people may be surprised by the answer.

To go anywhere with project management, you must have a plan, know some basic project management principles, and know how to get around in Microsoft Project. In this part, you check out your knowledge of project planning, you find out about the three basic ingredients of project management, and you see how Microsoft Project works to provide you with information.

Part II: Putting Your Project Together

Part I shows you what you need to know to begin a project. Part II shows you how to enter the information into Microsoft Project. In this part, you create tasks and set their duration. You customize the work calendar or make multiple work calendars for different groups. You create a schedule of events and define the relationships of the tasks in the schedule. You create deadlines and determine where you can permit slack. You identify who is going to do what for how much and when. Your project manager muscles start to show a little tone. You're ready to strut around in Microsoft Project.

Part III: Viewing Your Project

The place where your work starts to pay dividends is the use of project views. How much work is assigned to each resource? Which tasks are critical? How can you find a specific piece or group of information and exclude unrelated information? In Part III, you become familiar with the multitude of ways that Microsoft Project can organize and calculate your information. Searching and sorting information is surprisingly simple after you get the hang of it, and it's where you start realizing how smart you're getting to be with this project management stuff.

Part IV: Making Project 98 Work for You

After you enter the project information and find out how to view tables, charts, and forms, you're ready to trim the fat and build up areas of weakness. Is anything overbudgeted? How can costs be reduced? Is the schedule tight? Are resources being used in the best manner? In Part IV, you get to tweak and poke and test and mold till you're satisfied that you have a project that's ready to fly.

Part V: Project Management

When the project is off the ground, you keep it on course with Microsoft Project's tracking tools. Compare the actual course of events against the original plan. Update the project with up-to-the-moment status reports. Analyze variances in cost or work or time. Create interim plans. Customize your work environment to better suit your style and needs.

Part VI: Telling the World How It's Going

Ready to flaunt your expertise a little? Microsoft Project provides all kinds of nifty ways to communicate project status. In Part VI, you print views and reports. You find out how to isolate specific resource information. You turn your information into graphs and charts. And you say it all in different kinds of reports. What's more, if you don't like the options available to you, you can customize your presentation. You're wearing your project manager status well — it looks good on you.

Part VII: The Part of Tens

Part VII takes you to the toolshed and out on the highways and byways. You find out about the many Microsoft Project toolbars and you discover various services for your continuing growth as a project manager. If you're interested, this could even be a new career path.

Part VIII: Appendixes

The final part provides some basics about using data from other applications in Microsoft Project. I also show you how to load the sample project files from the *Microsoft Project 98 For Dummies* CD-ROM.

Icons Used in This Book

This icon signals something technically wild and wonderful (if you're into technospeak). It may be interesting and useful to you, but it's not essential to doing business in Microsoft Project.

Here's a friendly little shortcut on your road to project management success. This icon usually tells you a way to do your work more easily or more quickly.

This icon tells you that the information is worth committing to one of your memory banks. Otherwise, if you don't recall it, you'll have egg on your face and on the keyboard. Don't worry, the book doesn't have many of these icons.

In some parts of Microsoft Project, a keystroke or a mouse click can take you to a point of no return. This icon warns you when you're approaching one of those places.

Once in awhile, you'll see this icon. I included some sample files and some great resources on the CD-ROM to help you be a little less busy and a lot more organized in your project management.

Where to Go from Here

Project managers are decision makers. Here's your first one in this book. You can begin with Chapter 1 or Chapter 3. Or you can smorgasbord. In any case, have fun.

Part I

Basic Project Stuff

"WHAT DO YOU MEAN IT SORT OF IS AND ISN'T COMPATIBLE?"

In this part . . .

Basic project management knowledge and skills are important. They're especially important if you're going to do project management. That may not be as dumb as it first sounds.

Part I covers three kinds of information you should know to use Microsoft Project successfully. First, you need to have a workable plan. Simple, you say. Well, maybe so. But then again, maybe not. You need a project plan that can face reality eyeball to eyeball. You need contingencies for the unforeseen. You need also to assess the strength of the support you have for carrying this project to completion. Okay, I'll lighten up. The point is, using Chapter 1 to define your project's scope and clarify your goals might be worth your while.

Second, some technical terms and skills are common to project management but aren't the type of thing you pick up around the water cooler. You might want to double-check your understanding of these terms and your ability to perform the tasks they define. This part prepares you for things such as project phases and tasks, durations and task relationships, and resources and work.

Third, make sure that you understand some of the inner workings of Windows 95, how to run Microsoft Project, the use of the keyboard and the mouse, and the overall Microsoft Project environment.

Chapter 1

Basic Project Management

In This Chapter

- Finding out that your problems are actually projects
- Applying principles of project management
- Encountering the phases of your project
- Discovering the seven steps of an effective project plan
- Understanding commonsense project management concepts

My first exposure to the basics of project management showed me things I could do right away to improve my performance as a manager. All it took was embracing the discipline and putting the principles into practice.

Projects are as old as Noah's first shipbuilding contract, but project management is a dynamic, relatively young field — as in the latter half of this century. Project management has been around long enough, however, to have some proven, widely applied terms and practices that are insightful and logical. And, perhaps most important, Microsoft Project is based on them.

This chapter gives you some important background information, definitions, and explanations about project management. Hey! Don't break out the caffeine! A lot of this is interesting — and all of it is useful. In fact, you can start your project as you read this chapter. The *Microsoft Project 98 For Dummies* CD-ROM contains some useful evaluation forms. Using these forms, you can directly apply your insight into the building of your project.

As Complicated as You Need

If you're new to project management, you may be wondering just how complicated all this project management stuff is going to be. The answer may seem odd at first. Project management (and Microsoft Project) is as complicated as you need it to be. If you want to use Microsoft Project to plan and manage a snipe hunt, it's not complicated at all. If you need Microsoft Project to organize and manage an expedition to find the Sasquatch, you'll find that it can handle the complexities of even the largest quest.

This chapter is called "Basic Project Management" because it helps you with the fundamentals. For those who want to make project management a career, I include references to organizations dedicated to helping you do just that. (See Chapter 22.) But this chapter and this book aim at another goal: to help you understand and use Microsoft Project immediately and successfully as you manage your projects. To begin, you need to know what makes up a project.

Defining Your Project

Maybe the easiest way to define a project is to begin by saying what it isn't. Forgive my over-generalization, but a project isn't something you normally do. Project managers call the work you normally do *operations.* Work you don't normally do is often called a *project.*

For example, I usually spend my time sitting at a computer performing my normal work operations — writing letters, sending invoices, receiving phone calls, and so forth. That's normal operation. Today is different. I'm sitting at the same computer, doing what appears to be the same things, but I'm performing a project. I'm writing a book.

For work to be considered a project, it must meet four criteria. A project is *temporary, unique,* a *creation,* and a *product.*

Temporary

By definition, your project is *temporary.* It has a beginning and an end. It is not a place where you can hang your hat until the golden years.

Continuing with the book example, my project had a definite beginning with the submittal of the proposal to the publisher. This book project ends (for me) when it's approved in its final version for publication by or before the deadline.

A project is temporary also in that it usually involves a project team that exists for the sole purpose of the project.

Throughout this chapter, I ask some questions to help you define your project. If you want, answer them in your head or, better yet, complete the related form on the CD-ROM. Your answers to many of these questions will have a direct effect on the efficiency and outcome of your project.

ON THE CD

You can read the suggestions in this chapter and at the same time begin work on your project. Do this by using either Microsoft Word or WordPerfect to open `Defining.doc` or `Defining.wpd`, respectively, in the forms folder of the *Microsoft Project 98 For Dummies* CD-ROM. The Defining form is written to compliment the sections of this chapter. You may find it helpful to complete the Defining form and print it as a reference tool for upcoming tasks. You may want to print additional copies of the form for your team members. (See Figure 1-1.)

Questions:

Can you define your project's beginning and end?

When does your responsibility start, and what are the conditions that mark completion?

Who will you temporarily need for your project team?

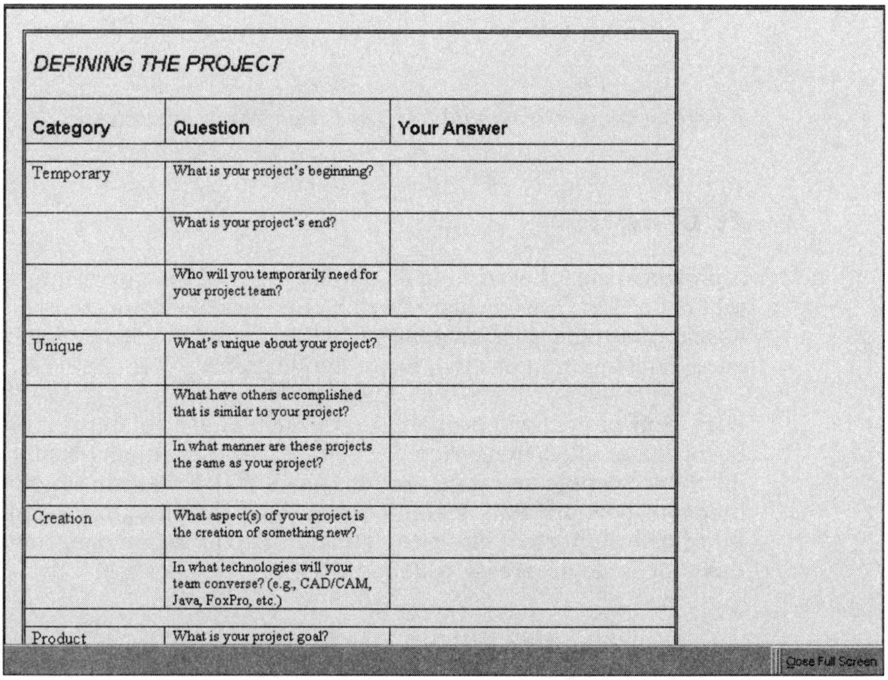

DEFINING THE PROJECT

Category	Question	Your Answer
Temporary	What is your project's beginning?	
	What is your project's end?	
	Who will you temporarily need for your project team?	
Unique	What's unique about your project?	
	What have others accomplished that is similar to your project?	
	In what manner are these projects the same as your project?	
Creation	What aspect(s) of your project is the creation of something new?	
	In what technologies will your team converse? (e.g., CAD/CAM, Java, FoxPro, etc.)	
Product	What is your project goal?	

Close Full Screen

Figure 1-1: The Defining form and other forms on the CD-ROM can help you and your team members begin the pick-and-shovel work for your project.

Unique

Your project is *unique*. Its characteristics and outcome are one of a kind.

Every project's product is different in some way from other products or services. If you're managing a project, you're developing something that hasn't existed before in just this way. It doesn't matter whether the project is engineering a Mars landing, planning a party, or researching a new strain of garbanzo beans. If it's a project, it's unique.

And so, using my book example, Dummies Press publishes oodles of fascinating and worthwhile books. But the *Microsoft Project 98 For Dummies* project has its own focus, deadlines, project team, marketing strategies, and so on. The product of this project is unique. And, carrying this further, books by other authors and publishers about the same subject are each unique in some way.

Questions:

What's unique about your project?

What have others accomplished that is similar to your project?

In what manner are these other projects the same as your project?

How are they different?

Are these similarities and differences strengths or weaknesses?

A creation

A project is an act of turning an unrelated set of resources into something that hadn't previously existed. I don't necessarily mean *creation* in a theological or artistic way. It's creative in that something is coming into existence. That creation has two major implications.

First, your project will probably go through phases of development to become a product or service. Second, because a project usually involves a number of people and organizations, each with a stake in the project's outcome, communication about your project's status throughout its phases is critically important and often difficult. The project management term for this process is progressive elaboration.

Progressive elaboration is the communication of a project's status in a manner that facilitates progress through the phases of a project. This can be tricky. The project manager has to communicate to the principals of a project in a manner that complements the unique technology and professional language of each. You use specifications to talk to engineers. You use models and simulations when talking to customers. You use reports when talking to investors.

I heard someone define writing as the act of pushing the pen into the unknown. Using my book example, the members of this project team and I are pushing this project through its stages of completion. Each stage has its expected product and a method of progressive elaboration for clear communication of the project's status. Microsoft Project is a wonderful tool to assist you in progressive elaboration about your project.

Questions:

What aspect of your project involves the creation of something?

What kinds of technology do you need to be conversant about in your project?

A product

A project's goal and only reason for existence is a *product* or service. The simplicity of this statement masks its significance. Maybe saying it as an equation will make it more obvious:

Project goal = product

Your project's sole reason for existence is its outcome. In the end, you and your adoring boss and coworkers will measure all of your project's value in the manner and to the degree that it accomplished its goal.

Questions:

How clear is your project's goal?

Is the goal attainable?

Does the goal need a reality check?

Defining Project Management

Consider your project's product or service as the project's target. Your goal is an arrow. The more carefully you craft a goal, the more likely its potential for accuracy of flight (see Figure 1-2).

Figure 1-2: William Tell of project management.

Two things are missing in this analogy: the bow and the archer. Consider your project team as your bow. The project team provides you the leverage needed to propel the arrow. Using the word *project* as a verb for a moment, your project team projects the goal toward its target.

The William (or Wilhelmina) Tell of this analogy is you, the project manager. The project manager keeps the goal (arrow) on course. If the goal is well-crafted and the project team has the resources to project the goal throughout its course, you, the project manager, become the key to hitting the target.

REMEMBER

Project management is the application of knowledge, skills, and tools to enable a project goal to hit its target.

As you'll see, Microsoft Project is a highly valuable management tool for you and your team. It helps you make sure that you have a good arrow, the right-sized bow, and a good target at which to aim. William Tell would be apple green with envy.

Projects Have Phases

It's time to leave the archery analogy to describe another important aspect of projects and project management. Projects have *phases*, as shown in Figure 1-3. Each phase has its own beginning, end, and desired outcome. All phases share the following traits:

- Each phase requires execution.
- Although the overall result of the project is a product, each phase has its own product, too. (The project management term for a product is a *deliverable*.)
- Each phase has its own phase-end review process.

A graphic representation of phases is repetitious cycles. A phase keeps coming back to a beginning point to move forward — like a wheel on an automobile.

Most projects have five to seven phases, but some have a lot more. Simple projects usually have at least three phases, as follows:

- Project planning phase
- Project execution phase
- Project closure phase

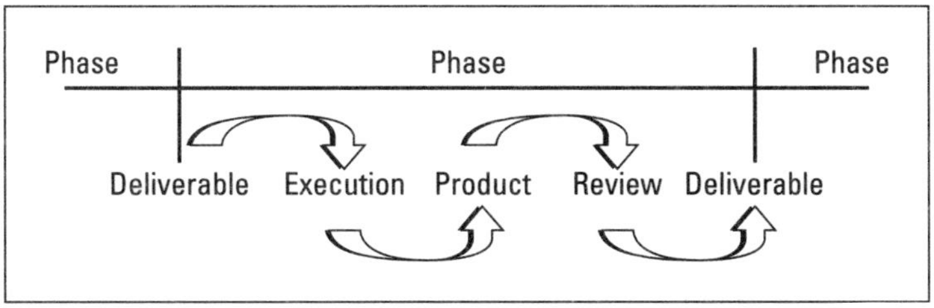

Figure 1-3: Each project phase is a cycle that builds on the deliverable (product) of the preceding cycle.

William Tell(s) about changing hats

If you are a project manager, you wear a lot of hats. Depending on the organization, in varying degrees you are responsible for the *development of the project plan.* This may include:

- Defining tasks, their sequence, and their duration
- Scheduling
- Resource planning (people, equipment, and materials)
- Organizational planning
- Cost estimating and budgeting
- Risk identification
- Quality planning
- Communication of planning

The project manager is responsible also for the *execution of the project plan,* which includes these tasks:

- Staffing
- Team building
- Contract administration
- Procurement
- Cost control
- Risk control
- Quality assurance
- Performance reporting
- Problem solving
- Change control

The *completion of the project plan* usually includes:

- Contract closures
- Administrative closures

In this simple example, the deliverable (remember, that's the project management term for a product) of the project planning phase is a plan. The project manager's job is to insure that someone is there in the second phase to translate the first phase deliverable (plan) in a manner that correctly continues the creative process through the second phase (execution), and so forth. Each phase ends with a deliverable that is the groundwork for the next phase to begin.

The deliverable of the last phase, the project closure phase, is the completion of the project. Upon review of all contracts and other administrative considerations, the bills are paid, the project team is disbanded, and the maintenance of the product is turned over to ongoing operations for the product's life. Although the product lives on, the project has ended. (In Chapter 5, you see how Microsoft Project uses phases to create task groupings.)

Microsoft Project is an excellent assistant during the project review and translation of each phase. Figure 1-4 is a realistic example of project phases, illustrating a more complex series of phases that build a successful project.

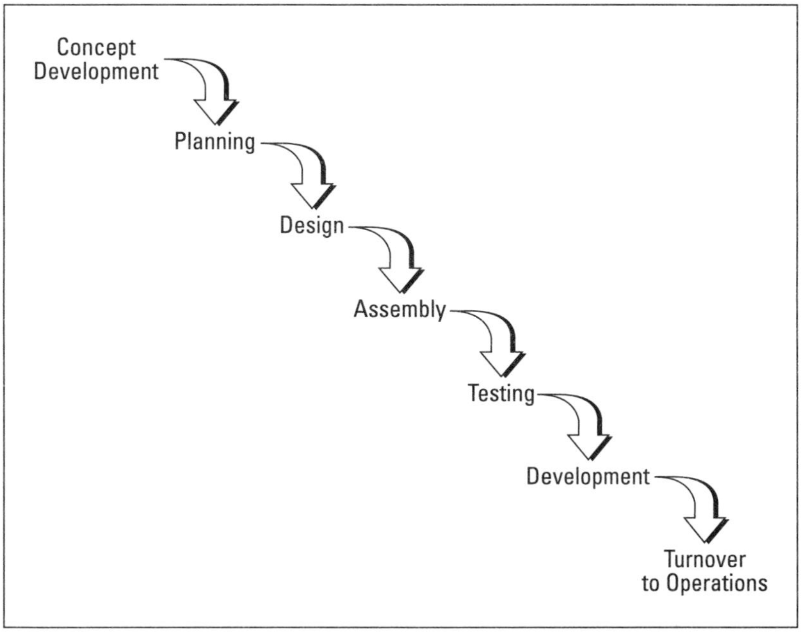

Figure 1-4: A project usually consists of several phases, each contributing to the successful overall outcome.

Seven Steps of an Effective Project Plan

Project managers are successful because they manage effective plans. Plans are effective if they are based on achievable goals. Well-developed plans and goals are like a high-octane fuel: They have all that it takes to keep a project engine running smoothly and efficiently.

What follows are some steps to better ensure the quality of your project and to prepare you for using Microsoft Project. I suggest you get paper and a pencil or open your word processor and answer the following questions.

The questions in this section are available also in a word processing file. To use the electronic form, open `7steps.doc` (in Microsoft Word) or `7steps.wpd` (in WordPerfect) in the forms folder of the *Microsoft Project 98 For Dummies* CD-ROM. Whether or not you use the form is your call. But please be sure to answer these questions. Although they're difficult to answer, in the long run you'll be glad you made the effort. (See Figure 1-5.)

SEVEN STEPS OF EFFECTIVE PROJECT PLANS (& ONE EXTRA)		
Category	Question	Your Answer
1. Scoping It Out	What is your project's scope?	
	What is the importance or need resolution of your project?	
	Who is your target customer, audience, or recipient?	
2. Identifying Stakeholders	Who are the stakeholders for your project?	
3. Determining the Quality	What are the explicit expectations about quality in your project?	
	Are there explicit expectations based on industry or government standards and regulations?	
	Are there any explicit policies?	
	What implicit expectations could affect your project?	
	What can you do to turn implicit expectations into explicit	

Close Full Screen

Figure 1-5: The 7steps form is a good tool for self-assessment and team building.

1. Scoping it out

A project's *scope* is a detailed description of what you are going to produce.

Questions:

What is your project's scope?

What is the importance or need of your project?

Who is your target customer, audience, or recipient?

2. Identifying stakeholders

Stakeholders are the organizations and individuals involved in or affected by a project.

Question:

Who are the stakeholders for your project?

3. Determining the quality

A business friend often says, "Anything worth doing is worth doing poorly." By this he means that if something is important enough to accomplish, it needs to be completed even if it falls short of perfection. Lowered standards may be acceptable in some situations but totally inappropriate in a lot of others. Everyone who has a stake in the project needs to agree on what yardstick of *quality* will be expected.

Questions of quality can be based on either explicit or implicit expectations. *Explicit expectations* involve standards overtly agreed upon by everyone involved. *Implicit expectations* are often the unwritten rules, opinions, and double standards that can turn a well-intended idea into a quagmire of inefficiency. Whenever possible, turn implicit expectations into explicit ones.

Questions:

What are the explicit expectations about quality in your project?

Are there explicit expectations based on industry or government standards and regulations?

Are there any explicit policies?

What implicit expectations could affect your project?

What can you do to turn implicit expectations into explicit expectations?

4. Listing constraints

Constraints are unavoidable time limitations imposed on your project. Typical constraints are deadlines or the availability of key resources or personnel.

Question:

What constraints can you identify for your project?

5. Fitting your organization's style

No project exists in a vacuum (unless you're planning a space walk). A project is never more important than the organization that supports it. But quite often, pressures within an organization can make a project tougher than anticipated.

Some organizations are function based; they have structures grouped by specialty, such as marketing, design, and accounting. Functional organizations are usually hierarchical. Each function has a boss, an assistant boss, and so on.

Other organizations are project based. They exist to perform projects. Most organizations exist somewhere between these ends of the continuum.

Questions:

From where or whom does your authority come for this project?

Does your project team have autonomy, or must team members receive approvals within their own hierarchy?

Is there agreement in your organization about your project goals?

Are there persons unrelated to the project who believe that they are stakeholders? If so, what will you do about it?

6. Facing risks

Risks are circumstances outside your influence that may have a positive or negative effect on your project.

Questions:

Are there any significant risks to your project?

If so, what can you do to prepare for their eventuality?

7. Setting goals

Using the answers to all these questions, set *goals* for your project. Make your goals detailed and as clear as possible. Write them in such a way that they will answer any major questions by stakeholders.

Question:

What are your project goals?

Commonsense Project Management Concepts

The primary concern of management is producing expected results. Although this may sound rather cold-hearted, some people skills are also fundamentally important to just about any management responsibility. These are often called *transferable skills*. As a project manager, knowing your relative strengths or weaknesses in these transferable skills is important. Very few people are strong in all of them.

Smart project managers know that the word *staff* should be taken literally — managers are expected to lean on their staff. Sharing leadership responsibilities can elicit strong character strengths from your associates. It's common sense that the project goal is more important than the pride of the project manager. This section introduces some transferable skills worth considering for your project.

Leadership

Leadership and management are not synonymous, but both are necessary. *Leadership* involves:

- Knowing and believing the vision — having a vision of where you're going and knowing what has to be changed to get there.
- Sharing the vision — communicating your goals and objectives so that they can be understood and acted upon.
- Bringing the vision to life — helping the project team own and interpret the vision in a manner that energizes them to overcome obstacles.

Communication

We measure *communication* by its effectiveness. Managing involves establishing and maintaining methods of effective communication. This often requires speaking and listening in the technical language of the stakeholder.

Negotiation

Negotiation is the grease that keeps projects moving smoothly. The ability to settle an argument and to successfully modify an agreement is critical to the success of most projects. Throughout a project, the project manager has to tweak plans to keep things on course.

Problem resolution

Problem resolution involves accurately identifying what a problem is and knowing what you're going to do about it. For some people, the problem-solving skill comes naturally and is an enjoyable part of their job. Other people hate any kind of confrontations or technical problems and will avoid them at any cost. A project manager needs to expect problems — they're part of the job.

Looking in the mirror and around you

Using your trusty pointing device and matrix tablet (formerly known as pen and paper) or your word processor, do yourself a favor by answering three important questions on the 7step form.

Questions:

What management skills are your strengths?

Would your associates agree with this?

What mix of people and skills are necessary for the proper management of your project?

Effective project managers share some important traits. Two of those traits are clarity about what they are going to do and a realistic awareness of what it will take to do it. After reading this chapter, you should be well on your way to exhibiting those project manager characteristics. A third important trait — the project manager's ability to identify and manage details — is the subject of Chapter 2.

Chapter 2

Tasks, Schedules, and Resources

In This Chapter

- Identifying major groups of related work
- Determining specific tasks in your project
- Setting the duration of time for tasks
- Marking milestones in your project
- Assembling and assigning resources to tasks

I'd like to begin this chapter by revealing something important about myself. I hate details. To me, details are crabgrass on the lawn of life. And this hatred of details makes me get warm and fuzzy about Microsoft Project. Whether or not I like it, the success of a project is in the attention given to details.

Identifying details is laborious. And managing the evolution of details in a project can be overwhelming. Fortunately, more than anything else, Microsoft Project is a powerful tool for identifying details, managing their relationship with other details, and tracking their evolution throughout a project.

Even on small projects, it's not possible or appropriate for the project manager to know all the details. But what is possible and necessary is to make sure that each detail is being attended to by someone.

Project management is a discipline that oversees the attention to numerous, often unrelated details in a way that ensures success. And success means that maybe you'll get that fire-engine-red Porsche for a Christmas bonus after all. Hey! Where does it say that project managers can't fantasize?

Stated briefly, here's what you need to know to handle details in a project manager sort of way. *Projects* are a series of small schedules (phases); these small *schedules* are groups of related tasks; *tasks* are individual items of work, each having a start and a finish (duration); tasks are accomplished by or with resources; *resources* perform work within allocated time and cost limitations.

Voilà! That's what a project manager does with details, and it's also a one-paragraph description of this book. For your reading pleasure, this chapter describes project management in a little more detail (ahem).

Starting with Categories and Phases

A good way to get to the details is by identifying categories or phases of a project. By *categories,* I mean things that naturally fit together. By *phase,* I mean a series of events that has to happen before another phase can begin. Table 2-1 lists some sample categories and phases.

Table 2-1 Sample Categories/Phases

Project Type	*Category/Phase*
Residential construction	Contract
	Design
	Lot preparation
	Footing and foundation
	Framing
	Electrical/mechanical rough-in
	Finishing
	Yard preparation
	Approvals
	Occupancy
	Contract completion
Video production	Contract
	Marketing
	Script development
	Graphics and animation development
	Preproduction
	Production
	Post-production
	Duplication
	Distribution
Event planning	Location preparation

Project Type	*Category/Phase*
	Award design
	Announcements
	Advance registration
	Catering contract
	Event management

On to Tasks

Categories and phases are helpful because they break the plan into major sections. Project management further breaks categories and phases into tasks. A brief definition of a *task* is a job that has a beginning and an end. A longer and more illustrative definition of a task is an element of work performed during the course of a project.

Tasks have a duration (a beginning and an end). Tasks may have a cost. And tasks have resource requirements; that is, someone has to do the task with something someplace.

Table 2-2 lists some samples of tasks for a residential construction.

Table 2-2 Task Samples

Category/Phase	*Task*
Contract	Customer selections
	Write specifications
	Write contract
	Signatures
Design	Plot plans
	Elevations
	Floor plans
	Mechanical plans
	Electrical plans
Lot preparation	Surveying
	Well drilling

(continued)

Table 2-2 *(continued)*

Category/Phase	***Task***
	Septic system
	Electrical service
	Natural gas service
	Excavation
	Landscaping
Footing and foundation	Footing
	Foundation
	Basement walls
	Basement drainage and floor
	Inspection
Framing	Wood framing
	Exterior sheathing
	Roofing
Electrical/mechanical	Plumbing lines
	Furnace and A/C ducts
	Electrical wiring
	Inspection
Finishing	Gypsum wallboard
	Stairway construction
	Painting
	Trim
Yard preparation	Sidewalks and driveway
	Landscaping
	Seeding
Approvals	Customer walkthrough
	Punch list corrections
Occupancy	Final inspection
Contract completion	Contract closure
	Administrative closure

Defining Duration

A brief definition of *duration* is the amount of time it takes to finish a task. A long definition of duration is the number of work periods it takes to complete a task. This does not include nonworking periods, such as evenings, weekends, and holidays. You can express a work period in minutes, hours, days, and weeks.

Using a simple example, you could measure a work period for carpenters in days. This measurement is based on a limited time period per day, such as 7 A.M. to noon and 1 P.M. to 4 P.M. In contrast, you may measure the duration for contract writing in hours.

Start estimating the duration for tasks when you create your project management plan.

As you'll see, Microsoft Project helps you keep track of task durations and judge their accuracy. Microsoft Project also helps you edit your duration estimates.

Table 2-3 shows an example of estimating duration as part of project planning.

Table 2-3 Estimating Duration

Category/Phase	***Task***	***Duration***
Contract	Customer selections	1 week
	Write specifications	1 day
	Write contract	3 hours
	Signatures	1 hour
Design	Plot plans	1 day
	Elevations	2 days
	Floor plans	2 days
	Mechanical plans	½ day
	Electrical plans	½ day
Lot preparation	Surveying	2 hours
	Well drilling	1 day
	Septic system	1 day
	Electrical service	1 day

(continued)

Table 2-3 *(continued)*

Category/Phase	*Task*	*Duration*
	Natural gas service	1/2 day
	Excavation	1 day
	Landscaping	1 day
Footing and foundation	Footing	1 day
	Foundation	2 days
	Basement	1 week
	Basement floor	1 day
	Inspection	1 hour

Defining Milestones

Perhaps you think of a mile marker when you see the word *milestone.* Or you may picture some great event, such as the first time you said the word *aluminum* correctly. In project management, both of these pictures are true. A milestone marks places in your project and denotes important events.

A *milestone* is the beginning or the completion of a significant event or series of events in a project. Usually, a milestone marks a major stage of completion in a project, often the completion of a deliverable. (Sorry I had to get technical on you.)

TECHNICAL STUFF

A *deliverable* is some outcome that must be produced as a stage of completion of a project. Examples of a deliverable may be a contract, an installed well, or an approved inspection.

Table 2-4 lists some planned milestones for a project.

Table 2-4 Planned Milestones

Category/Phase	*Task*	*Duration or Milestone*
Milestone	*Project begins*	*June 2*
Contract	Customer selections	1 week
	Write specifications	1 day
	Write contract	3 hours

Category/Phase	*Task*	*Duration or Milestone*
	Signatures	1 hour
Milestone	*Contract begins*	*(anchored) July 1*
Design	Plot plans	1 day
	Elevations	2 days
	Floor plans	2 days
	Mechanical plans	1/2 day
	Electrical plans	1/2 day
Milestone	*Plans completed*	*June 19*
Lot preparation	Surveying	2 hours
	Well drilling	1 day
	Septic system	1 day
	Electrical service	1 day
	Natural gas service	1/2 day
	Excavation	1 day
	Landscaping	1 day
Footing and foundation	Footing	1 day
	Foundation	2 days
	Basement	1 week
	Basement floor	1 day
	Inspection	1 hour
Milestone	*Inspection approved*	*(anchored) July 15*

In Table 2-4, note that the first milestone is the date when this project begins. Marketing dollars may have been invested, model homes built, and many hours spent by salespeople to turn a prospect into a customer. All of this may have happened before the first milestone. But as far as the project is concerned, its date of birth is June 2.

One of the desired outcomes of laying out a plan is to expose its seeming inconsistencies. For instance, look at the second milestone; the date (July 1) is later than the date of the third milestone (June 19). The design phase has to be incorporated into the contract phase so it can finish in time to be one of the deliverables of the contract phase. As you soon see, Microsoft Project is a whiz at keeping track of these kinds of complexities.

Observe, too, that due to the nature of the contract, the inspection milestone is a fixed, or anchored, date. The event can't be later or the contractor will be penalized. You can manage this easily with the assistance of Microsoft Project. You can associate some tasks to be dependent on the completion of others. You can assign other tasks to run concurrently. In the example, the well drilling, the electrical service, and the natural gas service can all happen at the same time.

Identifying Resources

Resources can be people and things. Who will do it? What equipment or facilities will be necessary? The identification, assignment, and management of resources are the trickiest part of project management. It's also one of the best features of Microsoft Project.

Using the residential construction example, Table 2-5 lists some sample resources.

Table 2-5 Sample Resources

Task	*Duration or Milestone*	*Resource*
Project begins	*Milestone: June 2*	
Customer selections	1 week	Sales, 4 half-days
Write specifications	1 day	Specifier, 1 day
Write contract	3 hours	Counsel, 3 hours
Signatures	1 hour	Sales, 1 hour, Conf. Rm.
Contract begins	*Milestone: July 1*	
Plot plans	1 day	Drafting, 1 day, CAD
Elevations	2 days	Drafting, 2 days, CAD
Floor plans	2 days	Drafting, 2 days, CAD
Mechanical plans	1/2 day	Contractor 1
Electrical plans	1/2 day	Contractor 2
Plans completed	*Milestone: June 19*	
Surveying	2 hours	Contractor 3, 2 hours
Well drilling	1 day	Contractor 4
Septic system	1 day	Contractor 4

Task	*Duration or Milestone*	*Resource*
Electrical service	1 day	Contractor 2
Natural gas service	1/2 day	Utility
Excavation	1 day	Contractor 5
Landscaping	1 day	Contractor 6
Footing	1 day	Contractor 5
Foundation	2 days	Contractor 5
Basement	1 week	Contractor 5
Basement floor	1 day	Contractor 5
Inspection	1 hour	City
Inspection approved	*Milestone: July 15*	

Although Table 2-5 is only one example of resource allocation, it provides insight into the type of project plan analysis you can make after you start plugging resources into tasks. For instance, look at the duration for customer selections. It's one week, but within that time only 4 half-days are set aside for staff input. A week is set aside to do tasks that are a few days in duration. This is a common situation.

Resources can be not only people, but also things. If something is necessary to perform a task, and if it's not automatically available, it can be included in the project plan. Using the preceding example, someone on the sales staff has to reserve the conference room for an hour on July 1. The room is used for many purposes by a variety of staff and customers. In such a situation, the conference room may be a managed resource.

Overallocation of resources is one of the most common problems in project management. As you allocate resources to tasks, you should double-check the availability of those resources and their commitment to other projects or operations. In the preceding example, drafting will devote 5 days within a 10-day period to this project. The builder may be wise to double-check the availability of these personnel to perform the tasks in the allotted time.

In addition to resource overcommitment to multiple projects, resources can also be overallocated in a single project. In our example, contractor 5 is responsible for 12 days of work in a 15-day period. You may need to ensure that the contractor has allotted enough labor and equipment to meet the milestone. To add to the concern, remember that foul weather is not reflected in the milestone.

Determining critical path

Two important scheduling terms of project management are critical task and critical path. A *critical task* is one that must be completed on schedule for the project to finish on time. If a critical task is delayed, the project completion date is also delayed. A project's *critical path* is comprised of a series of critical tasks. In Chapter 16, you use Microsoft Project to control critical tasks and critical paths.

Refining your project plan

By now, you've probably thought of some ways to develop your own project. Putting some thoughts together while they're fresh in your mind is a good idea. Here are some guidelines to help you:

1. **Identify the phases and categories of your project, using the previous examples.**
2. **Break your phases and categories into tasks.**
3. **Determine milestones and deliverables for your project.**
4. **Identify resources and their limitations.**
5. **Map the critical path of your project.**

So you have your phases. You've even broken them down (into tasks). Your durations are doable, and your milestones are reachable. You've determined the deliverables and identified the resources. You know the critical path and you've refined the project. Man! You are one serious project manager!

Chapter 3

Welcome to Microsoft Project

In This Chapter

- Get going in Microsoft Project
- What you see when you begin
- Using your mouse
- Selecting your tools from toolbars
- Getting help

Microsoft Project 98 is an easy-to-use project management software program. It's a member of the Microsoft Office 97 family and shares features such as toolbars, the Office Assistant (an animated help system), and Visual Basic for Applications (a sophisticated macro language) with other Office 97 programs. It's designed for use with Windows 95 (and higher) and Windows NT 4.0 (and higher) operating systems.

Even though Microsoft Project is easy to use, it is a powerful planning, analysis, management, and reporting tool. It gives you, your project team, and your stakeholders the ability to see both the forest and the trees of the most complex plans. With it, you can split a project into manageable parts without sacrificing or confusing relationships. It helps you identify risks and solve problems before they occur.

Starting Microsoft Project

I assume you've installed Microsoft Project 98 on your computer. If you haven't, don't cancel the rest of your year or anything. Installing the program is a snap:

1. **Click the Start button on your desktop.**
2. **Choose Run.**

   The Run dialog box appears.

3. **Type** d:setup.exe **and click OK.**

   If necessary, replace *d* with whatever your CD-ROM drive is. The installation wizard leads you through the rest of the setup. When you're finished, c'mon back!

To start Microsoft Project:

1. **Click Start (see Figure 3-1) on the taskbar at the bottom of the screen.**
2. **Click Programs.**
3. **Click Microsoft Project.**

Screens

When you start Microsoft Project, the Welcome screen appears, as shown in Figure 3-2. From here, you have several choices. You can:

- Learn while you work
- Watch a quick preview
- Navigate with a map
- Select an option to not show the startup screen again

TIP

The Navigate with a Map option uses an ingenious online graphical description of the process of building a project file. I suggest you look at the map now or at least remember that it's there for future use. Sometimes a map is all you need to keep your project on track.

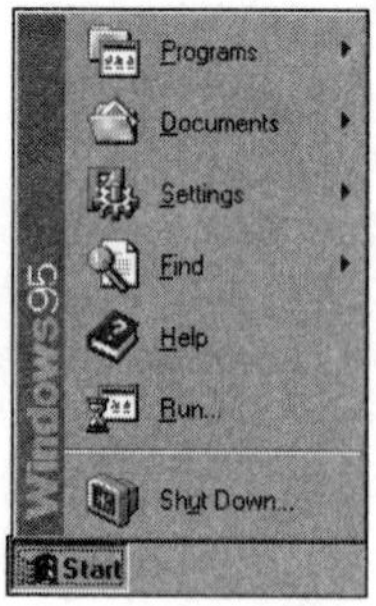

Figure 3-1: Click the Start button to begin.

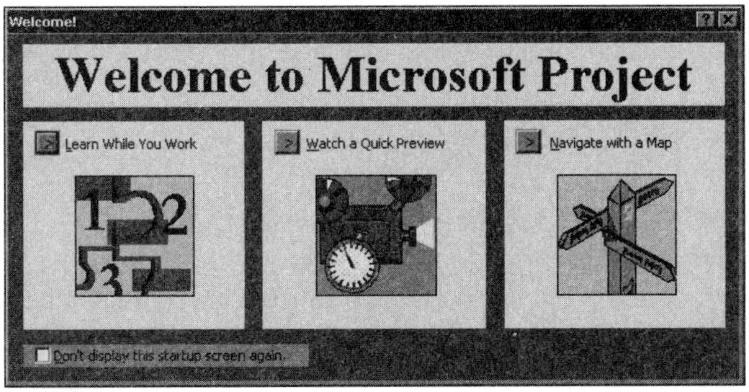

Figure 3-2: The Welcome screen is a helpful first view of Microsoft Project.

You may also appreciate the Watch a Quick Preview option. The Preview describes Microsoft Project in a nutshell. Like the map, a short tour can be a big help now and a refresher later. After you're finished, you can select the Don't Display This Startup Screen Again check box. Then select the X in the upper-right corner of the Welcome screen to close it. The default screen, or view, appears, as shown in Figure 3-3.

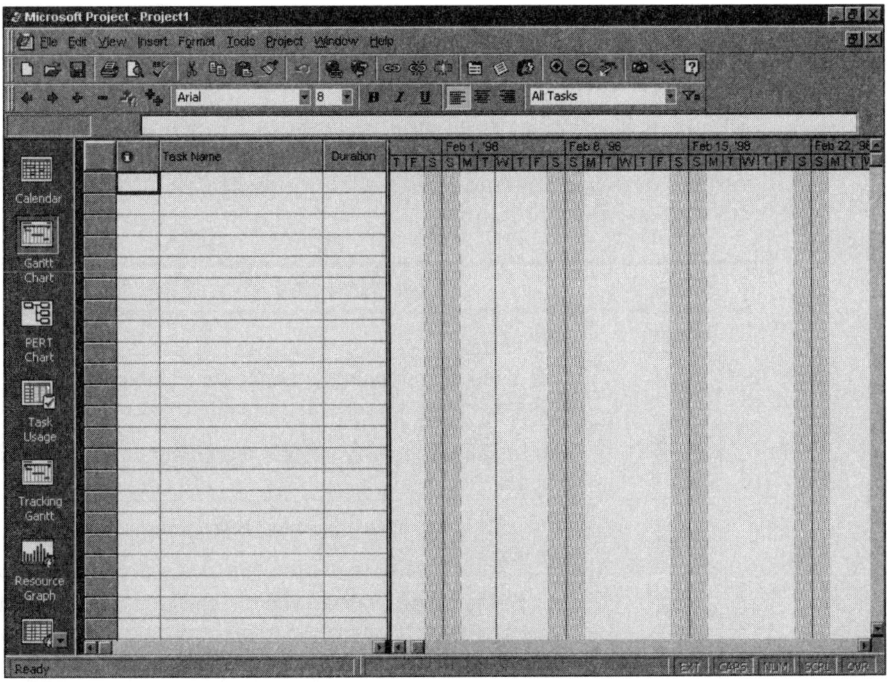

Figure 3-3: The Microsoft Project default screen is the Gantt chart.

A *view* is usually a chart or graph combined with a table and a filter. Using views, you can enter, organize, and examine information in a variety of formats.

Microsoft Project has three types of views:

- **Charts or graphs,** such as a Gantt chart, a PERT chart, a resource graph, or a calendar
- **Sheets,** which provide information in rows and columns like a spreadsheet
- **Forms,** which provide or solicit information about a task or a resource in a format similar to a dialog box

Microsoft Project's default view is called a *Gantt chart* (named after Henry Gantt, the person who first developed it). The default view, like just about everything else in Microsoft Project, can be changed.

To change the screen default, choose Tools➪Options. Click the View tab. In the Default View list, select a new default view and click OK.

A Cursory Look at Cursors

Microsoft Project has some unique cursors. They'll drive you bananas if you don't know what they mean. In other chapters, I discuss the significance of various cursor commands in detail. For now, Table 3-1 lists the different cursors and their functions.

Table 3-1 Cursors and Their Functions

Cursor	Function
	This is the default pointer. It appears all the time, except when one of the following cursors takes its place.
	The I-beam appears whenever the cursor crosses or rests in a text box.
	This pointer appears whenever the cursor is in the task detail area of a view.
	This pointer appears when you rest the cursor on the divider between parts of a view. You can then drag the divider horizontally.

Cursor	*Function*
	When the view is split by choosing Window➪Split, this pointer appears when you rest the cursor on the horizontal divider between parts of a view. You can then drag the divider vertically.
	This pointer appears when you rest the cursor on the edge of a column heading. You can then drag the column heading horizontally.
	This pointer appears when you rest the cursor on the line between rows in the Gantt chart. You can then drag the line to make the row height larger or smaller.
	This pointer appears in some views. It indicates that you can drag an object.

Double-clicking a portion of a view displays a dialog box relevant to the area you double-clicked. For example, double-click the task list area (the area where the plus cursor appears). The task information dialog box appears. Click Cancel.

Selection Bars

Microsoft Project selection bars (such as the title bar, menu bar, and toolbars) are similar in layout to other Microsoft programs, but they offer shortcuts to numerous features unique to project management. Maybe the best news is that you don't need a photographic memory or a degree in buttonology to use them.

The title bar

The top horizontal bar shown in Figure 3-4 is called the *title bar.* To the far left are the program's name and a Program icon for opening or closing the program. It's the same icon you'll find on the taskbar if you minimize the program. Next is the name of the current file. To the far right are the Minimize button, the Program window button, and the Close button.

The menu bar

The second horizontal bar, shown in Figure 3-5, is called the *menu bar.* The Resize window button controls the size of the current window, and the Project icon closes the current window. Both are labeled in Figure 3-5.

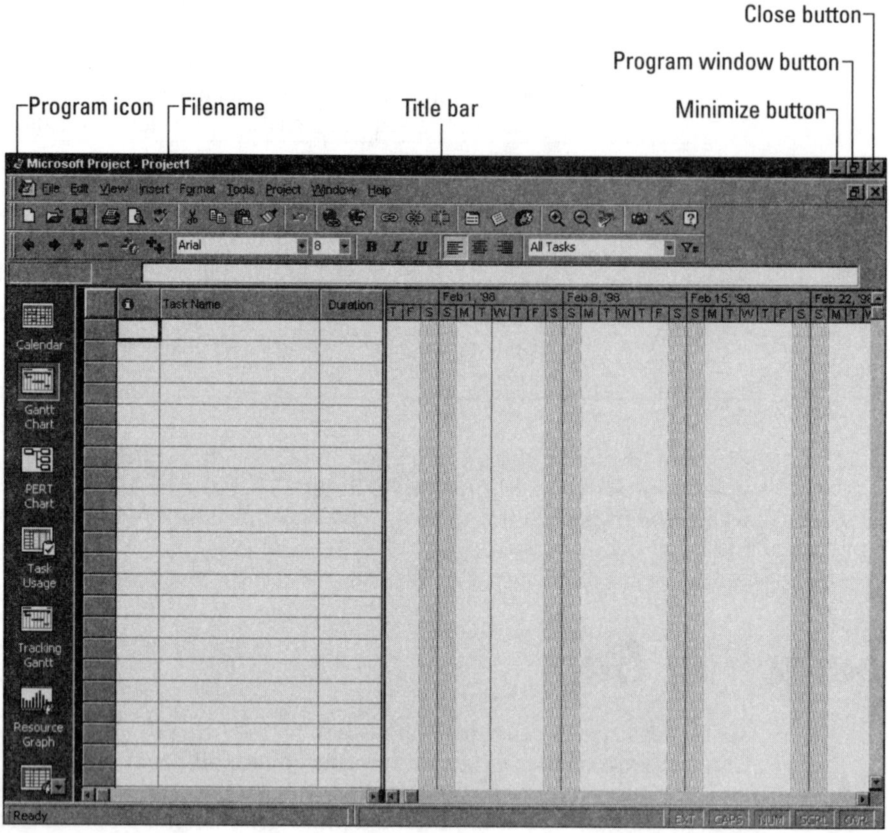

Figure 3-4: The title bar contains the project filename and window controls for the program.

Keeping Project from turning into a project

One of the strengths of any good software program is its ease of use. If it's designed well, you can concentrate on your work instead of on how to make the application function. The term designers use for the attention and vigilance you use to perform a task is *primary work.* The term for the attention and vigilance you use to make the software program function properly is *secondary work.*

As you can imagine, the greater effort expended to perform secondary work, the less vigilance and attention you'll have left to accomplish your actual job.

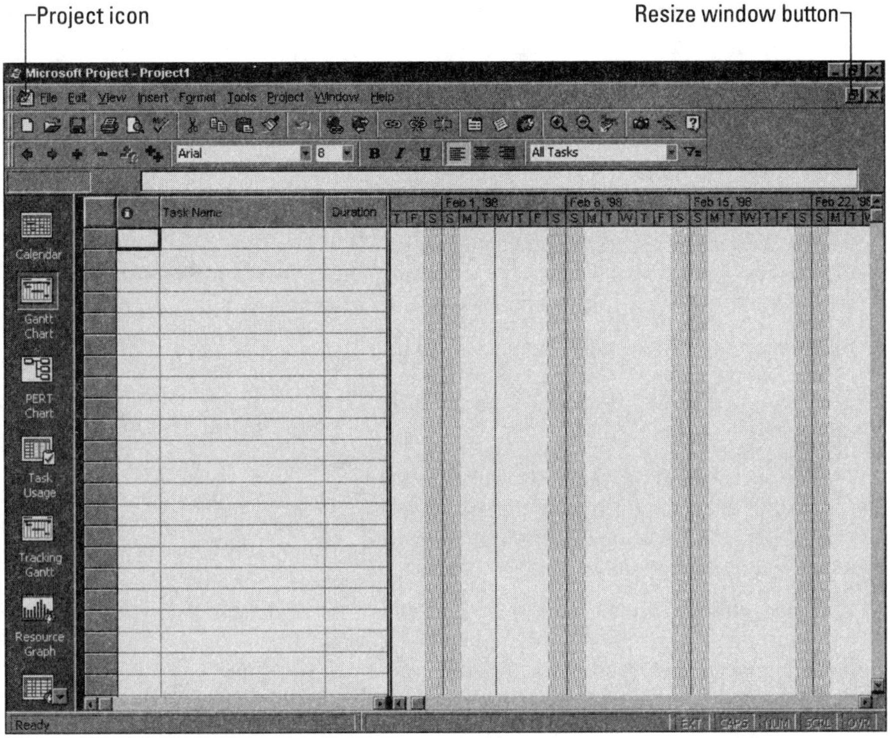

Figure 3-5: The menu bar groups related program commands into lists and sublists.

In Microsoft Project 98, you can load as many windows as you want. This enables you to work with or refer to numerous projects and subprojects at the same time, much like a word processor and multiple documents.

When you choose a menu item, a list appears. For example, choose Edit, and the Edit menu shows the possible selections, such as Cut Cell and Copy Cell. Note that some items are unavailable, such as Paste as Hyperlink, when certain criteria don't exist.

Now choose View⇨Calendar. The Gantt chart is replaced by a Calendar view. Choose View again. This time, the Calendar item has a check mark in front of it; this means that you are currently in the Calendar view.

Choose View⇨Gantt Chart again. The view changes back to its original view.

How Project 98 differs from earlier versions

Microsoft Project 98 has a number of new features and improvements that I describe in detail in other chapters. Here's an overview:

Task and resource usage views: You can now more quickly view resources and their assignments plus details of the costs or work-to-date of each resource. This is a nice addition.

Split tasks: You can now divide a task among resources and split a task in two on the Gantt chart. The task remains the same, but it is in portions with time in between.

Multiple critical paths: Although the Microsoft Project default is to display only one critical path, you can now display a critical path for each independent network of paths.

New and changed fields: Microsoft Project has increased its potential for specificity through the addition of oodles of new fields. (A field is a specific category of information, such as a start date, an actual cost, or a note.)

What-if analysis: Microsoft Project provides the project manager the opportunity to determine pessimistic, expected, and optimistic duration analysis.

Progress lines: You can create a visual representation of a project's status with progress lines on the Gantt chart. Progress lines are a kind of graph that points to the left for work behind schedule and to the right for work ahead of schedule. This improvement is a bit of a yawner— it just adds more lines to a Gantt chart.

Workgroup communications: Microsoft Project has some genuine communications improvements over previous versions. You can now send information to and receive information from team members through e-mail, an intranet, and the World Wide Web.

View bar: The default screen for Microsoft Project now provides a visual selection of views within a scrollable frame, much like frames on an Internet page. If you are unimpressed with this feature, you can hide it by right-clicking in the frame and deselecting the view bar.

AutoFilters: A hybrid of Microsoft Project filters, autofilters are visible in any sheet view. Each field in a sheet view has its own autofilter. The AutoFilter icon rests on the formatting toolbar, to the right of the filter text box.

The standard toolbar

The third horizontal row in Figure 3-6 is the *standard toolbar*. The toolbar contains most of the buttons necessary for performing basic functions in Microsoft Project.

Microsoft Project offers additional toolbars, which I describe in other chapters. These additional toolbars don't replace the standard toolbar. To add a toolbar, right-click anywhere on the toolbar and make your selection. To remove the additional toolbar, right-click anywhere on the toolbar and select from the shortcut menu the toolbar you want to remove.

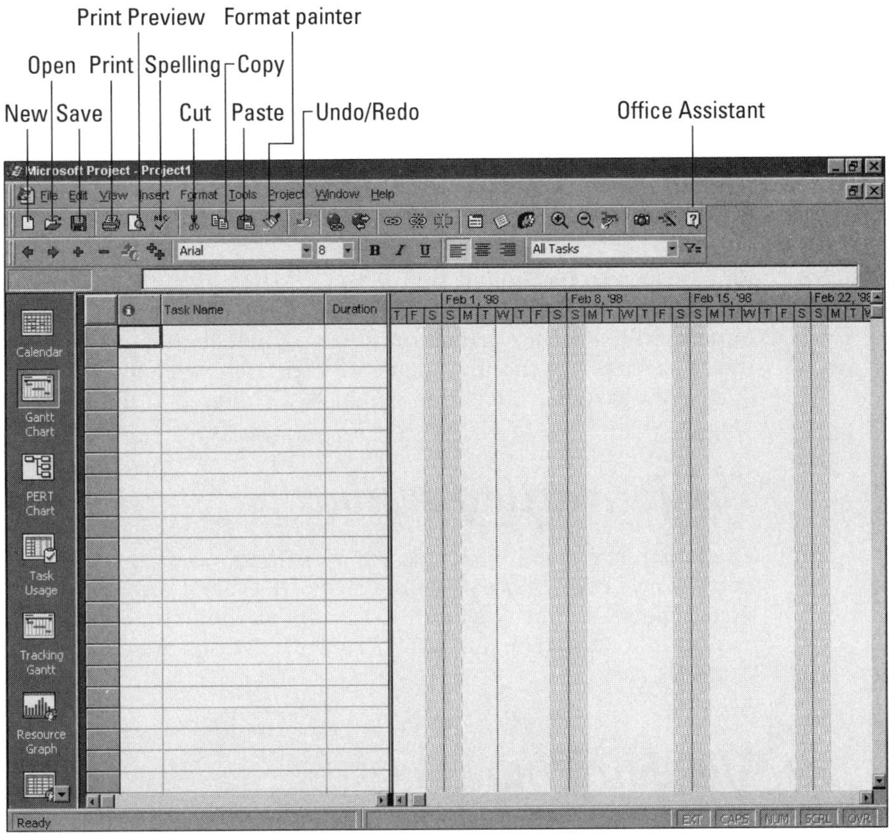

Figure 3-6: The standard toolbar displays the most commonly used commands.

The 11 buttons on the left of the standard toolbar and the one on the far right are common to most Microsoft Office applications:

New	Opens a new project window
Open	Opens the default or current folder
Save	Saves the active project
Print	Prints a copy of the active project with current print settings
Print Preview	Shows how the printed document will look
Spelling	Provides a spell check of your active project
Cut	Cuts a selection and puts it onto the Clipboard
Copy	Copies a selection
Paste	Pastes from the Clipboard, replacing the selection

Format painter	Copies and applies text format
Undo/Redo	Undoes or redoes the last command (unlike Word, Excel, and PowerPoint, which have separate Undo and Redo buttons)
Office Assistant	Opens Microsoft Project Help Topics

The other buttons on the standard toolbar are unique to Microsoft Project.

When you select a toolbar button to perform a basic operation, you don't have a choice of settings. For instance, if you click the Print button, the print options will be either default ones or your latest changes. You don't have the opportunity to modify the print properties. In contrast, if you choose File⇨Print from the menu bar, you have a choice of print properties.

The formatting toolbar

The fourth horizontal bar in Figure 3-7 is the *formatting toolbar.* The six buttons and two list boxes on the right are typical word processing selections. The seven buttons and the list box on the left are unique to Microsoft Project functions. The Microsoft Project functions are described in later chapters.

The entry bar

The empty bar between the formatting toolbar and the Gantt chart is the entry bar. The entry bar is an editing tool for writing or editing the contents of project tables and sheets. One use for the entry bar is for writing or modifying task names.

The view bar

The vertical bar on the left is the view bar. The view bar is a handy way to quickly change (you guessed it) views of your project. For example, click the Calendar button. The window now looks like a normal monthly calendar and is called the Calendar view. Click the Gantt Chart button, and the window returns to the Gantt Chart view.

You can hide the view bar by choosing View⇨View Bar, or by right-clicking in the view bar and choosing View Bar. For more on views, see Chapter 8.

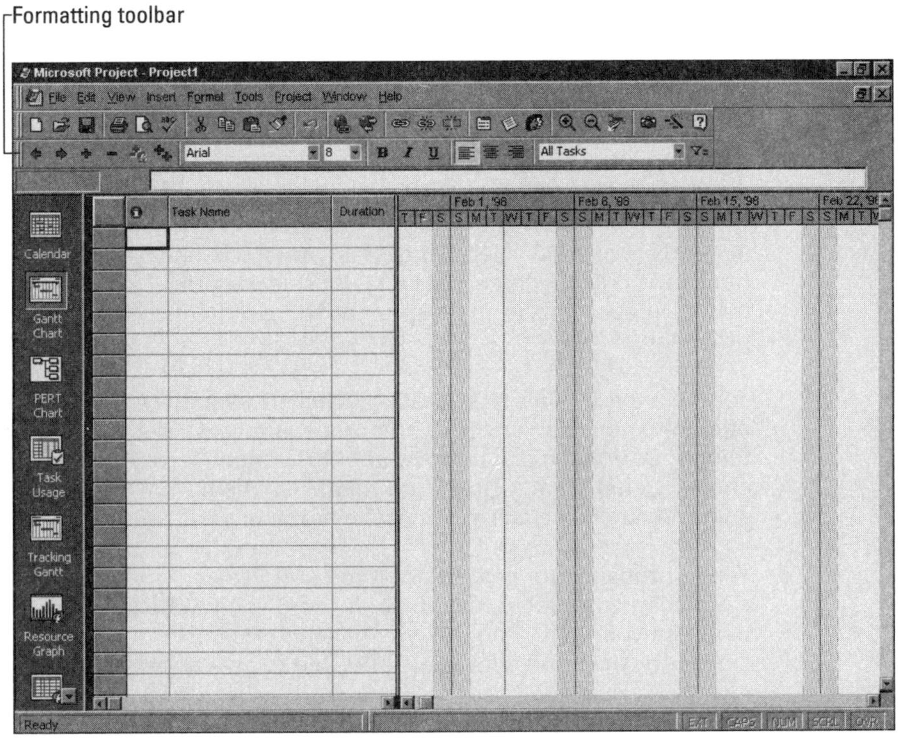

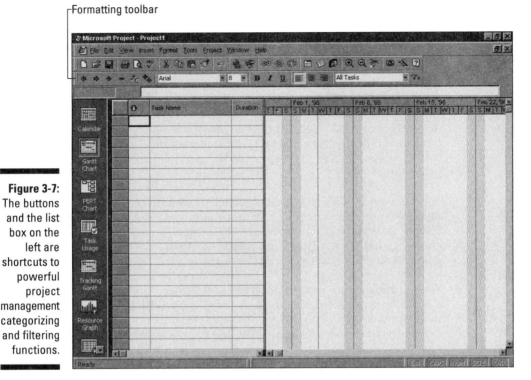

Figure 3-7: The buttons and the list box on the left are shortcuts to powerful project management categorizing and filtering functions.

What You Won't Remember

Microsoft Project has a bunch of buttons that provide great shortcuts to performing project management functions. The trick is knowing and remembering what these buttons are.

All the buttons are cleverly iconographic. But even after you've been using the program for a long time, it's sometimes hard to remember, for example, what the two faces and the finger pointing at the box are for. Not a problem! You can easily find out what the buttons are and what they do through two online help functions in Microsoft Project.

Tool tips

Tool tips are simple but immensely helpful little functions that identify each button on the toolbar. Place your mouse over one of the toolbar buttons (but don't click). In about a second, a descriptive phrase or word appears.

If the tool tip doesn't appear, it's probably turned off. To turn it on, choose View⇨Toolbars⇨Customize. Select the Show Screen Tips on Toolbars check box in the Options tab. While you're there, you can also try one of the Menu animations, such as Unfold. When you're finished, click Close.

Finding help

A greatly expanded selection of Help options is one of the winner innovations in Microsoft Office products. By selecting the Help menu, you'll get helpful suggestions from a variety of Microsoft Office Assistant Help procedures.

For instance, if you're a Microsoft Office 97 user, the Office Assistant is offered to you in a variety of humorous animated forms, such as the default Clippit. Or if you'd like to know about the function of a specific button, choose Help⇨What's This?, and then click the button you want to know about. A nutshell description of the purpose of the button appears.

You're probably not paid to use Microsoft Project — you're paid to perform a project management responsibility, and you've chosen Microsoft Project to lessen your load. The less you have to remember, to use Microsoft Project efficiently, the more effort you'll be able to give to being successful.

The techno-gurus who designed Microsoft Project had their act together in limiting the number of procedures you need to know to effectively use the program. Even so, some things have to be studied to be understood. And, depending on the comparative size of the left and right sides of your brain, you may prefer structured training to winging it. In either case, you can gain a lot of knowledge about the program through the built-in help options.

Knowing where you are

Escape! In Microsoft Project, one of the most important keyboard keys you can know is the Esc key. If you're hung up in a complex dialog box or you think you're getting into trouble with a complicated activity, the Esc key is a quick and easy way to return to a screen view. It cancels whatever you are working on.

Knowing what you're doing

As I mention, Microsoft Project offers a number of online aids to answer your questions or show you how to perform project management functions.

Click the Help Topics button or press F1 on the keyboard. The Help Topics dialog box appears. Following are instructions for each option in the dialog box. Feel free to explore any of them.

To find what kind of help is available:

1. **Click Help➪Contents and Index.**
2. **Click the Contents tab.**
3. **Double-click Creating a Project.**

   The dialog box displays a number of topics to assist you in the use of Microsoft Project.
4. **Double-click Getting Started: When Will Your Project Begin?**

   A multiple-choice graphical tutorial leads you through the steps of entering start or finish dates.
5. **To return to the Help Topics dialog box, click the Help Topics button.**

To check out Microsoft Project's Index option:

1. **In the Help Topics dialog box, click the Index tab.**
2. **In the text box, type** baseline.
3. **Double-click the words *an overview of.***

   A graphical text box appears explaining the purpose of a baseline. If you want, click the red tab or boxed phrase for further information.
4. **To return to the Help Topics dialog box, click the Help Topics button.**

To search for specific words and phrases in the help files:

1. **In the Help Topics dialog box, click the Find tab.**

   The first time you select the Find tab, Microsoft Project runs the Find Setup wizard to create a search database. (The search database needs to be created only once.) The wizard offers you three options, with a recommended default option to Minimize Database Size.
2. **You want to have the search database created, so click Next.**
3. **Click Finish.**
4. **In the text box, type** tracking toolbar.

   Microsoft Project lists all 13 topics it found relating to the tracking toolbar.

To return to the Gantt screen, click Cancel.

Knowing when and how to communicate with others

When all else fails, you can get live, free technical support. At the time of this publication, Microsoft provides two free technical support calls. (You pay for the call.) After that, support costs a chunk of change per call, so save this option as a last resort.

TIP

You'll need the product ID number if you ever have to call technical support. To find the product number, choose Help➪About Microsoft Project. Be smart and write down and file the number now, before you need help. That way, if you ever have trouble getting into the software program, you'll at least have the product number.

Technical support options

A number of technical support options are available short of the live telephone call:

1. **Choose Help➪Contents and Index.**
2. **Click the Contents tab.**
3. **Double-click Getting help.**
4. **Double-click Technical Support.**
5. **Double-click the one option, Technical Support.**
6. **If you are in the United States or Canada, select Product Support Within the United States and Canada. Otherwise, select Microsoft Technical Support Worldwide.**

   A listing of free support services appears.
7. **Close the Help dialog box to return to the Gantt screen.**

The services listed in Help topics aren't your only line of support. You can get help with your project in lots of ways. In Chapter 22, I list ten of them.

Wizards Are Everywhere!

Wizards are one of the great innovations of Microsoft Office products. Take full advantage of their assistance while you are learning to use Microsoft Project effectively. Doing so can greatly reduce your secondary work.

Remember, secondary work is the drain on your attention that keeps you from completing your task. In other chapters, I discuss alerts from the Planning wizard as they relate to specific tasks. (By *alert,* I mean that Microsoft Project will interrupt your work with a question from the wizard if the program detects that you are on the verge of making a mistake.)

To use the Planning wizard feature:

1. **Choose Tools➪Options.**
2. **Click the General tab.**
3. **Select all Planning Wizard check boxes if they are not already selected.**
4. **Click OK after you're finished.**

To see how a Planning wizard may work, click the Gantt Chart Wizard button on the standard toolbar. The wizard takes you through a series of steps to assist you in formatting the look and interactivity of your Gantt chart. When you're finished, click Format It to activate your changes.

Part II

Putting Your Project Together

The 5th Wave By Rich Tennant

I TOLD you not to build him too close to the monitor.

In this part . . .

After you define your project's scope and set the goals, you can create a schedule and start defining the relationships of the various project parts. In this part, using sample information, you develop tasks, set durations, add resources, outline your project, clarify relationships, and set times.

Be careful; you might find yourself craving the company of other project managers so that you can talk Gantt charts and resource pools.

Chapter 4

Creating a Schedule

In This Chapter

- Using Windows to manage files
- Putting your schedule in Project
- Changing your tasks
- Setting milestones
- Relating tasks

In this chapter, I introduce you to the procedure for creating a schedule in Microsoft Project. The procedure is friendly and straightforward. If you occasionally do a "big shop" at a grocery store, you're ready to tackle this type of work. Before you shop, you probably create a list of what you need. If you're familiar with the store, you probably order the list to match the layout of goods in the store's aisles. You order your project in Microsoft Project in much the same way. Instead of putting eggs and peanut butter in a cart, though, you enter a list of tasks into a file. And instead of planning your shopping by aisles, you make sense of your tasks' order by assigning time and associating responsibilities.

The first order of business is to mess around with some Windows stuff, such as creating a folder and saving a file. After that, it's time to do some scheduling. While you're there, will you pick up a quart of milk?

Start Microsoft Project, if necessary. If the Welcome dialog box appears, you can select the check box titled Don't Display This Startup Screen Again. Then click the Close (X) button.

The Office Assistant may open a Tip dialog box, offering a helpful hint about using Microsoft Project. Click Close to close the Office Assistant dialog box.

TIP: If you don't want to see a tip the next time you start the program, make sure the Office Assistant dialog box is closed and then choose Tools➪Options. Select the General tab and click to clear the Show Tips at Startup check box.

The screen displays a blank default Gantt chart. You can either begin a new project or open an existing one. In this chapter, I show you how to create a new project.

Description of the Practice Project

Suppose that you are a new project manager for Dream Homes, a small company dedicated to the custom design and construction of medium- to high-priced homes. Your project is the new home construction described in Chapter 2. You are building a home for Ferdinand and Isabella Smith. For the sake of the example, the current date is May 21, 1998. The start date of the project is June 2. The home must be completed and ready for occupancy on October 1. Others in your company scoff and say it can't be accomplished. Not you. With your knowledge of the industry and your newly acquired project management skills, it's a shoo-in (or a Smith-in).

Begin your project by clicking the New icon on the standard toolbar. The New icon is the blank sheet on the far left of the third row. The Project Information dialog box appears, as shown in Figure 4-1.

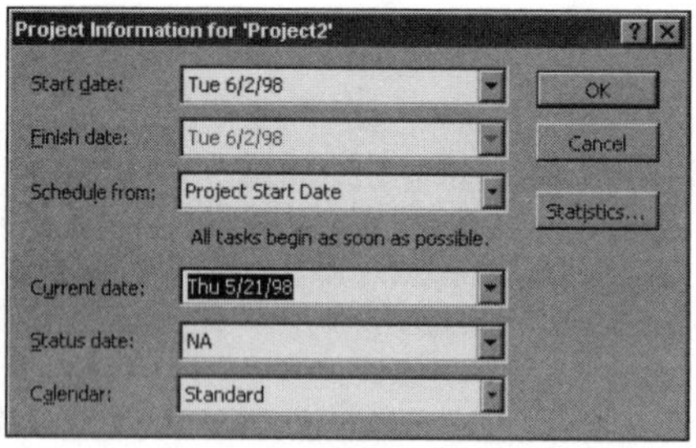

Figure 4-1: Use the Project Information dialog box to set the start and end date of a project.

1. **In the Start Date text box, type** June 2.

   If the current year is not 1998, type the current year.

2. **In the Current Date box, type** May 21 **or click the down arrow and select May 21.**

   If the current year is not 1998, select the appropriate year on the calendar or type the current year.

3. **Click OK.**

You don't need to type the time or the year. 8:00 A.M. is the default start time for all workdays, and the current year is the default year. You also don't need to worry about the finish date because it is adjusted based on your scheduling. After you set the start date, your schedule's length automatically sets the finish date. (Chapter 7 shows you how to change the default times on project calendars.)

Managing Files

File management in Microsoft Project conforms to the new features in Windows 95. If you're accustomed to working with Windows 3.1 or Windows for Workgroups, you'll find the new management tools easy to figure out and safer to use. They're especially helpful in Microsoft Project. For instance, you can use spaces and uppercase and lowercase letters for file names. Now you can create realistic names such as `My first project` instead of that crazy old eight-character alphabet soup `my1stprj`. You even get to bring deleted files back from the grave!

Creating a new folder

Forgive me if this sounds obvious, but in Windows 95, you keep files organized in *folders*. (If you were a Windows 3.1 user, you probably remember that folders used to be called directories.) Nothing is more embarrassing than reaching into a drawer to give a customer a pen and then discovering you've just handed over your toothbrush. (I hate it when that happens.) The same idea is true of computer files. You keep groups of related information in individual drawers (folders).

So what's in a name? Not much, I suppose. But in addition to the new name, Windows 95 enables you to manage folders with more freedom than before. That's significant.

One of the ways life is easier is that you can create a folder on the fly and without losing your train of thought. For instance, you can make a folder while in the Save mode. To do so:

1. **Click the Save button on the standard toolbar.**

   The File Save dialog box appears, as shown in Figure 4-2.

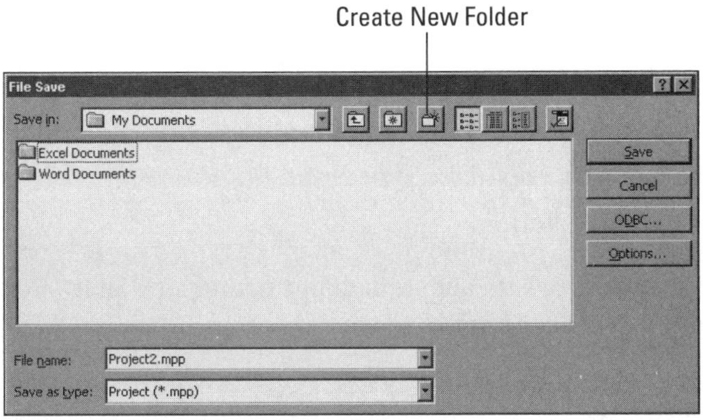

Figure 4-2: The File Save dialog box lists the current folder in the Save in text box.

Folders within the current folder (displayed in the Save in text box) are shown in the window.

2. **Click the Create New Folder button.**

   The New Folder dialog box appears, as shown in Figure 4-3.

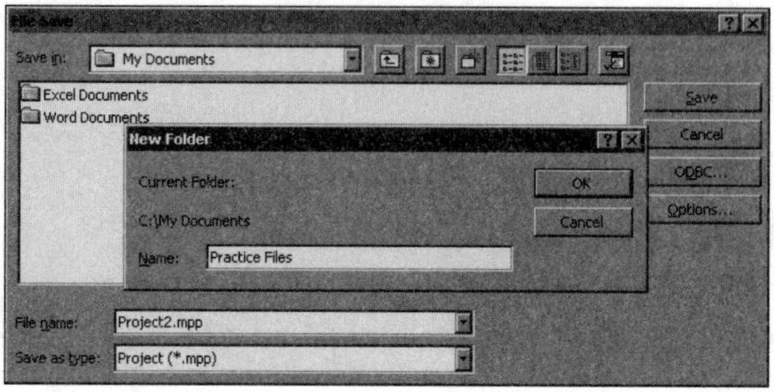

Figure 4-3: The New Folder dialog box shows the current folder.

3. **In the Name text box, type** Practice Files.
4. **Click OK.**

Windows 95 accepts file folder names with uppercase letters, lowercase letters, spaces, and up to 255 characters.

Saving a file

You've set a project start date. In so doing, you've begun a project plan. Kind of a heavy thought, huh? It isn't absolutely necessary to save your file at this time, but it's a good idea. That way, everything from this point forward isn't floating around in random memory. Your project will have a home.

I assume you're still in the File Save dialog box. If you're not, click the Save button on the standard toolbar. To save a file in your new folder:

1. **In the File Save dialog box, double-click the Practice Files folder.**
2. **In the File name text box, type** Smith Home.
3. **Click the Save button.**

The Microsoft Project title bar should now display the Smith Home project name, as shown in Figure 4-4.

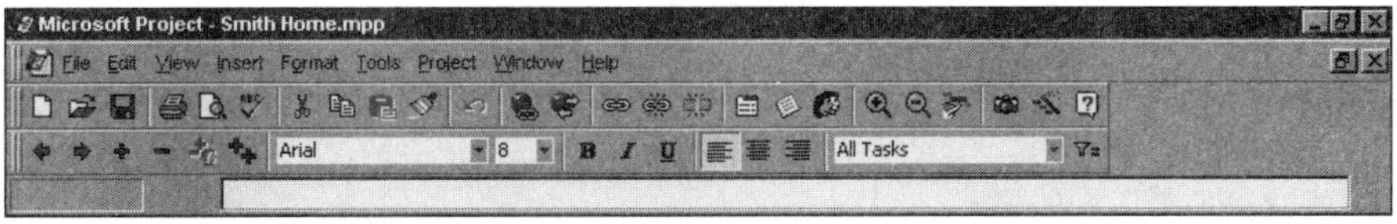

Figure 4-4: The Microsoft Project title bar displays the project's name.

Microsoft Project uses four file extensions: MPP (project), MPT (template), MPD (project database), and MPX (Microsoft Project exchange). The first, MPP, is the default project file extension. The next, MPT, is the template extension. You can save a file with the template extension as the basis for other projects. For instance, you can make a generic project containing all the tasks that are usually necessary to complete a project and then save it as a template. The next time you begin a similar project, you can open your template instead of starting from scratch. The MPD extension saves your entire project in a database format. You can open projects saved in the MPD format in Microsoft Access. The last file extension, MPX, is an ASCII, record-based text format used to transfer a file between applications that support the MPX file format.

Opening a project file

Although you're in the beginning stages of creating your own project file, it may be nice to sneak a peek at a finished project just to see an example of how all this stuff may appear when it's finished. Don't worry, you don't need to close your project. Microsoft Project will keep it loaded even if you open another project, which is kind of like walking and chewing gum at the same time.

To open a project file:

1. **Click the Open button on the standard toolbar.**

   The File Open dialog box appears, as shown in Figure 4-5. Your Practice Files folder should still be open. If it isn't, that's okay. Just double-click it.

2. **Click the Up One Level button.**

   The Look in text box probably says My Documents. It's the default folder for all Office files.

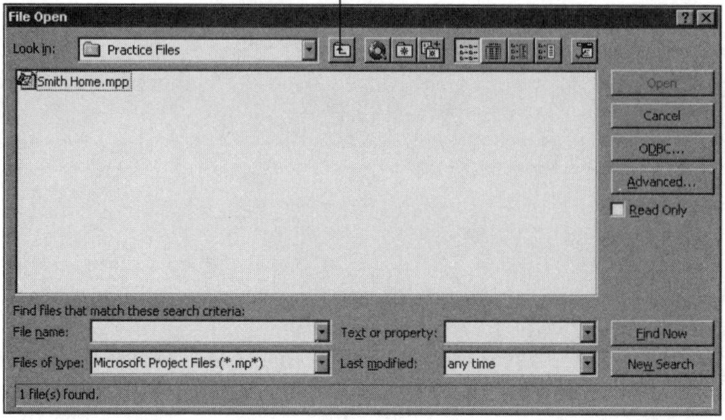

Figure 4-5: Notice that the File Open dialog box doesn't offer the Create a New Folder option.

3. **Click the Up One Level button again.**

   You're probably at the root directory (such as C:). If you're not there yet, click again.

4. **Double-click Program Files.**
5. **Double-click Microsoft Office.**
6. **Double-click Templates.**
7. **Double-click Microsoft Project.**
8. **Double-click the Event Planning.MPT file.**

   An event-planning template file is now the active screen, as shown in Figure 4-6.

The event-planning template is one of six template files that come with Microsoft Project. After you load a template file, you can use it like any other project. It's called a *template* because it lets you reuse existing information that's already created for you. In this event-planning file, a number of tasks and sample durations have already been created.

You're not going to work on this event-planning project. I asked you to load it so you could see a partially completed project plan and practice getting around a little in project folders.

The loading of the event-planning template didn't replace your Smith Home project. Don't believe me? Choose Window from the menu bar and you can see that the Smith Home project is still loaded.

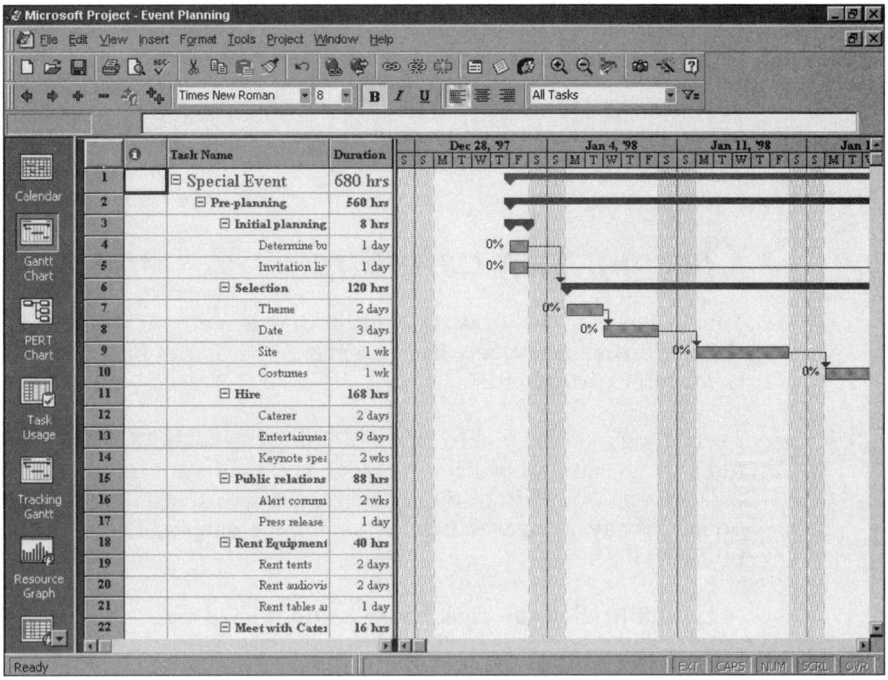

Figure 4-6: A new project called Event Planning appears.

Microsoft Project lets you open numerous projects at one time. This is for people who like walking into walls. Well, there *is* a good reason for all those projects being open at one time. In really big projects, instead of having one huge project file, you can break it into a bunch of bite-sized pieces called *subprojects*. When you do this, loading a lot of files at once is sometimes necessary.

Before closing the event-planning file, you may enjoy navigating it to see an example of what your project will soon be like. Be sure to check out the Calendar and PERT Chart views by selecting their respective Views on the view bar.

To close the `Eventpln.mpt` file, choose File⇨Close (or press Ctrl+F4). If a dialog box appears asking whether you want to save changes, click the No button. Smith Home should now be the active project window.

Making a Schedule

The first step in creating a schedule is to enter the project tasks.

In my explanation of schedule creation, I use common project management terms, such as task, duration, resource, constraint, and milestone. If you're not familiar with these project management terms and principles used by Microsoft Project, read Chapter 2 and check out the glossary. I also ask you to use your mouse to get around in Microsoft Project. If you need some more confidence in this, check out Chapter 3.

Customizing columns

Your screen should show the Smith Home project in Gantt Chart view. A Gantt Chart view actually has two parts — a Gantt chart on the right and a Gantt table on the left.

Everything's set for you to begin building the schedule. But because you're not a vanilla kind of project manager, you may want to customize your project. As you see in other chapters, you can customize your project in oodles of ways. One way is by changing the names of columns in the Gantt table. To do this:

1. **Double-click the Task Name column heading.**

   The Column Definition dialog box appears, as shown in Figure 4-7.

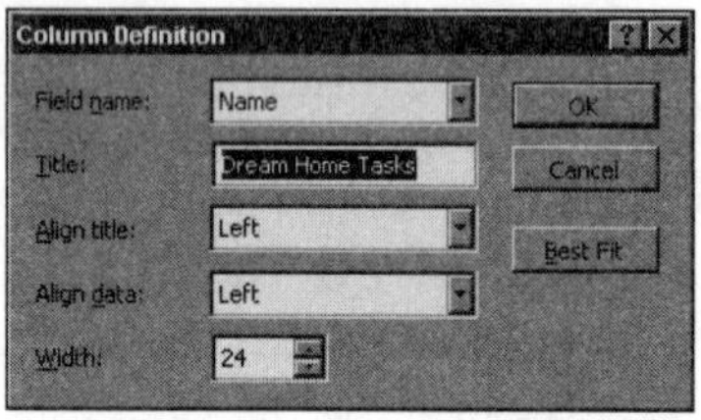

Figure 4-7: Use this dialog box to define the properties of your column.

2. **In the Title text box, type** Dream Home Tasks.
3. **Click OK.**

Creating a task

Microsoft Project offers more than one way to enter tasks. The simplest way to enter task information is cell by cell. In Microsoft Project, a *cell* is the intersection of a column and a row.

To enter a task:

1. **In the Dream Home Tasks column, move your cursor to the first cell and click.**

   The cell is highlighted.

2. **In the cell, type** Customer selections.

3. **Press Enter.**

   When you press Enter, the task resides in the cell. You've created the first task (see Figure 4-8).

Two other things happen. One, the next cell is highlighted. Two, a duration of one day appears next to the first task. The one-day duration is the default duration for all tasks. You can change that in a little while.

TIP: If you can't see the Duration column to the right of the Task Name column, drag the vertical bar separating the Gantt table and the Gantt chart to the right.

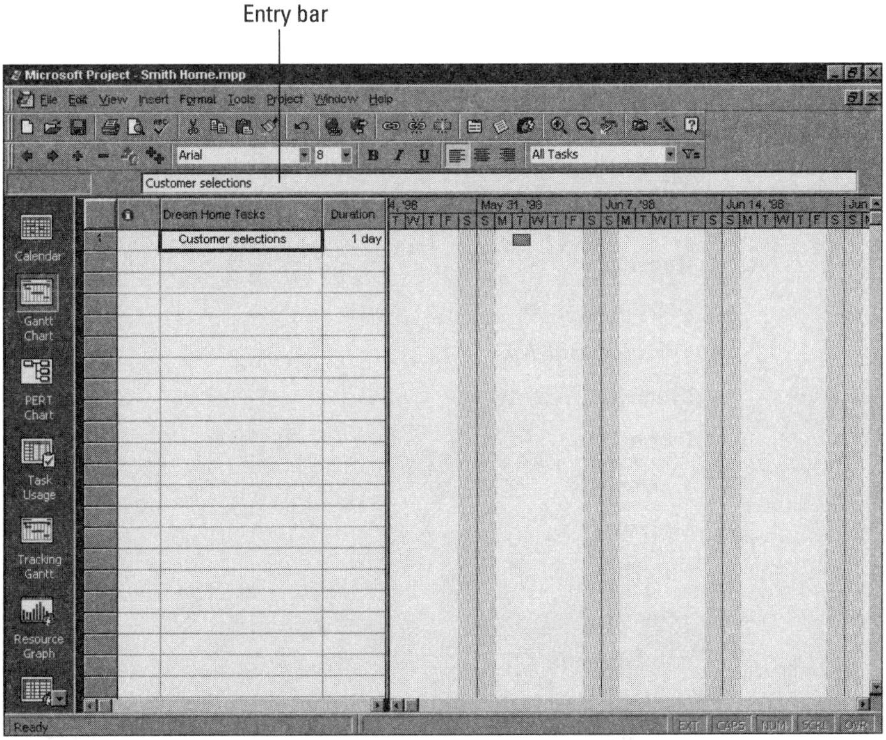

Figure 4-8: When you enter information in a cell, it also appears temporarily in the entry bar.

Now that you have the hang of this, how about entering a list of tasks? It's easy:

1. **Select the next empty task cell if it isn't already highlighted.**
2. **Type the task name.**

   All the tasks appear in the list following these steps.
3. **Press Enter.**
4. **Repeat for each task.**

Type the following tasks into successive task cells:

Write specifications

Write contract

Signatures

Plans

Water service

Electrical service

Excavation

Landscaping

Footing/foundation

Inspection

Wood framing

Roofing

Plumbing lines

Furnace and A/C

Electrical Wiring

Inspection

Wallboard

Stairway

Painting

Trim

Landscaping

Customer walkthrough

Punch list corrections

Final inspection

Contract closure

Administrative closure

If you make a mistake, the easiest way to correct it is to select the errant cell and retype the information in the entry bar (labeled in Figure 4-8) below the formatting toolbar. The entry bar displays the contents of the active cell. To make a change, highlight the word you want to correct in the entry bar text box and then type the correct word. When everything is the way you want, click the green * button. If you don't want to make the change, click the red X button.

TECHNICAL STUFF

The number to the left of each task is its ID. This number has two functions. It indicates the order of a task and is the unique identifier of the task. Because each task has its own ID, you can have multiple tasks with the same name.

Way to go! You've created an entire list of tasks. This process isn't the only way to create that list, but it's the simplest. After you've entered all the tasks in the list, press the Page Up key. This takes you to the top of the task list. So far, your project should look like Figure 4-9. The task column is filled with the Smith Home tasks.

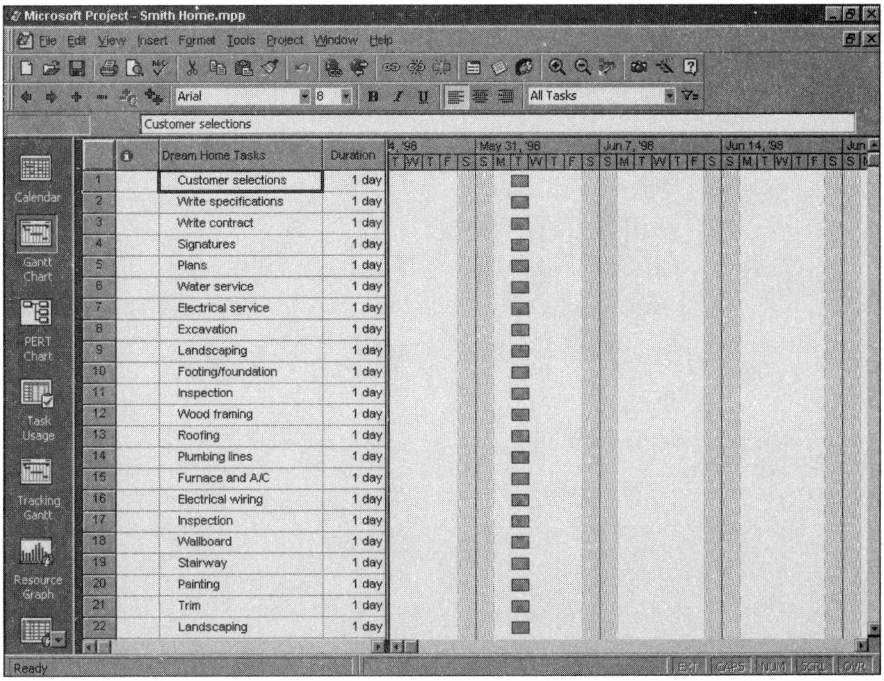

Figure 4-9: Notice that you have more than one inspection task, but each task has its own ID.

Entering durations

Duration is the amount of time it takes to finish a task. You can't have a schedule without estimating each task's duration. In this section, you do just that. Later, you discover some secrets to improve the accuracy of your estimates.

In Microsoft Project, you can use the following durations:

- m (minutes)
- h (hours)
- d (days)
- w (weeks)
- 0 (milestones)

If that last one is confusing, don't worry. You find out more about it later in the chapter.

TIP

Microsoft Project assigns five days to a workweek and eight hours to a workday.

You enter durations in the same way you enter task names. Simply select the cell, if necessary, and type. Press Enter, and the next cell is highlighted automatically. Type the following durations next to their respective tasks. (If you can't see the Duration column to the right of the Task Name column, drag the vertical bar separating the Gantt table and the Gantt chart to the right.)

Task	***Duration***
Customer selections	**1w**
Write specifications	**1d**
Write contract	**3h**
Signatures	**1h**
Plans	**6d**
Water service	**1d**
Electrical service	**1d**
Excavation	**1d**
Landscaping	**1d**
Footing/Foundation	**8d**

Task	*Duration*
Inspection	**1h**
Wood framing	**3w**
Roofing	**4d**
Plumbing lines	**3d**
Furnace and A/C	**3d**
Electrical wiring	**3d**
Inspection	**1h**
Wallboard	**1w**
Stairway	**4d**
Painting	**2w**
Trim	**1w**
Landscaping	**2d**
Customer walkthrough	**3h**
Punch list corrections	**4d**
Final inspection	**1h**
Contract closure	**1d**
Administrative closure	**2d**

Whew. You've entered all the durations. Press the Page Up key. Your project should now look like Figure 4-10.

Saving an active file

It's wise to frequently save your work as you add new information to your project. So be wise and click the Save button on the standard toolbar now.

The Planning wizard appears, as shown in Figure 4-11, and it asks whether you'd like to save a baseline for your project.

A *baseline* is a snapshot of your project plan. You use it as the basis of comparison between what you've planned and what actually happens after the project begins.

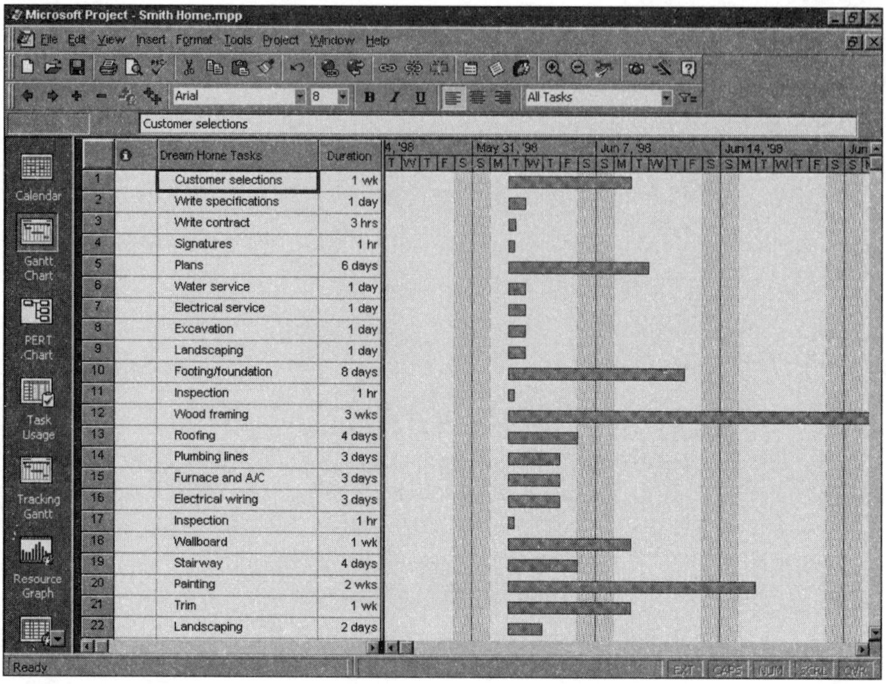

Figure 4-10: The Gantt chart shows duration by bar length; the bar length is relative to the timescale indicated at the top of the chart.

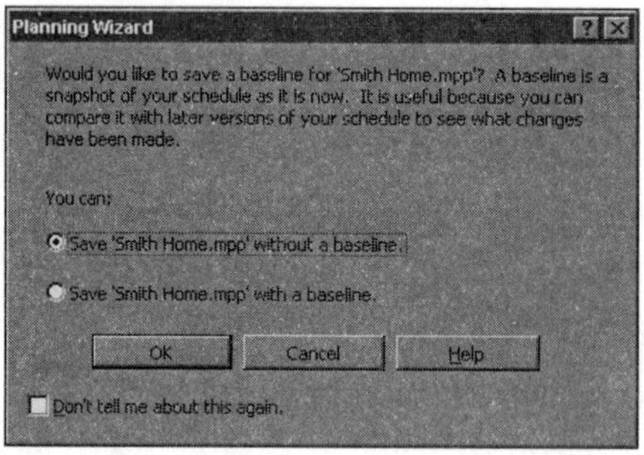

Figure 4-11: The Planning wizard offers to help you find out about baselines. You're welcome to select this option.

You haven't finished creating your project plan, so for now:

1. **Select the Save 'Smith Home.MPP' without a Baseline option.**
2. **Click OK.**

   You've resaved the file.

Editing Tasks

One of the nicest features of Microsoft Project is how easy it is to make changes. Adding, deleting, and moving tasks is a piece of cake. Even late into the project, the program can keep up with your changes and alert you to their effects on other aspects of the project.

You're only at the beginning of your project, but it's already time to make a few changes. Suppose that you've reviewed your tasks and you notice the following:

- The design of the home takes place after the contract signatures. Normally, design plans are part of the contract. You'll need to move the task.
- Water service and electrical service can be put in only after the foundation has been erected or poured. You need to move this small group of tasks.
- The landscaping task is listed twice. Sometimes there may be a good reason to list a task twice, but not this time. All landscaping work would be ruined in the early stages of construction. You need to delete one landscaping task and change the other's duration.
- You need to add some tasks with zero duration, specifically, milestones.

Moving a task

Moving a task and its duration is simple. To move Plans so that it precedes Signatures:

1. **Select task number 5.**
2. **Hold down your left mouse button and drag the cursor up until it rests on the line between tasks 3 and 4.**

   A gray line appears.
3. **Release the mouse button.**

   Task 5 has just become task 4 and vice versa.

Notice that the durations have automatically realigned with the new task positions.

Moving a group of tasks

You can move a group of tasks in much the same way that you move an individual task. *Your* next task, Mr. Phelps, if you accept it, is to move the Water service and Electrical service tasks so that they follow the Footing/Foundation task. To do so:

1. **Select the ID number of task 6.**
2. **Press and hold down the Shift key.**
3. **Select the ID number of task 7.**

   This highlights the block of tasks and their ID numbers.
4. **Release the mouse button and Shift key.**
5. **Click in the highlighted number area and then drag the cursor down until it rests on the line between tasks 10 and 11.**

   A gray line appears.
6. **Release the mouse button.**

   Tasks 6 and 7 are now tasks 9 and 10.

Good grief! That must be something like what the astronauts feel when they're trying to dock into a Russian spaceship. With a little practice, it gets less stressful.

Oops. Undoing changes

If you make a mistake or change your mind, you can undo your most recent action by clicking the Undo button on the standard toolbar.

Deleting a task

The final corrections (at this point anyway) are to delete one of the Landscaping tasks and change the other's duration. The Landscaping task at task 7 needs to go because, as mentioned, it occurs too soon.

To delete task 7 and its duration:

1. **Select anywhere on the task 7 row in the Gantt table.**

   When I say Gantt table, I mean the information on the left side of the vertical bar. The Gantt chart is on the right of the vertical bar.

2. **Press the Delete key.**

   That Landscaping task is gone. The tasks that followed now ripple into their new position.

3. **Change the duration of task 21, Landscaping, to 4 days by typing** 4.

   Days is the default duration.

Press the Page Up key. Your project should now look like Figure 4-12.

The new information is only temporary until you save it, so save your project again:

1. **Click the Save button on the standard toolbar.**
2. **Select Save 'Smith Home.MPP' without a Baseline.**
3. **Click OK.**

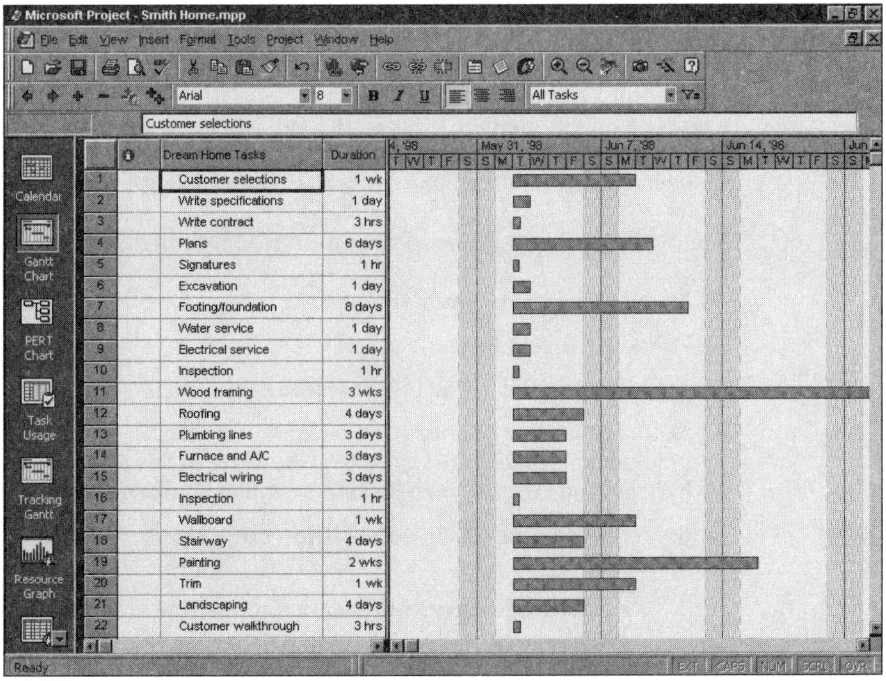

Figure 4-12: The edited Gantt chart shows all current changes.

Inserting tasks

Inserting a task or tasks is as simple as moving or deleting them. Just click an existing task and press the Insert key. Space is inserted for your new task at that point, and the former occupant of the cell moves to the next cell down. In the next section, I show you how to insert space for additional tasks — in this instance, project milestones.

Inserting milestones

A *milestone* is the beginning or completion of a significant event or series of events in a project. Milestones are places where you stop to assess your progress. Often, milestones occur when contractors should be finished with their responsibilities so that others can begin. Sometimes milestones are a place for changing some project team members.

On the Smith Home project, some milestones are linked to stage-of-completion commitments in the contract. Another contract stipulation is that occupancy must occur on or before October 1 of the same year.

In Microsoft Project, you designate a milestone by entering a duration of 0. To insert a milestone, you click in the cell where you want to insert the milestone and press the Insert key. The task that currently holds that place will trickle down one task line (as will all subsequent tasks).

To add your first milestone to the Smith Home project:

1. **Select task 1, Customer selections.**
2. **Press the Insert key.**
3. **Type** Project begins **as the milestone, and** 0d **as the duration.**

   Notice that after you leave the duration field, the Gantt chart creates a black diamond with the date 6/2, the start date you entered in Project Information. Your screen should look like Figure 4-13.
4. **Insert these other milestones into your project, all with a duration of 0d:**
   a. **Before Excavation, insert a milestone called** Contract begins.
   b. **Before Wood Framing, insert** Foundation stage complete.
   c. **Before Wallboard, insert** Framing stage complete.
   d. **Before Contract closure, insert** Finishing stage complete.
   e. **After Administrative closure, enter** Project complete.

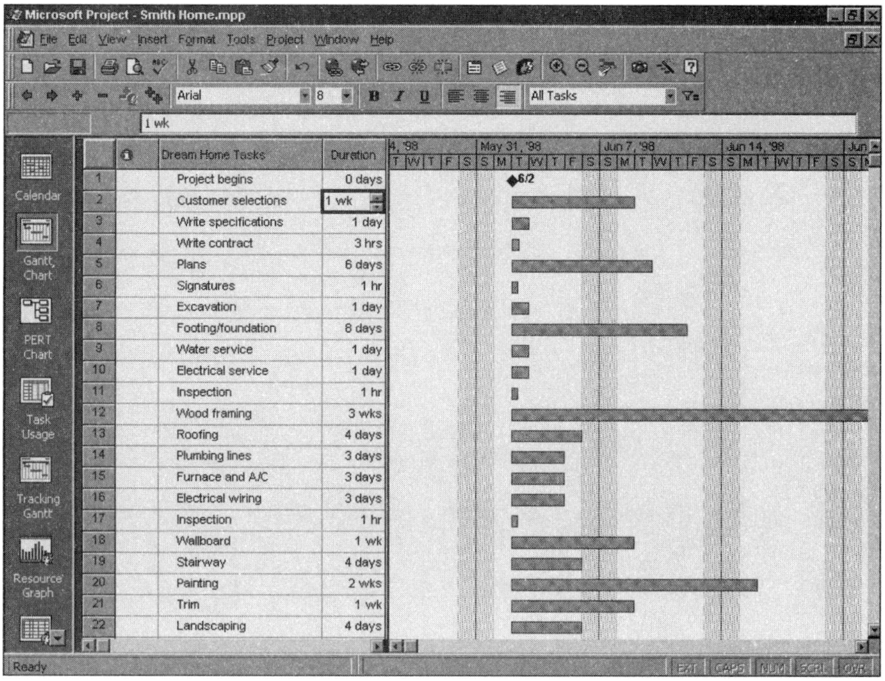

Figure 4-13: The default Gantt chart designation of a milestone is a black diamond.

TIP: You can scroll the Gantt table by clicking the scroll bar on the right of the Gantt chart.

5. **Press the Page Up key.**

   Your project should now look like Figure 4-14.

Don't be bothered by the fact that all the milestones have the same date as the project start date. You'll change those dates shortly.

Your project's value increases with each entry of information. Make sure you save your file frequently, or your Van Gogh may lose an ear. Click the Save button on the standard toolbar, select Save 'Smith Home.MPP' without a Baseline, and then click OK.

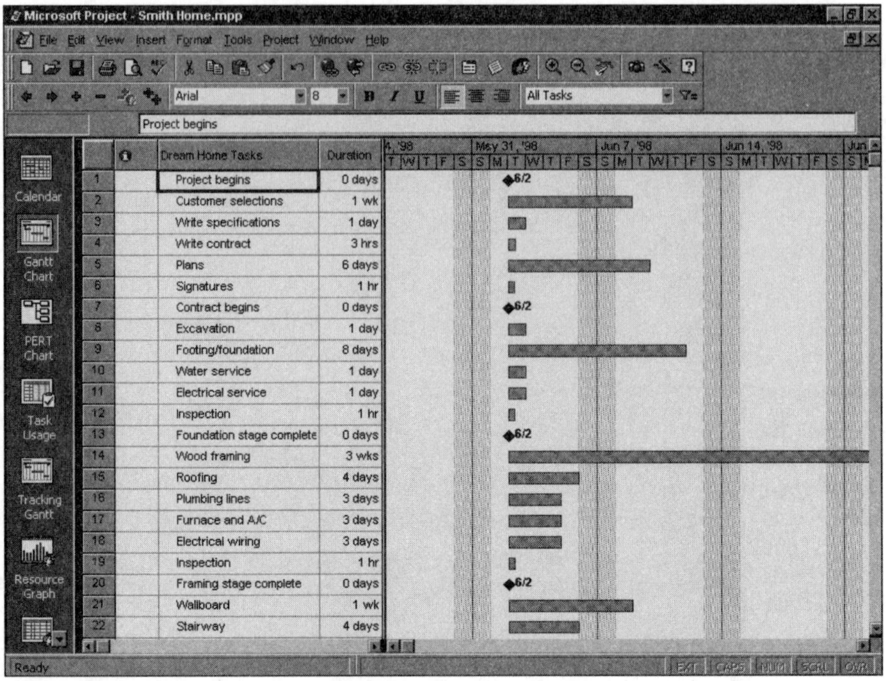

Figure 4-14: The milestones have been added, but their actual dates have not been set.

Linking Tasks

As you scan the project, you'll notice that all the project's tasks are set to start on the same date. The painters are going to have trouble getting to the second floor of a house that hasn't been designed yet. Hmm. Something is missing. Although the task durations are all relatively accurate, the overall project has no layout in time.

To add the element of time to a project, you link tasks. The default link is that a task will not begin until previous ones have finished. It's called a *finish-to-start* link. You can link two or all your tasks.

This chapter discusses the default finish-to-start link. To find out about other types of links, check out Chapter 6.

To link all the tasks on the Gantt chart:

1. **Select task 1, keeping the mouse button held down.**
2. **Drag the cursor through all the tasks.**

   All the tasks are selected.

3. **Click the Link Tasks button on the standard toolbar.**

Now the Gantt chart comes alive. Tasks are linked in the finish-to-start relationship and stretch out beyond the screen's width (unless you have a monitor shaped like a two by four). In Microsoft Project, what you see is called a *view*.

For now, you'll stay in the Gantt Chart view. Close the view bar for a while to provide more chart real estate. Simply right-click your mouse in the view bar area. A view list appears. Click View Bar to deselect it.

To view your links on the Gantt chart:

1. **Press the Page Up key until you return to the first task.**

   The Gantt chart looks much different now.

2. **Press the Page Down key once or twice until you see the last few tasks.**

   There seem to be no bars to the right of these tasks.

3. **Select the final task cell, Project Complete.**

4. **Click the Goto Selected Task button on the standard toolbar.**

The Gantt chart should look something like Figure 4-15. We have troubles. The project, in its current state, will finish on October 1, exactly the contractual finish date. That's unrealistically optimistic. What about that thing called rain?

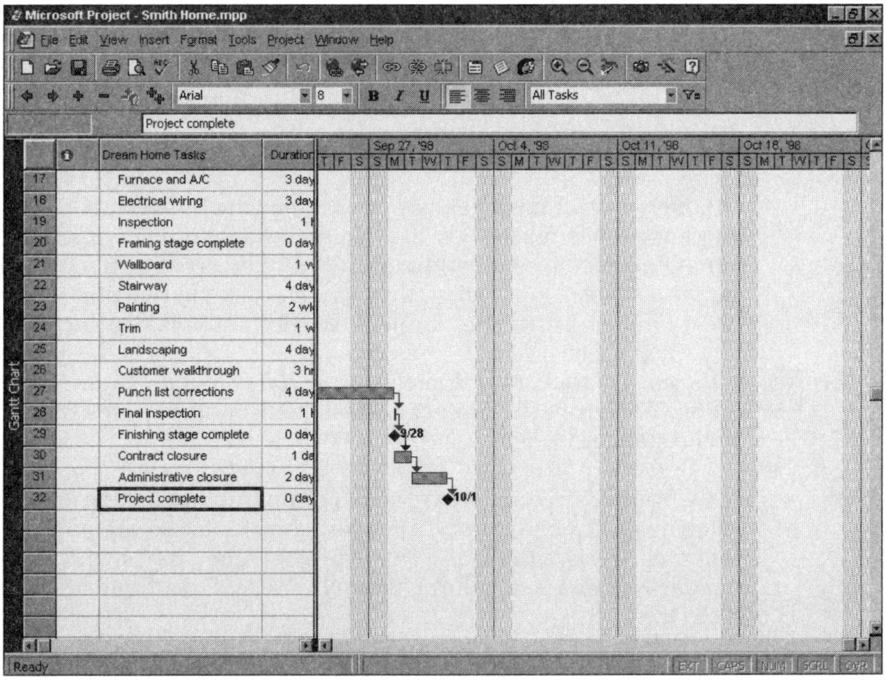

Figure 4-15: The Gantt chart shows the timescale projection of linked tasks.

Unless you know some weather magic, you need to do some project management magic to shorten the project's length. But like all other forms of magic, project management is really a craft. You need to know a number of disappearing tricks to make the Smith Home project realistically shorter. That's what this chapter and Chapters 5, 6, 7, and 16 are about — optimizing work through quality time management.

While you're looking at the chart, notice the lines with arrowheads. A line indicates a link. An arrowhead indicates relationship.

Unlinking tasks

One of the magic feats you need to know is how to unlink tasks. Sometimes you'll need to unlink tasks so that you can reorganize task relationships. Use the tasks in the Smith Home project to see how this works:

1. **Click the first task.**
2. **Click the Goto Selected Task button on the standard toolbar to see your task duration in the Gantt chart.**
3. **Select the first task, keeping the mouse button held down.**
4. **Drag the cursor down through all the remaining tasks.**

   All the tasks are selected.

5. **Click the Unlink Tasks button on the standard toolbar.**

   The project returns to its previous unlinked condition.

Undoing an action

Although project managers are pros at making things appear and disappear, they sometimes reach their hand in their hat and pull out something they weren't expecting. Or sometimes, if you're up close, you may hear them mutter a slight "Oops" when they saw a project in two. But you'll see no sweat on their brow. They know the Undo button is only a click away.

In the case of the Smith Home project, you can undo your most recent action. To restore the project to its linked condition, click the Undo button on the standard toolbar.

Phew. Your project should be linked again. All that linking and unlinking and relinking makes one thirsty. Time for a break. But before you get up from your chair, resave the Smith Home project. Click the Save button on the standard toolbar, select Save 'Smith Home.MPP' without a Baseline, and then click OK.

So you've created your schedule. Kind of makes your heart flutter to think of all those nicely arranged tasks and durations and milestones and links. And you've accomplished the tasks in a very short time, er, duration.

Chapter 5

Outlining Your Project

In This Chapter

- Creating summary tasks
- Promoting and demoting tasks
- Modifying the Gantt chart timescale
- Using outlining features

Microsoft Project provides a dynamic way to order, view, and control related groups of tasks. It does this through outlining.

In project management, an *outline* is an ordered structure for a project showing how some tasks fit into broader groupings, called *summary tasks.* Tasks grouped within a summary task are called *subtasks.* Project phases are sometimes reflected as task groups under specific summary tasks. Figure 5-1 is an example of a summary task and subtasks.

Why Microsoft Project (and You) Work Better with Outlines

Outlining your project into summary tasks and subtasks has strong benefits. One important advantage is that you can report on the project's progress using varying levels of detail. For instance, the bank may want to know only the current stage of construction and therefore needs only a summary task report. Or your procurement department may want a detailed report of only the upcoming phase of a project so that the materials can be delivered on time without unnecessary stockpiling of inventory.

With outlining, you're more likely to manage a project successfully because you associate tasks with their related activities and deadlines. For instance, a public utility will want a two-week lead time before installing the electric service. In addition, they will install the service only after you have completed the footing and foundation work. Your management of these two tasks will be easier if you associate them as subtasks of the same summary task.

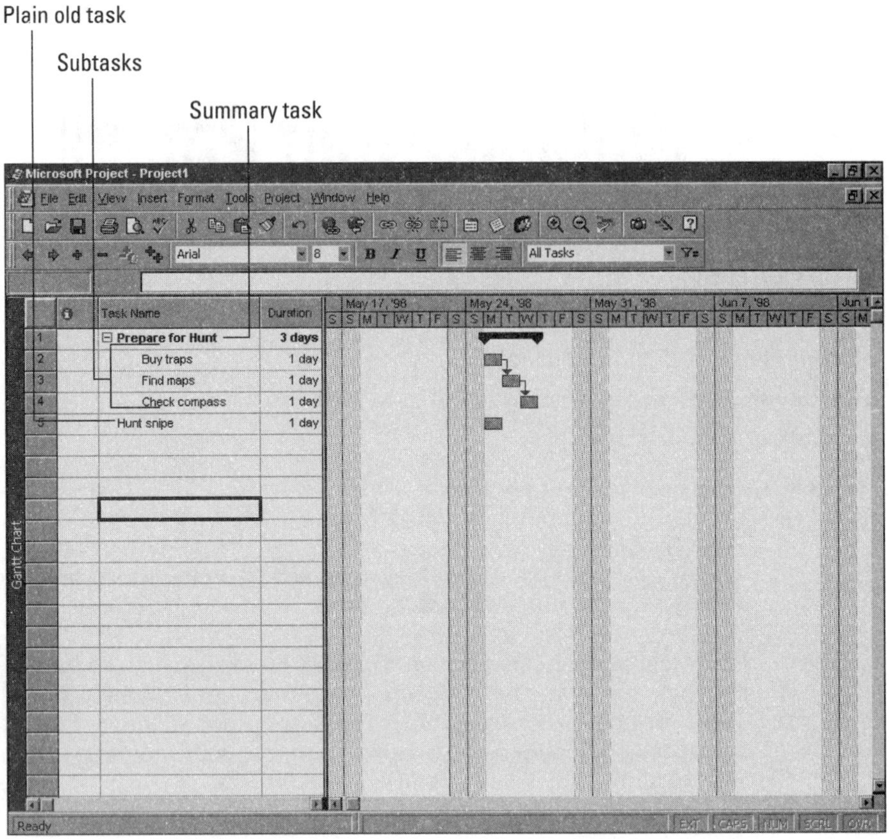

Figure 5-1: An example of a summary task and subtasks.

A summary task is just what its name implies: a summary of the duration, cost, and resources of all the subtasks related to the summary task. You can assess the overall status of a group of subtasks by looking at summary task information.

Types of Outlines

You can prepare two basic types of outlines: top-down outlines and bottom-up outlines. A top-down outline identifies a project by all its phases or major categories. These phases and categories typically become your summary tasks. After you list these major categories, you break the project down into a series or group of tasks within each category. These become your subtasks.

A bottom-up outline is the reverse. You list everything that needs to be accomplished in the project. Then you cluster, or order, the tasks into major phases or groups. The result is the same as for top-down outlining; you just get there from the opposite direction.

The project you develop in Chapter 4 is an example of a bottom-up outline. You develop the tasks, but do not identify the summary tasks and subtasks.

This chapter — and the rest of Part II — uses an example project file (Smith Home project) that you create in Chapter 4. If you haven't already created the file, check out Chapter 4.

Adding Summary Tasks

Your project, the Smith Home, is a bottom-up outline. You created the tasks, and now it's time to put them into summary tasks — kind of like putting sliced loaves of bread into wrappers. The wrapper doesn't add anything to the slices, but it contains them and tells all about them. Got any pumper-nickel projects?

In the bottom-up approach, you add summary tasks by inserting them (in the same way you insert any other task). Here goes:

1. **Click the Open button on the standard toolbar.**
2. **Double-click the Practice Files folder.**
3. **Double-click the Smith Home.MPP project file.**
4. **Select the Customer selections task and press Insert.**
5. **Type** Contract/Design**.**

This newly inserted task isn't a summary task yet. It becomes a summary task after you identify (demote) its subtasks.

Demoting Tasks

Demotion is not a popular word these days, but it's a rad term in project management. If you want to create a subtask, you demote it; that is, you place it under the hierarchy of a summary task. You don't need to furrow your brow, buy antacids, or close the office door to do it either.

Demoting tasks in Microsoft Project is simple. All you have to do is select the cell or cells you want to demote and click the right arrow on the standard toolbar. So roll up you sleeves and get ready to do some demoting.

To demote subtasks in your project:

1. **Move the cursor to the beginning of the Customer selections task.**
2. **Click and drag down to the end of the "Contract begins" milestone.**

   Tasks 3 through 8 are selected.

3. **Click the Indent button on the formatting toolbar.**

Your project should now look like Figure 5-2.

The following changes have taken place:

- The selected tasks have been indented to the right.
- The summary task, Contract/Design, has been changed to bold.
- The summary task duration is now the sum of the six subtasks.
- A summary bar is now in the Gantt chart. It begins with the start of the first subtask and ends with the finish of the last subtask and the date of the milestone.

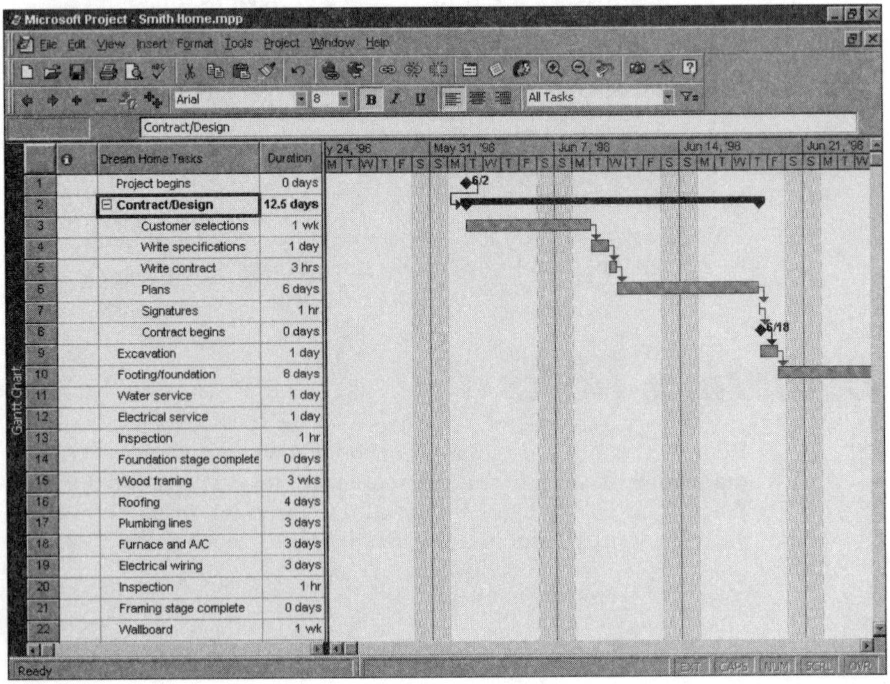

Figure 5-2: Tasks 3 through 8 are now subtasks of task 2.

You can demote as many levels as you want. A quick way to demote a task is with the mouse. Position the mouse cursor over the first letter of the task's name. The cursor turns into a right-left arrow. Holding down the left mouse button, drag the task to the right to demote it or to the left to promote it.

Now insert another summary task into your project:

1. **Select Excavation task and press Insert.**
2. **In the text box, type** Foundation Stage.
3. **Press Enter.**

Don't worry if Microsoft Project interprets that the new task is another subtask of Contract/Design. After you insert the task, you can modify its place in the hierarchy of the outline.

After all that tough demotion stuff, it's time to do some promotion.

Adjusting the width of the task column

All of a task's name doesn't have to fit in the task name cell. The full name still exists even if you can't see all of it. But for outlining and reporting, the schedule looks better if everything fits.

To make task names fit, you can either shorten the names or enlarge the task column to fit the longest task name.

For example, look at task 23 in Figure 5-5, Framing stage complete. It just doesn't fit. To make it and all the tasks fit, you can do one of four things:

- Drag the border between the Dream Home Tasks and Duration column headings to the right.
- Double-click the Dream Home Tasks heading. The Column Definition dialog box appears. For Width, enter a number larger than the current 24 (up to 128 characters).
- Double-click the Dream Home Tasks heading. In the Column Definition dialog box, choose Best Fit. The column is automatically sized based on the length of the task name.
- Double-click the border between the Dream Home Tasks and Duration column headings.

Promoting Tasks

To free the Foundation Stage task from the subtask category, you promote it. Task promotion is as simple as demotion. To promote the task:

1. **Select the Foundation Stage task.**

2. **Click the Outdent button on the formatting toolbar.**

   Foundation Stage moves to the left, indicating that it is no longer a subtask of Contract/Design.

Now that you have the hang of the outlining procedure, insert the following additional summary tasks:

1. **Select Wood framing, press Insert, and type** Framing Stage.
2. **Select Wallboard, press Insert, and type** Finishing Stage.
3. **Select Contract closure, press Insert, and type** Close Out Stage.

Demote the tasks that follow each new summary task as follows:

1. **Click and drag over the tasks that follow a new summary task.**
2. **After the group of tasks is selected, click the Indent button on the toolbar.**
3. **Repeat for each group of subtasks.**

When you have completed this process, press the Page Up key until you return to task ID 1.

You may notice hatch marks in the Duration column. This means the information in the cell is larger than the cell size. If you'd like to correct the column width, double-click the Duration column title and select Best Fit. You can also double-click the vertical border between the Duration column head and the column head to the right.

Changing the Gantt Chart Timescale

To improve your analysis of the project, you can zoom in and out on your Gantt chart by pressing the zoom buttons on the standard toolbar.

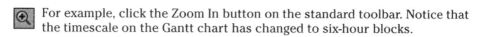

For example, click the Zoom In button on the standard toolbar. Notice that the timescale on the Gantt chart has changed to six-hour blocks.

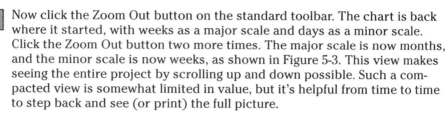

Now click the Zoom Out button on the standard toolbar. The chart is back where it started, with weeks as a major scale and days as a minor scale. Click the Zoom Out button two more times. The major scale is now months, and the minor scale is now weeks, as shown in Figure 5-3. This view makes seeing the entire project by scrolling up and down possible. Such a compacted view is somewhat limited in value, but it's helpful from time to time to step back and see (or print) the full picture.

If needed, you can zoom all the way in to quarter-hour intervals, and you can zoom all the way out to half-year intervals.

Click the Zoom In or Zoom Out button on the standard toolbar to return the Gantt chart timescale to the default days and weeks scale. Then save the file by clicking the Save button on the standard toolbar, selecting Save 'Smith Home.MPP' without a Baseline, and clicking OK.

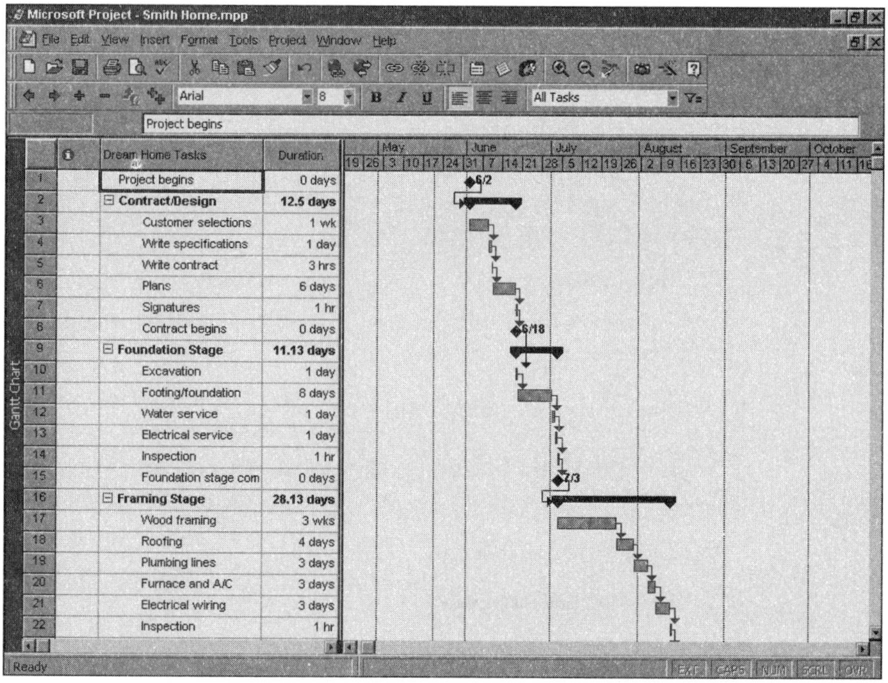

Figure 5-3: The Gantt chart with a timescale of months and weeks.

Editing Summary Tasks

I have good news and bad news about editing summary tasks. The good news is that you can move them, add them, and delete them like any other task (as I describe in Chapter 4). The bad news is that, if you're not careful, you may affect subtasks in a way you weren't intending. For instance, if you delete a summary task, you delete its subtasks, too.

But even the bad news isn't all bad. Microsoft Project warns you if you may be making a mistake.

Deleting summary tasks

Do you have a summary task that isn't as brilliant as it first appeared? Have circumstances changed and you need to cluster a few groups of subtasks under a single summary task? You can delete a summary task — carefully!

Because the Smith Home project is for practice, it's a good place to make your first attempt at deleting a summary task:

1. **Select the Foundation Stage summary task.**
2. **Press the Delete key.**

   The Planning wizard appears (see Figure 5-4). It warns you that Foundation Stage is a summary task and that deleting it will delete its subtasks as well. Pretty sharp, huh?
3. **Click Cancel.**

   You retreat from this point of no return. (Well, you could click Undo as a last resort.)

If the Planning wizard didn't appear:

1. **Click the Undo button on the standard toolbar.**

   This retrieves your deletion.
2. **Choose Tools⇨Options.**
3. **Click the General tab.**
4. **Select the Advice from Planning Wizard check box and all three of its subordinate check boxes.**
5. **Click OK.**

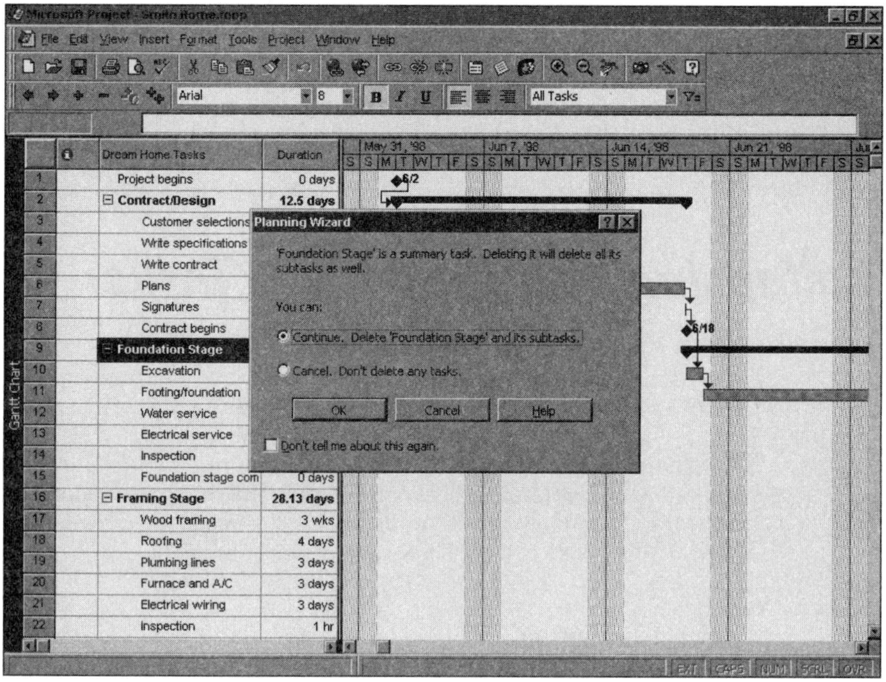

Figure 5-4: Click the Cancel button or the Cancel option to avoid deleting the summary task.

From now on, the Planning wizard will appear as I describe in the book. Leaving all the wizards on until you're proficient with the program is a good idea.

To delete a summary task without affecting the subtasks, you need to first promote the subtasks to tasks. You do this by selecting the tasks and then clicking the Outdent button on the formatting toolbar. You can then delete the summary task.

Moving summary tasks

If you move a summary task, you move its subtasks as well. Subtasks stick to their summary task like glue.

If you move a summary task into an existing summary group, the summary task and its children will become a subtask and sub-subtasks, respectively, of that group.

When you move a summary task, the move affects the relationships of subtasks to other tasks. The subtasks are groupies of the summary task. Where the summary task goes, its subtasks follow — even if this doesn't make sense to your schedule. You probably need to modify task relationships if you have already linked tasks. For information about changing task relationships, see Chapter 6.

Collapsing and Expanding Tasks

One of the great features of Microsoft Project is its flexibility in the presentation of information. For instance, after you have outlined a project, you can simply point and click to expand or collapse the project.

To collapse a summary task, you click the minus box to the left of the Summary task's name. For example, click the minus box next to the Foundation Stage summary task to collapse its subtasks, as shown in Figure 5-5. Repeat this process to collapse the other subtasks.

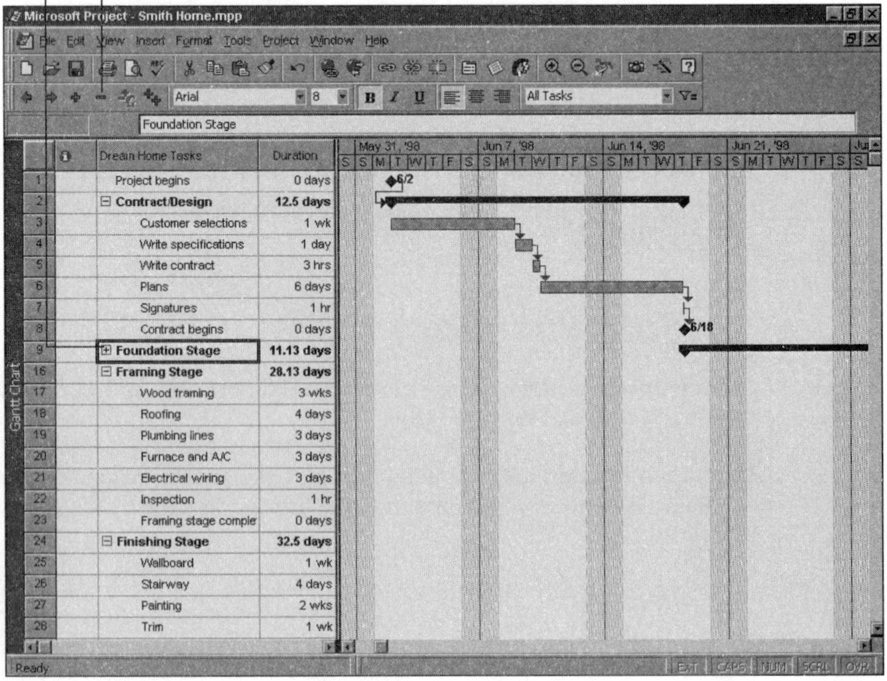

Figure 5-5: Click the Hide Subtasks button to collapse a summary task.

To expand a summary task, you click the plus box to the left of the Summary task's name. For example, click the plus box next to the Foundation Stage summary task to expand its subtasks, as shown in Figure 5-6.

To expand all subtasks, click the Show All Tasks button on the formatting toolbar.

Adding and Removing Outline Symbols and Numbers

You can remove the plus and minus symbols from summary tasks. You can also add or remove outline numbering, a feature similar to legal or regulatory outlining. You know the type — 1.1.1.1.1. instead of I.A.1.a.i.

TECHNICAL STUFF

The Outline option aligns according to a project management system called Work Breakdown Structure (WBS). In this system, tasks are organized to facilitate detailed reporting and tracking of costs. Each additional indent of a subtask is an increasingly detailed breakdown of project work.

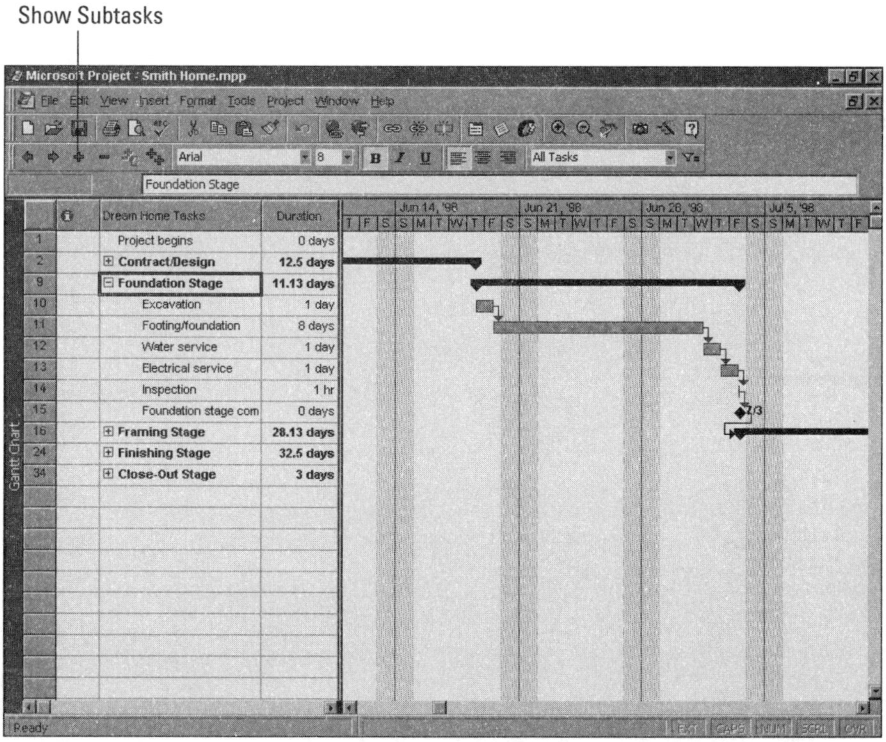

Figure 5-6: Click the Show Subtasks button to expand a task.

To activate the outline option:

1. **Choose Tools➪Options.**
2. **Click the View tab.**
3. **Click to clear the Show Outline Symbol check box.**
4. **Select the Show Outline Number check box.**
5. **Click OK.**

The tasks and subtasks are now associated with outline numbers, as shown in Figure 5-7. The outline numbers reflect the number of a summary task, the numbers of related subtasks, and the level of hierarchy within the summary task. This differs from a task ID. For instance, task ID 6 in outline numbering may be 2.4, which means it's the fourth subtask of summary task 2.

Now that you've gone to all this trouble to create your project, it would be simply *outlinedish* to risk someone tripping on your power cord or dropping a box of nails on your keyboard. Hey! Do you know what time it is? Right. It's time to save the file again. Click Save, select Save 'Smith Home.MPP' without a Baseline, and click OK.

After I outline a project, I'm always glad I did, even though the process is a pain in the subtask. In other chapters, you reap the rewards of those who toil. May all your tasks be promoted!

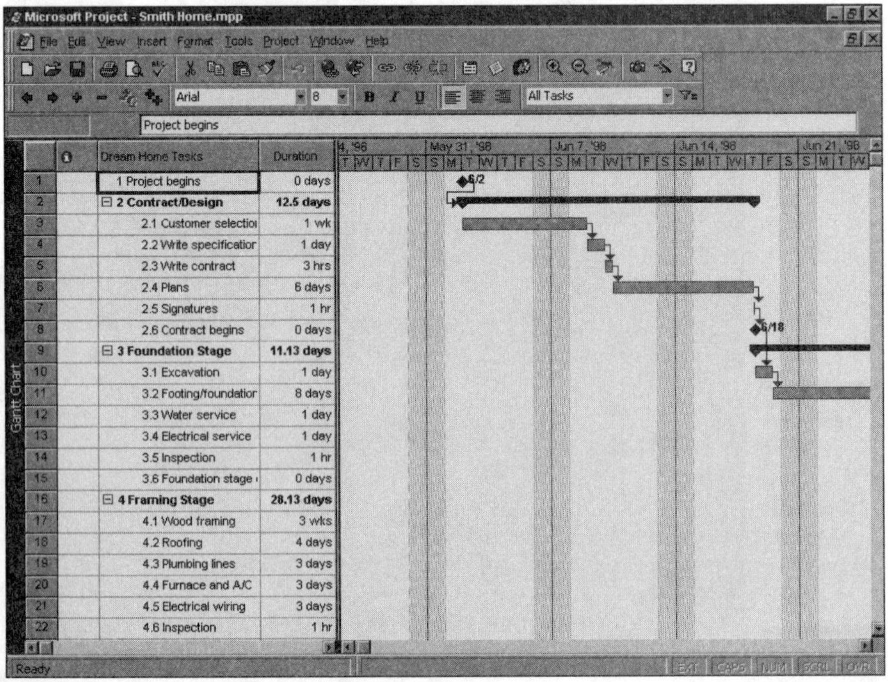

Figure 5-7: When you set outline numbers to be visible, they remain so until you clear the Show Outline Number check box.

Chapter 6

Task Relationships

In This Chapter

- Applying constraint to tasks
- Exploring the Gantt table
- Detailing task information
- Modifying task relationships

Microsoft Project is all about relationships — it's a master of whodunits (or whosgoingtodoits). As the project manager, you are the great storyteller. You get to choose the twists and turns and control the outcomes. The players of the story, the tasks, are *dependent* on other tasks to begin or finish. The tasks are also the cause of other tasks beginning — the predecessors. *The Predecessors!* What a title! You'll sell a million. Can I come to your file signing?

The success of your project is largely the result of the care you put into your task relationships. Sometimes the players are constrained by circumstances beyond their control. In this chapter, you have an opportunity to establish various task relationships and constraints in your project.

The example in this chapter is based on the Smith Home project file you create in Chapter 4 and further develop in Chapter 5. You use this example throughout Part II. If you haven't already created the file, you may want to follow the instructions in Chapters 4 and 5.

If it isn't already open, open `Smith Home.MPP` in the Practice Files folder.

Using Constraint and Feeling Good about It

Some tasks have to begin or end on certain dates. This may be due to the availability of a key consultant or limited access to an important piece of equipment. Other tasks can start just as soon as their predecessors finish. In either case, priorities govern the beginning and end of every task. In project management, these priorities are called constraints.

A *constraint* is a time limitation placed on a task. All linked tasks have constraints. Looking at your home building project, you can see that Microsoft Project linked each task to follow directly on the heels of its predecessor. Microsoft Project used its default constraint, called *As Soon As Possible*. Fortunately, you aren't limited to this constraint because reality isn't limited to it. In fact, Microsoft Project uses eight kinds of constraints, as listed in Table 6-1.

Table 6-1 Constraints and Their Descriptions

Constraint	*Description*
As Late As Possible (ALAP)	The task must start as late as possible without impeding the start date of subsequent tasks. This constraint has no actual constraint date.
As Soon As Possible (ASAP)	The task must start as early as possible. This constraint has no actual constraint date. This is the Microsoft Project default constraint for tasks.
Finish No Earlier Than (FNET)	The task must end no sooner than a certain constraint date.
Finish No Later Than (FNLT)	The task must finish no later than a certain constraint date.
Must Finish On (MFO)	The task must finish on a certain date. The date is anchored in the schedule.
Must Start On (MSO)	The task must start on a certain date. The date is anchored in the schedule.
Start No Earlier Than (SNET)	The task must start on or after your constraint date.
Start No Later Than (SNLT)	The task must start on or before your constraint date.

Microsoft Project used its ASAP constraint when it linked all the tasks in your home building project. Some remodeling is in order — not of the house, but of some task constraints:

- The ASAP default set the signing of the contract on June 18. It actually is scheduled for 11:00 a.m. on July 1.
- The contract begins at the signing of the contract, but the actual scheduled beginning of the work is July 7 at 8 a.m.

Microsoft Project usually provides multiple ways to enter information. One way is to enter information directly into the Gantt table. You'll use this method to change the contract signing constraint.

Using the Gantt Table

To take full advantage of the reporting capability of the Gantt table, you'll need to change the manner in which Microsoft Project displays dates and time. The default way is to show a day/date. You need to see time of day as well. To change this, select Tools⇨Options. Click the View tab. In the Date format box, select the day/date/time format (Fri 1/31/97 12:33 PM). Click OK.

The Gantt table presents your project plans in a table format. As you see in Part III, the table provides more information than you can shake a Gantt bar at. Who knows what lurks behind the Gantt chart? The project manager knows. That's you, or at least it will be you soon. Take a look:

1. **Select the vertical separator bar between the Gantt table and the Gantt chart.**
2. **Drag the bar to the right until it reveals all the columns, including Resource Names.**

   Two columns, the Start column and the Finish column, may be full of hatch marks.
3. **Double-click the right edge of each column heading to expand the column's width and change the hatch marks to dates.**

The subtasks of the Foundation Stage may still be collapsed, so click the Show All Tasks button on the formatting toolbar. Your screen should now look like Figure 6-1.

The Start date and time for the contract signatures is Thursday, June 18, 1998, at 11:00 a.m. You need to change it to Wednesday, July 1, 1998, at 11:00 a.m. Simply do the following:

1. **Double-click the Start cell for the Signatures task.**

   The Task Information box appears. This is a handy tool for making changes to a task.
2. **Select the entire Start Date text box.**
3. **Type** 7/1 11:00 am **in the text box.**

   If the current year is not 1998, enter the current year also, such as 7/1/99 11:00 a.m.

   Don't use periods with the *AM* designation.
4. **Click OK.**

   A Planning Wizard dialog box appears, as shown in Figure 6-2. The Planning wizard is alerting you that you are about to modify the relationship of the Signature task and its predecessor, the Plans task.

If the Planning wizard doesn't appear, click the Undo button on the standard toolbar. Then choose Tools➪Options. Select the General tab and then select the Advice from Planning Wizard check box. Make sure all the advice check boxes are checked. Click the OK button and repeat Steps 1 through 4.

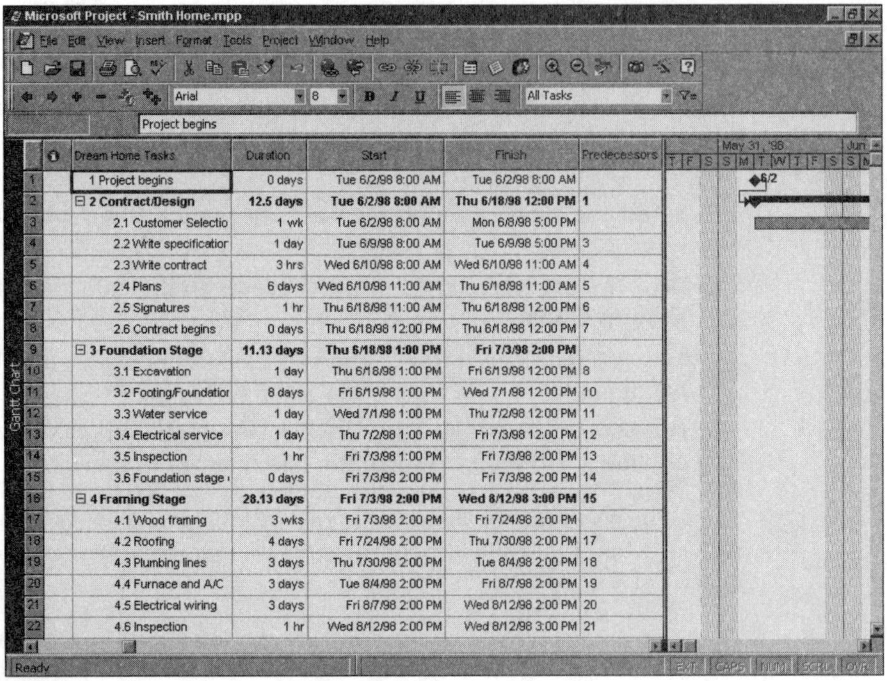

Figure 6-1: The Gantt table displays all its columns.

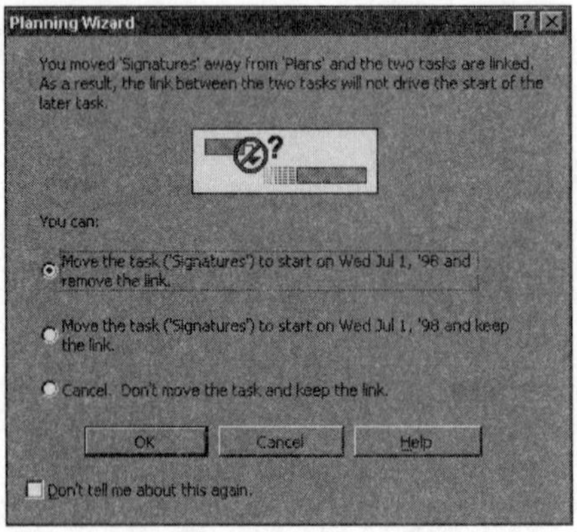

Figure 6-2: The Planning wizard asks whether you want to maintain a link even though you have changed a constraint.

5. **Select the second option, the one that moves the task and keeps the link.**
6. **Click OK.**

   You have changed a constraint from ASAP to SNET (Start No Earlier Than).

Notice that the indicator (i) column now contains a constraints indicator icon. If you place your cursor over the icon, a tool tip appears telling you that the task is now Start No Earlier Than as well as the constraint date.

Using the Task Information Box

One of the more efficient ways to assess and make changes to tasks is by using the Task form. As you are about to see, it puts all kinds of information at your fingertips simultaneously. You can access the Task form by selecting a task and then clicking the Task Information button on the standard toolbar.

But perhaps a better way to see the Task form is through a combination view. A *combination view* contains two views about information. The lower view, or pane, shows detailed information about the task or resource that is highlighted in the upper pane.

Before changing to a combination view, you need to expose more of the Gantt chart and less of the Gantt table:

1. **Select the vertical bar separating the Gantt table and the Gantt chart.**
2. **Drag the vertical bar to the left until it exposes only the Task Name and Duration columns.**
3. **Choose Window⇨Split to change to a combination view.**

   Your screen should now look like Figure 6-3.

Welcome to a combination view! In this crazy little world, you can see a portion of the Gantt table, the Gantt chart, and the Task form. This isn't exactly a view from Pike's Peak, but it's about the best that Microsoft Project has to offer.

You can manipulate each of the two windows and their sections. For example, to view a combination perspectives on one piece of information, do the following:

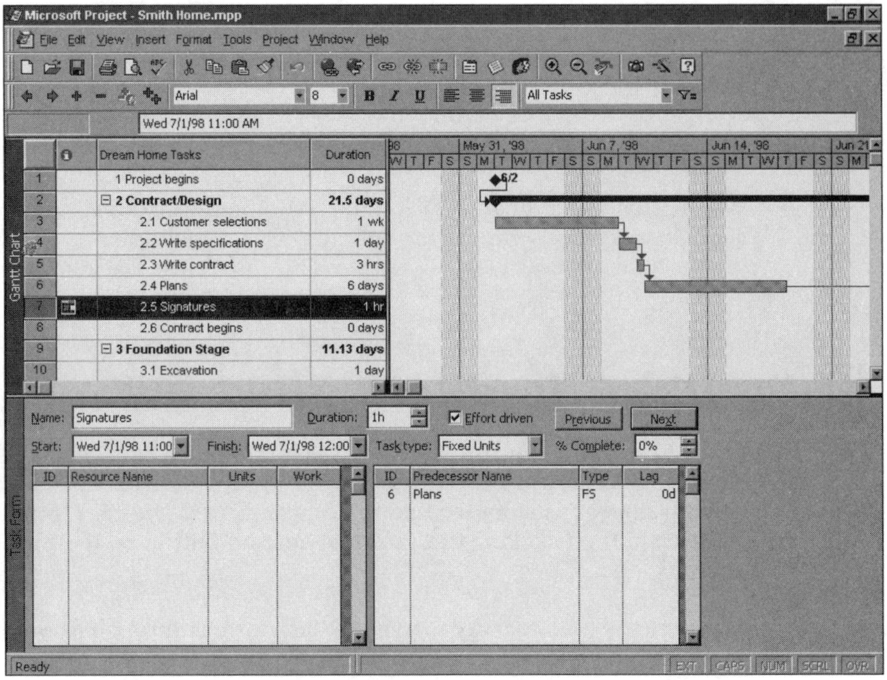

Figure 6-3: The screen is split, revealing the Gantt chart and the Task Information box.

1. **Select the Signatures task.**

2. **Click the Goto Selected Task button on the standard toolbar.**
3. **Click the Zoom In button on the standard toolbar a few times to see the bihourly timescale.**
4. **If necessary, click the Goto Selected Task button again to line up the view with the Signatures task.**
5. **After you're finished, click the Zoom Out button until you return to the weeks/days timescale.**

Next, you'll use the Task form in a combination view to change a duration and a task relationship. In the Gantt table, highlight one of the tasks. Then if necessary, in the task form, click the Next button until the Excavation task is highlighted and *Excavation* appears in the Name box of the Task form.

The Start date for the Excavation task is wrong. Excavation is the first task after the contract has been signed. As the schedule is currently written, the excavation is slated to begin right after lunch on the same day as the contract signing. Realistically, the excavation contractor will need a three-day lead time.

To change the excavation contractor's lead time, you need to change the constraints on the Excavation task. The standard Task form doesn't offer a constraint option, so first you need to change to the Task Details form:

1. **Choose View⇨More Views to change to the Task Details form.**

   A list box appears.

2. **Scroll through the list until you find Task Details Form and double-click it.**

   The Task Details form, shown in Figure 6-4, replaces the standard Task form.

3. **Under Constraint, click the down arrow.**

   A list box appears.

4. **Select Start No Earlier Than.**

5. **In the Date box under Constraint, type** 7/6.

   If the current year isn't 1998, type the current year also, such as 7/6/99.

6. **Click OK.**

   Notice that the start and finish dates for the task have changed in the Task Details form. Also notice that the Gantt chart has moved the Excavation date to Monday, July 6 (see Figure 6-5).

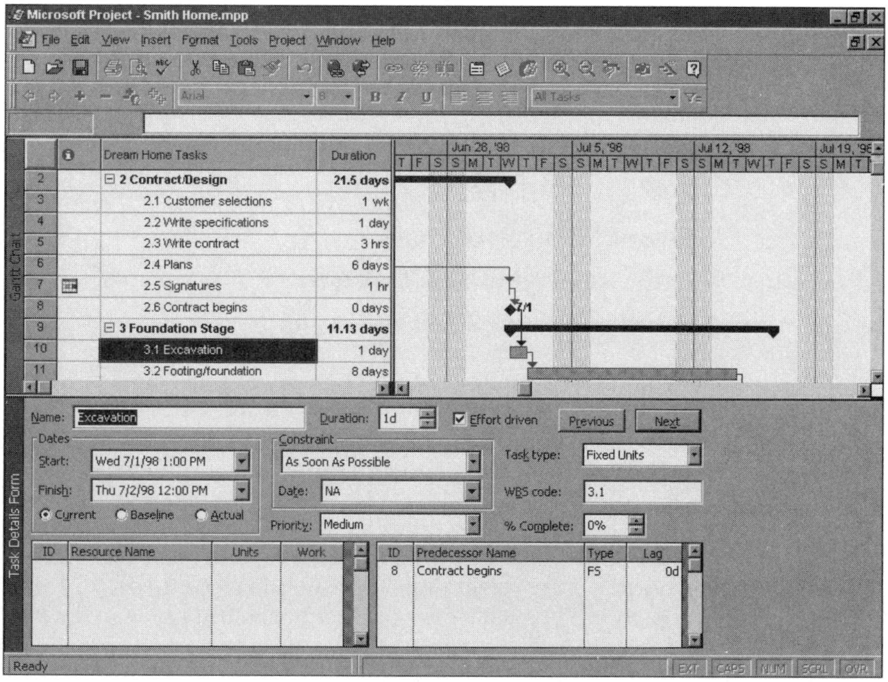

Figure 6-4: The Task Details form has constraint options.

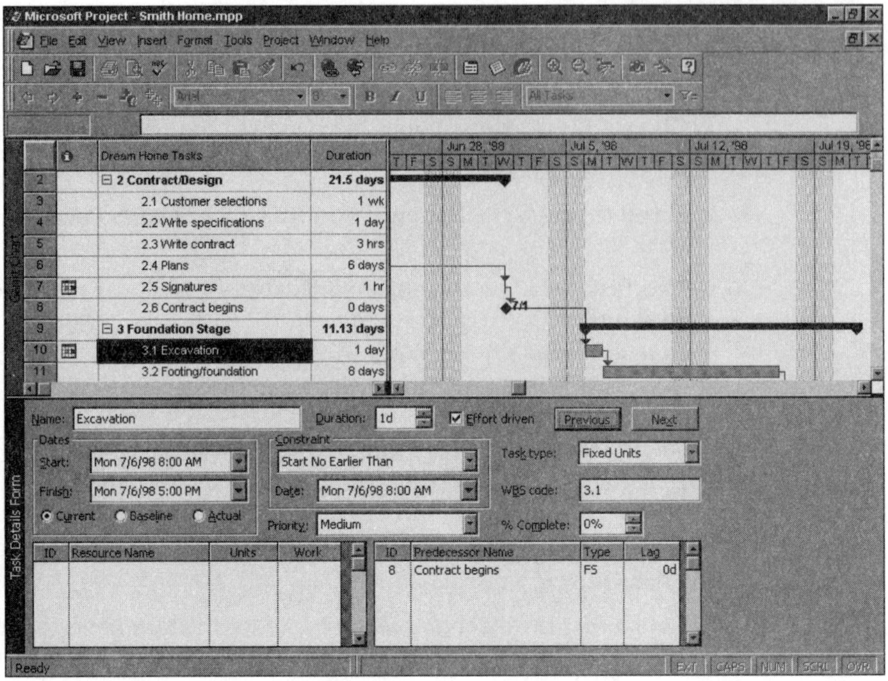

Figure 6-5: The changes to the start and finish dates are reflected in the Gantt chart.

While you're in the Task Details form, click Previous until you reach the Signatures task. Notice that the constraint change you made to Signatures is recorded in the list box under Constraints. Click Next until you're back to the Excavation task.

You won't be making any other constraint changes for now, so change the form view back to the standard Task form:

1. **Choose View⇨More Views.**
2. **In the list, double-click Task form.**

   You're back to the standard Task form.

While you're in the split view, you may want to see how you're doing with the projected completion date. Click anywhere in the Gantt chart. The vertical bar on the far left of the window is highlighted in color rather than appearing gray, which indicates that the Gantt window is the active view.

Press Page Down as many times as necessary until the final task, Project complete, appears. Select the Project complete task. The Task form probably says that the project finish date is Friday, October 16, 1998. This is unacceptable. The customer contract has a firm move-in date of no later than Thursday, October 1. You have some project management to do to meet this deadline. One of the ways you can do some time managing is by changing task relationships.

Press Page Up until the Excavation task appears again. Then click anywhere in the Task form to make it active.

Changing Task Relationships

You need to find ways to manage time. A project is seldom totally linear. More often than not, many tasks occur at the same time. Speaking of time, it's time to change some task relationships in your home building project. You can schedule tasks to happen concurrently. Water and electric service meet this bill (sorry, no pun intended). So those are the first relationships to change:

1. **Click Previous or Next until you reach the Water service task.**

   The Task form shows that the predecessor of Water service is Footing/foundation, ID 11. This is okay.

2. **Click Next.**

   You should be at Electrical service. Its predecessor is Water service, ID 12. To make Electric service occur concurrently with Water service, the Electric service and the Water service must share the same predecessor.

3. **Change the Electric service predecessor by selecting the ID column in the Task form and typing** 11.

4. **Click OK.**

   Notice that the predecessor name has changed to Footing/foundation.

5. **Click anywhere in the Gantt chart to activate the Gantt window to view the result.**

6. **With Electrical service highlighted, click the Goto Selected Task button on the standard toolbar.**

   Your screen should look similar to Figure 6-6.

Notice that the Gantt chart now assigns the same predecessor to Water service and Electric service. They both start on the same day. Because both tasks have the same duration, they also end on the same day. As you see a little later, this isn't always the case.

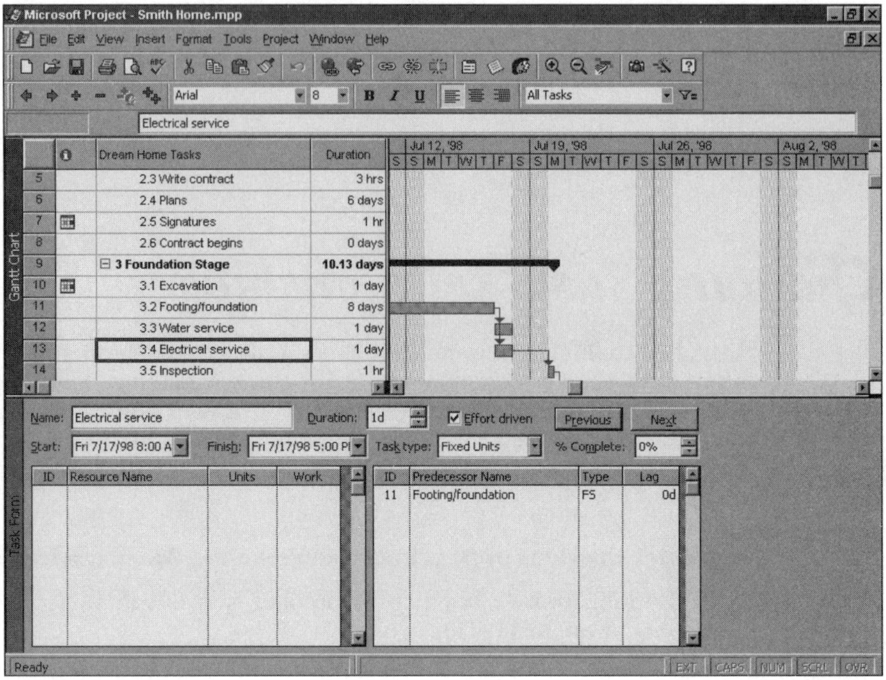

Figure 6-6: The Electric service and Water service tasks now share the same predecessor.

Lagging

Sometimes you need to make room in a project (and maybe in your life, if you're like me) to allow for some flexibility of time. You achieve loose time between dependent tasks by a process called *lagging*.

In the Task form, you can see that the Finish date and time for the Electrical service task is Friday, July 17, at 5:00 p.m. Click the Next button to arrive at the Inspection task. Its Start date is Monday, July 20, at 8:00 a.m. This is the next workday and the next work hour. You need to add some lag time to this task relationship.

Lag time can be in minutes, hours, days, or weeks. In the following, you add a one-day lag:

1. **Select the Lag column and type** 1d.
2. **Click OK.**

Notice that the Lag column now says 1d and that the start date has changed to Tuesday (see Figure 6-7). Also notice that the Gantt chart has changed to reflect the lag. In addition, because the Inspection task is a subtask of the Foundation Stage summary task, the summary bar has elongated. Way to go, you ol' project manager!

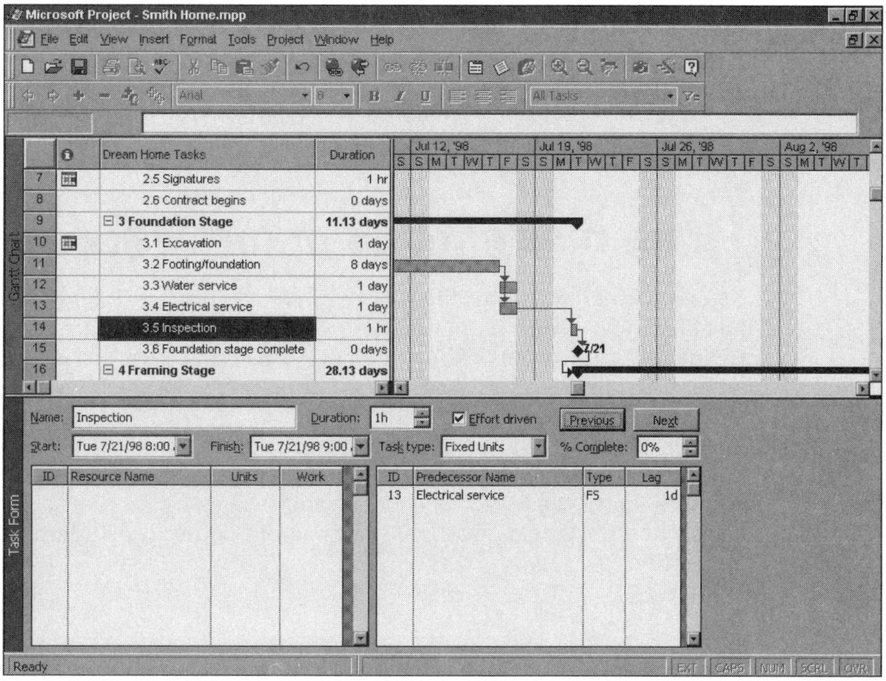

Figure 6-7: The Gantt chart shows a one-day lag.

Sharing predecessors

Using what you know so far, you need to make some task relationship changes in the Framing Stage. The Roofing, Plumbing lines, Furnace and A/C, and Electrical wiring tasks could share the same predecessor and, therefore, happen at the same time. For all these tasks, make Wood framing, ID 17, their predecessor:

1. **Click Previous or Next until you reach the task (such as Roofing).**
2. **Change the task's predecessor by selecting the ID column and typing** 17 **in the column.**
3. **Click OK.**
4. **Follow Steps 1 through 3 for the remaining tasks.**

After you're finished:

1. **Click anywhere in the Gantt chart.**
2. **Select the Electrical wiring task.**

3. **Click the Goto Selected Task button on the standard toolbar.**
4. **Scroll the Gantt chart until your screen appears similar to Figure 6-8.**

   The tasks should be stacked as you specified when you gave them all the same predecessor.

Fixing time glitches in the Task form

You've corrected one problem only to create another. Task ID 22, Inspection, has Electrical wiring as its predecessor. The problem is that the Electrical wiring task's duration is shorter than the Roofing task. Inspection can't occur until all Framing Stage construction subtasks are complete.

Sheesh. Does it feel like you're trying to rub out an ink spot? It's really not that bad. As you edit your project, changes sometimes require other changes. In this case, you have to change the Inspection task predecessor and provide a one-day lag as you did before the Foundation Stage inspection.

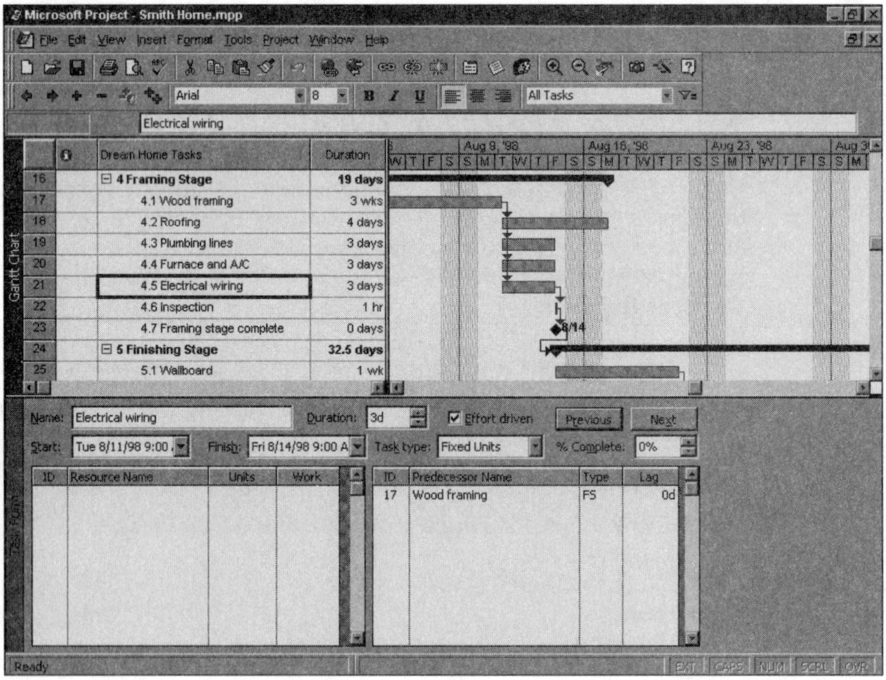

Figure 6-8: Four tasks share the same predecessor.

To edit the task:

1. **Click the Next button in the Task form until you come to ID 22, the Inspection task.**
2. **Change the predecessor ID to 18.**

   This ID is the Roofing task, the longest of the four preceding stacked tasks.
3. **Select the Lag column and type** 1d **in the column.**
4. **Click OK.**

Your project should now look like Figure 6-9. You've made big progress.

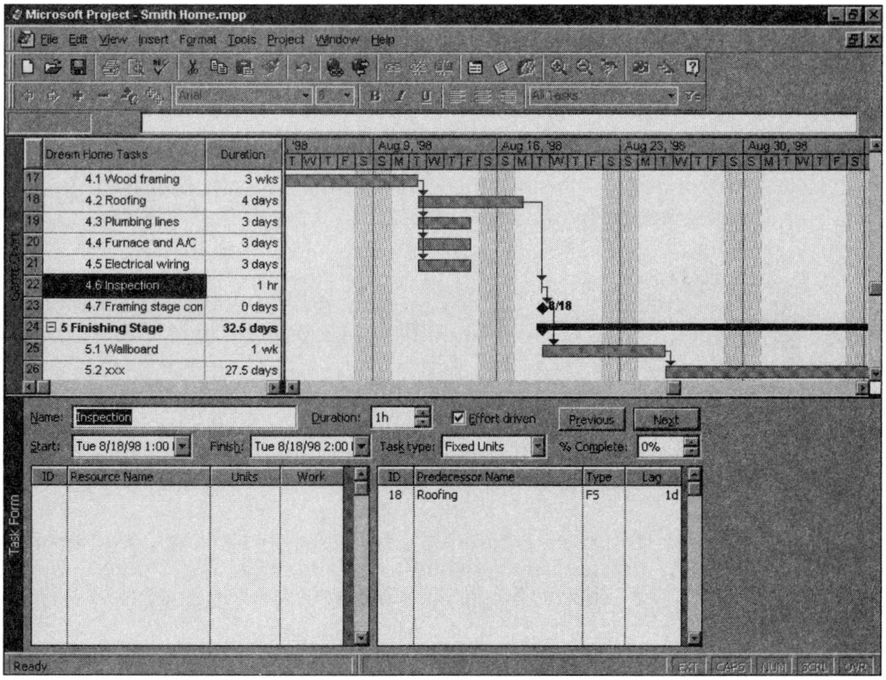

Figure 6-9: The corrected inspection date corresponds with the longest task of the group. In Microsoft Project, task relationships (links) can relate not only adjoining tasks but any tasks — even tasks in other projects!

Kinds of Task Relationships

Microsoft Project has four kinds of task relationships: finish-to-start, start-to-start, finish-to-finish, and start-to-finish:

- **Finish-to-start (FS)** relationships are the default Microsoft Project task relationship. It means that Task A must finish before Task B can begin. When you create a link, the default relationship is finish-to-start.
- **Start-to-start (SS)** relationships mean that Task B can't start until Task A does. An example of this is heating a store-bought pizza. Task A heats the oven. Task B puts the pizza in the oven.
- **Finish-to-finish (FF)** relationships mean that Task B cannot finish before Task A does. An example is a credit card sale. Task A delivers the product to the customer. Task B gets the customer to sign the credit slip.
- **Start-to-finish (SF)** relationships mean that Task B can't finish until Task A starts. An example of this is a temporary electrical generator that can't stop until power is turned on to a permanent electrical system.

As you've probably guessed by now, some task relationships in the home building project aren't the default finish-to-start relationship. Specifically, you need to change some relationship types in the Finishing Stage of the project.

The Wallboard task (ID 25) and the Stairway task (ID 26) should both start at the same time. They should have a start-to-start (SS) relationship.

The Painting task (ID 27) should also have a start-to-start (SS) relationship with the Wallboard task (ID 25), but it should lag by four days. That way, the wallboard crew can finish a portion of the house so that the painter can begin priming and applying the first coat.

The carpenter can begin doing the finish woodwork as soon as the paint dries. When one-third of the Painting task (ID 27) is completed, the Trim task (ID 28) should begin. This is also a start-to-start (SS) relationship.

The Landscaping task should coincide with the completion of the Painting task. This is a finish-to-finish (FF) relationship.

The Customer walkthrough task (ID 30) should follow the completion of the Painting task (ID 27) and should have a two-day lag. This is a finish-to-start (FS) and a lag.

This may seem like a lot, but it's not. Each of these conditions is normal in a project plan and is easy to perform (and understand) in Microsoft Project. Scout's honor.

To begin changing task relationships, start with the Wallboard and Stairway relationship:

1. **Click the Next button until the Task form reaches ID 26, the Stairway task.**

   The predecessor is already ID 25, Wallboard. But you need to change the Type.
2. **Select the Type column and type** ss.

   The letters *ss* stand for start-to-start.
3. **Click OK.**

   As the Gantt chart shows, the Stairway task has a start-to-start relationship with the Wallboard task.

Next, you change the Painting and Wallboard relationship. As mentioned, you need to set a start-to-start relationship of this task to its new predecessor, the Wallboard task (ID 25). And you need to set a four-day lag.

1. **Click the Next button until the Task form reaches ID 27, the Painting task.**
2. **Select the Predecessor ID column, and type** 25.
3. **Click OK.**
4. **Select the Type column, and type** ss.
5. **Select the Lag column, and type** 4d.
6. **Click OK.**

   As the Gantt chart shows, the Painting task has a start-to-start relationship with the Wallboard task and has a lag of four days.

Note the grayed areas of the Gantt chart, which indicate nonworking periods. By default, Microsoft Project considers Saturday and Sunday as nonworking days. See Chapter 7 to find out how to modify the default working schedules.

Next, you need to set a start-to-start relationship with the Trim task's existing predecessor, the Painting task (ID 27). In this case, you need some lead time.

Lead time is the opposite of lag time. With lead time, you give the predecessor a certain head start before the dependent task can begin. Lead time is expressed as a percentage or in minus minutes, hours, days, or weeks.

In this example, the Painting task should have a 33 percent lead before the Trim task starts. To change the Painting and Trim relationship:

1. **Click the Next button until the Task form reaches ID 28, the Trim task.**
2. **Select the Type column, and type** ss.
3. **Select the Lag column, and type** 33%.

   Microsoft Project interprets the percentage as a lead time for the Predecessor task.
4. **Click OK.**

   In the Gantt chart, the Trim task now has a start-to-start relationship with the Painting task and gives the Painting task a 33 percent lead.

The Landscaping task should coincide with the completion of the Painting task (ID 27). This is a finish-to-finish (FF) relationship:

1. **Click the Next button until the Task form reaches ID 29, the Landscaping task.**
2. **Select the Predecessor ID column, and type** 27.
3. **Click OK.**
4. **Select the Type column, and type** ff.

   The letters *ff* stand for finish-to-finish.
5. **Click OK.**

   In the Gantt chart, the Landscaping task now has a finish-to-finish relationship with the Painting task. Both tasks end at the same time.

You can change a task relationship also by double-clicking a link in the Gantt chart. Double-click anywhere on a link between tasks. The Task Dependency dialog box appears. The dialog box identifies the link from Task A to Task B. The Type box allows you to select a task relationship. The Lag box allows you to enter lag (or lead) time.

Next, the Customer walkthrough task should follow the completion of the Painting task (ID 27) and have a two-day lag. To change the Customer walkthrough and Painting relationship:

1. **Click the Next button until the Task form reaches ID 30, the Customer walkthrough task.**
2. **Select the Predecessor ID column, and type** 27.
3. **Click OK.**
4. **Select the Lag column, and type** 2d.
5. **Click OK.**

   You have completed your changes to the Finishing Stage.

Removing split and making your eyes horizontal again

Had enough of this magnificent combination view? Are your eyeballs working independently? Well, you have just about beat the living tar out of the Task form. Why not let it cool down for awhile and return to a single view?

To remove a split, choose Window⇨Remove Split or double-click the horizontal split-screen separator. The screen returns to a full Gantt chart. Scroll the Gantt chart so that the Finishing Stage summary task is near the top-left corner of the chart. Your Gantt chart should now look similar to Figure 6-10.

After all that work, it's time to resave the project file:

1. **Click the Save button on the standard toolbar.**
2. **Select Save 'Smith Home.MPP' without a Baseline.**
3. **Click OK.**

A task is to a project what dirt is to a garden. It isn't much to look at, but try growing a begonia without it. Tasks are the groundwork of a project — nothing happens without them.

But begonias need more than dirt; they need people and tools for planting, watering, and weeding. And so it is with a project. Tasks, left to themselves, usually don't bear worthwhile fruit. In project management lingo, the planters, waterers, and weeders are called resources. Properly managed resources can make a bouquet from a briar patch. To find out about resources, check out Chapter 7.

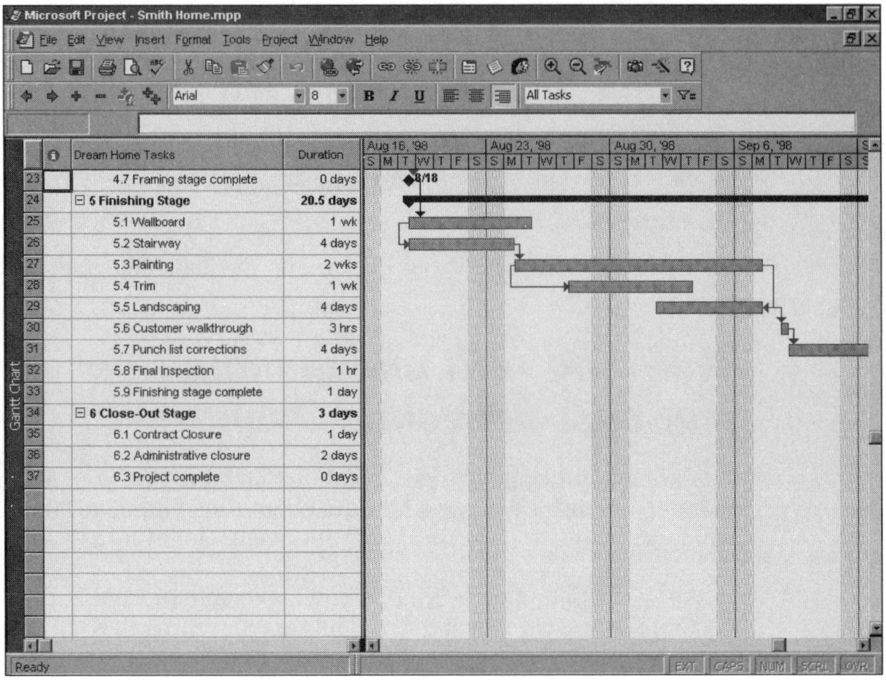

Figure 6-10: The Gantt chart shows the new task relationships in the Finishing Stage task.

Chapter 7

Resources

In This Chapter

- Identifying people and things as resources
- Making the most of what you have
- Relating resources to responsibilities
- Putting the details into resources
- Controlling time with multiple calendars
- Shortcut ways to assign resources

So, you're responsible for a project. Its success is important to you and your organization. If you get it right, the world will be put on notice that one serious strategist is in its midst. If you don't get it right . . . well, that's not an option.

The project needs to run like a machine. Deadlines must be kept and goals must be met. Of course, things won't always run like clockwork. People overbook, materials arrive late, equipment breaks down. But those events don't change the fact that the project has to meet its goals on time and on budget.

This situation isn't as bleak as it appears. It just means that getting your name into next year's Who's Who of project management may require managing your project resources.

What You and Your Chair Have in Common

Resources are equipment and the people who perform work on your project. However, in project management, resources aren't *every* piece of equipment and *every* person who performs work on your project.

For instance, ensuring that every member of the project team has a desk and a chair may be out of the scope of your project management responsibilities. That may be part of the operational givens of the organization that initiates the project. In contrast, if you and your project team need to meet in a conference room every Monday morning at 8:30, that conference room may be one of the resources of your project. You may need to manage the room's availability.

The same is true of people. It may be an operational given that the shipping department provides the people power to handle all incoming and outgoing mail and parcels. If you have a mass mailing that must go out on a certain date, however, the shipping department personnel have just become a project resource. The proper scheduling of and communication about that mailing is a project management responsibility.

The art of resource planning is a beauty to behold when performed well — and ugly to the bone when performed poorly.

Resources and Cost Estimating

You can't separate resources from their cost. Resources and cost are so interrelated that any decision about one usually affects the other. As you see here (and in Chapter 15), Microsoft Project makes it possible for you to work on both simultaneously. You can

- Determine whether the resource cost accrues up front, throughout the work, or at the end.
- Set hourly and overtime rates.
- Indicate flat per-visit charges.
- Establish that a resource is working on a contractual fixed cost.

Determining and managing the right quality, quantity, and availability of resources separates project managers from wanna-be's. But this isn't as scary as it may seem. A project manager isn't necessarily a walking encyclopedia of technical and managerial knowledge. More often, an effective project manager makes expert judgment by knowing how to get and use good information. Here are some tips.

Tie resources to tasks

Ensuring a successful marriage of resources to the project is much easier if you specifically assign resources to individual tasks or groups of tasks. As you'll soon see, Microsoft Project recognizes only resources tied to tasks.

Find out how the same thing was accomplished before

A man visiting Ernest Hemingway for the first time, so the story goes, was shocked by what he found. Everywhere, in every room, in every available space, he saw stacks and stacks of books. When the visitor asked Hemingway why he had so many books, the novelist simply said that a writer has to read. The significance of this story to you, the project manager, is that the easiest and safest step to success is to find out how similar projects have been accomplished by experts (who happen to be people just like you).

Remember your goal

A new project manager may be tempted to spend hours developing a dynamite set of goals and objectives and then file them somewhere as though they were unrelated to the reality of the moment. Nothing could be further from the truth. As you assign resources, they should directly relate to your goals, objectives, and project scope. If they don't, be warned! The horse is getting out of the barn. Back up, take a deep breath, meet with your project team, and solve the discrepancy immediately.

Create a resource pool

You can find out the details about the resource pool in a little bit, but consider this for now: A *resource pool* is the sum of people and equipment you have available for your project. Some resources are unlimited in their availability; others are specific as to when and to what degree they can be utilized. Some carry no direct cost to your project, some are a fixed cost, and others are available a la carte. Prepare the list accordingly.

Know your limitations

Knowing your limitations means that you should be well versed in company policy about rentals, consulting fees, equipment purchases, and the like. Near misses count only in horseshoes and hand grenades. Be sure that you know what is and isn't expected.

A real-life blunder illustrates my point. A friend of mine once managed a multimillion-dollar video production project that involved stakeholders in Los Angeles, Indianapolis, and Washington, D.C. The project deadlines were killers, and approval for all production phases required signatures from all three stakeholders. Therefore, overnight delivery of materials was an almost daily occurrence. At the conclusion of the highly successful project, my friend received a negative performance appraisal because he had violated his company's policy regarding overnight deliveries.

Get help

Expert judgment is more often than not a team achievement. See whether other parts of your organization can give you expert counsel about company policies and guidelines. Find out whether any professional or trade associations can shed some light on standard practices that may affect your project. One good way to learn about trade associations is by searching the Internet.

If you're not a regular cruiser on the Net, you can find out how to perform powerful searches in *The Internet For Dummies,* 5th Edition (written by John Levine, Carol Baroudi, and Margaret Levine Young and published by IDG Books Worldwide, Inc.).

Resource-Driven and Fixed-Duration Tasks

Microsoft Project assumes that you are working with resource-driven tasks unless you tell it otherwise. If you increase the amount of resources assigned to a *resource-driven task,* the task will be shorter in duration. For example, if it takes two people six hours to unload boxes of oranges from a truck, four people could do it in three hours. In contrast, a *fixed-duration task* is unaffected by resources. For example, the procedure of signing a mortgage takes an hour. If 15 people were in the room, it would still take an hour.

You use the Task form to designate a task as fixed duration. From the Gantt Chart view, choose Window⇨Split. Select the appropriate task and then select the Fixed option on the Task form. Now the task duration will remain the same no matter what changes you make to the task's resources.

Hitching Resources to Tasks

Before you go through all the trouble of assigning resources to tasks, you may ask yourself whether you really need to do so. Some projects don't need that kind of specificity. If you don't associate resources to tasks, Microsoft Project does its schedule calculations by using the project's task duration and task relationship information.

In most cases, you'll find a real value in assigning resources to tasks. Microsoft Project is a trooper, keeping track of and automatically updating even the most complex resource and cost relationships. By assigning resources to tasks, you can:

- Keep your hands on costs
- Determine when too many or too few resources are allocated to a task
- Find out when resources are scheduled to be in two places at one time
- Track the stages of completion of a task by various resources
- Understand and report with accuracy

The example in this chapter is based on an example project file (Smith Home project) that you create in Chapter 4 and further develop in Chapters 5 and 6. You use this example throughout Part II. If you haven't already created the file, you may want to follow the instructions in Chapters 4, 5, and 6.

Using the Assign Resources dialog box

In Microsoft Project, resources can be hitched to tasks in a number of ways. The simplest way is by using the Assign Resources dialog box. This dialog box directly associates a resource list to a specific task.

The dialog box has two columns: Name and Units. *Name* is the title you assign to a resource. *Units* is a quantity of resource units dedicated to the selected task. Microsoft Project's default unit assignment is 1. This means 1 unit (person or equipment) is assigned 100 percent of its time per day throughout a task's duration.

You use the Smith Home project to look at the Assign Resources dialog box and to practice assigning resources:

1. **Open Smith Home.MPP in the Practice Files folder if it isn't already open.**
2. **Select task 3, Customer selections.**

3. **Click the Assign Resources button on the standard toolbar.**
4. **In the Name box, type** Sales **and press Enter.**

So far, you've created a resource, but you haven't assigned it to the task. Before you do, determine the unit assignment of the resource. The Customer selections task has a duration of 1 week. Although the selection process may take a week, the resource allocation is quite different. Of the entire sales force of ten full-time employees, you're assigning one person one-fourth of her or his time to this customer. The unit designation for this is 0.25. Type **0.25** in the Units box and press Enter. See Figure 7-1. (If your unit designation appears as a percentage, select Tools⇨Options. Click the Schedule tab, and change the Show Assignment Units as: list box to Decimal.)

Three changes have occurred :

- A check mark appears next to the resource name in the Assign Resources dialog box. The check mark indicates the resource assignment.
- The resource name appears next to the taskbar on the Gantt chart.
- The unit allocation appears next to the resource name on the Gantt chart.

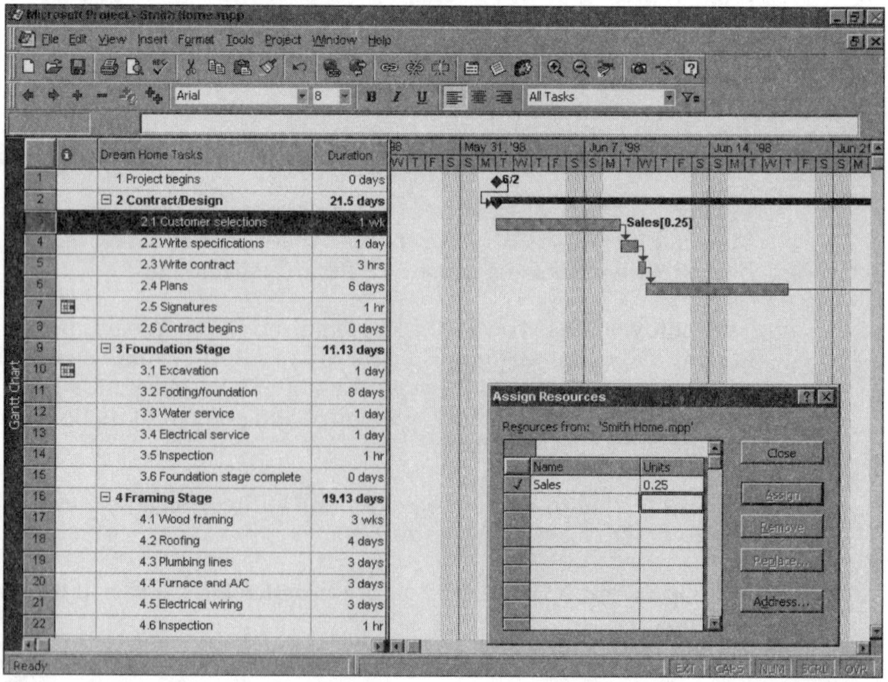

Figure 7-1: The resource is named, and a unit designation is assigned. The Gantt chart tags the resource and units to the right of the taskbar.

The first time you assign resources and their units to a task, Microsoft Project assumes that the resource assignment equals the duration you first estimated. After you assign a resource and unit designation, the task becomes a resource-driven task by default. Therefore, if you change the units, the task duration changes automatically. If this is not what you want, you can make the duration unchangeable (regardless of the resources or units) by converting the task to a fixed-duration task.

The resource pool

A fast and easy way to prepare your project for resource assignments is by creating a resource pool. A *resource pool* is a set of resources assembled for assignment to project tasks.

To create a resource pool for the Smith Home project:

1. **Highlight the Customer selections task, if it isn't already selected.**
2. **Click the Assign Resources button on the standard toolbar.**
3. **In the Name column, type** Specifications.
4. **Select the next line and type** Counsel.
5. **Repeat Step 4 for the following:**

   Drafting

   Excavation Contractor

   Water Utility

   Electric Utility

   Building Inspector

   Framing Crew

   Plumbing Contractor

   Mechanical Contractor

   Electrical Contractor

   Wallboard Crew

   Paint Crew

   Finish Carpenters

   Project Manager
6. **After you're finished, scroll back to the top of the list.**

   The Assign Resources dialog box should look like Figure 7-2.

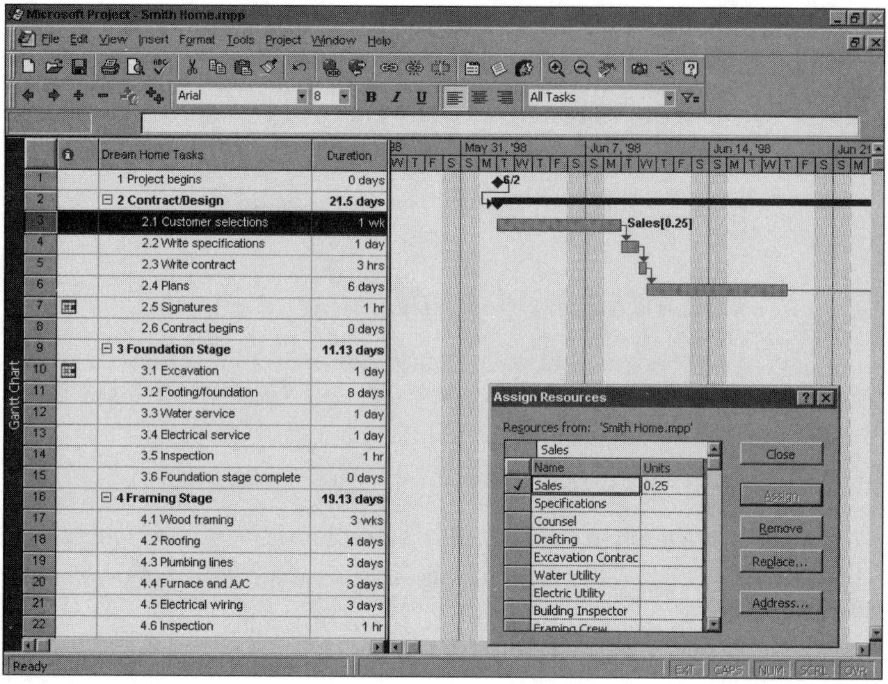

Figure 7-2: The check mark next to Sales indicates that it's the only resource in the pool assigned to the highlighted task, which is Customer selections.

A smart way to enter resources is by title rather than by a person's name and by specialty rather than by a company name. This gives you some leeway for changes in personnel and contracts.

Creating a resource pool is a major step in resource allocation. This is a good time to save the project file:

1. **Click the Save button on the standard toolbar.**
2. **Select Save 'Smith Home.MPP' without a Baseline.**
3. **Click OK.**

Resource details

Microsoft Project lets you get as detailed about your resources as your project requires. Some resources may be assigned staff whose salaries are not directly attributed to the project budget. Other resources may be hourly workers who directly affect the budget. And still other resources may be contractors who are working against a fixed amount. Whatever the case, the details are manageable.

If you close the Assign Resources dialog box, open it again by highlighting a task and selecting the Assign Resources button on the standard toolbar. Double-click Framing Crew, and the Resource Information dialog box appears, as shown in Figure 7-3.

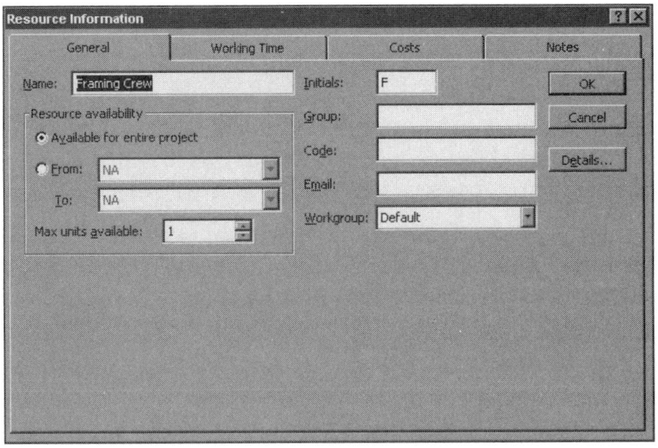

Figure 7-3: Use the Resource Information dialog box to enter as much or as little information as you choose.

The Resource Information dialog box is divided into four groups of information, each with its own tab. In the dialog box, you can enter a number of details specific to this resource. These details are true of this resource no matter which task you assign the resource to. Some of these details include the following:

- ***General tab***
  - **Name.** All resources are identified by their name or their initials.
  - **Initials.** A substitute for the Name field. This can save you some keystrokes when you're assigning resources.
  - **Max Units Available.** The total number of units available for the project. The number can range from 0 to 100. Microsoft Project uses this number when calculating whether you have enough resources for a task or multiple simultaneous tasks.
  - **Group.** The name of a resource group. Any resource using this group name will be part of the group. (For instance, you may put water and electric service in a group called Utilities.) Then you can sort by the group name.
  - **Code.** An alphanumeric code for the resource. This is a helpful tool for accounting.

- ***Working Time tab***
  - **Base Calendar.** Microsoft Project offers three flavors of base calendars: Standard, Night Shift, and 24 Hours. These three calendars are based on default settings. For instance, the Standard work calendar is Monday through Friday, from 8 a.m. to 5 p.m. with one hour for lunch and no holidays.
- ***Costs tab***
  - **Standard Rate.** The cost for regular work. Microsoft Project's default multiplier in this box is hours. If you type 15, for example, it interprets that to mean $15/hour. Possible time units are minutes (m), hours (h), days (d), and weeks (w).
  - **Overtime Rate.** The cost for overtime work. Use this if the resource expects an overtime rate for overtime work. Like Standard Rate, enter an amount followed by a time unit abbreviation.
  - **Per Use Cost.** The cost per use fee. An example of this is the building inspector's fee of, say, $65 per visit.
  - **Cost Accrual.** When the cost for the resource actually occurs. The three choices are Start (incur total actual cost as the tasks using this resource start), Prorated (incur actual costs as the tasks using this resource progress), and End (incur total actual cost as the tasks using this resource end). Microsoft Project defaults to an Accrue at Prorated cost unless you specify otherwise.

Using the Resource Information dialog box, assign the following details to the Framing Crew resource:

Option	***Value***
Initials	FC
Group	Carpenters
Max units available	16
Standard Rate	10
Overtime Rate	15

Click OK when you're finished.

The General and Costs tabs of the Resource Information dialog box should now look like Figures 7-4 and 7-5, respectively. Click OK. The Resource Information dialog box automatically interprets rates as a per-hour amount unless you use m for minute, d for day, or w for week.

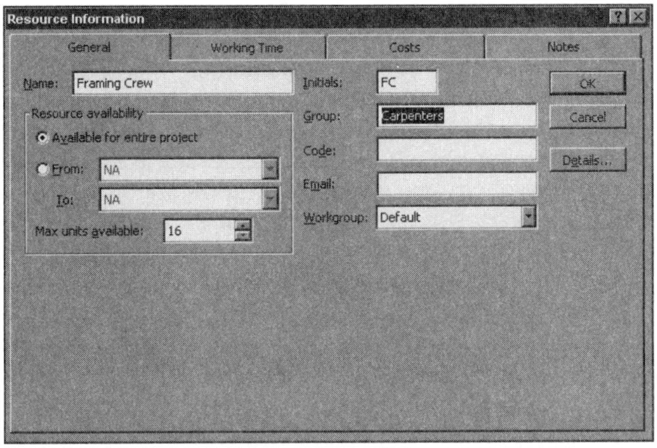

Figure 7-4: The General tab of the Resource Information dialog box.

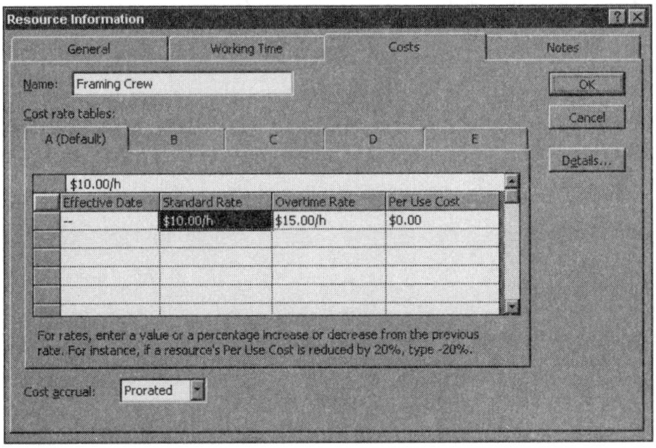

Figure 7-5: The Costs tab of the Resource Information dialog box.

Dragging a resource

An easy way to assign resources from the resource pool is by dragging them. Using the home building project as an example:

1. **Scroll the Gantt chart to the top.**
2. **Select Specifications from the resource pool.**
3. **Move the cursor to the leftmost column of the Assign Resources dialog box.**

   The cursor changes into a face.
4. **Click and drag the cursor over the Write specifications task.**
5. **Release the mouse button.**

The screen should look like Figure 7-6. The Specifications resource is now checked. Note that a unit of 1 is associated with the resource for that task. In addition, the Gantt chart lists the resource name.

The drag feature automatically assigns a unit of 1 to the resource. After you've assigned the resource, change the task units to modify the task duration. So, if you're planning an initial unit assignment of something other than 1.0, don't use the drag feature. Instead, enter a unit value in the Units column of the Assign Resources dialog box and click the Assign button.

Assigning a resource to multiple tasks

Using the resource pool, you can assign a resource to several tasks at the same time. If the tasks are grouped sequentially, select the first task, hold down the Shift key, and select the last task in the sequence. Release the Shift key. All the tasks in the sequence should be highlighted.

If the tasks are not grouped sequentially, select the first task, hold down the Ctrl key, and select the tasks you want. When you have selected the final task, release the Ctrl key. All the nonsequential tasks you selected should be highlighted.

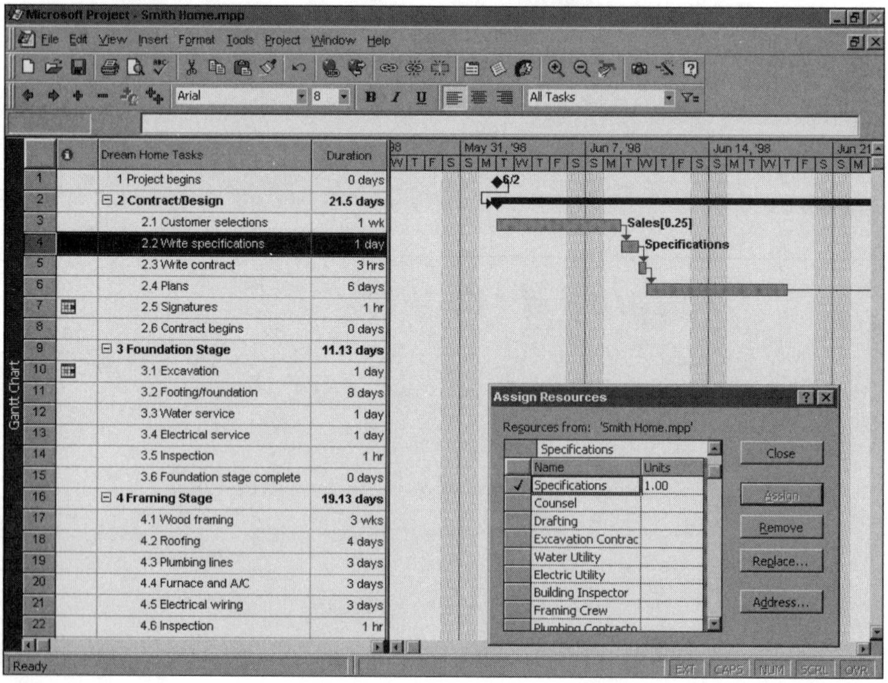

Figure 7-6: The Specifications resource in the Assign Resources dialog box is now checked, indicating that the resource has been assigned to the Write specifications task.

After you select the tasks, select the resource from the resource pool. If you want, you can add a unit assignment. When you are satisfied with your selections, click the Assign key.

Note that you can also assign multiple resources to a single task, and assign multiple resources to multiple tasks.

Using the home building example, you assign two resources to three tasks. It just so happens that the project manager and the building inspector must both perform the inspection task. Make some preliminary changes to the Gantt Chart view and then assign the resources to the tasks:

1. **Scroll the Gantt chart until the first Inspection task, task 14, is the topmost visible task.**
2. **Select task 14.**

3. **Click the Goto Selected Task button on the standard toolbar.**

4. **Click the Zoom Out button twice.**

   The timescale is now months and weeks.
5. **Drag the Assign Resources dialog box to the upper-right corner of the screen.**

   This gives you a fuller view of the Gantt chart.
6. **Select the first Inspection task, task 14 (if it isn't still selected).**
7. **Hold down the Ctrl key and select the other two Inspection tasks, tasks 22 and 32. Then release the Ctrl key.**
8. **In the Assign Resources dialog box, select Building Inspector.**
9. **Hold down the Ctrl key, scroll to the bottom of the resource pool, and select Project Manager. Then release the Ctrl key.**
10. **Click the Assign button in the Assign Resources dialog box.**

    The Gantt chart and the Assign Resources dialog box should look like Figure 7-7. Assigning multiple resources to a task doesn't affect the task's duration. But a change of units in a multiple resource assignment, just like in a single resource assignment, changes the task's duration unless the task is a fixed-duration task.

11. **Click the standard toolbar's Zoom In button twice.**

    The Gantt chart is restored to its normal timescale.
12. **Click the Close button in the Assign Resources dialog box.**

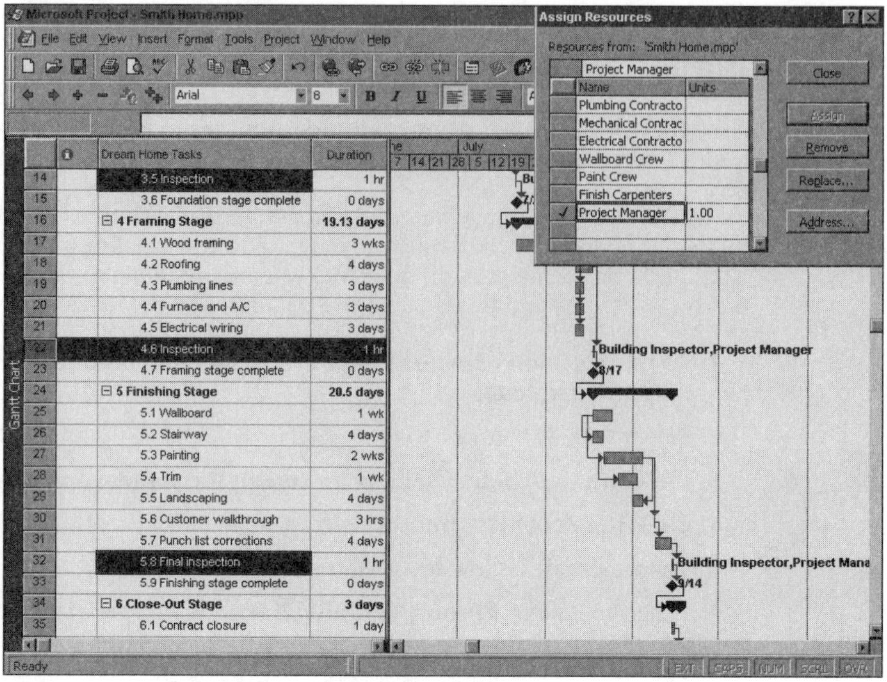

Figure 7-7: Assigning multiple resources to a task.

Removing and adding resources

Changing resource assignments can be simple or tricky depending on when in the project you do it. Early on, changing resource assignments is a piece of hot-fudge ice cream cake. Select the task in the Gantt table, click the Assign Resources button on the standard toolbar, select the resource in the resource pool, and click the Remove button.

You need to change a few things in the home building example. First, an important person is missing from the resource pool, namely the project foreman. Second, the project foreman rather than the project manager should perform the inspection tasks with the building inspector. To make these changes:

1. **Select the three Inspection tasks (if they aren't still selected).**

   To do so, select the first Inspection task, task 14. Hold down the Ctrl key and select the other two Inspection tasks, tasks 22 and 32. Then release the Ctrl key.

2. **Click the Assign Resources button on the standard toolbar.**
3. **In the first empty Name box, type** Project Foreman.

4. **Select Project Manager and click the Replace button.**

   The Replace With dialog box appears.

5. **Select Project Foreman and click OK.**

6. **Close the Assign Resources dialog box.**

The three inspection tasks change to show the removal of the project manager and the addition of the project foreman to each task.

Deleting a resource

Deleting a resource from the resource pool requires that you work in the Resource Sheet view. This view is especially helpful in summarizing details about all resources. You can also use it to make changes to resources.

To change to the Resource Sheet view, reopen the view bar by right-clicking the far-left vertical bar and selecting View Bar from the shortcut menu. Scroll the bar to show Resource Sheet and select it. Or, if you want, you may choose View⇨Resource Sheet. The screen now looks like Figure 7-8.

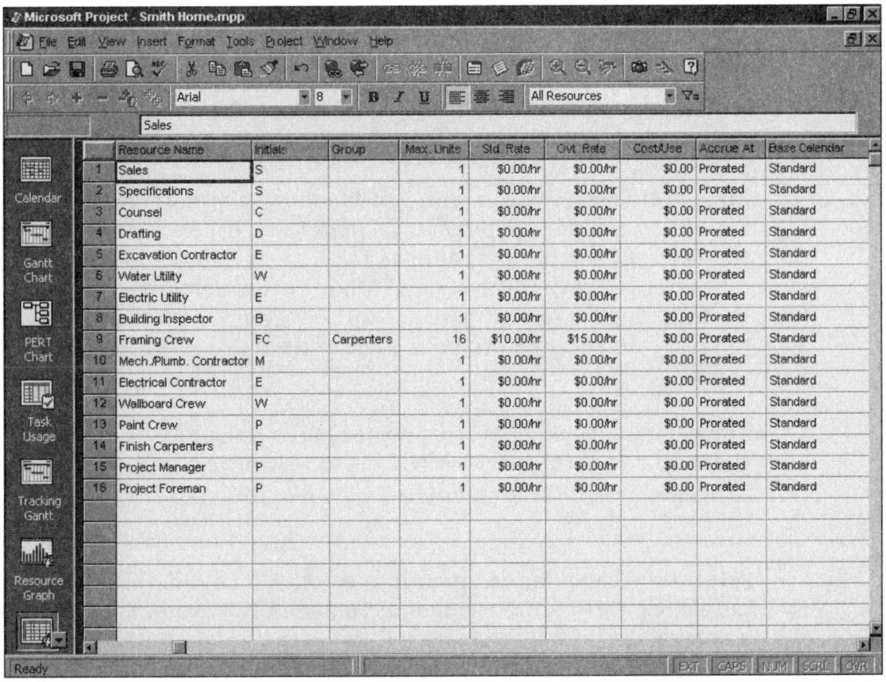

Figure 7-8: The resource sheet displays information about each resource. Notice the details of resource 9, Framing Crew.

In the home building example, the Plumbing task and the Furnace task will now be performed by a single contractor. Therefore, you must delete a resource and modify a resource name:

1. **Select resource 10, Plumbing Contractor.**
2. **Press the Delete key.**

   The Plumbing Contractor resource is deleted.
3. **Select the new resource 10, Mechanical Contractor.**
4. **In the Resource Name box, type** Mech./Plumb. Contractor.

A new combined resource replaces two previously distinct resources. After you've had a chance to look over the resource sheet, change back to the Gantt Chart view by clicking the Gantt Chart button on the view bar.

You did some heavy-duty project plan development. You made major resource assignments, added some resource details, and did some editing. This is a good time to save the project file: Click the Save button, select Save 'Smith Home.MPP' without a Baseline, and then click OK.

More Than One Calendar

It's not unusual for various resources to have different expectations about working hours and working days. Microsoft Project is an excellent tool for managing time with more than one clock.

Microsoft Project works with two kinds of calendars: project calendars and resource calendars. A *project calendar* (also called a *standard calendar*) is the default calendar that applies to all tasks and resources. This calendar measures duration by assigning Monday through Friday as working days and by assigning 8 a.m. to 5 p.m. as working hours, with one hour off for lunch at noon. By default, the project calendar does not include any holidays. What a grump!

You can change any part of a project calendar or all of it. You can make it so that any day of the week with a *y* in the name is a day off. Or you can schedule a siesta from noon to 3 p.m. It's up to you and your understanding, totally cool boss.

A resource calendar can march to the beat of a different drummer. You can customize the resource calendar to match the availability and work times of a specific resource. For instance, using the home building example, you can create a resource calendar for painters and wallboarders so that the two groups work at separate times. Why? Painters hate dust. And you can assign a special holiday just for the wallboard crew so that they can observe the invention of the screw gun.

It's time to make some changes to the home building example. You need to include some holidays that everyone knows and loves. In addition, you need to accommodate some groups who want to work different hours. Finally, you need to make some specific changes to a particular resource calendar. In the next sections, you

- Modify the project calendar.
- Create a second base calendar.
- Create a resource calendar.

Modifying the project calendar

First, add some holidays to the project calendar. The house is being built in the United States, so add July 3 and September 7 as nonworking days:

1. **Choose Tools⇨Change Working Time.**

   The Change Working Time dialog box appears, as shown in Figure 7-9.

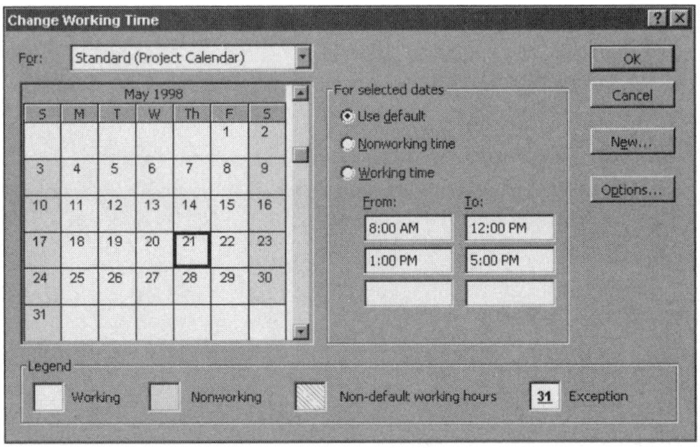

Figure 7-9: Shaded days represent default nonworking days.

2. **Manipulate the scroll bar until you come to July 1998.**
3. **Select July 3.**
4. **Under For Selected Dates, select the Nonworking Time option.**
5. **Repeat this process for Labor Day, September 7.**
6. **Click OK.**
7. **Select task 10, the Excavation task, to see the effect of your change on the available workdays.**

8. **Click the Goto Selected Task button on the standard toolbar.**

   The Gantt chart indicates that Friday, July 3, is a nonworking day. The day is gray on the chart, as shown in Figure 7-10. The changes to the project calendar could have adjusted all tasks after July 3 to be one day later. That didn't happen here, however, because task 10 is already scheduled to begin on Monday, July 7.

Gray is a rotten color for a nonworking day! In Chapter 9, you can customize the look of your Gantt chart. May all your nonworking days be sunny and sky blue!

Remember to save the project file again: Click the Save button, select Save 'Smith Home.MPP' without a Baseline, and click OK.

Creating a new calendar

Having another calendar to complement the project calendar is often necessary. Stop! Don't throw this book at the computer. Multiple calendars are simple to understand and use in Microsoft Project.

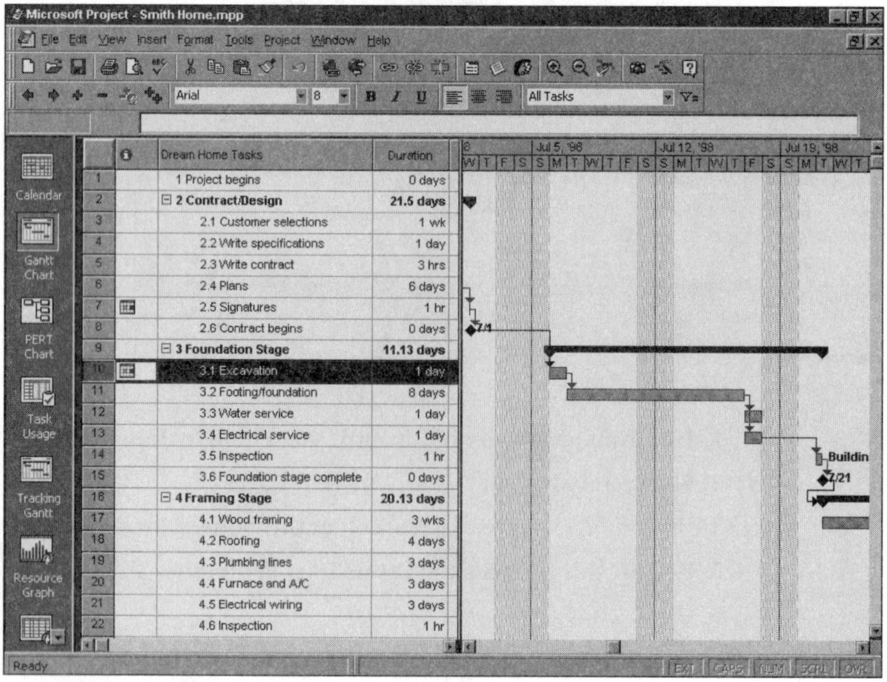

Figure 7-10: July 3 is now a nonworking day.

Sometimes you have groups of resources with things in common. For instance, in the home building example, all the construction folks want to arrive at the job at 7 a.m., have half an hour for lunch, and leave in mid-afternoon. In contrast, the office folk want to arrive at work at 8 a.m., have an hour for lunch starting at noon, and leave at 5 p.m. — the standard calendar working hours.

To resolve this, you need to create a second calendar, called a *base calendar.* You create it by first duplicating the project calendar. This way, any changes to the project calendar, such as holidays, will be carried over to the new calendar. Simple, right? An example should remove any mud or muddle:

1. **Choose Tools⇨Change Working Time.**

   The Change Working Time dialog box appears.

2. **Click the New button.**

   The Create New Base Calendar dialog box appears.

3. **In the Name box, type** Construction Hours Calendar**.**

4. **Make sure that the second option (Make a Copy of) is selected, and that it reads Make a Copy of Standard Calendar, as shown in Figure 7-11.**

   Anything you did to the standard calendar is carried over to the Construction Hours calendar. In this case, the July 3 and September 7 nonworking days are included.

5. **Click OK.**

The creation of a new calendar doesn't replace the standard calendar. All resources base their working hours and days on the standard calendar, until selected otherwise.

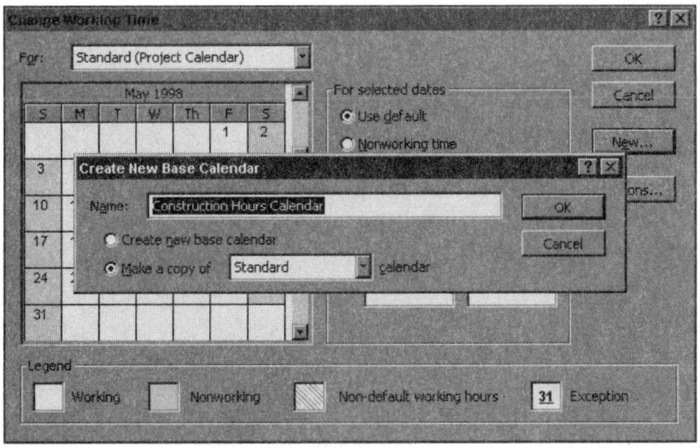

Figure 7-11: The Create New Base Calendar dialog box.

Now change the working hours for the Construction Hours calendar:

1. **Select the columns for working days by clicking on M (Monday) and dragging horizontally to F (Friday).**
2. **Under For Selected Dates, select Working time.**
3. **In the Working Time area, type** 7:00 AM **in the From box and** 11:00 AM **in the To box.**
4. **On the next line in the Working Time area, type** 11:30 AM **in the From box and** 3:30 PM **in the To box.**

   Your screen should look like Figure 7-12.
5. **Click OK.**

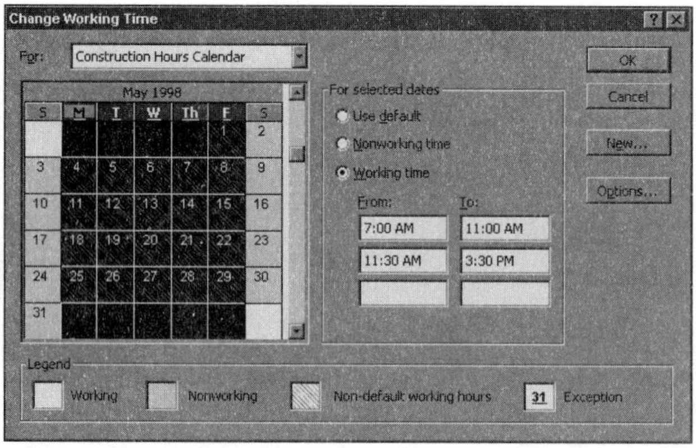

Figure 7-12: Use the Change Working Time dialog box to create a custom work schedule that includes changes made in the standard calendar.

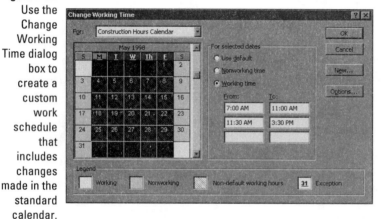

The last step is to apply this calendar to all appropriate resources. An easy way to do this is in the Resource Sheet view:

1. **Select Resource Sheet View on the view bar.**
2. **In the Base Calendar column, select the cell for resource 5, Excavation Contractor.**

   A down arrow appears next to the text box.
3. **Click the down arrow.**

   Four choices appear, as shown in Figure 7-13.

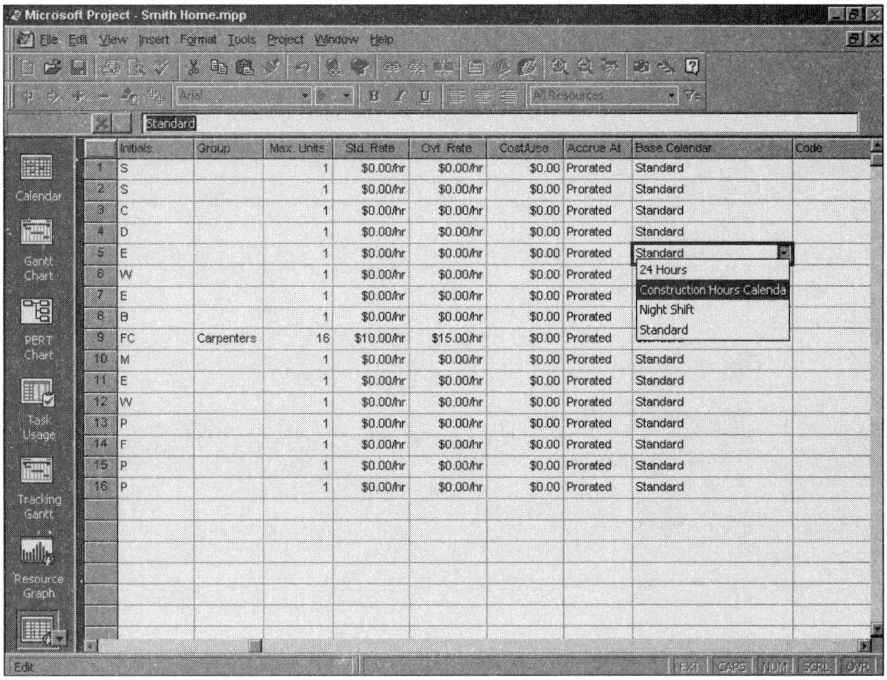

Figure 7-13: The text box lists the base calendars for the project. Three calendars are defaults, and Construction Hours Calendar is the one you created.

4. **Select Construction Hours Calendar.**

   Construction Hours Calendar replaces *Standard* in the Base Calendar cell for resource 5, Excavation Contractor.

5. **Double-click the column title cell, Base Calendar, and then choose Best Fit or double-click the right vertical edge of the column head.**

   The default column size was too small to fit the full name of the calendar. Best Fit corrects that.

6. **Follow Steps 2 through 4 for resources 6, 7, 9–14, and 16.**

   The results should look like Figure 7-14.

After you review your changes, return to the Gantt Chart view.

Creating a resource calendar

Now that you've modified the standard calendar and created an additional base calendar, creating a resource calendar will be easy. National Screw Gun Awareness Week, here we come! Using the home building example:

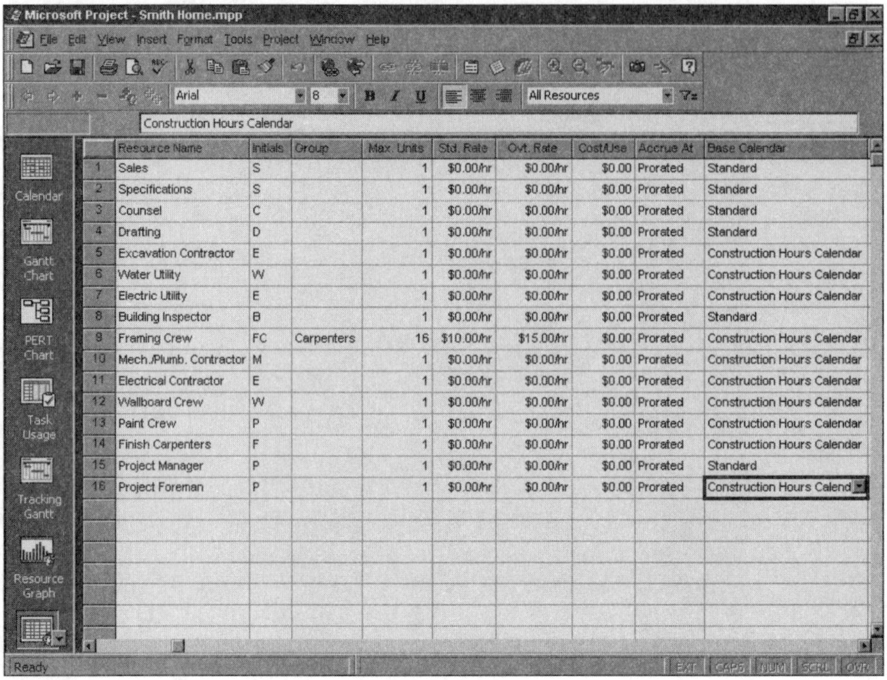

Figure 7-14: The Resource Sheet shows the changes. Microsoft Project automatically records these changes to any view that displays work times.

1. **Choose Tools⇨Change Working Time.**
2. **In the For box, select the Wallboard Crew resource.**

   Notice that the working days for a resource calendar are a light shade of gray.

3. **Scroll to July 1998.**

   The week beginning July 5 is the beginning of the wallboard workers' national holiday.

4. **Drag across the whole week to highlight it.**
5. **Under For Selected Dates, select the Nonworking time option.**

   The wallboarders are now free to attend the National Screw Gun Olympics. Fortunately, your schedule didn't need them that week anyway.

6. **Click OK.**

   You've just modified a resource calendar!

Save the project file: Click the Save button, select Save 'Smith Home.MPP' without a Baseline, and then click OK.

Another Way to Assign Resources

Another easy and effective way to assign resources to tasks is by using the Task form. To do so:

1. **Choose Window⇨Split.**

   The Task form appears in the lower half of the screen.

2. **Click Previous or Next until you come to task 5, Write contract.**

3. **Select the space below the Resource Names column title.**

   A highlighted box appears. In addition, a down arrow appears to the right.

4. **Click the down arrow to the right of the box.**

   A list of the resources in the resource pool appears, as shown in Figure 7-15. Earlier versions of Microsoft Project provided a drop-down list in the entry bar at the top of the screen. Microsoft Project 98 provides the drop-down list in its related text box. In this case, it offers the contents of the resource pool.

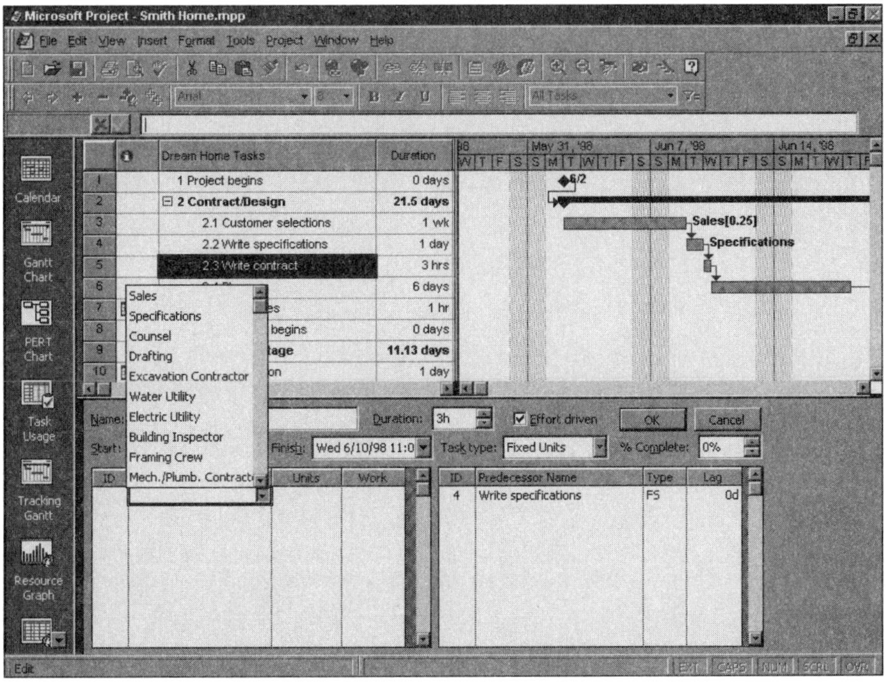

Figure 7-15: A list of resources in the resource pool appears.

5. **Click Counsel.**

   The resource now appears below Resource Names.

6. **Click OK.**

You can enter as many resources as you want in the Resource Names column. They all become assigned to that particular task. When you're back in the single view, you can still see the resource assignments by highlighting the task and clicking the Goto Selected Task button on the standard toolbar.

Save the project file a final time: Click Save, select Save 'Smith Home.MPP' without a Baseline, and then click OK.

Part III

Viewing Your Project

The 5th Wave — By Rich Tennant

"HOW'S THAT FOR FAST SCROLLING?"

In this part . . .

How many project managers does it take to change a lightbulb? Sorry, that's operations. Okay. How many lightbulbs does it take to change a project manager? Now, that's a good question. A project manager often needs all kinds of light shed on a subject before there's enough clarity to make a change. In project management, you add light to a subject by changing views.

In this part, you learn how to view charts, tables, and graphs. You use and customize the Gantt Chart view, the PERT Chart view, the Calendar view, and the Resource view. You find out about filters. And you work with multiple projects.

Chapter 8

Kinds of Views

In This Chapter

- Making sense of views
- Getting around in views
- Using views to see where you are (and aren't)

In the foggy stages of a project, the project manager, like a pilot, wants ready access to a map and an intelligent navigator. Microsoft Project has a powerful way to keep you on the right path — views.

Views are to project management what flying by instruments is to a pilot. One perspective can't give you all the information you need. One reading may indicate that you're right on schedule with a full retinue of resources. But another reading may show that the resources are headed into a maze of conflicting tasks.

A *view* is the way you display project information. Microsoft Project has two major classifications of views: task views and resource views. This chapter is about task views. To find out about resource views, check out Chapter 9.

Open the sample project file called `Chapter 8.MPP` from the Project folder. To do so, start Microsoft Project (if necessary) and then

1. **Click the Open button on the standard toolbar.**
2. **Open the Project folder on your hard drive or on the *Microsoft Project 98 For Dummies* CD-ROM.**
3. **Double-click Chapter 8.MPP.**

   The file opens.

Triangulation and project management

One of the biggest breakthroughs in modern mapmaking was the adoption of the triangulation technique. *Triangulation* is based on the idea that you can pinpoint an object's location to a fraction of an inch by observing it from three vantage points. Although the concept of triangulation is simple and has been around for hundreds of years, it needed a technology to make it possible. Through the use of orbiting satellites, triangulation has greatly reduced the margin of error in determining the precise location of points on the earth's surface.

This concept of triangulation is a helpful way to relate project management and its dependence on technology. You want to know how a project is progressing and you use your computer to do the job. The technology of Microsoft Project and its multiple vantage points (views) enable you to more precisely analyze the moving target of an ongoing project.

The three major categories of views are

- Charts
- Tables
- Forms

This chapter contains helpful descriptions and illustrations of these views.

Task Views

Microsoft Project bases its views on two kinds of information: task views and resource views. A *task view* presents information about tasks. Among the task views are Gantt Chart, PERT Chart, Calendar, Task Usage, Tracking Gantt, and various task tables and task forms.

A *resource view* presents information about resources. Among the resource views are Resource Graph, Resource Sheet, Resource Usage, and resource forms. This chapter deals with task views. Chapter 12 is about resource views.

The Gantt Chart view is a task view and also the default view of Microsoft Project. The default Gantt chart is actually a table and a bar chart. The bar chart shows tasks and their durations.

In the example for this chapter, a baseline has been added to the Gantt chart. Chapter 17 describes the reason and procedure for adding a baseline. For the present discussion, think of a *baseline* as a snapshot (a point of reference) of how the project manager predicts the project will occur. After you set the baseline, any updating of information reflects actual events compared against the baseline. (For details on using and customizing the Gantt chart, see Chapter 9.)

Using the Chapter 8 example, check out the task view. To do so:

1. **Select task 18, Roofing.**
2. **Click the Goto Selected Task button on the standard toolbar.**

The Gantt chart has black bars inside blue bars. The blue bars indicate the time you allotted for each task; the black bars indicate the actual progress of the task. Figure 8-1 shows that

- The Wood framing task has been completed.
- The Roofing task is partially completed.
- The Plumbing lines task hasn't started.
- The Furnace and A/C task has just begun.
- The Electrical wiring task is almost finished.

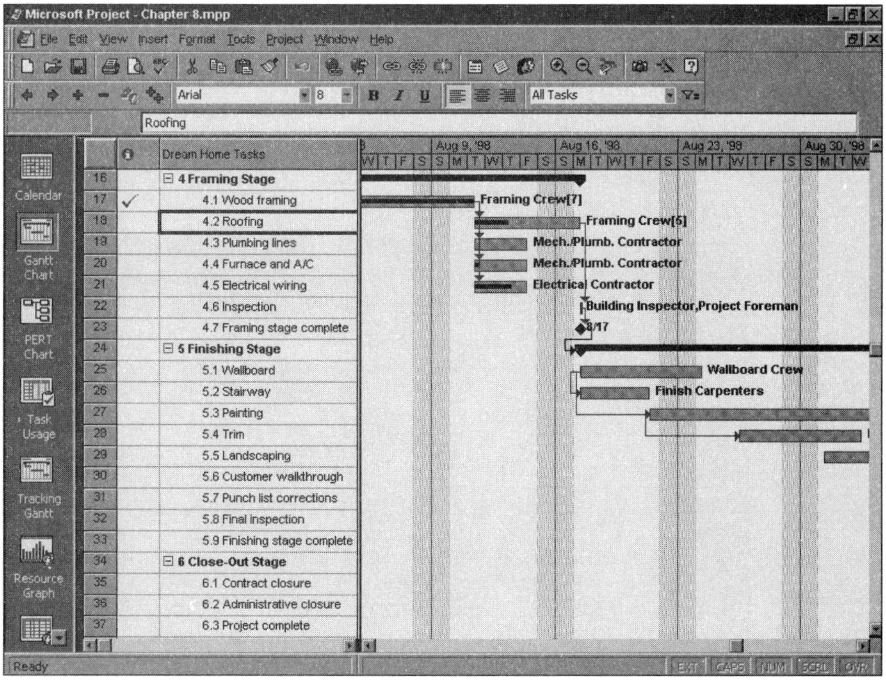

Figure 8-1: The task duration is the lighter (blue) bar. Progress is reported with the darker (black) bar.

Task Tables

Microsoft Project provides task tables and resource tables. Task tables can be seen either in the Gantt Chart view or in the Task Sheet view (the table minus the Gantt chart). Among these task tables are Entry, Cost, Schedule, and Summary.

Entry table

The Gantt chart's default task table is the Task Entry table. To see it in all its glory, place your mouse cursor over the vertical bar separating the table and the bar chart. The cursor changes to two vertical bars and two arrows. Click and drag the vertical bar to the right until the entire table is visible, as shown in Figure 8-2.

TIP: This view's real estate is maximized by deselecting the view bar and setting each column to Best Fit. Also, if a table column has hatch marks instead of information, move the cursor to where the column titles join and double-click when the cursor turns into a two-faced arrow.

The Task Entry table reflects the information that appears in bar chart form in the Gantt chart.

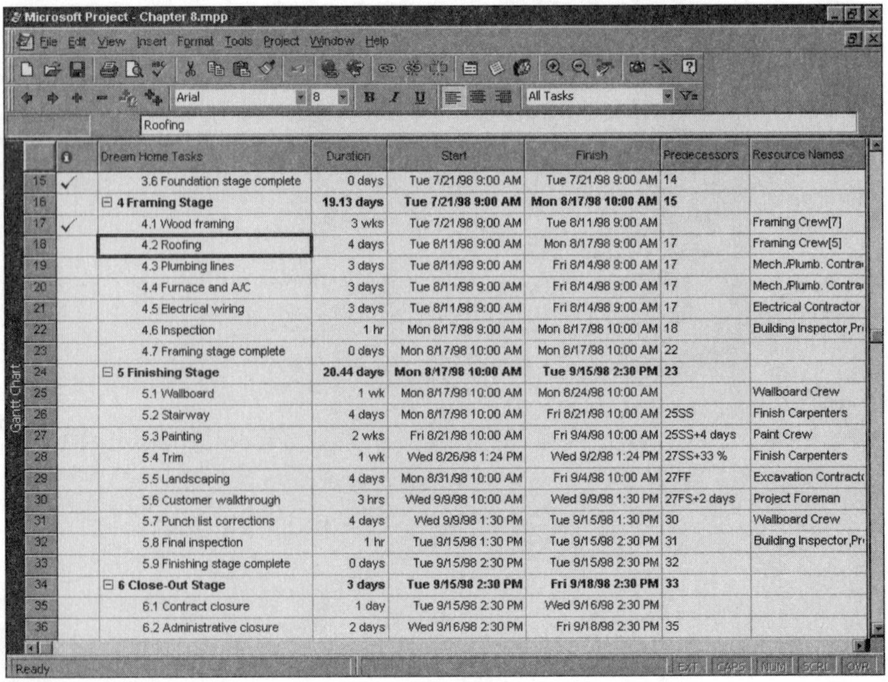

		Dream Home Tasks	Duration	Start	Finish	Predecessors	Resource Names
15	✓	3.6 Foundation stage complete	0 days	Tue 7/21/98 9:00 AM	Tue 7/21/98 9:00 AM	14	
16		**⊟ 4 Framing Stage**	**19.13 days**	**Tue 7/21/98 9:00 AM**	**Mon 8/17/98 10:00 AM**	**15**	
17	✓	4.1 Wood framing	3 wks	Tue 7/21/98 9:00 AM	Tue 8/11/98 9:00 AM		Framing Crew[7]
18		4.2 Roofing	4 days	Tue 8/11/98 9:00 AM	Mon 8/17/98 9:00 AM	17	Framing Crew[5]
19		4.3 Plumbing lines	3 days	Tue 8/11/98 9:00 AM	Fri 8/14/98 9:00 AM	17	Mech./Plumb. Contra
20		4.4 Furnace and A/C	3 days	Tue 8/11/98 9:00 AM	Fri 8/14/98 9:00 AM	17	Mech./Plumb. Contra
21		4.5 Electrical wiring	3 days	Tue 8/11/98 9:00 AM	Fri 8/14/98 9:00 AM	17	Electrical Contractor
22		4.6 Inspection	1 hr	Mon 8/17/98 9:00 AM	Mon 8/17/98 10:00 AM	18	Building Inspector,Pr
23		4.7 Framing stage complete	0 days	Mon 8/17/98 10:00 AM	Mon 8/17/98 10:00 AM	22	
24		**⊟ 5 Finishing Stage**	**20.44 days**	**Mon 8/17/98 10:00 AM**	**Tue 9/15/98 2:30 PM**	**23**	
25		5.1 Wallboard	1 wk	Mon 8/17/98 10:00 AM	Mon 8/24/98 10:00 AM		Wallboard Crew
26		5.2 Stairway	4 days	Mon 8/17/98 10:00 AM	Fri 8/21/98 10:00 AM	25SS	Finish Carpenters
27		5.3 Painting	2 wks	Fri 8/21/98 10:00 AM	Fri 9/4/98 10:00 AM	25SS+4 days	Paint Crew
28		5.4 Trim	1 wk	Wed 8/26/98 1:24 PM	Wed 9/2/98 1:24 PM	27SS+33 %	Finish Carpenters
29		5.5 Landscaping	4 days	Mon 8/31/98 10:00 AM	Fri 9/4/98 10:00 AM	27FF	Excavation Contract
30		5.6 Customer walkthrough	3 hrs	Wed 9/9/98 10:00 AM	Wed 9/9/98 1:30 PM	27FS+2 days	Project Foreman
31		5.7 Punch list corrections	4 days	Wed 9/9/98 1:30 PM	Tue 9/15/98 1:30 PM	30	Wallboard Crew
32		5.8 Final inspection	1 hr	Tue 9/15/98 1:30 PM	Tue 9/15/98 2:30 PM	31	Building Inspector,Pr
33		5.9 Finishing stage complete	0 days	Tue 9/15/98 2:30 PM	Tue 9/15/98 2:30 PM	32	
34		**⊟ 6 Close-Out Stage**	**3 days**	**Tue 9/15/98 2:30 PM**	**Fri 9/18/98 2:30 PM**	**33**	
35		6.1 Contract closure	1 day	Tue 9/15/98 2:30 PM	Wed 9/16/98 2:30 PM		
36		6.2 Administrative closure	2 days	Wed 9/16/98 2:30 PM	Fri 9/18/98 2:30 PM	35	

Figure 8-2: You can access the Entry table in the Gantt Chart view. It's the default table.

To change a default view, choose Tools➪Options. Click the View tab. In the Default View list box, select a new default view. Click OK. The next time Microsoft Project starts, it will open to the new default view.

Cost table

Another task table available in the Gantt Chart view is the Task Cost table. To access it, choose View➪Table: Entry. The Task Table list appears, as shown in Figure 8-3.

Select Cost. The Task Cost table, shown in Figure 8-4, provides information on the cost of the project's tasks.

Notice task 18, the Roofing task. Based on the predicted duration and the per-hour fee for each unit of the Framing Crew resource, the predicted total labor cost of the Roofing task is $1,600. The actual cost so far is $752.00, and $848.00 remains.

A glance at the tracking bar in the Gantt Chart shows that the work performed to date may be running over budget. This is the beauty of multiple views and tables. The Cost table gives one form of information, and the Gantt chart interprets that information graphically. In actuality, the budget for the task is okay based on another table — the Summary table.

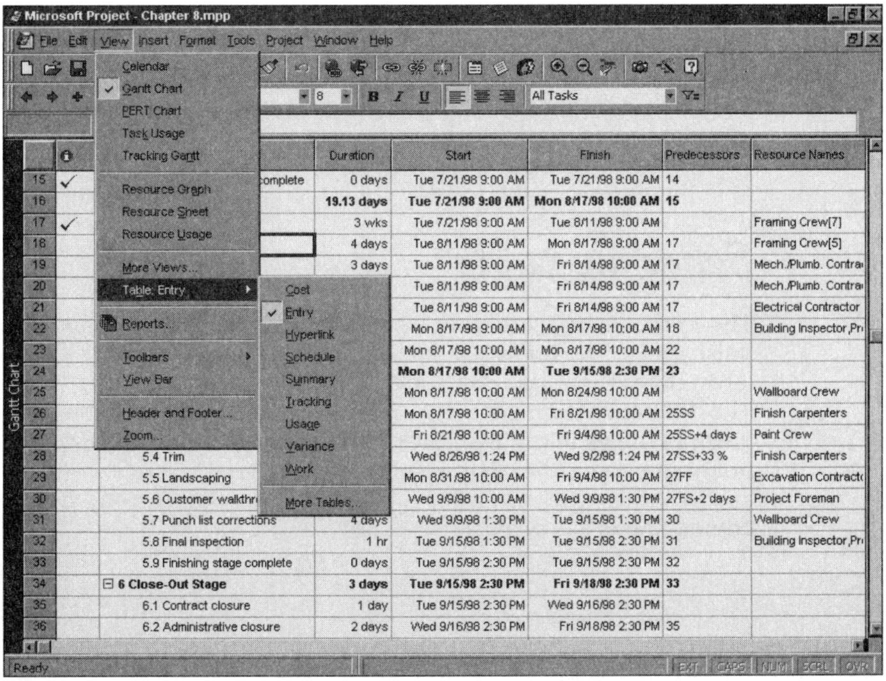

Figure 8-3: The Task Table list shows the most commonly used task tables.

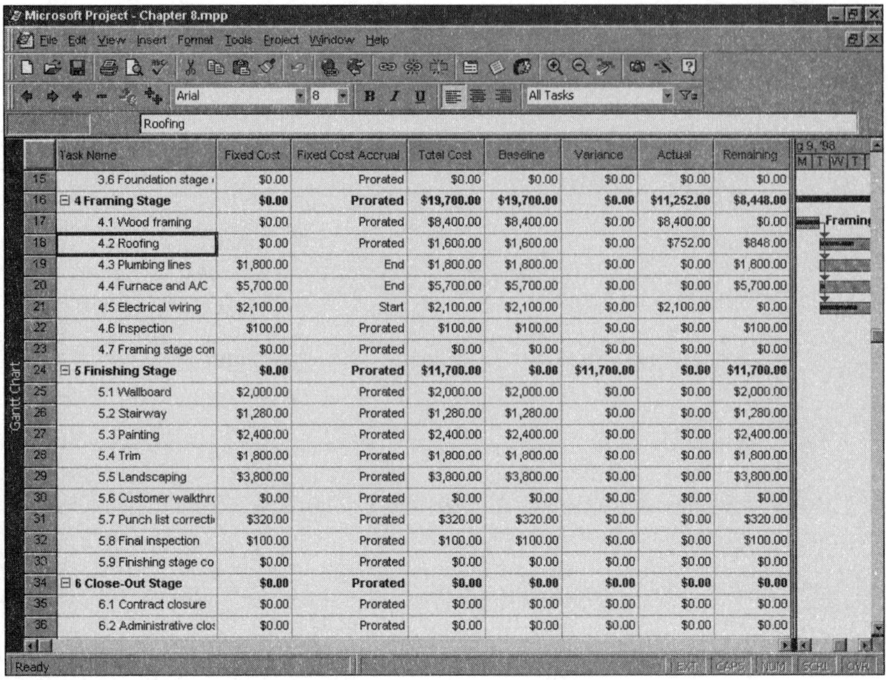

	Task Name	Fixed Cost	Fixed Cost Accrual	Total Cost	Baseline	Variance	Actual	Remaining
15	3.6 Foundation stage	$0.00	Prorated	$0.00	$0.00	$0.00	$0.00	$0.00
16	**4 Framing Stage**	**$0.00**	**Prorated**	**$19,700.00**	**$19,700.00**	**$0.00**	**$11,252.00**	**$8,448.00**
17	4.1 Wood framing	$0.00	Prorated	$8,400.00	$8,400.00	$0.00	$8,400.00	$0.00
18	4.2 Roofing	$0.00	Prorated	$1,600.00	$1,600.00	$0.00	$752.00	$848.00
19	4.3 Plumbing lines	$1,800.00	End	$1,800.00	$1,800.00	$0.00	$0.00	$1,800.00
20	4.4 Furnace and A/C	$5,700.00	End	$5,700.00	$5,700.00	$0.00	$0.00	$5,700.00
21	4.5 Electrical wiring	$2,100.00	Start	$2,100.00	$2,100.00	$0.00	$2,100.00	$0.00
22	4.6 Inspection	$100.00	Prorated	$100.00	$100.00	$0.00	$0.00	$100.00
23	4.7 Framing stage con	$0.00	Prorated	$0.00	$0.00	$0.00	$0.00	$0.00
24	**5 Finishing Stage**	**$0.00**	**Prorated**	**$11,700.00**	**$0.00**	**$11,700.00**	**$0.00**	**$11,700.00**
25	5.1 Wallboard	$2,000.00	Prorated	$2,000.00	$2,000.00	$0.00	$0.00	$2,000.00
26	5.2 Stairway	$1,280.00	Prorated	$1,280.00	$1,280.00	$0.00	$0.00	$1,280.00
27	5.3 Painting	$2,400.00	Prorated	$2,400.00	$2,400.00	$0.00	$0.00	$2,400.00
28	5.4 Trim	$1,800.00	Prorated	$1,800.00	$1,800.00	$0.00	$0.00	$1,800.00
29	5.5 Landscaping	$3,800.00	Prorated	$3,800.00	$3,800.00	$0.00	$0.00	$3,800.00
30	5.6 Customer walkthr	$0.00	Prorated	$0.00	$0.00	$0.00	$0.00	$0.00
31	5.7 Punch list correcti	$320.00	Prorated	$320.00	$320.00	$0.00	$0.00	$320.00
32	5.8 Final inspection	$100.00	Prorated	$100.00	$100.00	$0.00	$0.00	$100.00
33	5.9 Finishing stage co	$0.00	Prorated	$0.00	$0.00	$0.00	$0.00	$0.00
34	**6 Close-Out Stage**	**$0.00**	**Prorated**	**$0.00**	**$0.00**	**$0.00**	**$0.00**	**$0.00**
35	6.1 Contract closure	$0.00	Prorated	$0.00	$0.00	$0.00	$0.00	$0.00
36	6.2 Administrative clo	$0.00	Prorated	$0.00	$0.00	$0.00	$0.00	$0.00

Figure 8-4: Fixed costs can be based on contractual agreement.

Summary table

The Task Summary table summarizes how the project is doing task by task. To access it, choose View➪Table: Summary. In Figure 8-5, notice how Microsoft Project summarizes that the Framing Stage category is 71 percent complete, while its subtasks show stages of completion ranging from 0 percent to 100 percent complete.

Schedule table

The Task Schedule table shows task information about scheduled start and finish dates. To access it, choose View➪Table: Schedule. It also shows the latest dates that tasks can start and finish without messing up the schedule. The difference between the planned start and finish and the latest start and finish is shown in the two slack columns shown in Figure 8-6. *Free slack* is how much slack Microsoft Project allows a task before it conflicts with the successor task. *Total slack* is how much slack the task has until it delays the completion of the project.

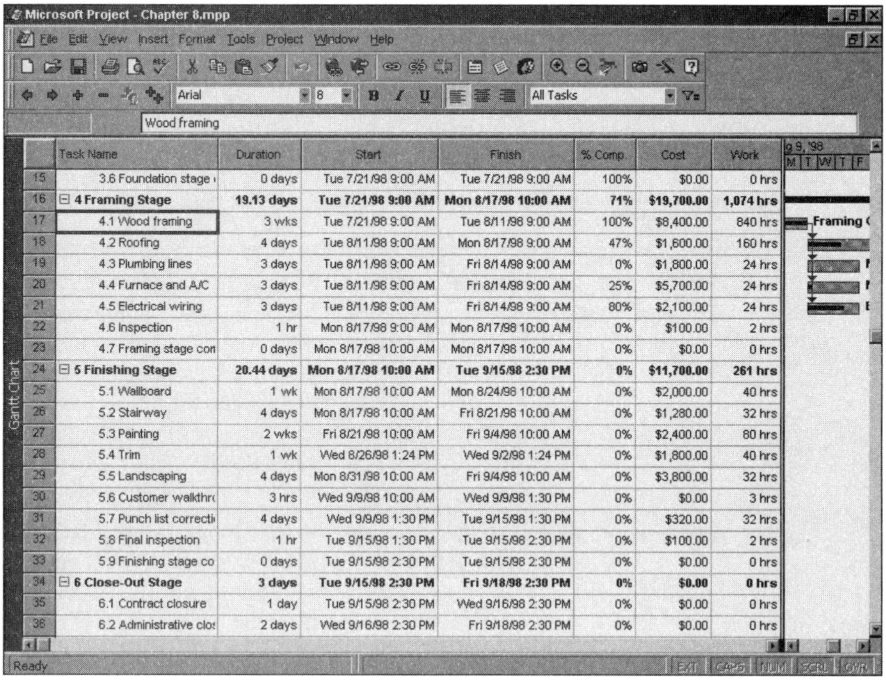

Figure 8-5: The % Comp. column displays the sum of all work to be performed by all resources for each individual category and its subtasks.

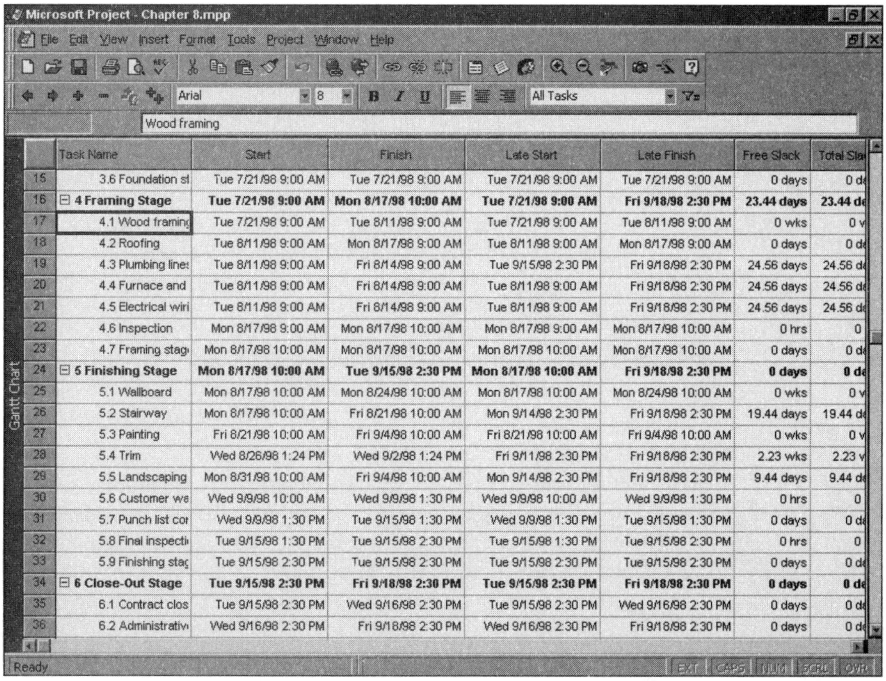

Figure 8-6: The Schedule table. Late Start and Late Finish dates are Microsoft Project estimates of how late a task may start and finish without negatively affecting the schedule.

Other task tables

Eight other task tables are available in the Gantt Chart view, shown in Table 8-1. If they aren't visible when you select View⇨Table, select View⇨Table⇨More Tables.

Table 8-1 Task Tables

Table	*What It Does*
Tracking table	Shows actual information about the progress of a project's tasks. You can keep your finger on the pulse of the schedule and the money being spent. Information includes the actual start and finish dates, the percentage of completion, the actual and remaining duration, the actual cost, and the actual amount of work performed.
Variance table	Shows how the actual start and finish dates vary from the planned (baseline) start and finish dates in terms of task duration. The default measurement for this table is days.
Work table	Displays the variance between estimated work and actual work for individual tasks (similar to the Variance table). It also shows the percentage of completed work and remaining work. The default measurement for this table is hours.
Baseline table	Shows the baseline information for each task's duration, start and finish dates, hours of work, and cost.
Constraint Dates table	Shows the constraint type of each task. Unless you specify otherwise, Microsoft Project assigns a default As Soon As Possible constraint type to all tasks. The table also lists any specific constraint dates.
Delay table	Assists in leveling resources. Leveling, discussed in Chapter 16, is a way of stretching out task durations to lessen resource allocation at a given time.
Earned Value table	Compares work and cost amounts, including cost of budgeted work and scheduled work. Scheduled data is sometimes different than budgeted data because it can be based on updated information. The column abbreviations refer to the following: BCWS is Budgeted Cost of Work Scheduled; BCWP is Budgeted Cost of Work Performed; ACWP is Actual Cost of Work Performed; SV is

Table	What It Does
	Earned Value Schedule Variance; CV is Earned Value Cost Variance; BAC is Budgeted at Completion; FAC is Forecast at Completion.
Export	Transfers a Microsoft Project file to another application, such as a spreadsheet.

You can also create your own table in Microsoft Project. To find out more, see Chapter 13.

Task Usage View

The Task Usage view lists in one quick visual reference the task and its associated resources, the amount of work each resource has performed over time, plus duration and start/finish dates. (See Figure 8-7.) The sheet portion of the view is mostly task information; the chart portion of the view is mostly resource information. In Chapter 13, you see the real power of this view when used with special filters.

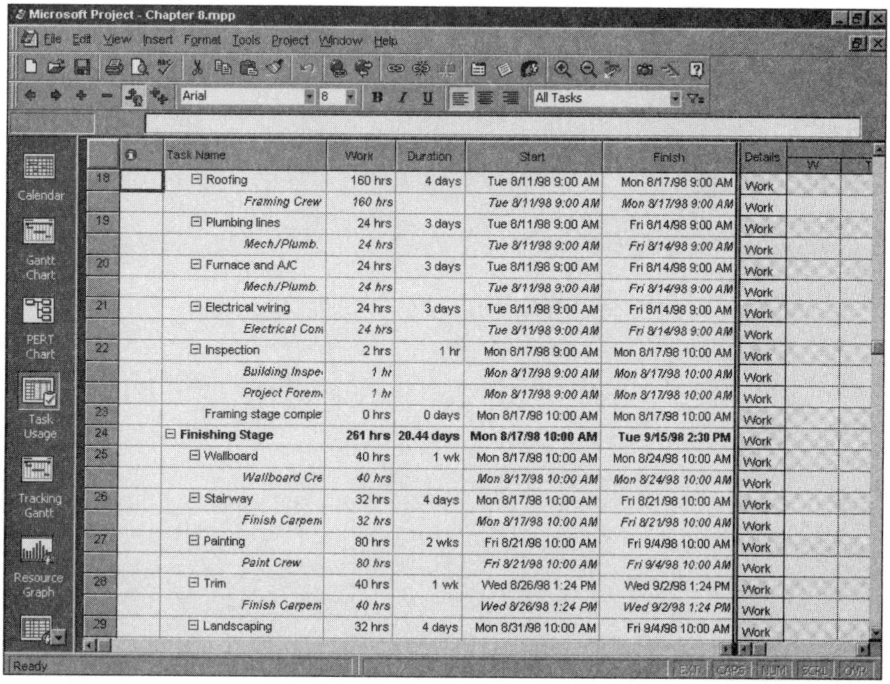

Figure 8-7: The Task Usage View is new to Microsoft Project 98. This view addresses the need for a visual representation of the resource work and costs of each task in increments of time, such as hours.

Tracking Gantt View

No, "Tracking Gantt" isn't a search for Henry. Rather, it's a useful method for getting a quick visual overview of the status of tasks in comparison to their baselines. (See Figure 8-8.) Combine it with the Tracking table (described in Table 8-1) and you're behind the wheel of a powerful engine. Enough said here — the Tracking Gantt is discussed in more depth in Chapter 17.

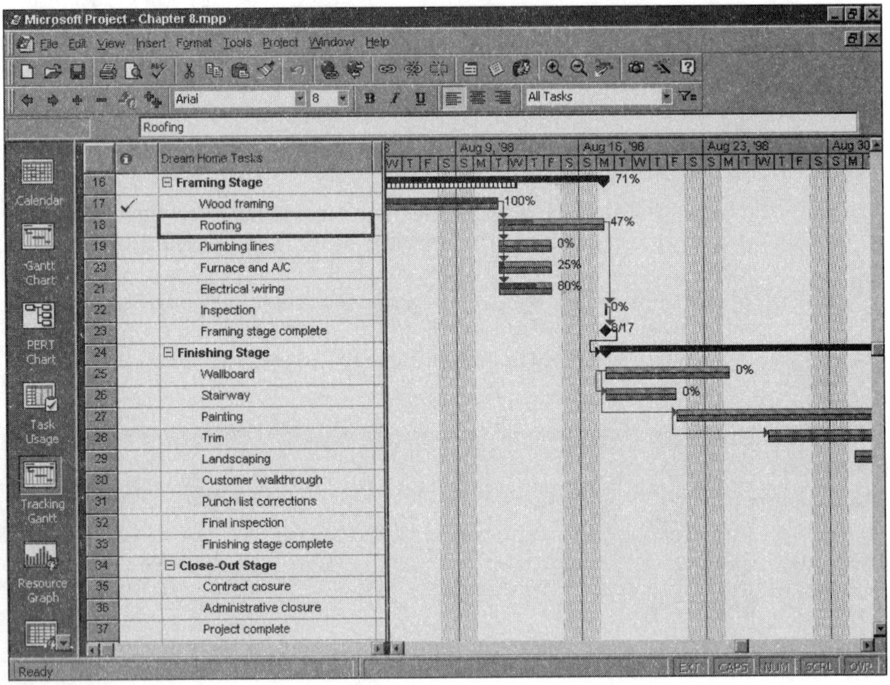

Figure 8-8: The Tracking Gantt view shows Summary tasks and their progress, task baselines and their progress, and critical progress.

Task Sheet View

If you'd like to work on tasks without seeing the Gantt bar chart, select the Task Sheet view, which presents information in a spreadsheet format. To change to the Task Sheet view:

1. **Choose View⇨More Views.**

   The More View list appears.

2. **Double-click Task Sheet.**

   The Entry table fills the Task sheet, as shown in Figure 8-9.

The Task sheet shows details about each task. It's your call whether you want to use this view or the Gantt Chart view. The methods for entering and editing information are identical in both views.

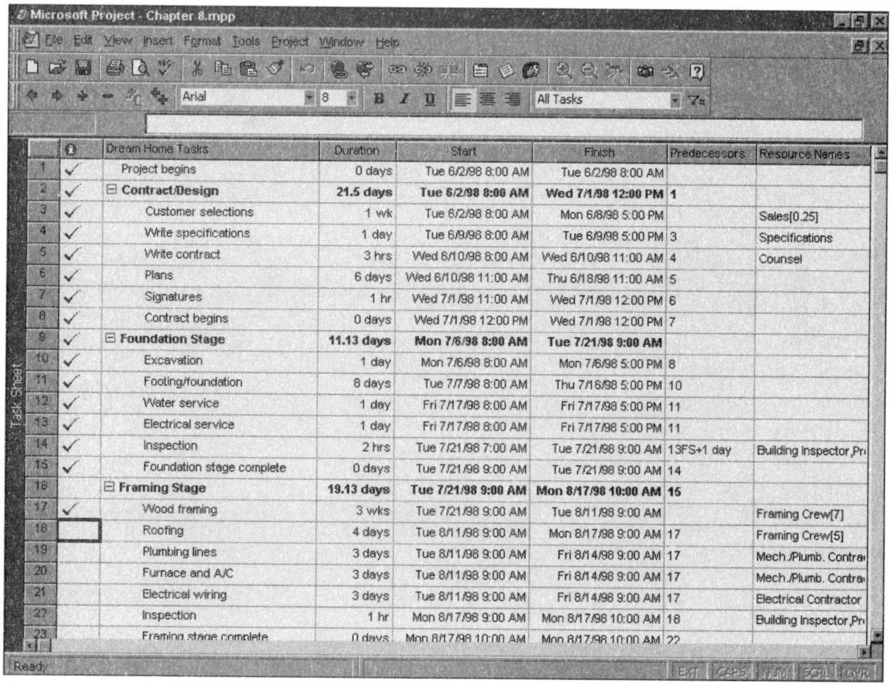

Figure 8-9: The same task tables available to the Gantt Chart view are available also to the Task Sheet view.

Calendar View

As mentioned, the Gantt chart is the default task view in Microsoft Project. Another task view is the Calendar view. The default Calendar view is a monthly calendar showing tasks in bar form, as shown in Figure 8-10. The length of the bar indicates the task's duration.

The Calendar view is a helpful communications tool for printing schedules. The Calendar view can be the primary way to manage small projects. To access the Calendar view, select the Calendar view icon on the view bar or choose View⇨Calendar.

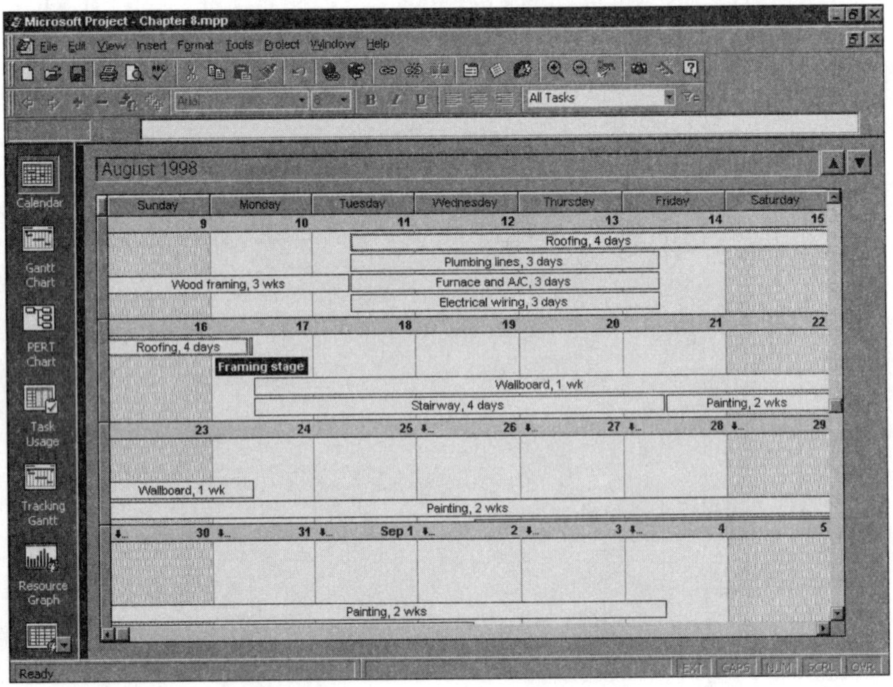

Figure 8-10: Use the up and down arrows to change month views. The familiar method of presentation makes it easy for you to view and edit tasks and durations.

PERT Chart View

In addition to the Gantt Chart view and the Calendar view, Microsoft Project also provides the PERT Chart view, shown in Figure 8-11. The PERT chart is a network diagram displaying all tasks and their relationships. To display the PERT Chart view, select the PERT Chart view icon on the view bar or choose View➪PERT Chart.

You can use the PERT chart to create and edit your schedule, create and undo links, set durations, and assign resources to tasks. To uncover the details about PERT charts, read Chapter 10.

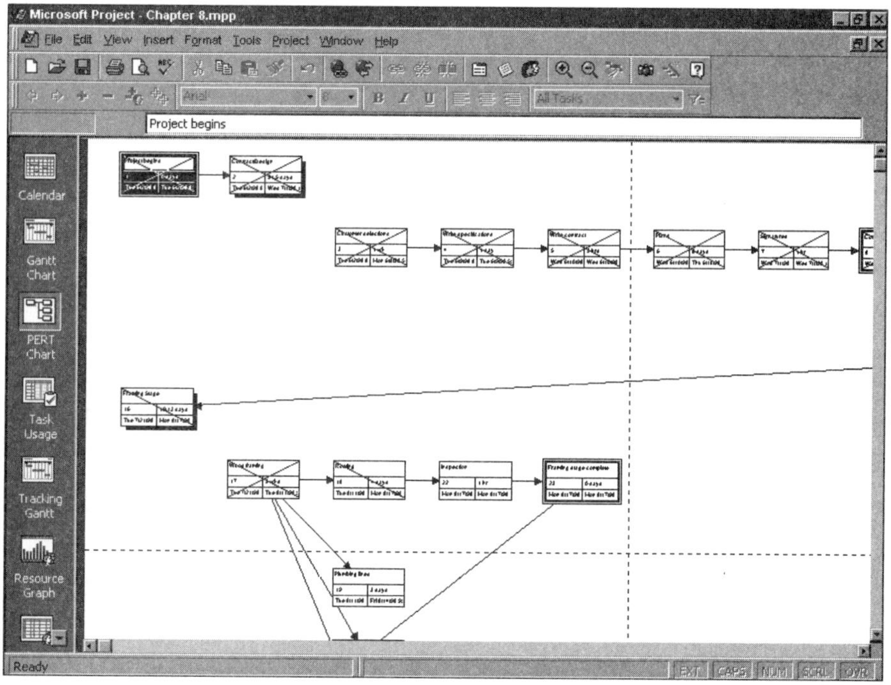

Figure 8-11: To change the layout of the PERT Chart view, choose Format➪Layout.

Chapter 9

The Gantt Chart

In This Chapter

- Using the Gantt chart for fun and profit
- Fast ways to a good-looking chart
- Mousing around in the Gantt chart
- Making time fit the project

Early in the 19th century, Henry Gantt introduced a new way to show information in a bar chart and spreadsheet fashion. Voilà! The man was immortalized. Now, whenever project managers discuss their work, they indirectly pay homage to him. Just as Henry Gantt's creation was a winner, what you do with his chart in Microsoft Project may make you a winner, too.

In this chapter, you kick the tires and get behind the wheel of the Gantt chart. You find out the neat little options just waiting for you, and you modify the chart to emphasize and segregate various kinds of information. Ole Henry may have been the first to fiddle with this kind of chart, but you're going to make the Gantt chart sing.

Start Microsoft Project, if necessary. Then, to open the sample project file called `Award Program 9.MPP`, do the following:

1. **Click the Open button on the standard toolbar.**
2. **Open the Project folder on your hard drive or on the *Microsoft Project 98 For Dummies* CD-ROM.**
3. **Double-click Award Program 9.MPP.**

Gantt Chart Text, Notes, and Graphics

Microsoft Project offers general text editing features and specialized formatting functions. Use these to polish your Gantt chart for on-screen readability, aesthetics, and reporting.

To practice, you'll correct a few errors in the example file. In addition, you'll improve the overall look and effectiveness of the information in several ways. The result will be a work of project management art.

Choosing words and speling corectly

One of the fastest ways you can make a negative impact on those you're most trying to impress is by misusing a word. Never use a word unless you're absolutely sure you know what it means. When you have a choice between a common word or an obscure word, use the common one. And make sure you spell the word correctly. Microsoft Project doesn't offer help in word selection, but it does provide a spell checker.

To use the spell checker, click the Spelling button on the standard toolbar or press F7. The Spelling dialog box appears, as shown in Figure 9-1. The location of the word as a task or a resource is shown in the Found In box. Perform the corrections as needed.

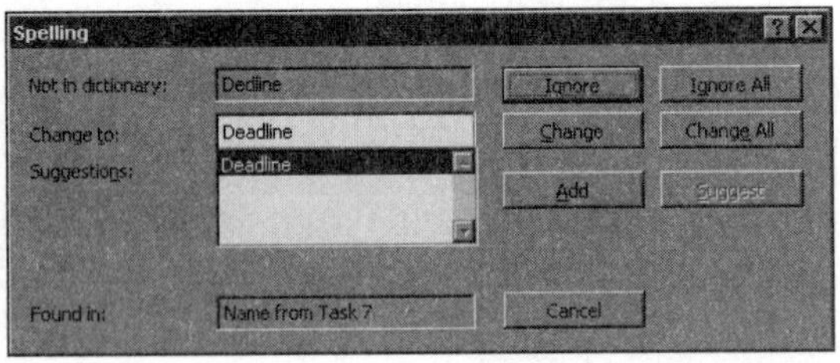

Figure 9-1: The spell checker displays the word it determines was misspelled.

Just as in any word processing application, Microsoft Project's spell checker doesn't catch everything. Task 15 has the article *an* that should be the conjunction *and.* You'll have to correct that the old-fashioned way: Highlight the task and change the text in the entry bar.

Customizing text

What's black and white and read all over? The traditional answer is a newspaper. With Microsoft Project, it never has to be a Gantt chart. Colorful changes to text can result in easy-to-read, visually pleasing information. The formatting toolbar is the ticket for making changes to fonts, font sizes, and colors.

Using the Award Program example, you change all category headings to 12-point Times New Roman. The headings are already boldface, and you'll leave them that way. To change the font style:

1. **In the Filter list box on the formatting toolbar, select Summary Tasks.**

   The summary tasks are now the only tasks listed, as shown in Figure 9-2. (Chapter 13 discusses the Summary task filter and others in detail.)

2. **Highlight the summary tasks by clicking task 1 and dragging the mouse cursor through task 16.**

   The four tasks are highlighted.

3. **In the Font list box on the formatting toolbar, select Times New Roman.**

   The font of the four tasks changes to Times New Roman.

4. **In the Font Size list box on the formatting toolbar, select 12.**

   The font size of the four tasks changes to 12-point, as shown in Figure 9-3.

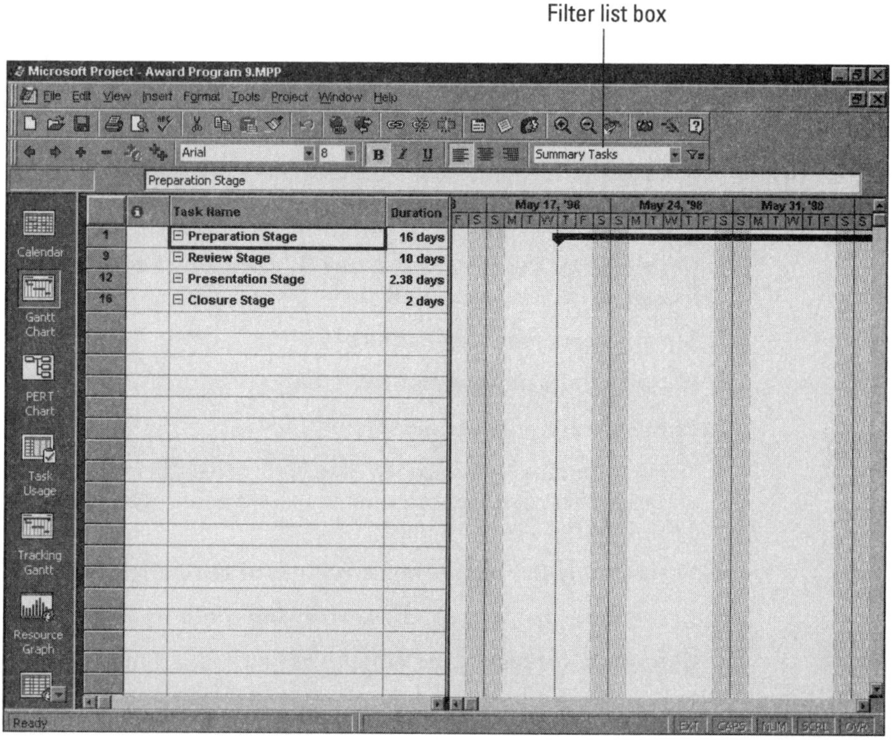

Figure 9-2: The Summary Tasks filter isolates and displays only summary tasks, hiding subtasks and milestones.

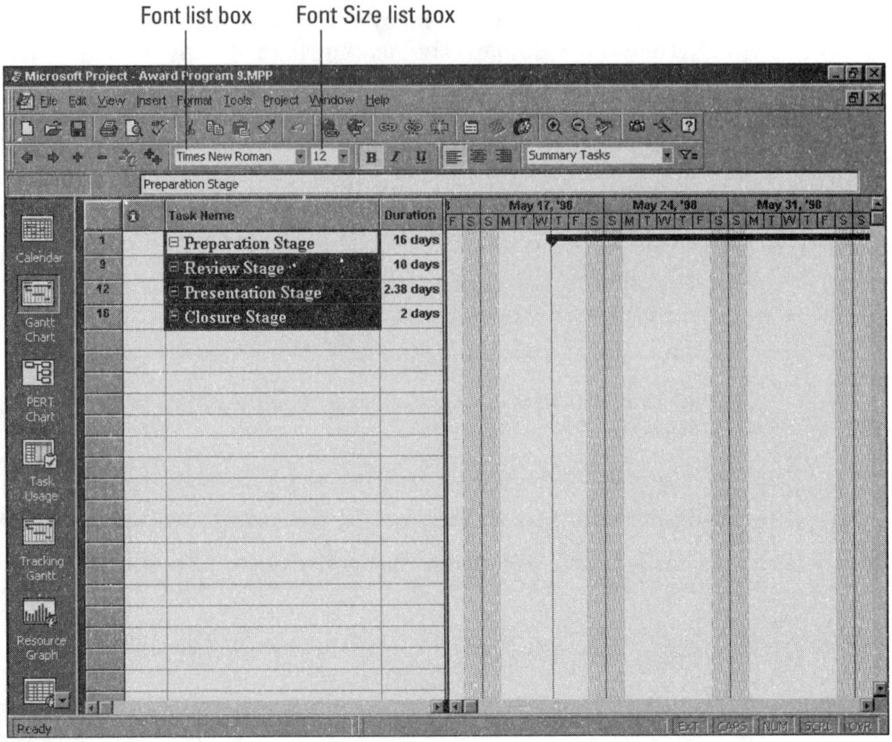

Figure 9-3: The formatting toolbar has some of the features commonly found in a word processor.

Not bad! But how about changing the Summary Task color, too? Not a problem, Ganttologist. To change the text color:

1. **Highlight all the summary tasks (if necessary) by clicking task 1 and dragging the mouse cursor through task 16.**

   The four tasks are highlighted.

2. **Right-click in the highlighted area.**
3. **In the shortcut menu, select Font.**

   The Font dialog box appears (see Figure 9-4). The dialog box should already show that the selected tasks have changed from 8-point Arial to 12-point Times New Roman.

4. **In the Color list box, select Green, and then click OK.**
5. **In the Filter list box on the formatting toolbar, select All Tasks.**

   The summary tasks are highlighted in a new color.

The number of available fonts may vary from one computer to the next. If you intend to share your project file, stick to commonly used fonts so that you can be sure how your project will look on another computer.

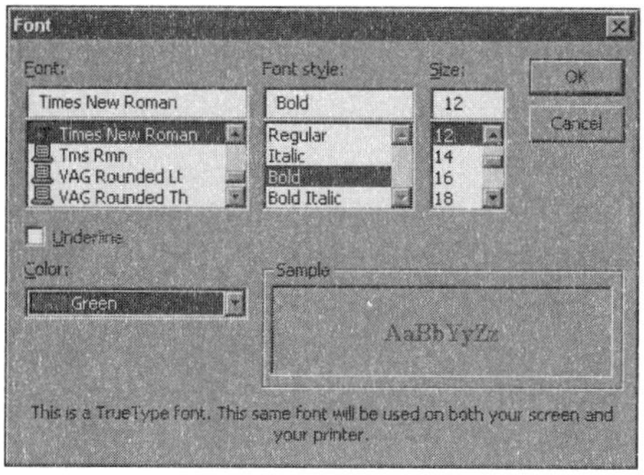

Figure 9-4: You can change the font and its style, size, and color in the Font dialog box.

Adding notes

Sometimes you need to write yourself or others a note about a task, a resource, or the entire project. To write a note about a particular task in the Gantt Chart view, you use the Task Notes button on the standard toolbar.

In the following, you use the Award Program example to attach a note to a task:

1. **Select any task.**
2. **Click the Task Notes button on the standard toolbar.**

   The Task Information dialog box appears, set to the Notes tab, as shown in Figure 9-5.
3. **In the Notes section, type your message.**
4. **Click OK.**

   A note indicator appears next to the task number.

You can view the note at any time by placing your cursor over the note indicator or by selecting the task and then clicking the Task Notes button.

To delete a note, highlight the task and choose Edit⇨Clear⇨Notes.

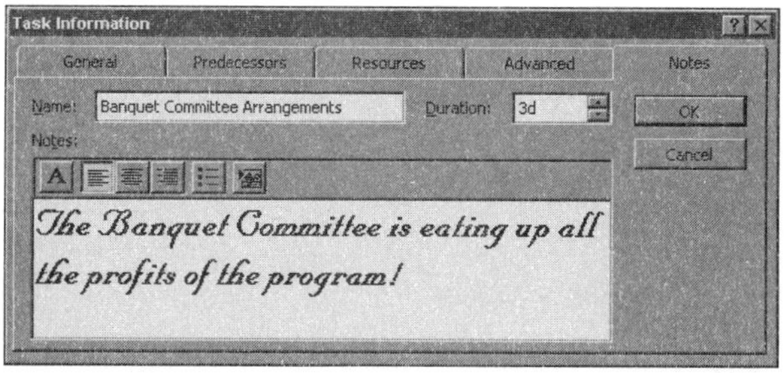

Figure 9-5: Enter task details, such as resources, predecessors, and start and finish dates.

Drawing and adding graphics

You can draw on the Gantt chart with a limited set of drawing tools. To access the drawing toolbar, right-click anywhere on the toolbar and choose Drawing from the list. Frankly, I think you'll be disappointed with what you can do, but go for it if you're interested. To remove the drawing toolbar, right-click the toolbar and choose Drawing again. The toolbar disappears.

Adding graphics would be more effective. If you have a graphics program, you can use its clipboard to copy a graphics file. Then you simply use the Paste command in Microsoft Project to insert the graphic in the Gantt chart.

For example, you can put a graphic in the Award Program's Gantt chart. To do so, use the standard Paint program that comes with Windows 95. If you have a graphics program, feel free to use it instead.

To add the graphic into the Award Program's Gantt chart:

1. **On the Windows desktop, click Start and then click Programs.**
2. **Choose Accessories⇨Paint.**

   The Paint application appears, as shown in Figure 9-6. Although it's a limited paint program, it's good for copying and pasting graphics.
3. **Choose File⇨Open.**
4. **Change to the Project folder, which is on your hard drive or on the *Microsoft Project 98 For Dummies* CD-ROM.**

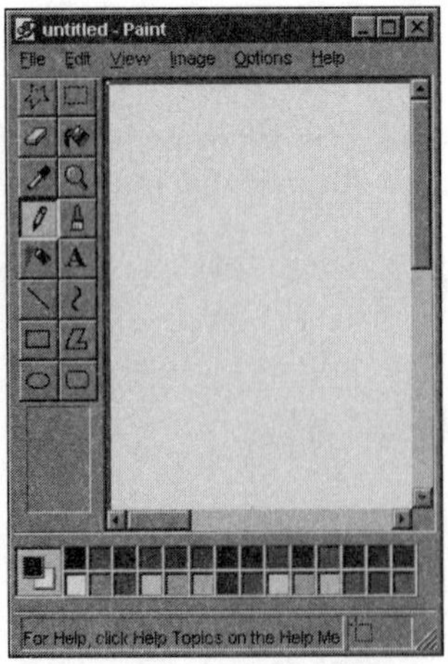

Figure 9-6: The Paint application recognizes only BMP and PCX extensions.

5. **Double-click award.bmp.**

   An award graphic is now in the Paint application.

Now that you have this priceless work of art in the Paint application, you need to copy it to the clipboard for use in Microsoft Project. You can use the same procedure to insert a company logo, a relevant graph, or a photo that identifies the project.

To copy and paste the award graphic into the Microsoft Project file:

1. **On the Paint menu bar, choose Edit⇨Select All.**
2. **On the Paint menu bar, choose Edit⇨Copy.**
3. **Click anywhere in the Project window to make it active.**

   Microsoft Project should now be the active screen.
4. **Choose Edit⇨Paste Special.**

   The Paste Special dialog box appears.
5. **Double-click Bitmap Image.**

   The Gantt chart should now look like Figure 9-7. If you want, you may close the Paint application.

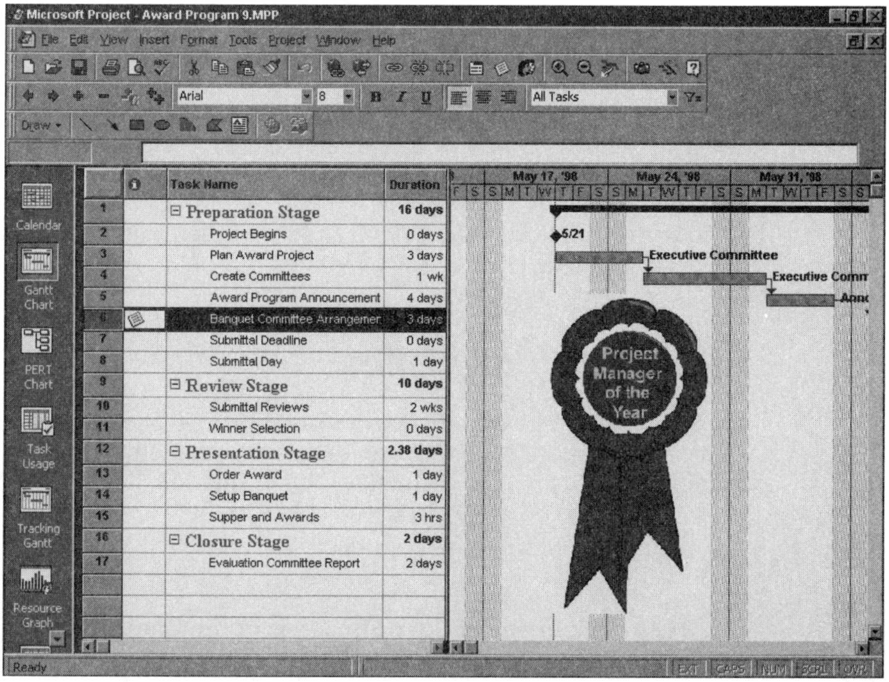

Figure 9-7: After you paste a graphic into the Gantt chart, you can easily drag it around. To edit the graphic, right-click the figure and then choose Edit.

Customizing the Look of the Gantt Chart

You can change the way your Gantt chart looks without modifying the information you've entered. Doing so won't put you on the inside track for winning an art award, but it will make working with task information less of a task. You and your associates may be spending oodles of hours working on your project, so you may as well like the way it looks.

Changing gridlines

Gridlines are horizontal and vertical lines that appear in the Gantt Chart view and some other views. You can change the look and frequency of gridlines to aid in the reading of the Gantt chart. To do so:

1. **Right-click in one of the white areas of the Gantt chart (not the Gantt table).**

   A list box appears.

2. **Choose Gridlines.**

   The Gridlines dialog box appears.

3. **With Gantt Rows highlighted, click the Normal Type box's down arrow. Select a line type.**

4. **In the Normal Color box, select the color you want for the Gantt row lines.**

5. **Click OK.**

   The gridlines appear with the selected color, as shown in Figure 9-8. Don't worry, if you don't like the color — you can change it easily.

To clear the gridlines, repeat Steps 1 to 3 and then select the blank box at the top of the list.

Changing bar styles

Changing bar styles has nothing to do with the trend toward micro breweries. A *bar style* is the way in which you depict duration on the Gantt chart. Sometimes it's helpful to customize the information. If that's what you want to do, the Bar Styles dialog box is the place to be.

To modify bar styles:

1. **Right-click in one of the white areas of the Gantt chart (not the Gantt table).**

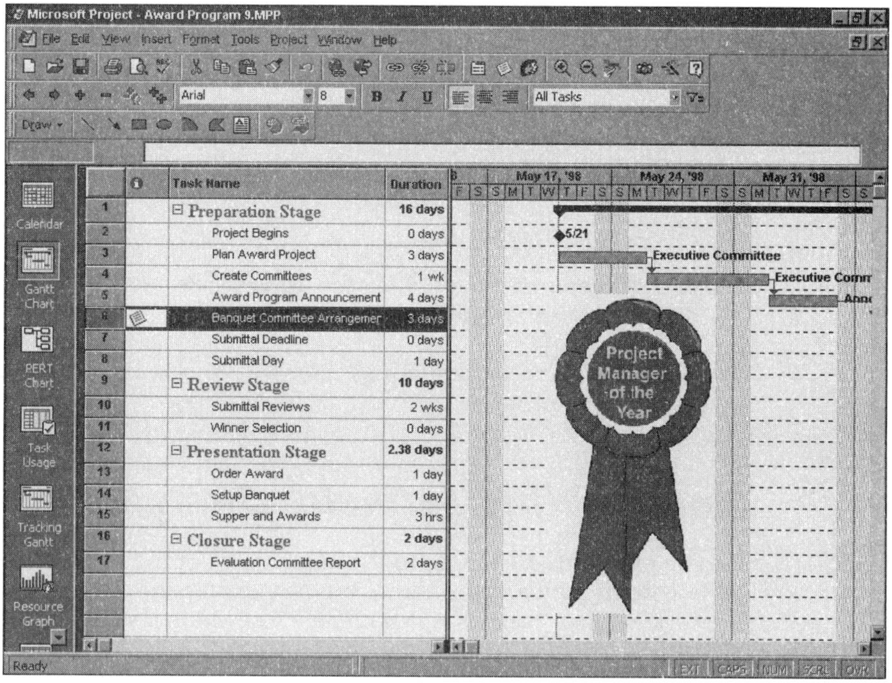

Figure 9-8: Here's one of the many ways you can customize the Gantt chart's gridlines.

2. **In the list box, select Bar Styles.**

   The Bar Styles dialog box appears.

3. **Select Summary from the Names list.**

   You can use the Bars selections for changing the Start shape, the Middle bar, and the End shape of all summary bars in the Gantt chart. For now, don't make any changes to the summary bars. That way, you can follow along with the next example.

4. **Click Cancel.**

Individual bar style changes

I ask you to click Cancel in the preceding set of steps because I want to show you something else. Sometimes it's neat to modify individual elements of the bar chart.

For example, you can choose a different color for each summary bar. To do this:

1. **Right-click the summary bar for task 1, Preparation Stage.**

2. **Choose Format Bar.**

   The Format Bar dialog box appears.

3. **Choose the Bar Shape tab.**

4. **Change the middle bar color to something other than black.**

   You can change anything else you want as well.

5. **Click OK.**

6. **Follow Steps 1 through 5 for the other three summary bars, using a different color or pattern for each.**

With each summary bar a different color, you may find it easier to identify the stages of the project.

Making other cosmetic changes

You can make other changes to the appearance of the Gantt chart. By right-clicking in the general chart area, you can change the color and look of nonworking time. Your days can finally be sky blue if you want! By double-clicking a particular area or element, you can change the look of that specific feature.

Changing links

One more double-click makes it possible for you to change more than a look. By double-clicking a link, you can modify the schedule.

For example, the Award Program has a scheduling blunder. The Announcement Committee is supposed to meet the day after it's formed, which is unrealistic. You need to create a one-week lag between tasks 4 and 5. To create this lag:

1. **Double-click the link between tasks 4 and 5 on the Gantt chart.**

   The link is the graphic depiction of the relationship of tasks 4 and 5. The link's Task Dependency dialog box appears.

2. **In the Lag box, change the lag time from 0d to** 1w.

   See Figure 9-9.

3. **Click OK.**

   All projects following task 4 move up one week.

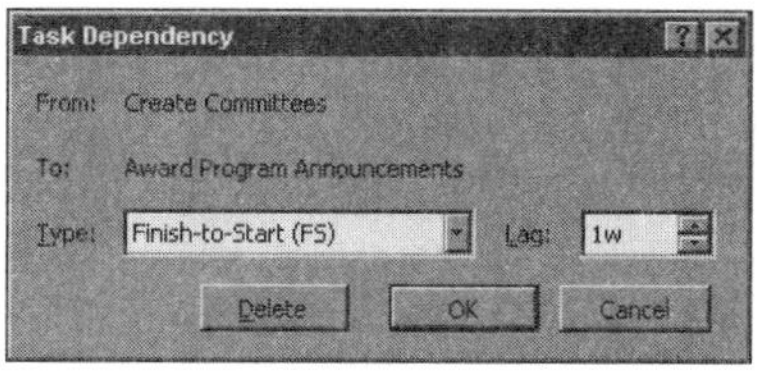

Figure 9-9: You can change the task relationship as well as the lag time.

Using the Mouse

You can use your mouse to solicit information from or change information in the Gantt chart. For instance, click and hold in the middle of a task bar. Do the same for a summary task and then a milestone. An information box reports the start and finish times of each task. These kinds of readouts are helpful when you're scanning the various stages of a project. By dragging the task duration bar right or left, you can move the entire task duration to new start and finish dates.

Getting Time on Your Side

In project management (and in life), the proper use of time is never easy. Microsoft Project can't solve all your time challenges, but at the very least, it can tell you whether time is helping or hurting your project. One of the time tools provided by Microsoft Project is the timescale.

The *timescale* is the indicator at the top of the Gantt chart (refer to Figure 9-8). Time is shown in major and minor increments. Major time increments are in the upper row of the timescale. For instance, the current setting shows a major timescale of one week. The date indicated is the first day of the week (Sunday). The second row is the minor timescale. The current setting shows individual days.

I'm not going to ask you to modify the timescale. But you may need to at some other time, so here's what it's all about:

1. **Double-click the timescale area of the Award Program's Gantt chart.**

   The Timescale dialog box appears, as shown in Figure 9-10.

2. **Click the Timescale tab, if it isn't already chosen.**

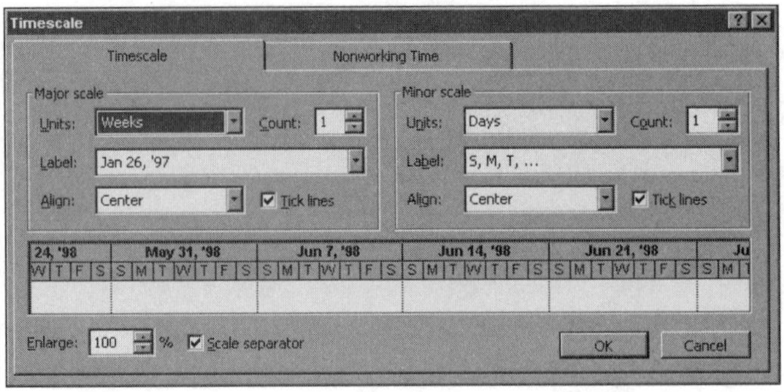

Figure 9-10: The Timescale dialog box offers settings for working and nonworking time.

The default setting of the timescale is weeks in the major scale and days in the minor scale. Notice the default manner of depicting time in the major and minor scales. The major timescale time lists month, day, and year. The minor timescale time lists an abbreviation for days.

The Count box under both Major Scale and Minor Scale affords you the opportunity to depict measurements of time sequentially or by skipping. Skipping is performed by changing the count from 1 to some other number. For instance, if the major setting is months (January, February, March), you can show every other month (January, March, May) by changing the count to 2. After you've checked out the settings in the Timescale dialog box, click Cancel to maintain the default settings.

Chapter 10
The PERT Chart

In This Chapter

- Understanding a PERT chart
- Getting around in a PERT chart
- Working with tasks in a PERT chart
- Working with relationships in a PERT chart

I wish I could tell you that the PERT chart was designed by Henry Gantt's Aunt Pertha, but she probably wasn't responsible (unless she worked for the U.S. Navy in the late 1950s). The PERT in PERT chart stands for *Program Evaluation and Review Technique* — I'll stick with the acronym.

Microsoft Project offers the PERT chart as one of its views because you can use it to

- Review project tasks in a graphical format.
- Study task relationships in a close-up view or a wide view.
- Edit tasks.
- Link tasks.
- Create schedules.
- Perform analysis.

In this chapter, you tinker with a sample PERT chart file. To begin, start Microsoft Project (if necessary). Then:

1. **Click the Open button on the standard toolbar.**
2. **Open the Project folder on your hard drive or on the *Microsoft Project 98 For Dummies* CD-ROM.**
3. **Double-click PERT Sample 10.MPP.**

Basics of the PERT Chart

PERT charts are weak on duration and strong on relationship. As you're about to see, PERT charts are like flowcharts, making it easy for you to concentrate on the implications of the links between tasks. On the flip side, PERT charts don't give you a lot of visual representation of the lengths of tasks or the timeline.

To see this mastery of the intricacies of relationship, choose PERT Chart on the view bar or choose View⇨PERT Chart. The Gantt chart is replaced by the PERT chart, as shown in Figure 10-1.

Zooming the view

One of the first things you need to know in a PERT Chart view is where to find the zoom controls so that you can see the whole picture as well as the details. You can use the Zoom In and Out buttons on the standard toolbar to perform this function. But you may like the PERT zoom feature better. To use the PERT zoom feature:

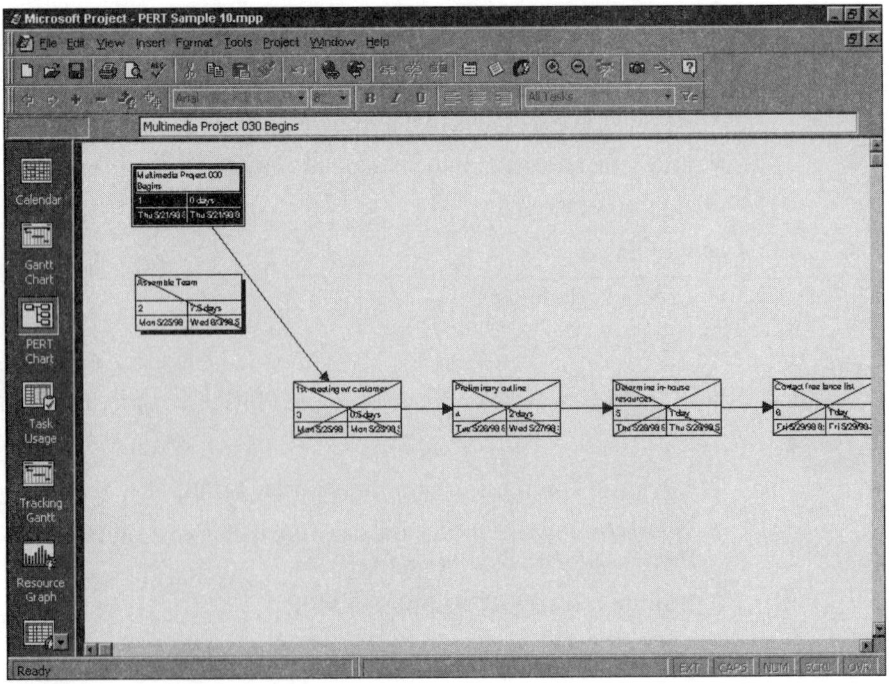

Figure 10-1: The lines and arrows in the PERT chart indicate the tasks' relationships.

1. **Choose View⇨Zoom.**

   The Zoom dialog box appears.

2. **Select Entire Project and then click OK.**

   Most of the picture appears, as shown in Figure 10-2.

Reading the view

The Entire Project view shows a number of aspects of the PERT chart. Each box, or *node,* is an individual task. Predecessors are always to the left of and above successors. Summary tasks are always to the left of and above their subtasks.

Click the Zoom In button on the standard toolbar once. At this level of magnification, you can see that some task boxes contain two diagonal lines, some contain a single diagonal line, and some have no diagonal line. Two diagonal lines mean the task is completed. A single diagonal line indicates a task is partially completed. No diagonal line means the task hasn't begun yet.

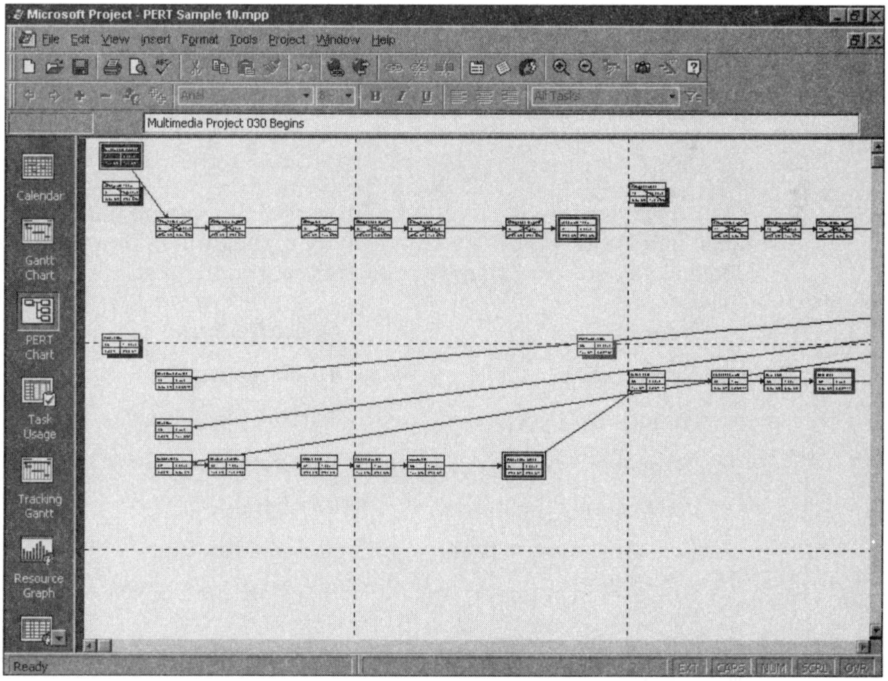

Figure 10-2: To see more of the PERT chart, use the Zoom dialog box or the Zoom In and Zoom Out buttons on the standard toolbar.

Note that a summary task has a single diagonal line if some but not all of its tasks have double diagonal lines.

An easy way to understand the various box frames and colors is by accessing the Box Styles dialog box. To do so:

1. **Double-click anywhere in the blank area of the PERT Chart view.**

   The Box Styles dialog box appears.

2. **Click the Borders tab.**

   The screen looks like Figure 10-3.

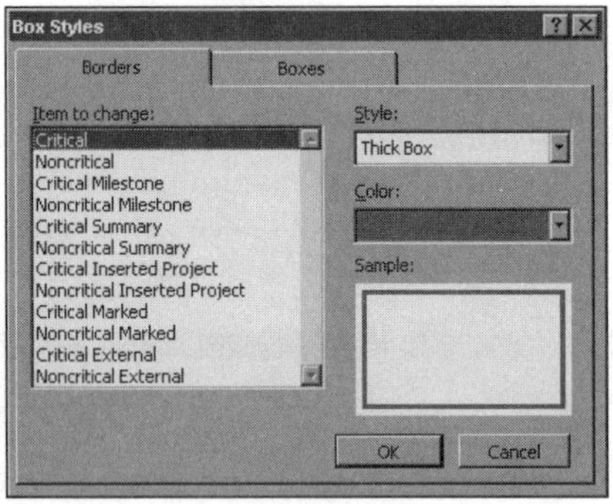

Figure 10-3: The shapes and colors of the nodes communicate just as much information as the text within them.

The Box Styles dialog box is an editing tool, but it also illustrates the meaning of node colors and shapes. By highlighting different Items to Change, you see how they're represented graphically:

Item	*Default shape*
Critical task	Thick red border
Noncritical task	Narrow black border
Critical milestone	Red frame
Noncritical milestone	Black frame
Critical summary task	Red shadow box
Noncritical summary task	Black shadow box

You can use the Box Styles dialog box to change the styles or color of any of these items.

Viewing task information

In addition to illustrating and interpreting the meaning of node borders, the Box Styles dialog box tells you about the information contained in the nodes.

To see what's in your nodes (no mirror is necessary), click the Boxes tab of the Box Styles dialog box. The Boxes tab is node mission control. Each PERT node box has five fields, as shown in Figure 10-4. Each field contains default information. Field 1 is usually used for the task name, as shown here. Fields 2 through 5 contain default information. But you can choose something else for each field if you want.

To practice changing box information, modify field 2:

1. **Select field 2.**
2. **From the choices in the list box, select Resource Group.**
3. **Click OK.**

   The Resource Group has replaced the task ID.

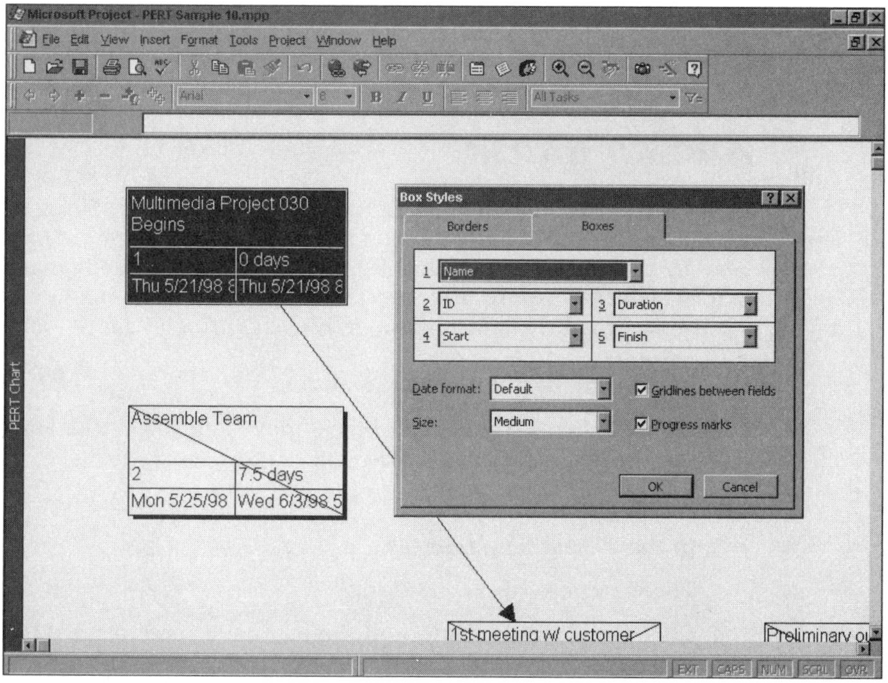

Figure 10-4: In addition to changing box information, you can modify the box design.

Some tasks don't have a resource group assignment. The PERT chart indicates this by using nodes with an empty resource group field.

Viewing task relationships

Click the Zoom Out button on the standard toolbar until the PERT chart is nearly a full view again. This view will assist in comparing task relationships.

Task relationships appear as red and black lines. Red lines represent *critical path relationships* (tasks that must be completed on time to keep the project on schedule). Black lines represent *noncritical path relationships* (tasks that have slack and can be completed later than their finish date). Critical path is described in detail in Chapter 16.

Editing Tasks and Relationships

Adding a task or changing a link on the PERT chart is simple. And don't worry about the way the changes will affect the Gantt chart. Microsoft Project is keeping records for you. Any changes to a task or a link in the PERT Chart view appear also in the Gantt Chart view and are recorded in relevant tables.

Adding a task

In this section, you add a task to the sample project file. Suppose that you need to add a storyboard meeting for staff and freelancers. This means you need to add a storyboard task after task 23 — Create preliminary tests, and before task 24 — Approvals. If you want, you can zoom in once or twice to more easily read the information in the tasks. To add a new task:

1. **Return the ID number to the nodes.**

   Right-click in a blank area of the screen, and select Box Styles. In the list box for field 2, select ID. Then click OK.

2. **Select Edit⇨Go To.**

3. **In the ID text box, type** 23.

   The view goes to task 23.

4. **Click the Zoom In button on the standard toolbar until the screen looks like Figure 10-5.**

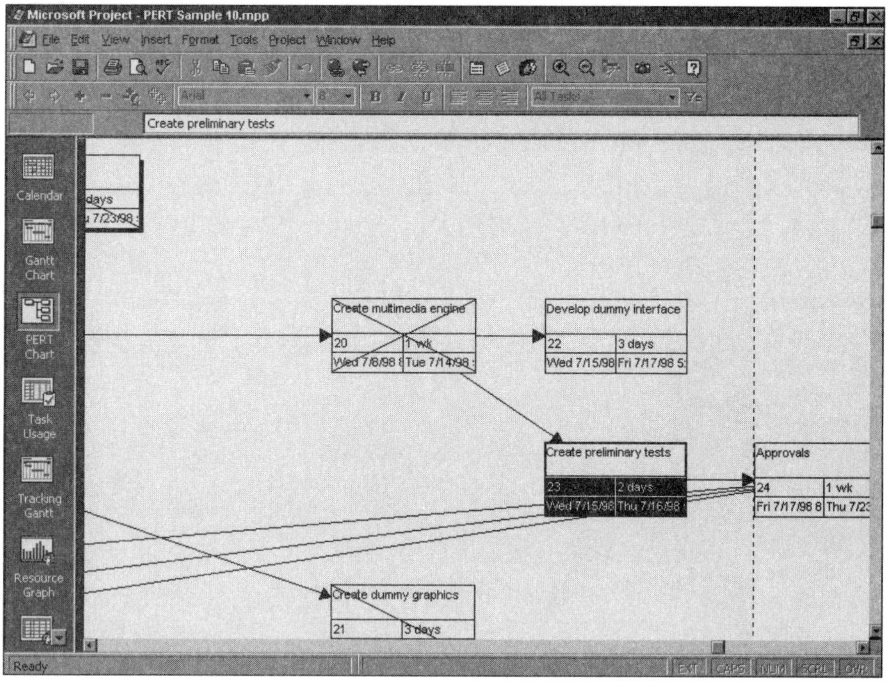

Figure 10-5: If you first select a task, the Zoom In and Zoom Out buttons focus on the selection.

5. **Draw a task box next to the Develop dummy interface task by clicking to the right of the task and dragging a box (see Figure 10-6).**

   TIP: Another way to create a new task box next to an existing task is by selecting the existing task and then pressing the Insert key.

6. **Double-click the new task box.**

   The Task Information dialog box appears.

7. **Select the General tab, and in the Name text box, type** Storyboard.
8. **Give the task a 1-day duration.**
9. **Click the Resources tab.**
10. **Select the first Resource Name text box. Use the drop-down list to select a resource.**
11. **Select the second Resource Name text box and do the same procedure as Step 10 to select another resource.**
12. **Continue adding resources until all except the Customer have been selected.**
13. **Click OK.**

    The new task box contains the task information, as shown in Figure 10-7.

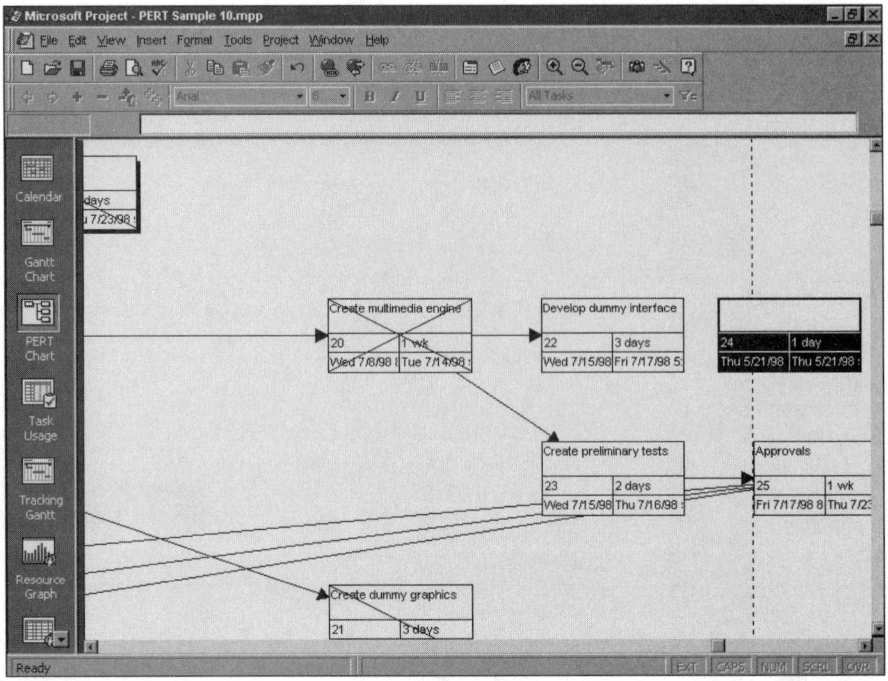

Figure 10-6: An empty, unlinked task node now exists to the right of the Develop dummy interface task.

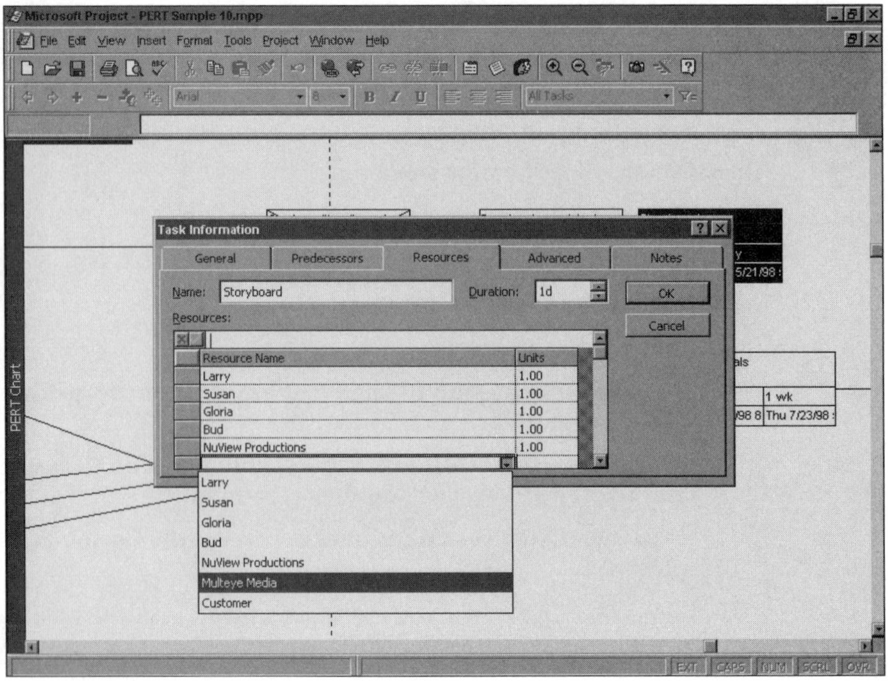

Figure 10-7: Whether you are in a PERT Chart view or any other view, there is only one list of available resources for a project.

Creating a link

To link a new task to its predecessor, its successor, or both, you click in the middle of the predecessor task and drag to its new relationship. If you don't understand what I mean by *linking,* you may want to connect with Chapter 6.

Using the sample project file:

1. **If necessary, click the Zoom Out or Zoom In button to show the boxes around the new task (Storyboard), and to easily read their information.**
2. **Place your mouse cursor on the Create preliminary tests task.**
3. **Hold down the left mouse button, drag to the task you have just created, and then release the mouse button.**
4. **Hold down the left mouse button, drag from your new task (Storyboard) to Approvals, and then release the mouse button.**
5. **Place the mouse cursor on the link between Create preliminary tests and Approvals. Double-click.**

   The Task Dependency dialog box appears.
6. **Click the Delete button.**

   See Figure 10-8. You've just created two relationships and deleted one.

Changing the layout

You may find a different layout easier to read. Choose Format⇨Layout. The Layout dialog box appears. Two link format layout options are available. Select the link format on the right, as shown in Figure 10-9.

Click OK. The task relationships are now shown in orthogonal lines, as shown in Figure 10-10.

Sorry. I was just itching to use my big word. To make something *orthogonal,* you make it perpendicular with right angles. So now you can hang out your shingle as an orthogonist.

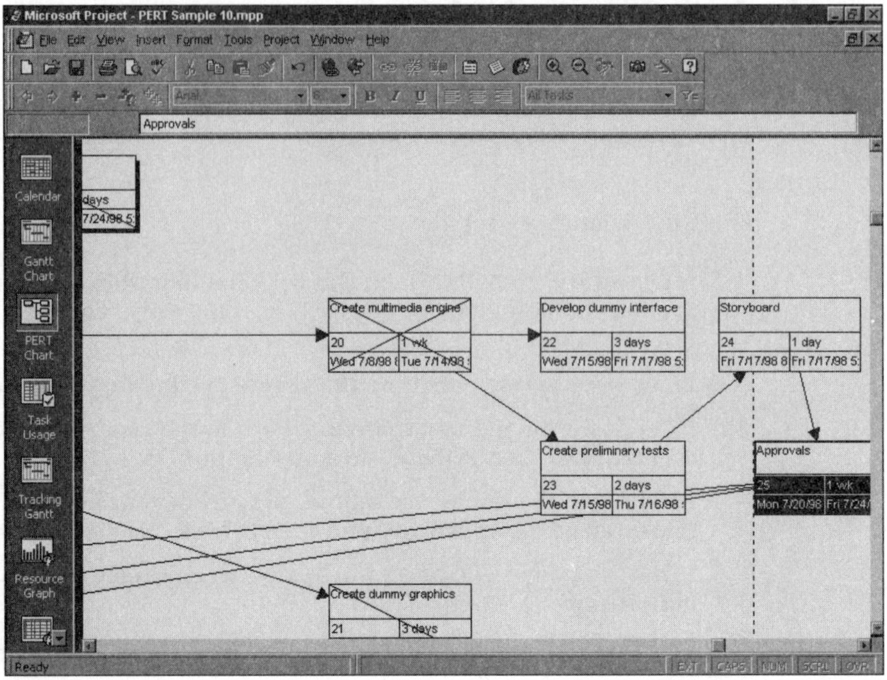

Figure 10-8: The changes you just made appear also in the Gantt chart.

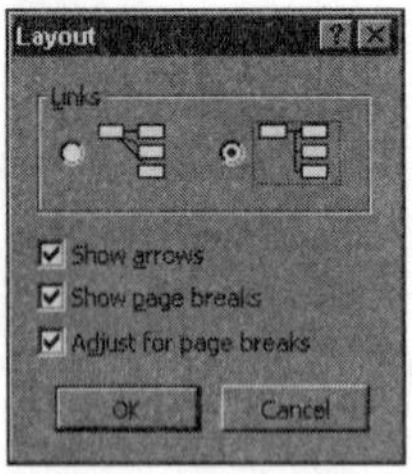

Figure 10-9: The two link layout options don't modify the task relationships in any way.

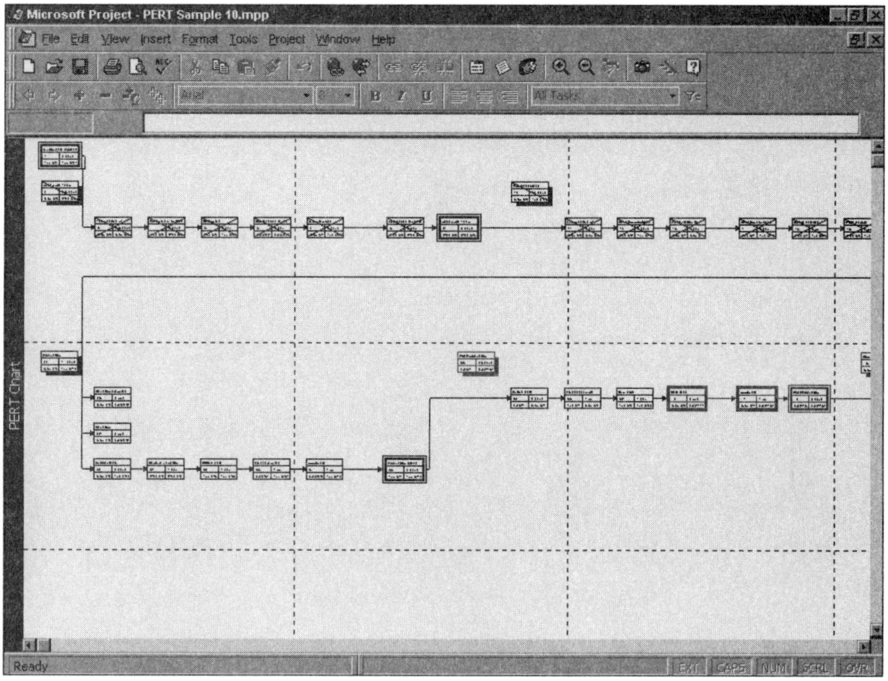

Figure 10-10: Changing the layout of the PERT Chart doesn't affect the task relationships.

Chapter 11
The Calendar

In This Chapter

- Cheering and complaining about the Calendar view
- Creating a schedule in the calendar
- Comprehending the calendar
- Cruising the calendar
- Customizing the calendar

The beauty of the Calendar view is also its liability. On the positive side, the Calendar view lets you see and present your work in a familiar manner. On the minus side, the Calendar view limits how much information you can present at a time. Ah, life! You can, however, do lots of things with the Calendar view if you work within its limitations.

The Calendar view can be helpful in two major ways. First, the Calendar view is a whiz at creating simple projects. Second, the Calendar view is a great tool for viewing, segregating, and reporting more complex projects. Accordingly, this chapter is divided into two major sections. The first focuses on how to create a simple project using the Calendar view. The second section deals with using the Calendar view for existing, more complex projects. If you want to skip the first section and go right to the second section, have at it!

Making a Simple Schedule with the Calendar View

The planner industry has nothing to worry about with Microsoft Project's Calendar view. Planners and Calendar view are for entirely different purposes. They're Appaloosas and orangutans.

Using the Calendar view, you can make a fully functioning project. You can create and track a schedule of tasks and establish their resources. After you create a project in the Calendar view, you can view it in the Gantt Chart view, resource views, graphs, and in combination views. You can also make reports from projects you create in Calendar view.

Creating a project using the Calendar view

Creating a project in Calendar view is fun, in a project manager sort of way. To begin, you need to switch views:

1. **Start Microsoft Project.**

   The program opens in the Gantt Chart view.

2. **Choose View⇨Calendar or select the Calendar button on the view bar.**

   Welcome to the Calendar view.

Here's the project: Simultaneously begin to develop a Web page and a company brochure. Then simultaneously contact trade associations, send mailers, distribute flyers, perform Web-search sign-ups, and amend database forms. For the date, assume that today is May 21, 1998.

TIP: Microsoft Project uses the current date as the default project start date if you don't specify a start date. To specify a start date, choose Project⇨Project Information. The Project Information dialog box appears. To set a new project date, change the Start Date.

Here's how you plan the project in the Calendar view: Begin by pressing the Insert key seven times. This creates seven tasks. The task boxes stack on top of each other in the start date box on the calendar, as shown in Figure 11-1.

Notice that the task boxes take up more space than is allowed in the date window. A down arrow in the date's shaded areas tells you that some tasks are hidden. You access the hidden task boxes by zooming or by exploding the date window. Zooming magnifies the entire calendar. Exploding the date window magnifies only one date.

You access the hidden tasks by exploding the date window. Double-click the gray date bar of the date that holds the task boxes. A task list appears, as shown in Figure 11-2. The check marks indicate the tasks visible in the window.

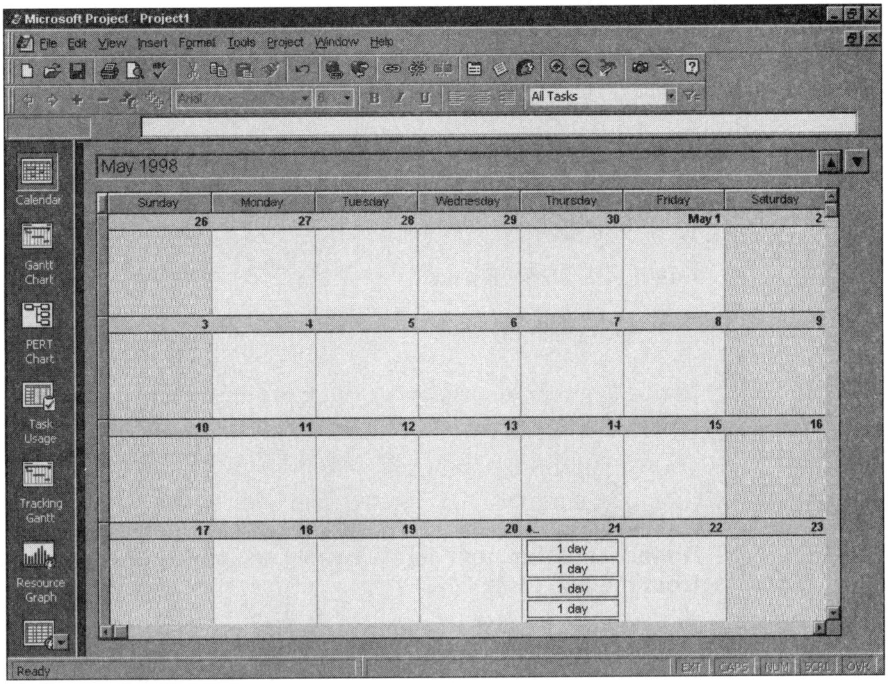

Figure 11-1: Each inserted box is an unnamed task. By default, each task begins on the start date and has a duration of one day.

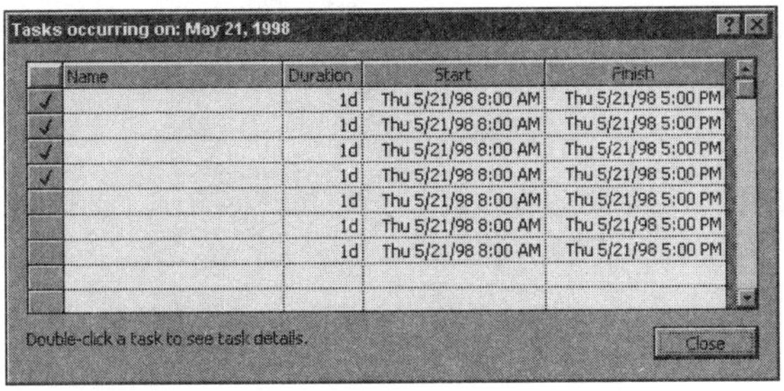

Figure 11-2: Another way to access the task list is by right-clicking the date bar and then selecting Task List.

Entering task information

Now that you have the task list on the screen, I'll show you a shortcut for entering task information. You'll use this method to enter the following tasks:

Develop Web Page

Publish Brochure

Contact Trade Associations

Send Mailers

Distribute Flyers

Web Page Search Sign-ups

Amend Database Forms

To enter these task names:

1. **In the Name column, double-click the first empty name box and type** Develop Web Page**.**

   The Task Information box should look like Figure 11-3.

2. **Click OK.**

3. **Double-click the next empty name box, and type the next task name from the list. Click OK.**

4. **Repeat Step 3 for the remaining tasks.**

   When you finish, you have names in all seven task boxes. The result should look like Figure 11-4.

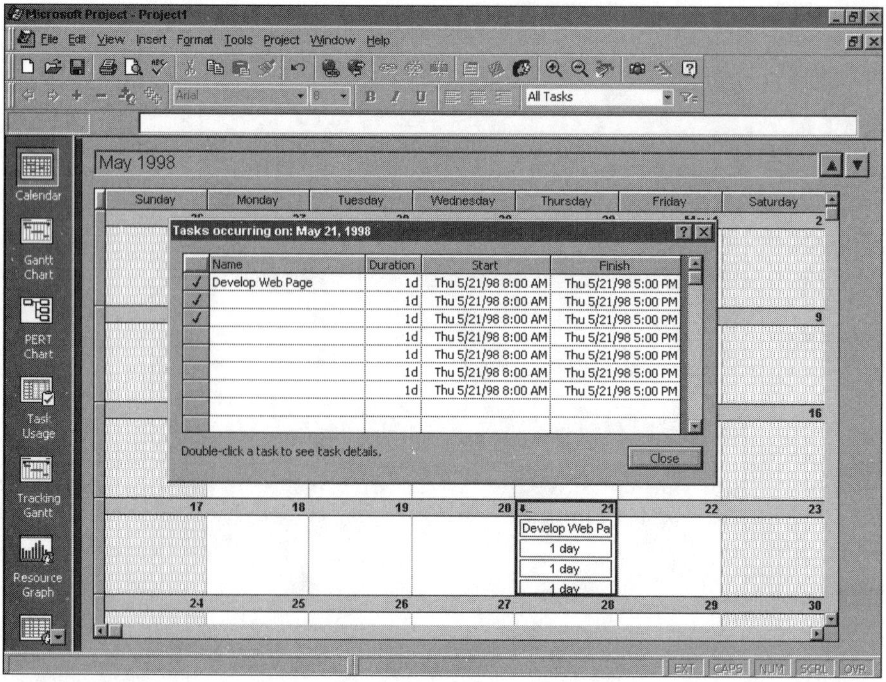

Figure 11-3: The Task Information box is the same in the Calendar view and the Gantt Chart view.

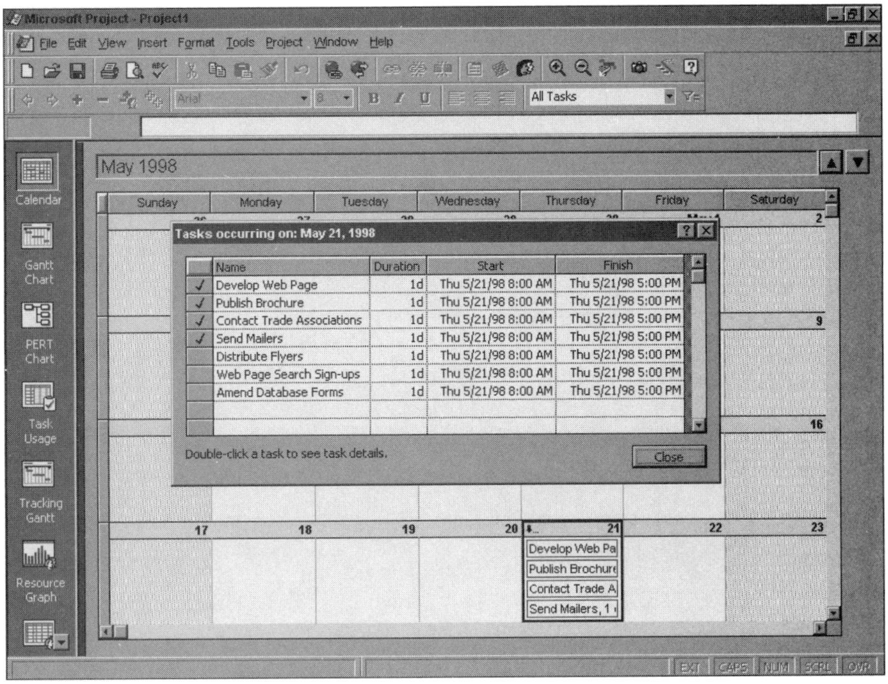

Figure 11-4: You can see and modify all tasks occurring on a certain date, including hidden ones.

5. Click Close to close the task list box.

Zooming the calendar

The default Calendar view shows four successive weeks. You can change that view from four weeks to two weeks with the Zoom In button.

Click the Zoom In button on the standard toolbar once. The view changes to a two-week interval. If your start date is in one of the latter two weeks on the calendar, the tasks disappear. That's because the Zoom In command focuses on the first two weeks of the calendar. To expose your start date, use the scroll bar or press the Page Down key once. The calendar should now look like Figure 11-5.

If you want, you can open the task list again to see all tasks with check marks. To do so, simply double-click the date bar of the date that holds the task boxes.

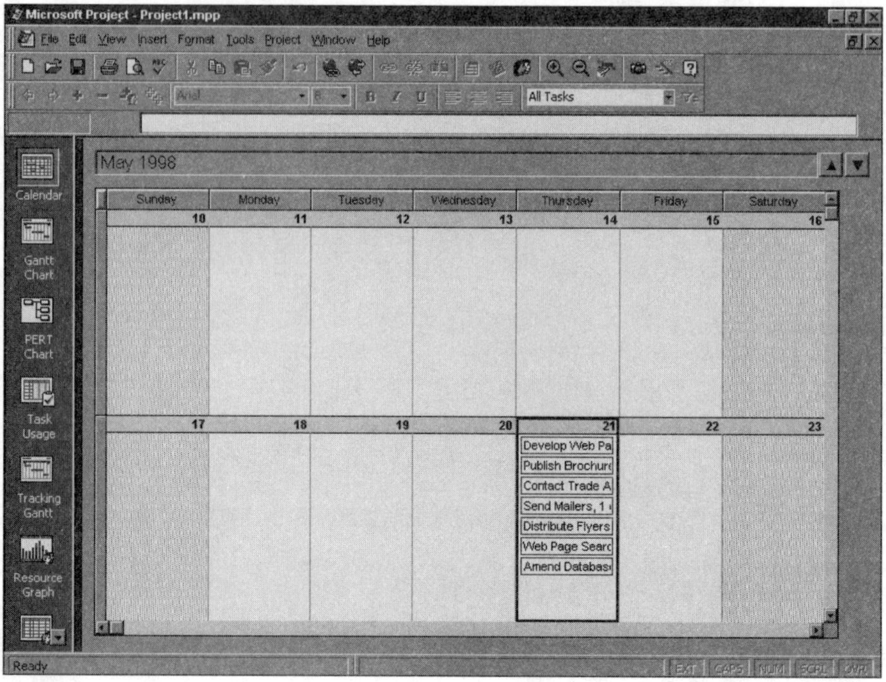

Figure 11-5: The Zoom In button enlarges the view size of each date box and exposes all the tasks in the project start date.

Adding duration in the Calendar view

You can change durations to the seven tasks you entered in two ways: by using the Task Information dialog box or by dragging. In this section, you try out both ways. It'll be fast and fun. Well, kind of fun anyway.

Here are the durations you need to add:

Develop Web Page: 2 weeks

Publish Brochure: 3 weeks

Contact Trade Associations: 2 days

Send Mailers: 2 days

Distribute Flyers: 2 days

Web Page Search Sign-ups: 2 days

Amend Database Forms: 2 days

To add these durations, do the following:

1. **Click the Zoom Out button on the standard toolbar once.**

   You're back in the four-week view.

2. **Double-click the first task, Develop Web Page.**

   The Task Information dialog box appears.

3. **In the Duration box, type** 2w **and click OK.**

   You've just entered a two-week duration for the Develop Web Page task using the Task Information dialog box.

4. **Move the mouse cursor to the right edge of the second task, Publish Brochure.**

   The cursor changes to a vertical bar and a right arrow.

5. **Click and drag downward.**

   A task information caption balloon appears. In the balloon is a duration reading.

6. **Drag down and back and forth until the duration reading is 15d (three work weeks). Release the mouse button.**

   You've entered a duration using the drag method. The second task, Publish Brochure, should now show a 15d duration.

7. **Click the Zoom In button on the standard toolbar once.**

   The screen returns to the two-week view.

8. **If necessary, scroll or press the Page Up key to expose the starting date.**

9. **Using the dragging technique, give each of the remaining tasks a 2-day duration.**

   The resulting view should look like Figure 11-6.

Linking tasks in Calendar view

Linking tasks is simple in Calendar view: You select the tasks and use the Link button. In Calendar view, like in Gantt Chart view, the default relationship type is finish to start.

Using this example, change a number of relationship types. Here are the relationships:

ID	*Task Name*	*Predecessor*	*Type*
1	Develop Web Page		
2	Publish Brochure	1	Start to start

(continued)

(continued)

ID	*Task Name*	*Predecessor*	*Type*
3	Contact Trade Associations	2	Finish to start
4	Send Mailers	3	Finish to start
5	Distribute Flyers	3	Finish to start
6	Web Page Search Sign-ups	3	Finish to start
7	Amend Database Forms	3	Finish to start

You can use the Task Information dialog box to enter this information. To get you started, I show you how to add information for the Publish Brochure task:

1. **Double-click the Publish Brochure task.**

   The Task Information dialog box appears.

2. **Click the Predecessors tab.**

3. **Select the first empty box under the Task Name column.**

   A small down arrow becomes active next to the text entry box.

4. **Click the down arrow.**

   A list of all the tasks appears, as shown in Figure 11-7.

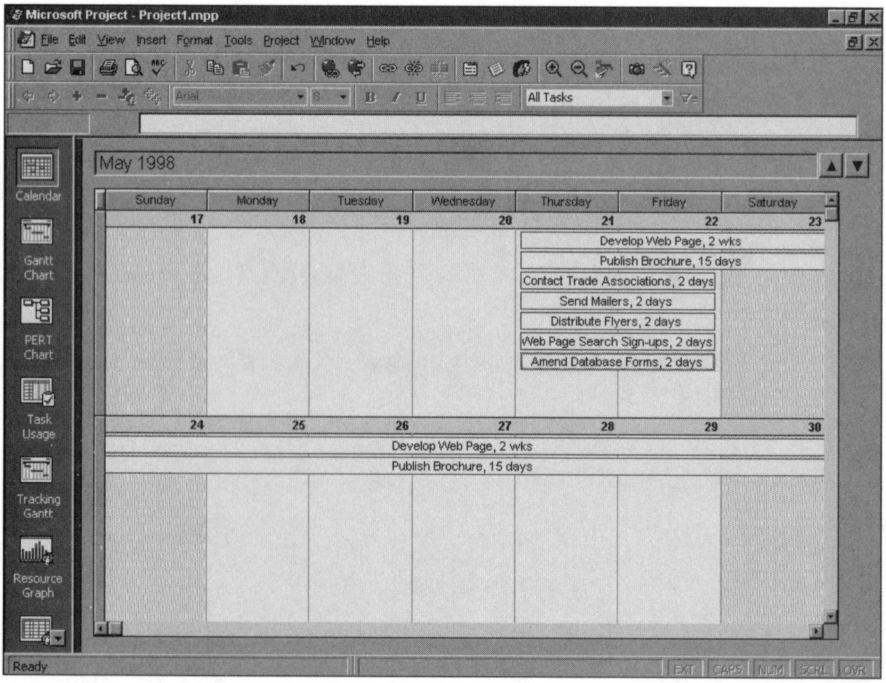

Figure 11-6: The tasks appear in stacked order because they don't have predecessors or successors yet.

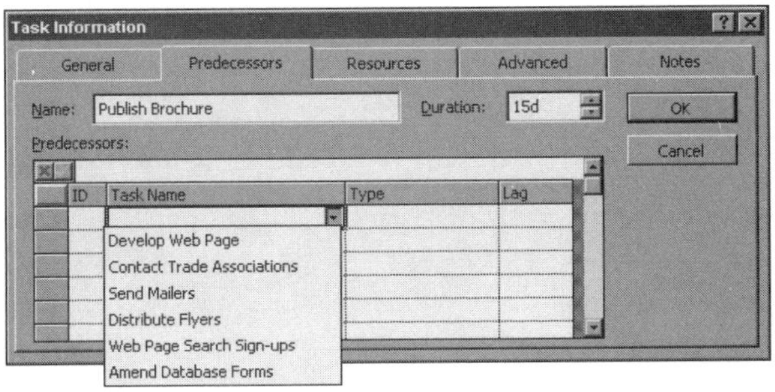

Figure 11-7: You can type the information in the box, but selecting from the list is usually faster and safer.

5. **Select Develop Web Page.**
6. **Select the first empty box under the Type column.**

   A small arrow becomes active next to the text entry box.
7. **Click the down arrow.**

   A list of all the relationship types appears.
8. **Select Start-to-Start and then click OK.**
9. **If necessary, press the Page Up key.**

Now complete the information for the tasks using these steps and the table preceding them as a guide.

Fitting the information to the calendar

After you finish entering task information, click the Zoom Out button on the standard toolbar once to change the screen to month view. Then scroll until the last full week of May and the first three weeks of June are in view. Notice in Figure 11-8 that some tasks are partially or totally hidden. Tasks remain vertically hierarchical even though they are separated horizontally.

You can modify the task layout to better fit tasks in the calendar boxes. To do this:

1. **Choose Format⇨Layout.**

   The Layout dialog box appears.
2. **Select the Attempt to Fit as Many Tasks as Possible option.**
3. **Click OK.**

   The screen should now look like Figure 11-9.

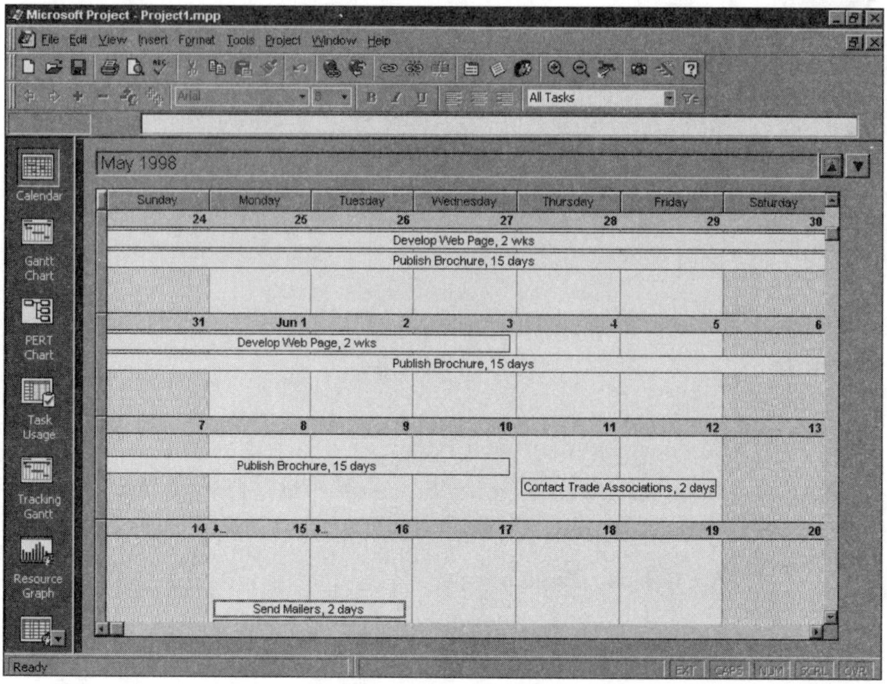

Figure 11-8: Linked tasks don't have connecting lines in the Calendar view as they do in the Gantt Chart view and the PERT Chart view.

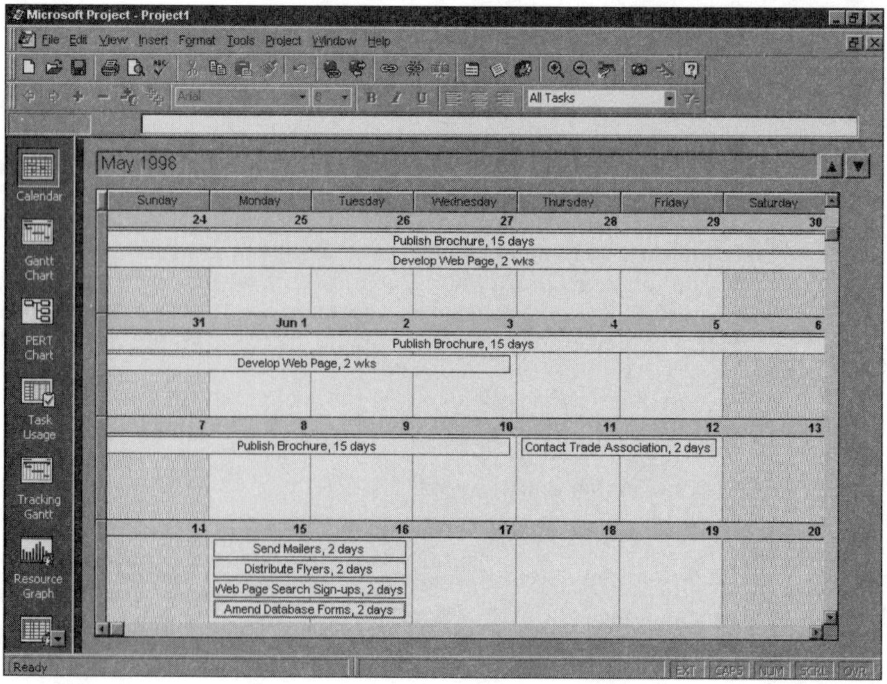

Figure 11-9: The Attempt to Fit as Many Tasks as Possible option optimizes space to display tasks.

Save this project file in your Practice Files folder as follows:

1. **Click the Save button on the standard toolbar.**
2. **Change folders to the Practice Files folder.**
3. **Save the project using a name such as Small Calendar.**
4. **If you want, close the file by choosing File⇨Close.**

Using the Calendar View for Existing Projects

The Calendar view can be used with existing projects. Sometimes it's a convenient tool for reviewing and reporting a portion of a project's schedule. Be aware, though, that Calendar view has its strengths and weaknesses. It handles small amounts of information well, but quickly becomes unwieldy for more complicated projects.

If you're working with an existing project, adding or editing tasks in the Calendar view can be messy. For instance, if you add a task to the middle of a project in the Calendar view, it will be messed up in the Gantt view. The task will be linked as you indicated, but it will be listed as the lowest ID number. Who needs such problems! It's safer to add or edit the task in the Gantt view. Then come back to the Calendar view to see your task nestled safe and warm where you want it.

In this section, you use the Calendar view to analyze an existing project. Open the sample project file called `Calendar 11.MPP` from the Project folder on the *Microsoft Project 98 For Dummies* CD-ROM as follows:

1. **Click the Open button on the standard toolbar.**
2. **Open the Project folder on your hard drive or on the *Microsoft Project 98 For Dummies* CD-ROM.**
3. **Double-click Calendar 11.MPP.**
4. **If the file doesn't open in Calendar view, choose View⇨Calendar.**

Cruising the calendar

Notice that the calendar opens to the project start date, as shown in Figure 11-10. The month is in the upper-left corner. The default view displays four weeks. Nonworking days are shaded gray.

Try cruising around a bit. You can do so in four ways:

- Click the up and down arrows to move from month to month.
- Click the scroll bar to slide your calendar up or down. When you click the scroll box, an information box appears that alerts you to the dates visible on the screen.
- Press Page Up and Page Down to move from month to month. (This is the same as clicking the up and down arrows on the screen.)
- Press Alt+Home and Alt+End to jump to the start or the end of the project, respectively.

When you finish cruising, press Alt+Home to return to the beginning of the project.

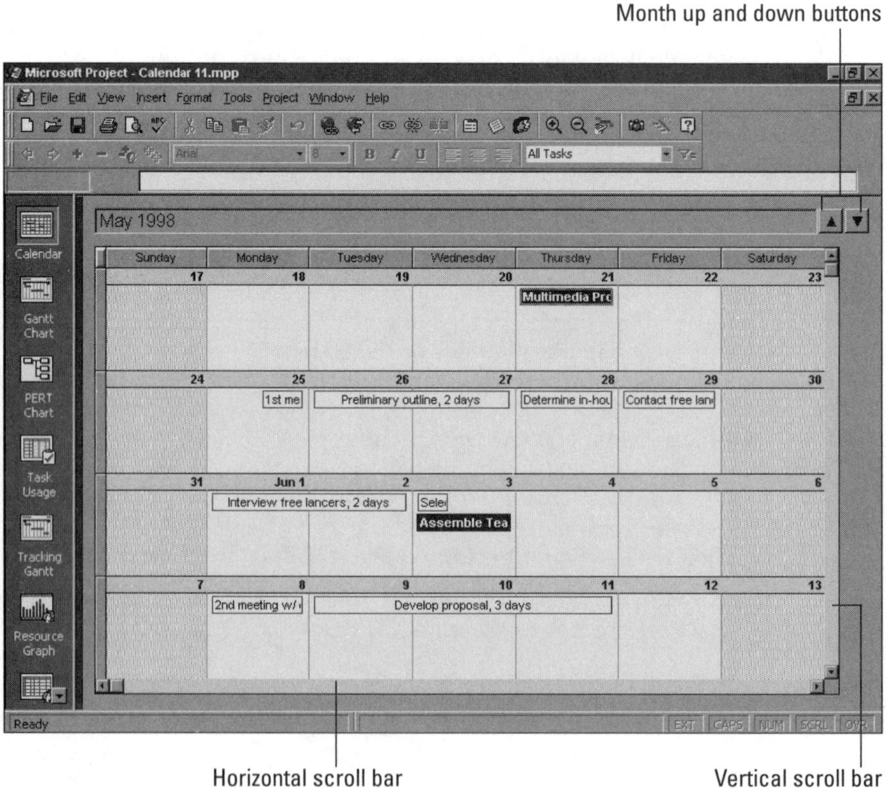

Figure 11-10: The Calendar view presents tasks in a bar style format. By default, the text consists of the task name and its duration.

Zooming to make it fit

Using the down arrow, change the Calendar view to August. The entire month isn't showing. You can either scroll down to see the final week, or you can make the month fit on the screen by zooming.

You can zoom with the Zoom In and Zoom Out buttons on the standard toolbar, but you get better results using the Zoom dialog box. Try this:

1. **Right-click anywhere in the white, unused portion of any date box.**

   A shortcut menu appears.

2. **Choose Zoom.**

   The Zoom dialog box appears, as shown in Figure 11-11.

3. **Select Custom.**

4. **In the Weeks box, type** 5.

5. **Click OK.**

   The Calendar view shows five weeks.

The default zoom in and zoom out increments are 1, 2, 4, and 6 weeks. You can customize your view in weeks, or you can set a view based on specific start and finish dates.

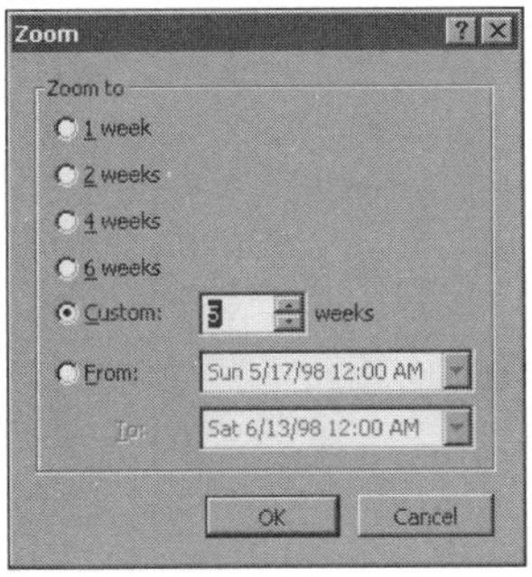

Figure 11-11: The practical limitations of custom zoom are directly related to the number of tasks appearing on any given day.

Making it fit with layout

You still have a problem. You can see all the weeks, but you can't see many of the tasks. Notice the down arrows in date boxes. The down arrows indicate that tasks occur on those dates, but the tasks are not currently visible. This can be corrected using a layout command. But you have to make a decision. Do you want to see all the weeks of the month or all the tasks on each day?

For this example, you change the layout to display all the tasks on each day. First, return to a four-week view:

1. **Right-click anywhere in the white, unused portion of any date box.**

   The shortcut menu appears.

2. **Choose Zoom.**

3. **Select the 4 Weeks option and then click OK.**

To make the tasks all appear in their respective days, begin by changing the calendar layout.

1. **Right-click anywhere in the white, unused portion of any date box.**

   The shortcut menu appears.

2. **Choose Layout.**

   The Layout dialog box appears, as shown in Figure 11-12.

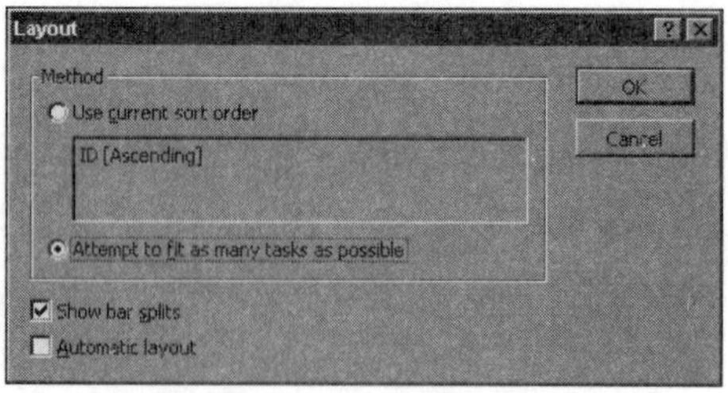

Figure 11-12: You can modify the layout in three ways. For details, click Help.

3. **Select the Attempt to Fit as Many Tasks as Possible option, and then click OK.**

   Some of the tasks now appear, as shown in Figure 11-13.

You have one more thing to do to maximize the view: Make the week rows tall enough to show as many tasks as possible. To do this, you use the automatic resizing feature.

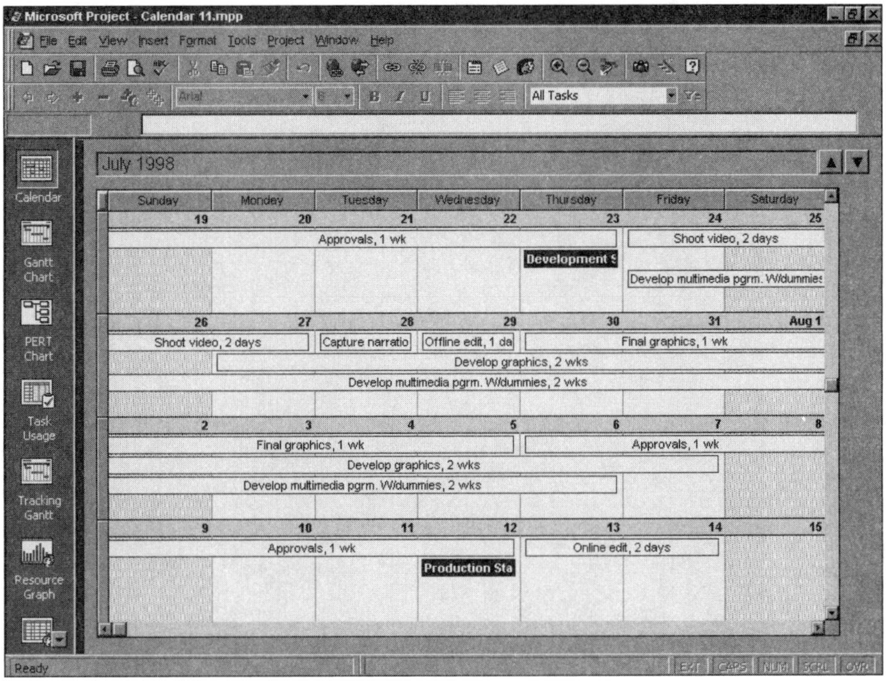

Figure 11-13: The Layout command fits as many tasks as it can into the date boxes.

1. **Place the mouse cursor over any horizontal line at the bottom of a week row.**

   The cursor turns into a horizontal line with an up and down arrow.

2. **Double-click.**

   Voilà! The tasks all fit into their date boxes.

Notice in Figure 11-14 that Microsoft Project calculated the space necessary and pushed the weeks down slightly.

Viewing a day

Notice that June 3 has two tasks so small there's little text identification. You can see what they are and simultaneously view all the other tasks on that day by double-clicking the day's date bar. When you do, you see that the short task is a half-hour meeting. The highlighted task turns out to be a milestone. (See Figure 11-15.) The check marks indicate that all the tasks are now visible.

If you want, save this file. Give it another name so that you can use the original file again.

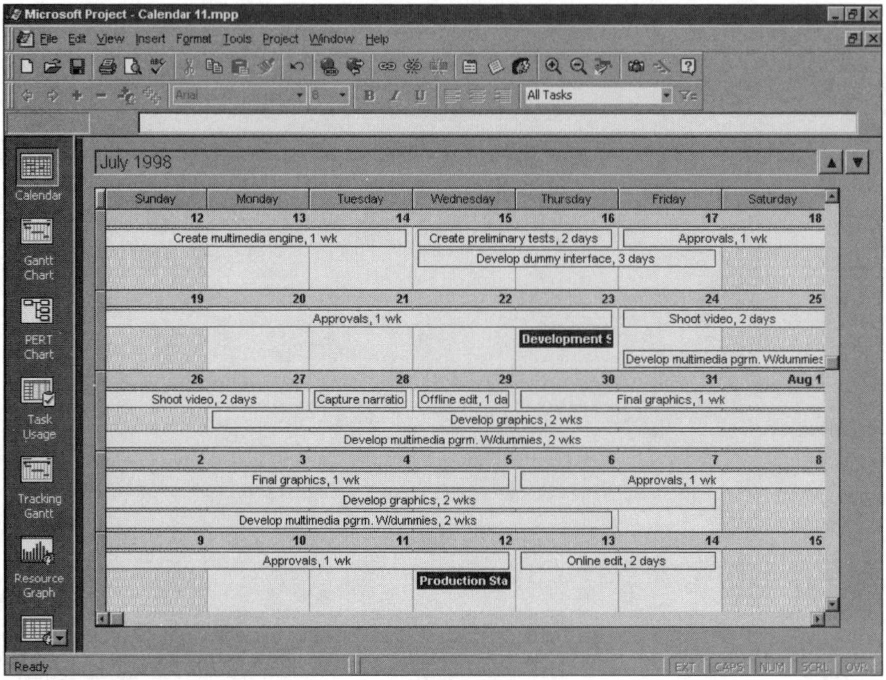

Figure 11-14: The Calendar view is now maximized to show all the tasks.

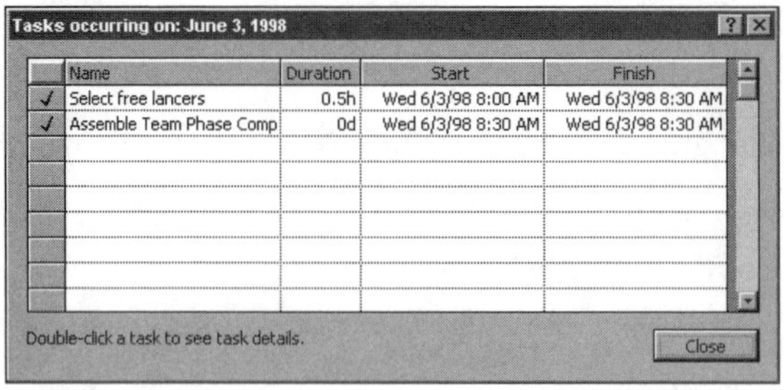

Figure 11-15: The date list box shows all the tasks occurring on that day.

Chapter 12

Resource Views

In This Chapter

- Using the Resource Sheet view
- Using the Resource Usage view
- Using the Resource Graph view

Chapter 8 explains the reasons for and importance of views, especially task views. Resource views have their place, too. Sometimes isolating resource information is helpful — as when you have an allocation problem. Each resource view displays information from a different perspective. Two of the views, Resource Sheet and Resource Usage, let you enter and edit resource information. The other view, the Resource Graph view, is for graphical illustration rather than for entering or editing information.

In this chapter, you use the sample project file called `Chapter 12.MPP` to view and manipulate resource information. Open the sample project file from the Project folder, as follows:

1. **Click the Open button on the standard toolbar.**
2. **Open the Project folder on your hard drive or on the *Microsoft Project 98 For Dummies* CD-ROM.**
3. **Double-click Chapter 12.MPP.**

   The file opens in the Gantt Chart view.

Resource Sheet View

The Resource sheet, like the Task sheet, is in spreadsheet form. The sheet lists resources and their related details such as initials, group designations, and maximum units (see Figure 12-1). You can use the sheet to enter and edit resource details. To access the Resource Sheet view, choose View➪Resource Sheet or select the Resource Sheet button on the view bar.

Adding information to the Resource sheet is similar to entering information in spreadsheet cells. You can insert rows and columns. You can also enter information at the first available open space at the bottom of the list.

Two of the greatest features of the Resource sheet are its sorting and filtering capabilities. I discuss sorting and filtering at length in Chapter 13. For now, experiment with a few options.

Sorting

Microsoft Project automatically assigns an identification number to each resource. By default, the Resource sheet is ordered by this ID. But this order simply reflects the order in which the resources were entered. If there's a significance to this order, great. Often, however, the default order has no special value. You can increase the value of the Resource Sheet view through sorting.

As an example of sorting, change the view to make the resources appear in alphabetical order. To do this:

1. **Choose Project⇨Sort.**

   The Sort list appears.

2. **Select by Name.**

   The view is now based on the alphabetical order of the resource names, as shown in Figure 12-2.

Filtering

In addition to changing the sort order, you can change the filter of the Resource Sheet view. Whether you realize it or not, Microsoft Project is always filtering your information — not like your mother, but more like an administrative assistant. Microsoft Project isn't hiding anything from you; it's controlling the amount of information it thinks you want to see at any given time.

The default filter for the Resource Sheet view is All Resources. You see this designation in the Filter list on the formatting toolbar shown in Figure 12-2. Here's an example of using a filter:

1. **Click the down arrow next to the Filter list on the formatting toolbar.**
2. **Select the Group option.**

   A Group entry box appears.

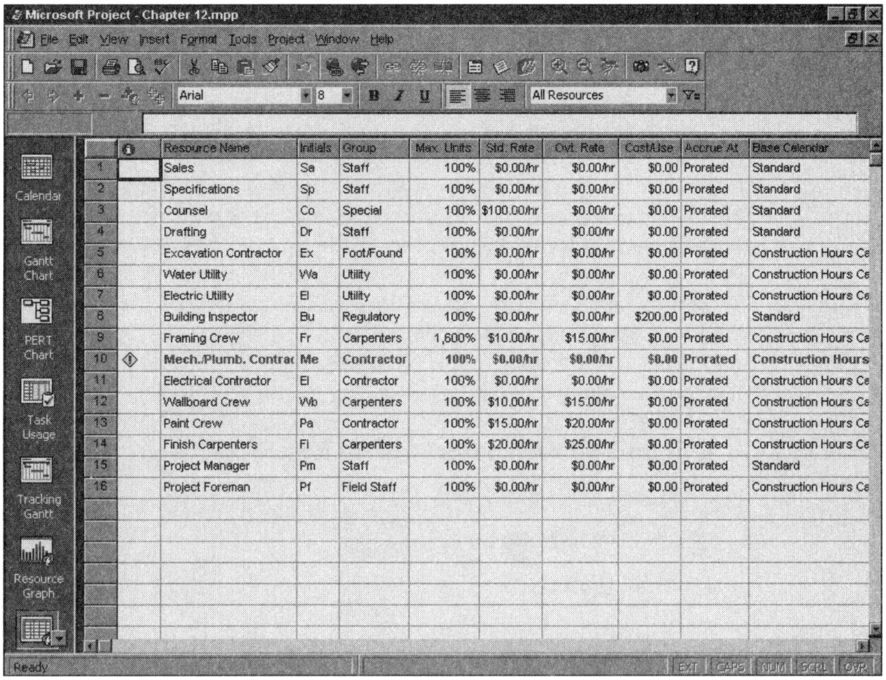

		Resource Name	Initials	Group	Max. Units	Std. Rate	Ovt. Rate	Cost/Use	Accrue At	Base Calendar
1		Sales	Sa	Staff	100%	$0.00/hr	$0.00/hr	$0.00	Prorated	Standard
2		Specifications	Sp	Staff	100%	$0.00/hr	$0.00/hr	$0.00	Prorated	Standard
3		Counsel	Co	Special	100%	$100.00/hr	$0.00/hr	$0.00	Prorated	Standard
4		Drafting	Dr	Staff	100%	$0.00/hr	$0.00/hr	$0.00	Prorated	Standard
5		Excavation Contractor	Ex	Foot/Found	100%	$0.00/hr	$0.00/hr	$0.00	Prorated	Construction Hours Ca
6		Water Utility	Wa	Utility	100%	$0.00/hr	$0.00/hr	$0.00	Prorated	Construction Hours Ca
7		Electric Utility	El	Utility	100%	$0.00/hr	$0.00/hr	$0.00	Prorated	Construction Hours Ca
8		Building Inspector	Bu	Regulatory	100%	$0.00/hr	$0.00/hr	$200.00	Prorated	Standard
9		Framing Crew	Fr	Carpenters	1,600%	$10.00/hr	$15.00/hr	$0.00	Prorated	Construction Hours Ca
10	◈	**Mech./Plumb. Contrac**	**Me**	**Contractor**	**100%**	**$0.00/hr**	**$0.00/hr**	**$0.00**	**Prorated**	**Construction Hours**
11		Electrical Contractor	El	Contractor	100%	$0.00/hr	$0.00/hr	$0.00	Prorated	Construction Hours Ca
12		Wallboard Crew	Wb	Carpenters	100%	$10.00/hr	$15.00/hr	$0.00	Prorated	Construction Hours Ca
13		Paint Crew	Pa	Contractor	100%	$15.00/hr	$20.00/hr	$0.00	Prorated	Construction Hours Ca
14		Finish Carpenters	Fi	Carpenters	100%	$20.00/hr	$25.00/hr	$0.00	Prorated	Construction Hours Ca
15		Project Manager	Pm	Staff	100%	$0.00/hr	$0.00/hr	$0.00	Prorated	Standard
16		Project Foreman	Pf	Field Staff	100%	$0.00/hr	$0.00/hr	$0.00	Prorated	Construction Hours Ca

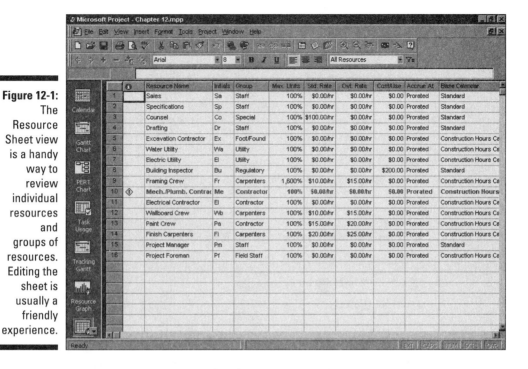

Figure 12-1: The Resource Sheet view is a handy way to review individual resources and groups of resources. Editing the sheet is usually a friendly experience.

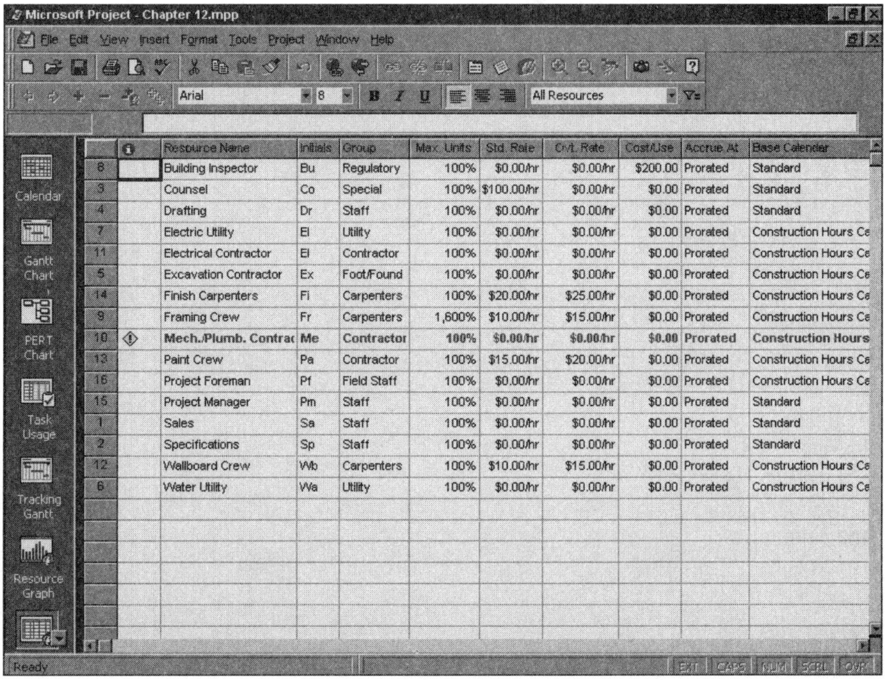

		Resource Name	Initials	Group	Max. Units	Std. Rate	Ovt. Rate	Cost/Use	Accrue At	Base Calendar
8		Building Inspector	Bu	Regulatory	100%	$0.00/hr	$0.00/hr	$200.00	Prorated	Standard
3		Counsel	Co	Special	100%	$100.00/hr	$0.00/hr	$0.00	Prorated	Standard
4		Drafting	Dr	Staff	100%	$0.00/hr	$0.00/hr	$0.00	Prorated	Standard
7		Electric Utility	El	Utility	100%	$0.00/hr	$0.00/hr	$0.00	Prorated	Construction Hours Ca
11		Electrical Contractor	El	Contractor	100%	$0.00/hr	$0.00/hr	$0.00	Prorated	Construction Hours Ca
5		Excavation Contractor	Ex	Foot/Found	100%	$0.00/hr	$0.00/hr	$0.00	Prorated	Construction Hours Ca
14		Finish Carpenters	Fi	Carpenters	100%	$20.00/hr	$25.00/hr	$0.00	Prorated	Construction Hours Ca
9		Framing Crew	Fr	Carpenters	1,600%	$10.00/hr	$15.00/hr	$0.00	Prorated	Construction Hours Ca
10	◈	**Mech./Plumb. Contrac**	**Me**	**Contractor**	**100%**	**$0.00/hr**	**$0.00/hr**	**$0.00**	**Prorated**	**Construction Hours**
13		Paint Crew	Pa	Contractor	100%	$15.00/hr	$20.00/hr	$0.00	Prorated	Construction Hours Ca
16		Project Foreman	Pf	Field Staff	100%	$0.00/hr	$0.00/hr	$0.00	Prorated	Construction Hours Ca
15		Project Manager	Pm	Staff	100%	$0.00/hr	$0.00/hr	$0.00	Prorated	Standard
1		Sales	Sa	Staff	100%	$0.00/hr	$0.00/hr	$0.00	Prorated	Standard
2		Specifications	Sp	Staff	100%	$0.00/hr	$0.00/hr	$0.00	Prorated	Standard
12		Wallboard Crew	Wb	Carpenters	100%	$10.00/hr	$15.00/hr	$0.00	Prorated	Construction Hours Ca
6		Water Utility	Wa	Utility	100%	$0.00/hr	$0.00/hr	$0.00	Prorated	Construction Hours Ca

Figure 12-2: Notice that the resource ID number stays with the resource. This prevents the sort process from messing up your resource assignments to tasks.

3. **In the entry box, type** Staff.
4. **Click OK.**

   The Resource Sheet view is now filtered to show only the Staff group, as shown in Figure 12-3.

Play with the Resource Sheet view, sorting and filtering all you want. After you're finished and before you turn out the lights, please put the Resource Sheet view back the way you found it.

To return the Resource Sheet view to its original order, you simply choose Project⇨Sort By ID. But because your inquiring mind can't settle for the mundane, I'll introduce you to the Sort By list. In Chapter 13, you use this list to do some powerful segregating of information. For the present:

1. **In the Filter list, select the All Resources filter.**
2. **Choose Project⇨Sort.**

   The Sort list appears.
3. **Select Sort By.**

   The Sort dialog box appears.

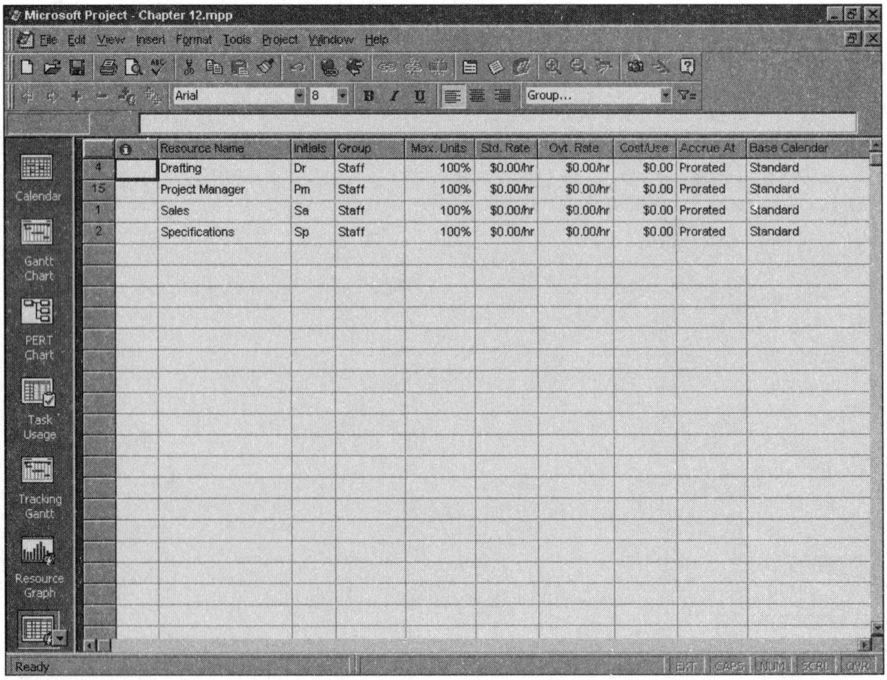

Figure 12-3: The filtering options in the Filter list are only a fraction of the filtering options available.

4. **In the Sort By list, click the down arrow and scroll to select Unique ID, as shown in Figure 12-4.**
5. **Click the Sort button.**

   The Resource Sheet view is back to its original condition.

Return to the Gantt Chart view, and then you can turn out the lights.

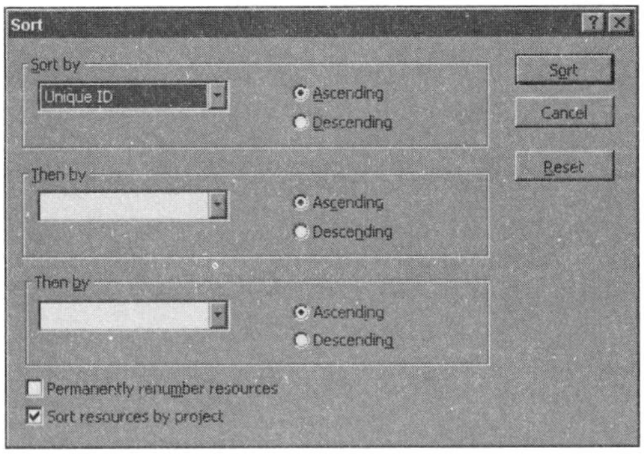

Figure 12-4: Be careful when using the Sort dialog box. Before you perform a sort, decide whether you want to permanently renumber resources.

Resource Usage View

From the Gantt Chart view, change to the Resource Usage view by choosing the Resource Usage icon on the view bar or by choosing View⇨Resource Usage. The Resource Usage view displays a combination view, as shown in Figure 12-5.

The default right window is a timeline depiction of the date and the amount of work performed by individual resources. The Details column identifies the information as work. In fact, you can list any combination of six types of details:

1. **Choose Format⇨Details.**

   The Details list appears.

2. **Select any combination of detail types.**

   Your choices are Work, Baseline Work, Cost, Actual Work, Overallocation, Remaining Availability, and Cumulative Work.

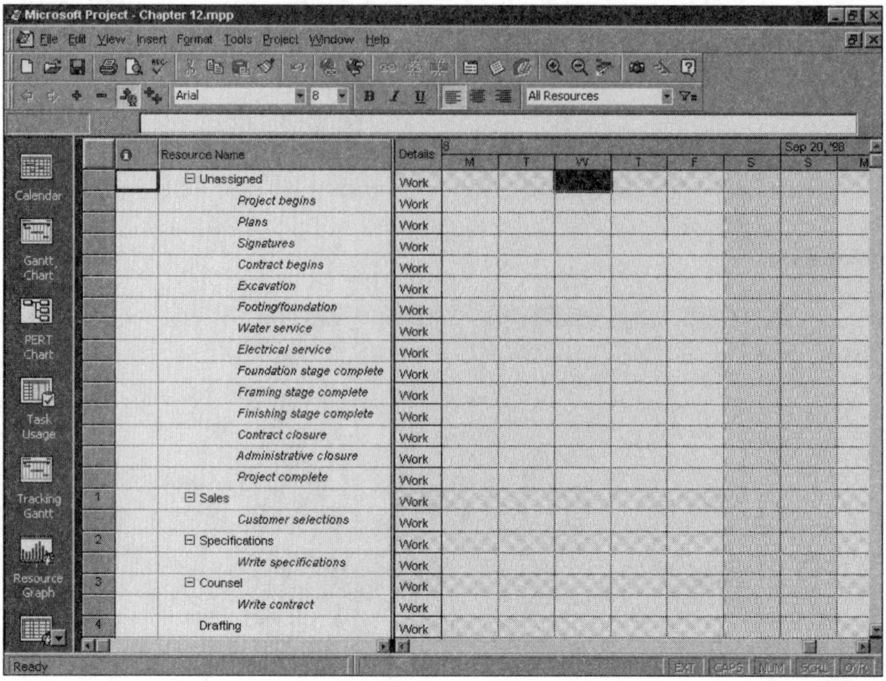

Figure 12-5: You can scroll information in either window with the scroll bars.

3. **If you're not satisfied with these detail options, you can choose Format➪Detail Styles.**

   The Detail Styles dialog box appears. Select any available detail and then click Show. If you want, you can also move the detail order and customize the text and background color for each detail.

4. **Click OK to accept your changes or click Cancel to reject your changes.**

The left screen can display any of five tables. The default table is the Usage table, which associates resources with their tasks. The indicator column displays resource-relevant information. As an example, scroll the view to Resource 10. Place the cursor over the indicators to read their messages.

To change tables, choose View➪Table. If you want, drag the vertical bar between the timeline and the table to the right until you expose all the details in the particular table. Six of the tables follow:

Table	*Does This*
Cost resource table	Shows information about resources, including cost, baseline cost, variance, actual cost, and amount remaining.
Entry resource table	Shows the resource's initials, group, maximum units, rate, overtime rate, cost per use, accrual method, relevant calendar, and code.
Hyperlink resource table	Creates shortcuts and associates them with a resource. Use it to jump to your computer files, files on a network, your organization's intranet, and the World Wide Web.
Summary resource table	Displays the assignment of resources, including the group name, the maximum units, the peak unit usage, the rates, the cost, and the work performed in hours.
Usage resource table	Lists your project's resources.
Work resource table	Shows various calculations about work, including percent completed, overtime, baseline, variance, actual, and remaining calculations.

One way to make use of the Resource Usage view is by splitting — not as in leaving the scene, but as in splitting the screen into two views. To do this, choose Window➪Split. A Resource Usage form appears in the lower view, as shown in Figure 12-6.

To try out the split view, highlight the Framing Crew resource name in the upper view. The form in the lower view reports the task information related to this resource.

After you finish checking out this split view, restore the screen by choosing Window➪Remove Split. This returns the Gantt Chart view.

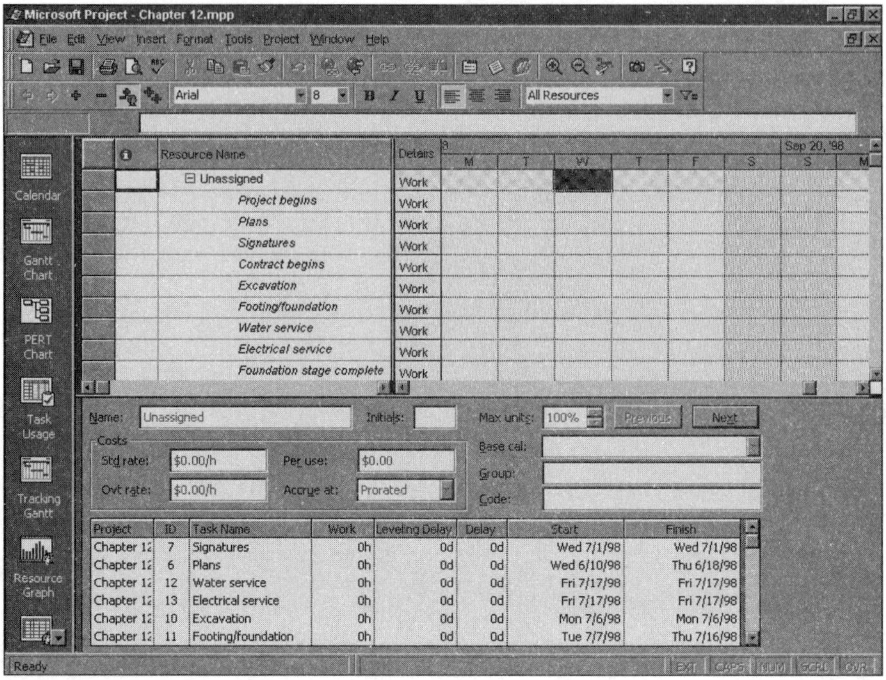

Figure 12-6: You can change the active view by pressing F6. The highlighted bar on the far left of the screen tells you which view is active.

Resource Graph View

The Resource graph shows information about the allocation or cost of resources in measurements of time. Use it for reviewing allocations for a single resource or a group of resources.

The best way to use this graph is in a split view with the Resource Usage view. To do this:

1. **Choose View ⇨Resource Graph, or select Resource Graph View on the view bar.**

   The Resource Graph view appears.

2. **Select Window⇨Split.**

3. **Select the lower pane, and choose Resource Usage View on the view bar.**

   The Resource Usage Chart appears in the lower split window, as shown in Figure 12-7.

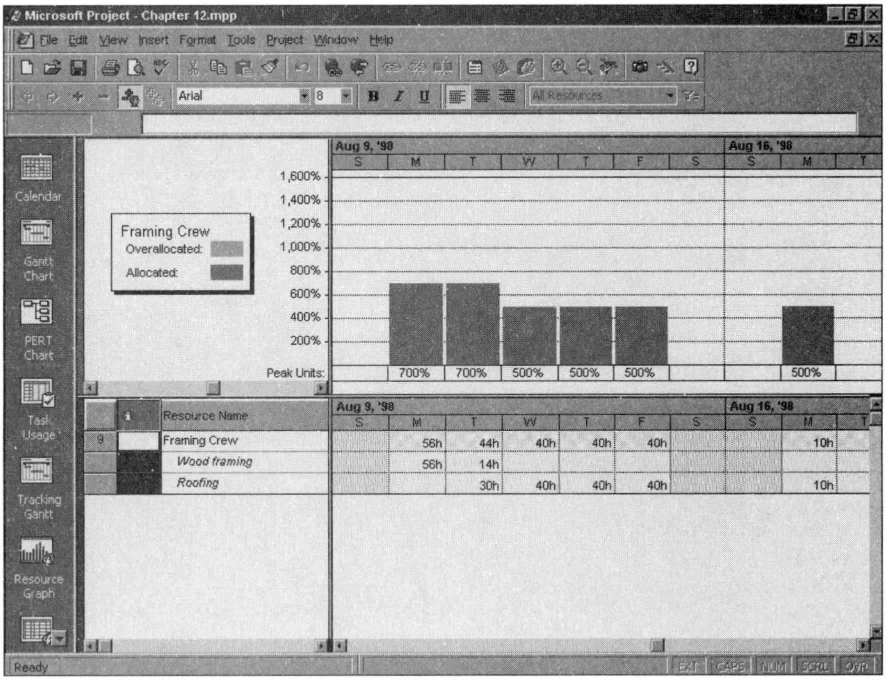

Figure 12-7: The upper view is the Resource Graph view, and the lower view is the Resource Usage view.

You can use this split view to compare the graphical chart with work in hours. If you want, you can edit work amounts to correct over-allocation problems or to simply spread the fun around to more people. To do this, first drag the vertical bar in the Resource Usage view until you expose the Work column. Select a work cell, and change the units of time. The change also appears in the Resource Graph view.

One helpful use of this split view is in correcting overallocation of work. Overallocation occurs when you assign more resource time than is available (for instance, assigning ten hours of work in an eight-hour day).

In the Resource graph, click the right arrow of the horizontal scroll bar in the left box until the Mech./Plumb. Contractor appears. As shown in Figure 12-8, the upper window displays the overallocated resources in percentages of time, and the lower window displays indicators and actual work in hours.

When you're finished with this view, remove the split window. If you've modified the file, you can save it — but use the Save as command and give the file another name. This way, you can use the original `Chapter 12.MPP` file again.

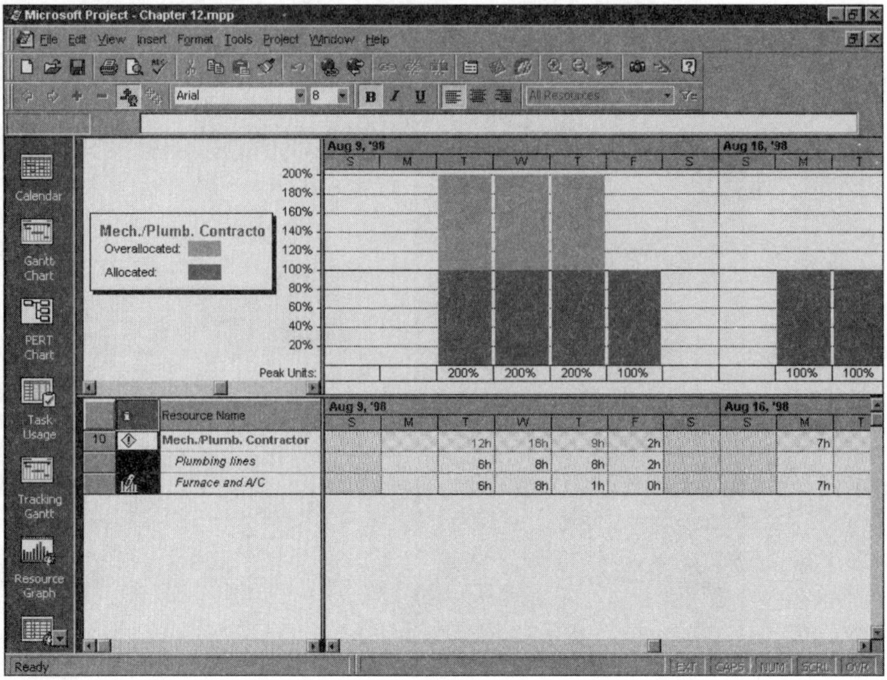

Figure 12-8: The Resource graph displays the resource (left) and a timeline chart (right). The Resource Usage view identifies the resource and tasks (left) and work details (right).

Chapter 13
Using Filters

In This Chapter

- Finding facts fast with filters
- Using standard filters
- Editing the facts that filters filter
- Creating filters to suit your fancy
- Making sense of sorting

So you have this beautiful, huge project. Tasks are in order and resources are assigned. Relationships are set and durations are as tight as a drum. You know how to look at the project from about every view the human brain can imagine.

Life is good — at least for an hour or so. Then you get a memo from a stakeholder requesting a listing of all resources whose tasks will occur on Tuesdays in odd weeks of all summer months. While you're still trying to figure out what an odd week is, you get a call from a contractor wanting to know whether there could be any slippage of other tasks and, if so, how they will affect her start date. Oh, and she has to know right now. And while your ear is still ringing from that one, your boss rushes in wanting a list of all tasks that cost more than $1,500, starting with the most expensive and ending with the least expensive.

Big deal! Why don't they ask for something complicated? All they want you to do is some filtering and sorting. So what are you going to do the second half of this hour?

Filtering and sorting are two of the best reasons for using software programs in project management. Quite often, you need to establish criteria for relating and finding certain details. In such situations, the least important project information may be what you needed the most just a few minutes ago.

A measurement of the worth of a project-management software program is its capability to solicit, associate, and interpret a group of facts from a mass of project information. With Microsoft Project, you can perform this with surprising ease and creative freedom.

A filter segregates information using predetermined criteria. A helpful analogy is the use of filters in photography. Choose a particular color filter, and all blue color is eliminated from a picture. In contrast, by choosing a saturation filter, all colors are screened from a picture by a predetermined percentage. As long as you use the same filter, you establish temporary group relationships that include some classes of visual information and exclude others. Using the same filter, you get the same visual relationships no matter where you point the camera.

In Microsoft Project, filters work in much the same way. For instance, you can choose a filter that allows the display of only unfinished tasks. Or you can choose a filter that displays all tasks with a duration greater than three days.

Sorting doesn't filter information. A sort sets a task order based on your criteria. Unlike filtering, you don't segregate information. Instead, with a sort, you order the information in a different way. For instance, you can sort the tasks in alphabetical order by task name.

It's possible to both filter and sort. For example, you can use a filter that lists only tasks whose costs are based on hourly rates. Then you can sort the filtered tasks by the amount per hour in ascending or descending order.

ON THE CD

By the end of this chapter, you'll be able to filter and sort like a first-class detail sleuth. To begin sleuthing, you use the sample project file called `Chapter 13.MPP`:

1. **Click the Open button on the standard toolbar.**
2. **Open the Project folder on your hard drive or on the *Microsoft Project 98 For Dummies* CD-ROM.**
3. **Double-click Chapter 13.MPP.**

   The file should open to the Gantt Chart view. For the sake of illustration, the timeline of the Gantt chart should be quarters over months.

Using Standard Filters

A filter segregates and associates project information to provide you with the specific facts you need. The underlying ingredients of a filter are test and value criteria. When you select a filter, you're saying you want to see all the tasks or resources with values that meet the conditions of a certain test. For example, the test may be that you want to see all tasks with a duration value greater than one week. Microsoft Project then searches the project databases and finds and displays all tasks with values that conform to that test criterion.

Microsoft Project provides a bunch of standard filters — 51 in all. These filters will probably meet most of your needs. But if you're like most project managers, sooner or later, you'll need to create a new filter or two. Fortunately, creating a new filter is almost as easy as using a standard one. As you may guess, though, it's best to find out how the standard filters work before you jump into the creative mode.

Whatever view your file happens to be in (except the PERT chart), you're looking at information provided through a standard filter. For example, if your file is in the Gantt Chart view, you're looking at tasks through the default All Tasks filter.

Knowing which filter is active is easy. Just look at the Filter box on the formatting toolbar, as shown in Figure 13-1.

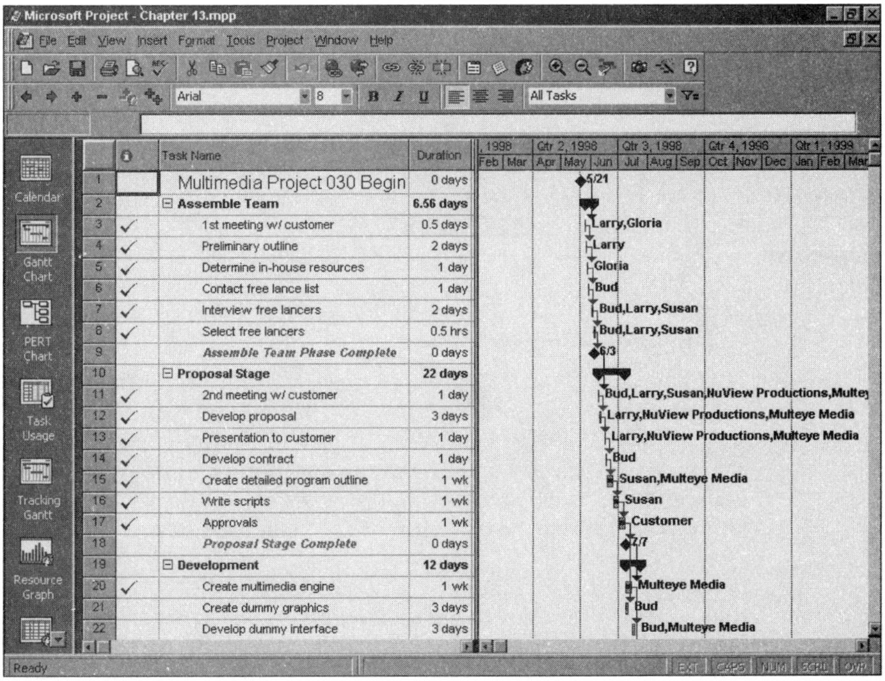

Figure 13-1: The Filter box displays the current filter selection, All Tasks.

In most views, you can access standard filters and new filters by using the Filtered For command, the Filter box, the More Filters command, or the AutoFilter command. Although all four choices provide access to filters, they each offer distinct ways to use those filters.

The Filtered For command

The Filtered For command changes the active task or resource view to display information that meets the selected filter criterion. In the following, you use the Filtered For command to display all completed tasks:

1. **Choose Project⇨Filtered for: All Tasks.**

   The Filtered For submenu appears, as shown in Figure 13-2. The submenu lists nine commonly used filters.

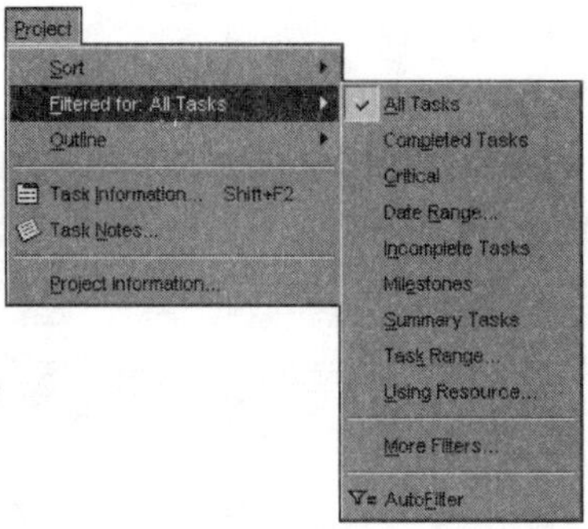

Figure 13-2: In addition to the nine most commonly used filters, the submenu can display any filter you create.

2. **Choose Completed Tasks.**

   The Gantt chart displays all tasks that have met the test of completion, as shown in Figure 13-3.

The view you just selected from the submenu can be referred to as an isolated filter view. An *isolated filter view* shows only those tasks or resources that meet the criterion of the selected filter.

In the Filtered For command, you can show either an isolated filter view or a highlighted filter view. A *highlighted filter view* is different from the isolated filter view in one major way. It identifies the tasks or resources that meet the filter criterion and displays them in a highlighted manner among all the other tasks or resources.

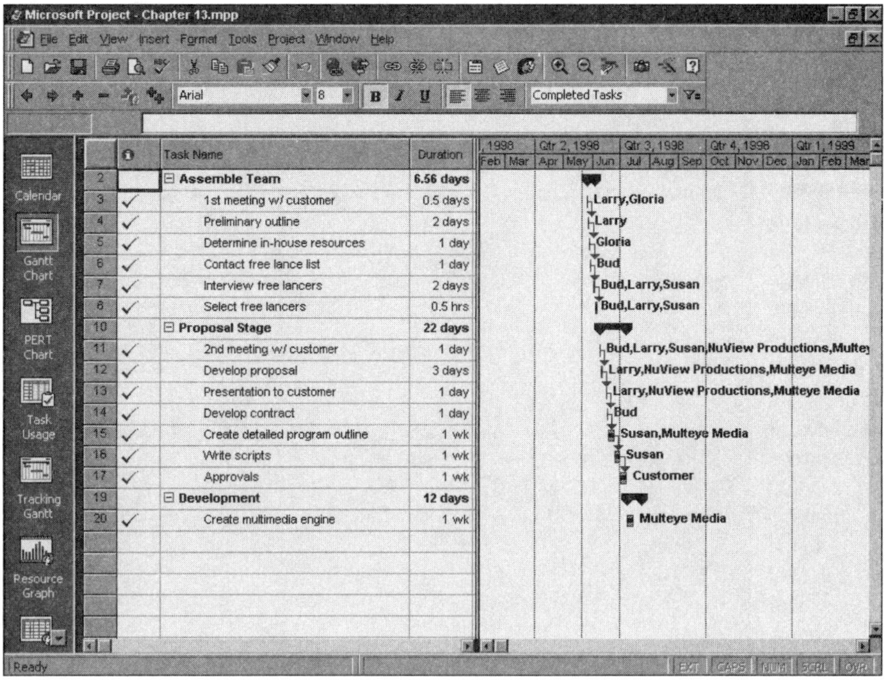

Figure 13-3: The Gantt Chart view displays only those tasks containing values that equal the test of completion.

Using the Filtered For command, select a filter in the highlighted filter view:

1. **Hold down the Shift key.**
2. **Choose Project⇨Filtered for: Completed Tasks.**

   The submenu appears.
3. **Choose Incomplete Tasks.**

   The Gantt chart displays all the tasks but highlights all incomplete tasks, as shown in Figure 13-4.

The Filtered For command lists a submenu of up to 20 commonly selected filters, including filters created by you. Later in this chapter, I show you how to create a filter and list it in this submenu.

TIP

You can revert the screen to the default filter by pressing F3.

The Filter box

The Filter box serves two purposes. It displays the current filter and provides a list of all task filters in task views or all resource filters in resource views. To use the Filter box:

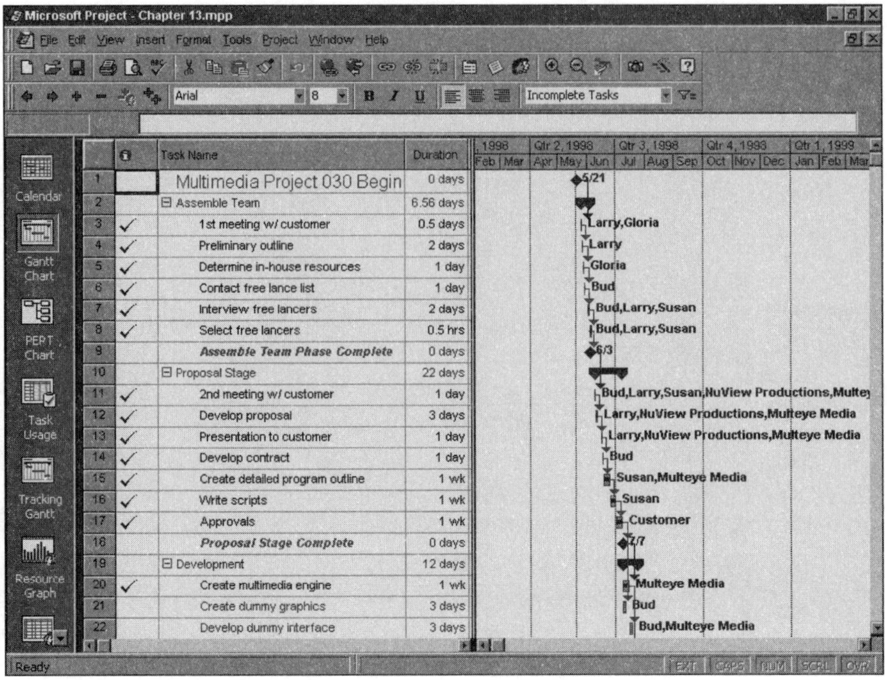

Figure 13-4: The highlighted filter view uses a font difference to designate the tasks or resources that conform to the selected filter criterion.

1. **Click the down arrow next to the Filter list box on the formatting toolbar.**
2. **Select the Unstarted Tasks filter.**

   Two things happen. The highlighted filter disappears and is replaced by an isolated view of the Unstarted Tasks filter.

The Unstarted Tasks view displays all tasks meeting the test of the Actual Start Date equaling NA (not applicable). By comparison, any started or completed task has an Actual Start Date not equaling NA because a date has been entered into the Microsoft Project database field. If you would like to view and compare this field:

1. **Press F3.**

   The filter returns to the All Tasks filter.
2. **Choose View⇨Table⇨Tracking.**

   The view changes to the Tracking table.
3. **Drag the vertical separator bar to the right to expose the full Tracking table.**

Look at the Act. Date (Actual Start Date) column. Tasks whose Act. Date field is NA are the tasks that appeared when you chose the Unstarted Tasks filter.

When you are finished with the Tracking table:

1. **Choose View⇨Table⇨Entry.**
2. **Drag the vertical separator bar back to the left so that it rests on the right edge of the Duration column.**

Remember, the Filter box always displays the current filter. The Filter box also contains all available task or resource filters as well as any filters you created.

You can't use the Filter box to access the highlighted filter view.

The More Filters command

The More Filters command is a misleading name — more than more filters may be better. The command displays a dialog box that is like a command central for filters -- it provides a number of options for selecting, highlighting, editing, creating, and organizing filters. To access the dialog box:

1. **Choose Project⇨Filtered for: All Tasks.**

   The Filtered For submenu appears.
2. **Choose More Filters.**

   The More Filters dialog box appears, as shown in Figure 13-5.

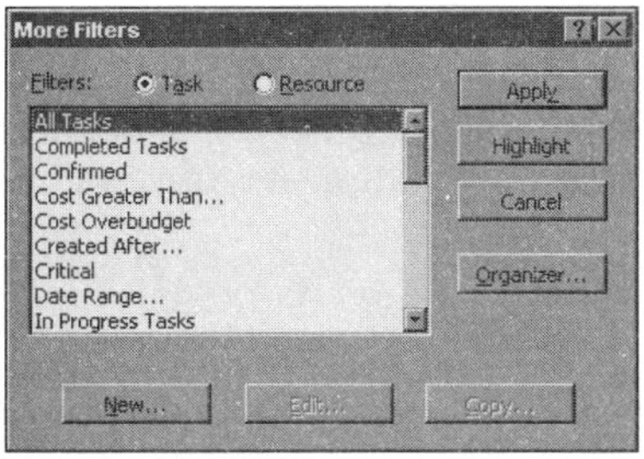

Figure 13-5: The More Filters dialog box.

Using the More Filters dialog box, you can perform many functions. (I describe these later in this chapter.) In addition to these creative opportunities, you can select either an isolated filter view or a highlighted filter view.

To select the isolated filter view, choose a filter and then click the Apply button. To select a highlighted filter view:

1. **In the More Filters dialog box, select the In Progress Tasks filter.**
2. **Click the Highlight button.**

   The In Progress Tasks filter identifies the tasks that meet this criterion.

The AutoFilter command

The AutoFilter command is a nifty little feature. AutoFilters are a helpful way to filter task or resource information in individual columns of sheet views. That may sound technical, but it's not. To use the AutoFilter command:

1. **Select the AutoFilter icon on the formatting toolbar.**

   A down arrow appears in the Task Name and Duration columns.

2. **Click the Task Name down arrow.**

   The AutoFilter analyzes the project file and displays the available Task Names. In addition, the AutoFilter offers All and Custom, as shown in Figure 13-6. The box displayed by the AutoFliter contains task or resource information unique to the selected field.

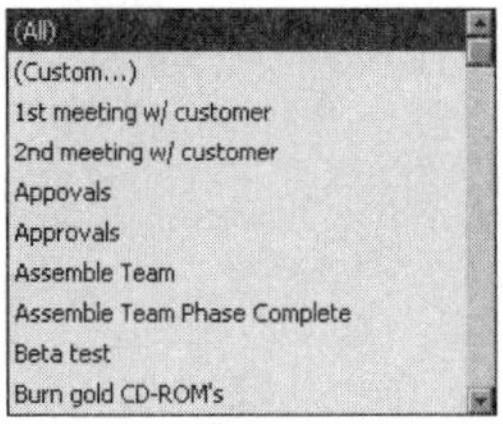

Figure 13-6: The AutoFilter offers All and Custom.

3. **In the AutoFilter box, select one of the task names.**

   The AutoFilter displays all criteria that equal the task name you selected. The color of the column name (in this case, Task Name) changes to blue, which indicates that the information is based on the use of that column's AutoFilter.

4. **Press F3 to restore the project to the default all tasks filter.**

Where have autofilters been all my life? Could it be that they are available for all columns in a table? Yep. Well, almost. Drag the vertical bar in the Gantt chart to the far right. Notice that an AutoFilter is available for every column except the Indicator column. Every sheet view provides this feature.

One of the most significant features of AutoFilter is the Custom command. It's an advanced feature that anyone can use almost immediately:

1. **Select the Finish column's AutoFilter.**

   The AutoFilter box displays all available project criteria equaling *Finish.*

2. **Select Custom.**

   The Custom AutoFilter dialog box appears, as shown in Figure 13-7.

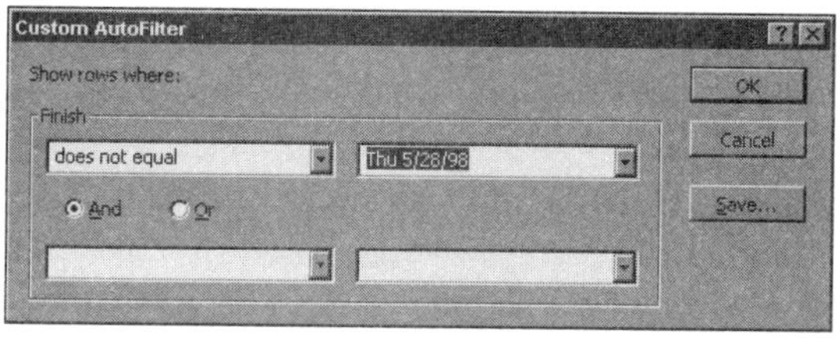

Figure 13-7: The Custom AutoFilter.

3. **Click the down arrow in the list box below Finish.**

   You are offered a number of comparison operators (such as *does not equal*).

4. **Select a comparison operator other than *equals*.**

5. **Click the down arrow in the text box to the right of the comparison operator.**

   The text box lists all the criteria in this project file's Finish field. By selecting one of the criteria, you are telling the AutoFilter to operate on that criteria based on the comparison operator to the left (such as *does not equal*). Pretty neat, huh?

6. **Click OK.**

If you want to do some more advanced AutoFiltering, use a second basis of comparison. In the Custom AutoFilter dialog box, select the And option or the Or option. Then add an additional comparison and its criteria, as shown in Figure 13-8. (The left conditions are the comparison and the right conditions are the criteria unique to that project file.) By setting two comparisons, you can, for example, bookend Finish dates to show those that are after one date and before another.

Lastly, you can save your custom AutoFilter so that it becomes a permanent filter option. Note, however, that your custom filter doesn't become your default filter for that column:

1. **If you closed the Custom AutoFilter, open it again.**

   If the information is gone, enter your double comparison again or use the one in Figure 13-8.

Figure 13-8: The Custom AutoFilter dialog box.

2. **Choose Save.**

   A Filter Definition dialog box appears. (See Figure 13-9.)

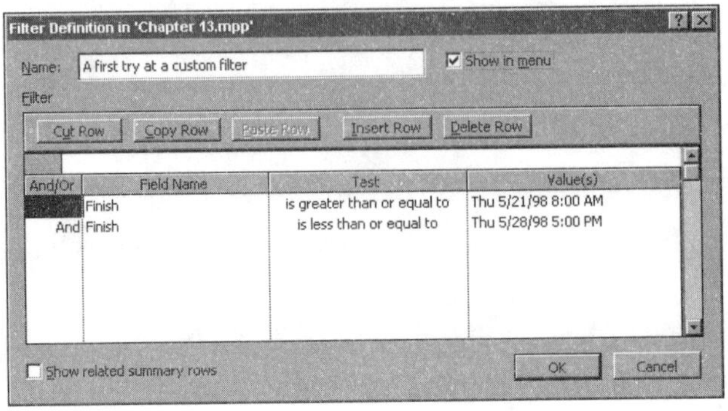

Figure 13-9: The Filter Definition dialog box.

3. **Give your custom filter a name.**

   Select a name that will be easy to remember.

4. **Select the Show in Menu check box.**

   This will make the custom filter available in the Filter For box.

5. **If you want, make more changes to the filter.**

6. **Click OK in the Filter Definition dialog box, and again in the Custom AutoFilter dialog box.**

   Two things have happened. Your view is now based on the custom criteria, and your custom filter has been added to the Filtered For menu.

7. **To see your custom filter, choose Project⇨Filtered for.**

   The Filtered For box now includes your custom filter, as shown in Figure 13-10.

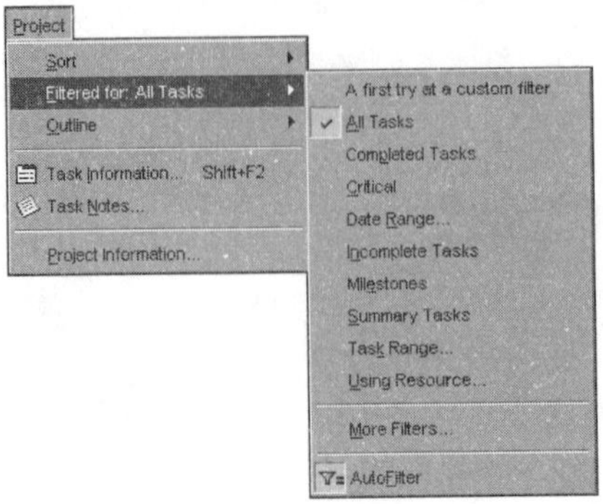

Figure 13-10: By saving the custom filter, you'll be able to access the filter at any time throughout the life of the project.

You can remove your custom filter at any time by choosing Tools⇨Organizer. The Organizer dialog box appears. Select the Filters tab. In the right column, select your custom filter and choose the Delete button.

When you finish checking out the custom filter option, press F3 to return to the default All Filters. Choose the AutoFilter icon to turn off the AutoFilters option. The icon acts as an on/off toggle.

Customizing the highlighted display

Sometimes modifying the look of your project view is necessary or simply more enjoyable than the default appearance. In this section, you change the color of the highlighted filter, which has a default text color of blue. First, highlight a filtered selection:

1. **Choose Project⇨Filtered for: All Tasks.**
2. **Choose More Filters.**
3. **Select one of the filters, such as Incomplete Tasks.**
4. **Click the Highlight button.**

For easier reading, change the text style of the highlighted filter:

1. **Choose Format⇨Text Styles.**
2. **In the Item to Change list box, select Highlighted Tasks.**
3. **Select the Underline option.**
4. **In the Font Style list box, select Bold Italic.**
5. **In the Color list box, select Purple (or another color).**

   The Text Styles dialog box should look like Figure 13-11.

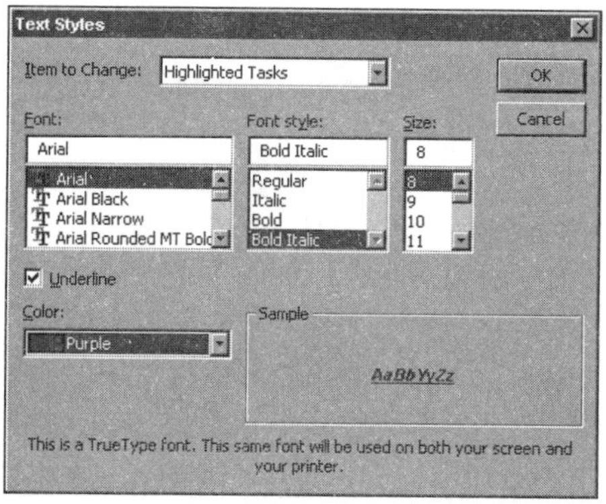

Figure 13-11: Use this dialog box to modify the default settings for all text categories in the Gantt chart.

6. Click OK.

The highlighted filter view displays the modified highlighted text.

Types of filters

The two major classifications of standard filters in Microsoft Project are task filters and resource filters. The task filters are accessible in all task views except the PERT Chart view. The resource filters are accessible in all resource views. Tables 13-1 and 13-2 describe the task and resource filters available.

In split views, filters work for only the upper view. And filters always apply to an entire project file. If you select a filter and then select a second filter, the second filter analyzes the entire file, not just the product of the first filter.

Table 13-1 Types of Task Filters

Task Filter	*Shows*
All Tasks	All tasks; this is the default filter
Completed Tasks	All completely finished tasks
Confirmed	Tasks agreed upon by requested resources
Cost Greater Than	Tasks that will cost more than the amount you designate; this is an interactive filter
Cost Overbudget	Tasks with a cost greater than their baseline amount
Created After	Tasks created by you after the date you designate; this is an interactive filter
Critical	Critical tasks
Date Range	Tasks between two dates you specify; this is an interactive filter
In-Progress Tasks	Tasks that have started but haven't finished
Incomplete Tasks	Tasks that aren't finished (including those that haven't started)
Late/Overbudget Tasks Assigned To	Tasks assigned to resources you designate that are over the budget you set or will finish after the date you had set; this is an interactive filter
Linked Fields	Tasks with text linked to other applications
Milestones	All milestones
Resource Group	Tasks associated with resources belonging to the group you specify; this is an interactive filter

Task Filter	*Shows*
Should Start By	Tasks that should have started by the date you specify, but haven't started; this is an interactive filter
Should Start/Finish By	Unfinished tasks based on a range set by you in the filter; this is an interactive filter
Slipped/Late Progress	Slipped or slow tasks
Slipping Tasks	Tasks that aren't finished and are behind schedule
Summary Tasks	Tasks with subordinate tasks
Task Range	Tasks within a range of task IDs you specify; this is an interactive filter
Tasks with Attachments	Tasks with objects or notes in the note box
Tasks with Fixed Dates	Tasks with a constraint other than As Soon As Possible and tasks that have already started
Tasks/Assignments With Overtime	Tasks where resources are working overtime
Top Level Tasks	The uppermost-level summary tasks; this filter is for projects with summary tasks within summary tasks
Unconfirmed	Tasks that have requested but unconfirmed commitment
Unstarted Tasks	Tasks that haven't started yet
Update Needed	Tasks that have experienced change and need to be sent for update or confirmation
Using Resource In Date Range	Tasks that start or finish within a timeline you determine and related to resources you designate; this is an interactive filter
Using Resource	Tasks that use the resource you specify; this is an interactive filter
Work Overbudget	Tasks with scheduled work greater than their baseline work

Table 13-2 Types of Resource Filters

Resource Filter	*Shows*
All Resources	All resources in your project file
Confirmed Assignments	Resources who have acknowledged their assignments; this is used with workgroups
Cost Greater Than	Resources that will cost more than what you designate; this is an interactive filter

(continued)

Table 13-2 *(Continued)*

Resource Filter	***Shows***
Cost Overbudget	Resources with a scheduled cost greater than the baseline cost
Date Range	Resources with assignments within two dates you specify; this is an interactive filter
Group	Resources associated with the group you specify; this is an interactive filter
In Progress Assignments	Resources who have started assignments but haven't completed them
Linked Fields	Resources with text linked to other applications
Overallocated Resources	Overallocated resources
Resource Range	Resources within the range of ID numbers that you specify; this is an interactive filter
Resources with Attachments	Resources with objects attached or notes in the note box
Resources/Assignments With Overtime	Resources or their assignments that are working overtime
Should Start By	Resources who should have started by a date you specify
Should Start/Finish By	Resources who should have started or finished by a date you specify; this is an interactive filter
Slipped/Late Progress	Resources associated with tasks that have slipped behind their baseline scheduled finish date or are late
Slipping Assignments	Resources with delayed assignments and incomplete tasks
Unconfirmed Assignments	Resources who have not responded with commitment to assigned tasks; this is associated with workgroups
Unstarted Assignments	Resources who have committed to assignments but have not yet begun them; this is associated with workgroups
Work Complete	Resources who have completed their tasks
Work Incomplete	Resources who have not completed their tasks
Work Overbudget	Resources with scheduled work that's greater than the baseline work

Using interactive filters

An interactive filter is one that asks you a question or questions and then goes hunting for the information you want. You can tell many of the interactive filters in the filter list boxes by the ellipsis marks (...) following the filter name, such as Should Start by. . . .

Using the `Chapter 13` example, you find all tasks whose resource is Bud. Then you use the highlighted filter option to display those tasks among all the others. To do this:

1. **Press and hold down the Shift key.**

   You should continue holding down the Shift key until the last step.

2. **Choose Project⇨Filtered for⇨Using Resource.**

   The interactive question box appears.

3. **Use the down arrow to scroll to the Bud resource, and select it.**

4. **Click OK and then release the Shift key.**

The Using Resource filter appears in the highlighted rather than isolated option. In addition, the filter box on the formatting toolbar displays the Using Resource selection, as shown in Figure 13-12.

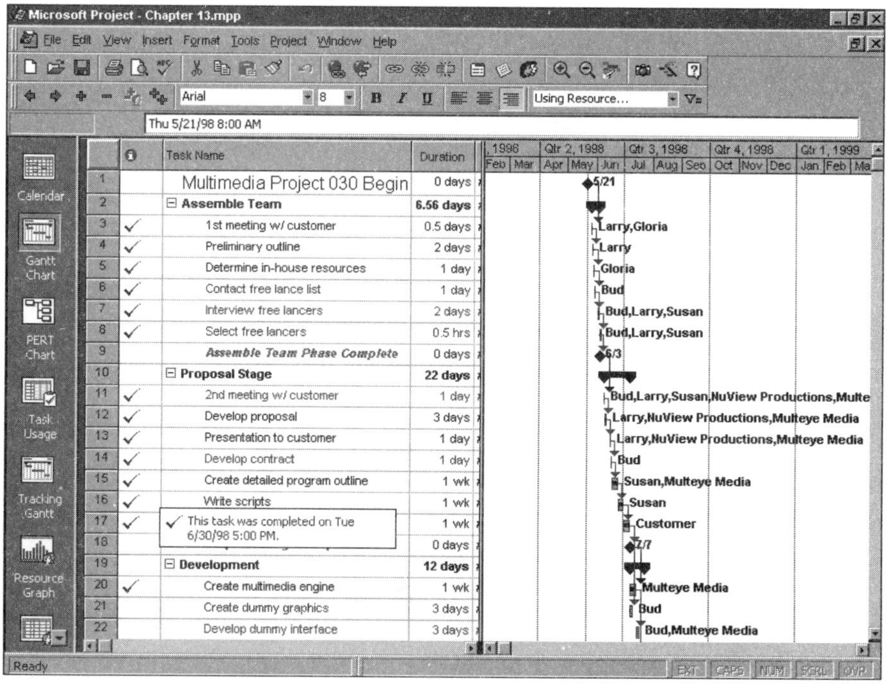

Figure 13-12: Interactive filters are especially helpful because you can use one filter to define a variety of values.

Creating Your Own Filters

So you've given Microsoft Project the benefit of the doubt. You've checked out all the task and resource filters, but none scratches the precise itch you have for details about your project. You're not a vanilla kind of project manager. You want some flavor and characteristics in your work. No problem — create your own filter.

Follow a few rules, and Microsoft Project will help you make your project as personal as you want. You don't have to tell anybody it's easy — go ahead and impress your stakeholders!

Creating a filter by editing an existing one

The easiest way to create a new filter is by editing an existing one because most of the work has already been accomplished. A slight change to an existing filter can make it work differently and look unique.

Using the `Chapter 13` example, you can edit an existing filter to create a new one that shows the final week before the project completion. To do this:

1. **Choose Project⇨Filtered for⇨More Filters.**

   The More Filters dialog box appears.

2. **Click the Task option.**
3. **Select Task Range and then click the Copy button.**

   The Filter Definition dialog box appears, as shown in Figure 13-13. Copy of Task Range is a temporary name for the copy of the Task Range filter. All the changes you make will be to the copy; the original filter remains intact.

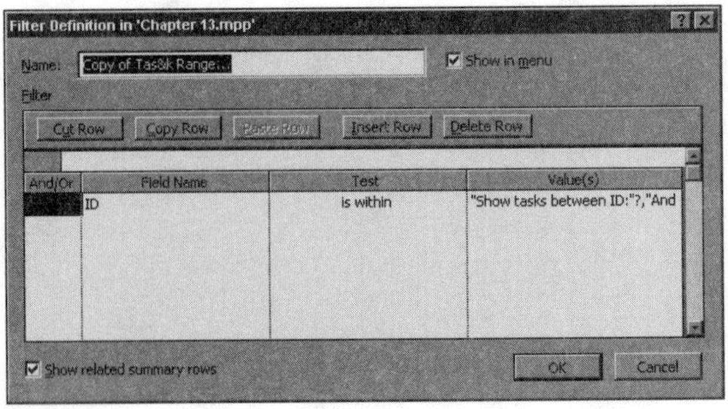

Figure 13-13: This dialog box provides a number of options for customizing and applying filters.

4. **In the Name box, type** Completion Date **(or whatever you want).**

   The Field Name is already ID, so leave it.

5. **In the Test column, select *is within*.**

   A small down arrow appears next to the text box.

6. **Click the small down arrow and select *equals*.**

   This is the Test list box, as shown in Figure 13-14.

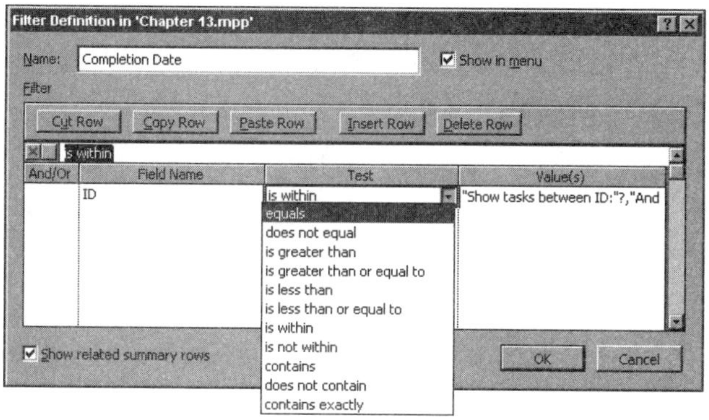

Figure 13-14: The Test list box contains 11 choices that make up the basis for choosing filter criteria.

7. **In the Value(s) column, select "Show Tasks Between ID:"?,"And ID:"?**

8. **Drag across the text in the text box above the column names and then press the Delete key.**

9. **In the text box above the column names, type** 45.

   Notice that the Show in Menu check box is selected. By leaving this box checked, your new filter will appear in the Filtered For submenu.

10. **Click OK.**

    Your new Completion Date filter appears in the More Filters dialog box, as shown in Figure 13-15.

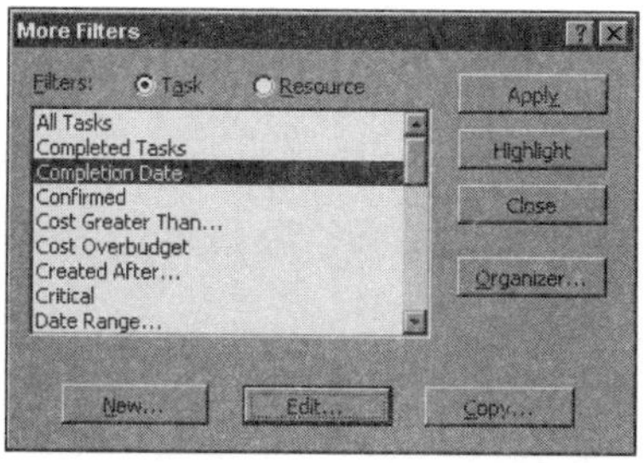

Figure 13-15: Your Completion Date filter is added to all the standard filters.

11. Click the Apply button.

Your new filter searches for all tasks equaling ID 45. The Completion Summary task and the Distribute milestone appear, as shown in Figure 13-16. By default, Microsoft Project displays the summary task when the filter finds one of the summary task's subtasks.

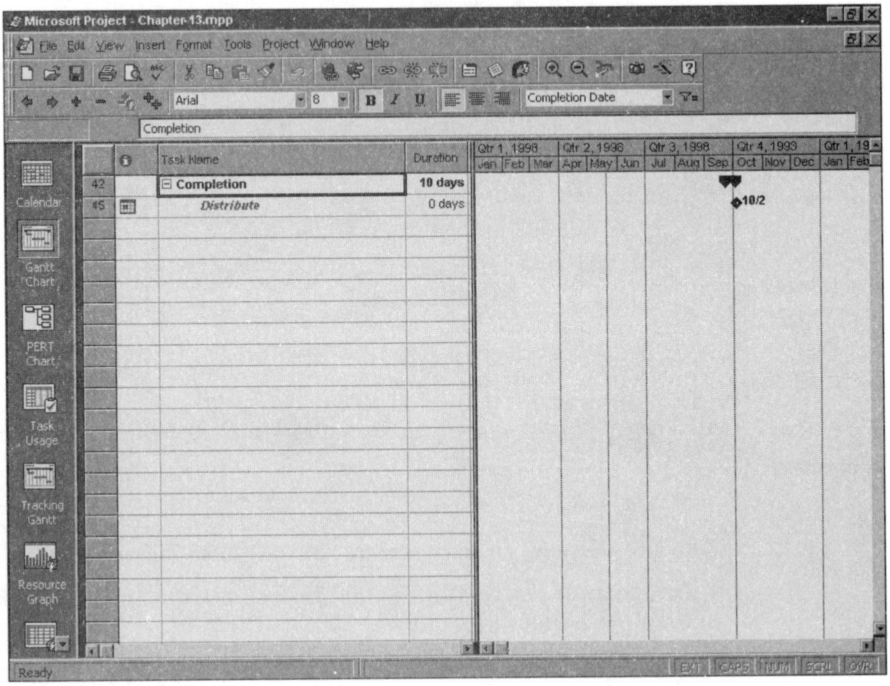

Figure 13-16: The filter displays the sole task that meets the filter criterion of all task IDs equaling 45.

Creating a filter from scratch

You create a new filter in much the same way as you copy and edit one, except you choose New Copy in the More Filters dialog box. In this section, you use the `Chapter 13` example to create a filter that lists all tasks with the NuView Productions resource. To do this:

1. Press F3 to return to the All Tasks filter.

This step isn't necessary; it simply cleans the slate back to the default setting.

2. Choose Project⇨Filtered for: All Tasks⇨More Filters.

The More Filters dialog box appears.

3. Click the New button.

The Filter Definition dialog box appears, as shown in Figure 13-17.

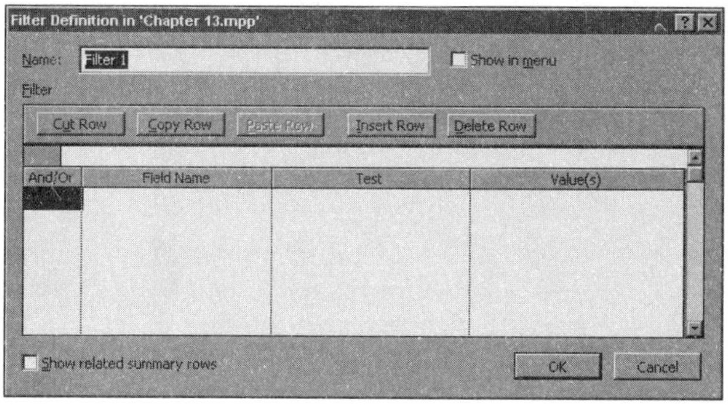

Figure 13-17: When you use the Filter Definition dialog box to create a filter from scratch, all the columns are empty.

You use the Filter Definition dialog box to set the criteria for selecting tasks or resources. After you create your filter, you'll be able to use it for both isolated and highlighted views. To create the Building Inspector filter:

1. **In the Name text box, type** NuView Schedule.

   This becomes the filter's name.

2. **Select the Show in Menu option.**

   This way, your new filter will appear in the Filtered For submenu.

3. **Select the Field Name text box.**

   A down arrow appears to the right of the text edit box.

4. **Click the down arrow and scroll to select Resource Names.**

   You could have simply typed the field name, but this way you ensure that the name is accurate.

5. **Select the Test text box, click the down arrow, and scroll to select Contains.**

   The Contains test displays or highlights tasks and resources that contain a value. The value is the next thing to set.

6. **Select the Value(s) text box.**

7. **Click the text edit box above the column names.**

   You know it's active when a red x and a green µ appear to the left of the box.

8. **In the text edit box, type** Nu.

9. **Click the green arrow to accept the text.**

10. **Check your work; it should look like Figure 13-18.**

11. **After you are satisfied, click OK.**

    The More Filters dialog box contains your nifty new filter.

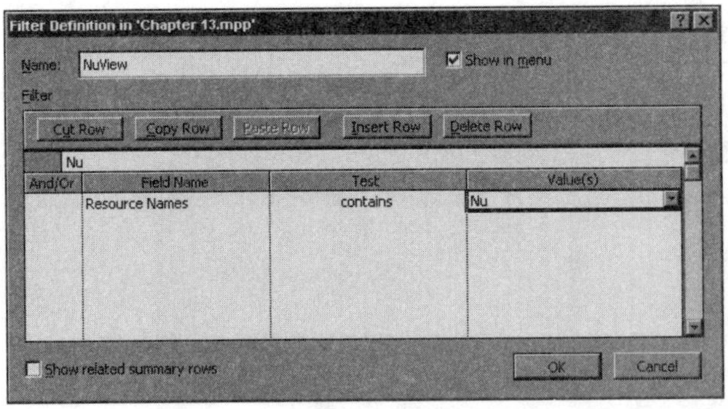

Figure 13-18: Does your work look like this?

12. Click the Highlight button.

All the tasks that meet the criterion of your new filter are highlighted.

Sorting Your Project

Sorting tasks and resources is another way to control the display of project information. Sorting, unlike filtering, doesn't isolate or single out information. Instead, it changes the order of tasks in a descending or ascending manner based on the criteria of a particular field or fields. Is that confusing enough? Actually, it's not that bad.

By default, Microsoft assigns ascending ID numbers to tasks as you enter them into a project file. Task ID 1 is 1 simply because you entered it first. The same is true for task ID 2, 3, and so on. By using the sort option, you can use another criteria for ordering tasks.

The Sort feature works with whatever is in the active display. If you've already applied a filter to a project, the Sort feature works with the tasks or resources that resulted from the filter criteria.

WARNING!

Before you resort to sorting, be sure you know whether you want to maintain the original task ID relationships. The dialog box offers you the option of permanently renumbering tasks. If you choose to let the sort renumber tasks, it can do some strange and not-so-wonderful things to your task relationships. (In fact, allowing tasks to be renumbered may have been the inspiration for the invention of spaghetti.)

Types of sorting

In this section, using the `Chapter 13.MPP` example, you play with the ways Microsoft Project can sort your information. You practice sorting by name and duration.

First, change to the Task Sheet view by choosing More Views at the end of the view bar. Scroll to select the Task Sheet view, and then click the Apply button. If necessary, expand any hatch-marked columns by double-clicking the right edge of the column headings.

Now, to use the Sort command:

1. **Choose Project⇨Sort⇨ Sort By.**

   The Sort dialog box appears, as shown in Figure 13-19.

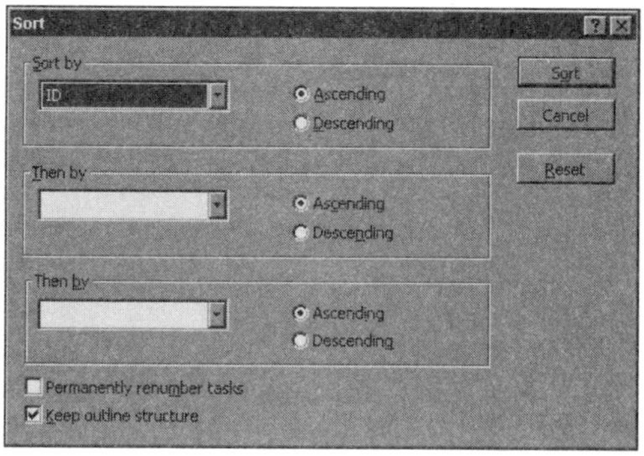

Figure 13-19: The Sort dialog box lets you order tasks or resources based on as many as three fields.

2. **In the Sort By list box, select Name.**
3. **Make sure that the Permanently Renumber Tasks check box is unchecked.**
4. **Click the Sort button.**

   The project is sorted to show all names in alphabetical order while maintaining summary task and subtask relationships, as shown in Figure 13-20.

At the bottom of the Sort dialog box are two check boxes. The first is unchecked by default. The second is checked by default. With these defaults, Microsoft Project will not reassign ID numbers to tasks when you sort them. And all sorts will keep subtasks within their summary tasks.

Press Shift+F3 to return to the default ascending ID order. This time, order all the tasks by their duration, from longest to shortest, without keeping the outline structure. To do so:

1. **Choose Project⇨Sort⇨Sort By.**
2. **In the Sort By list box, select Duration.**
3. **Next to the Sort By box, select Descending.**
4. **Uncheck the Keep Outline Structure check box.**

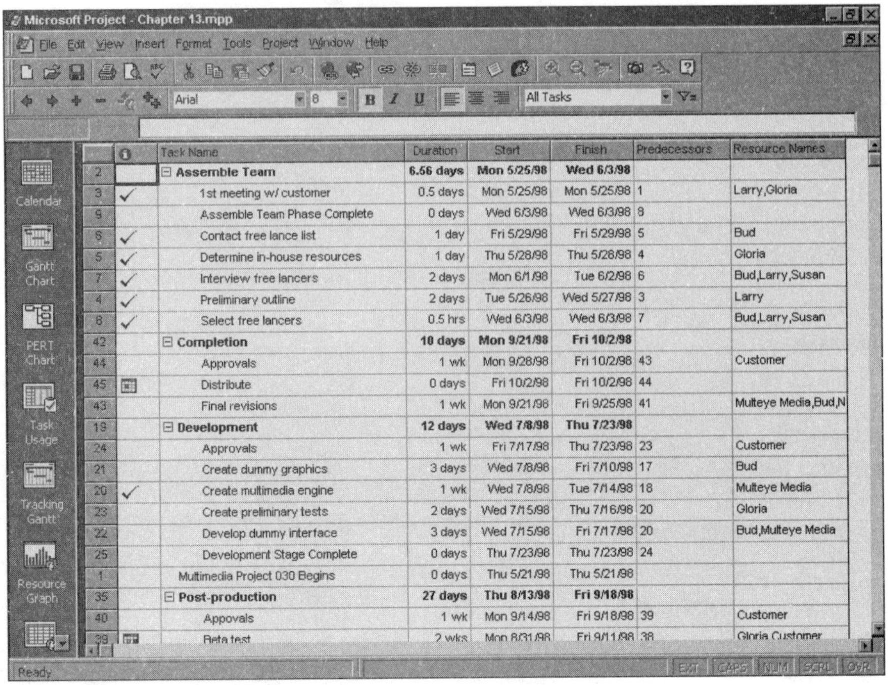

Figure 13-20: The Sort command orders the names in ascending order.

5. **Click the So̲rt button.**

   The display should look like Figure 13-21.

When you finish reviewing the sort, press Shift+F3 to restore the default sort order.

Sorting with multiple fields

The Sort command lets you order information by multiple criteria. An example of a multiple field sort is ordering groceries by category and then by price. The first criterion is ordering by category in ascending alphabetical order, such as fruit, produce, vegetable, and so on. The second is ordering the items in each category by cost in descending order, such as bananas at 49 cents a pound, oranges at 39 cents a pound, and apples at 28 cents a pound. (You can tell how often I buy the groceries in my family!)

Using the `Chapter 13` example, sort all the resource groups alphabetically in ascending order and sort all the individual resources by their standard rates in descending order. First, you need to change to the Resource Sheet view, so select the Resource Sheet icon on the view bar or choose V̲iew⇨Resource S̲heet on the menu bar.

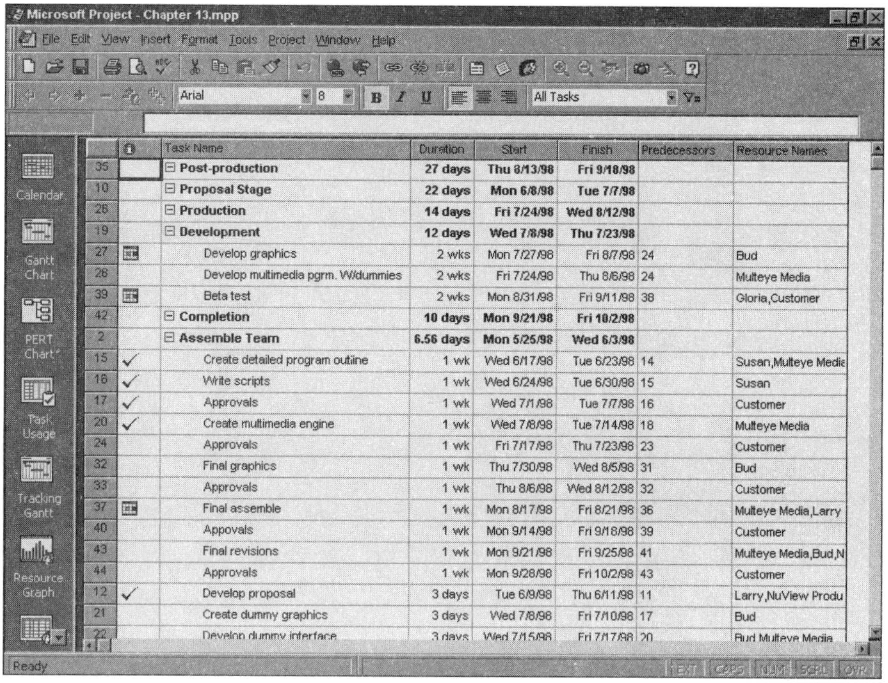

Figure 13-21: The Sort command sets all tasks in a descending duration order. The Subtasks are freed from their summary tasks in this sort.

To sort the resources:

1. **Choose Project➪Sort➪Sort By.**
2. **In the Sort By list box, select Resource Group.**

   Use the default Ascending order.

3. **In the Then By list box, select Initials.**
4. **Next to the Then By box, select Descending.**
5. **Make sure that the Permanently Renumber Resources check box is unchecked.**
6. **Click the Sort button.**

   The sort should look like Figure 13-22.

Filtering and sorting are two of the most powerful tools that Microsoft Project has to offer you for mastering and controlling your project information. In this chapter, you touched on each of the basics — using standard filters, isolating and highlighting filters, editing filters, creating new ones, sorting, and multiple sorting.

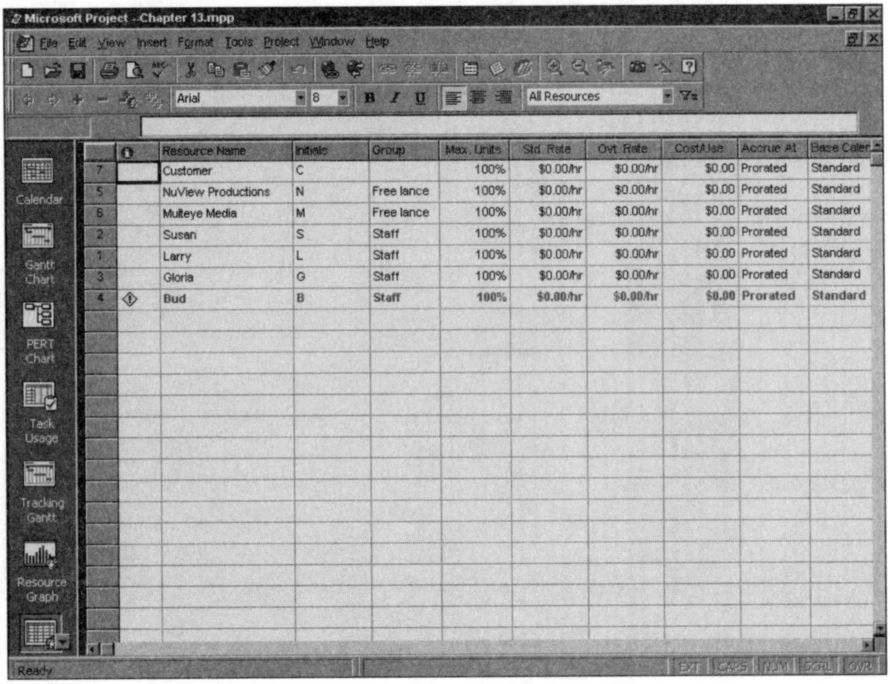

Figure 13-22: The Sort command has ordered the resource groups in ascending alphabetical order. The resources within each group are ordered by initials in descending order.

Part IV

Making Project 98 Work for You

"IT'S NOT THAT IT DOESN'T WORK AS A COMPUTER; IT JUST WORKS BETTER AS A PAPERWEIGHT."

In this part . . .

Now you focus on the endgame of the project plan, the final moments before project commencement. This involves a review of the original project scope and goals and a comparison of those early expectations with the current status. In this part, you learn to optimize your project plan, resolve cost and work overallocations, and level resource conflicts. You find out how to identify the critical path and how to crash the project's schedule.

This is where the fruit of all your efforts begins to show.

Chapter 14

Multiple Projects

In This Chapter

- Assembling multiple projects
- Using Windows for multiple views
- Creating multiple views of the same file
- Making a workspace
- Consolidating a project
- The value of subprojects
- Sorting your project

So you're not a single-project kind of manager. You have a few balls in the air. However, it seems like there are more things to do than there are resources or time to do them. And worse yet, you're not sure whether everything is okay or whether problems are lurking. Simplification sounds very attractive.

Microsoft Project can't make the world slow down, but it can reduce the chances of resource and time collisions. One way it does this is through the management of multiple projects. You are about to see some simple ways to hold the reins on projects that would otherwise pull your attention and resources in conflicting directions.

You work with multiple projects in the chapter, so you need to start by — you guessed it — opening a few project files. To do so:

1. **Click the Open button on the standard toolbar.**

   The File Open dialog box displays the contents of the Winproj folder.

2. **Open the Project folder on your hard drive or on the *Microsoft Project 98 For Dummies* CD-ROM.**

3. **Double-click Sample1 Chapter 14.MPP.**

   The file opens in the Gantt Chart view.

4. **Double-click Sample2 Chapter 14.MPP and then double-click Sample3 Chapter 14.MPP.**

   These project files open in the Gantt Chart view, too.

Using Multiple Open Project Files

To display files, Microsoft Project uses standard Windows conventions, which are the best way to begin using multiple projects. Choose Window, and the Window menu appears, as shown in Figure 14-1. You have four window choices. Unhide appears dimmed because it is unavailable. It becomes available only after Hide is activated. Next, the menu lists Split, which is the default combination view option.

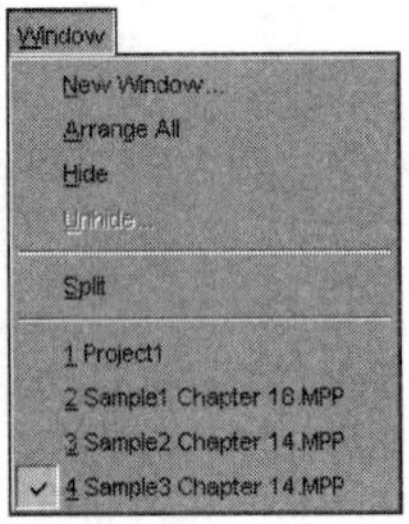

Figure 14-1: The Window menu activates display relationships of open files.

Following these options is a list of the currently open project files. You can load as many project files as you want but only nine appear in this menu. The rest are accessible by a More command that becomes visible after you open the ninth file.

Hiding and unhiding

Hiding a file is not the same as closing it. By hiding a file, you remove its name from the Window menu, even though the file remains open. As an example, hide the Project1 window as follows:

1. **If you don't have an opened Project1 window, click the New button on the standard toolbar.**
2. **Choose Window⇨1 Project1.**

   The active window becomes Project1 in full expanded view.

3. **Choose Window⇨Hide.**

   Project1 disappears.

4. **Choose Window.**

   Project1 has disappeared from the menu and the Unhide option has become active. Exciting, huh?

5. **Choose Unhide.**

   The Unhide dialog box appears, as shown in Figure 14-2. This is where you can practice magic and make the hidden file reappear.

6. **For our purposes, click the Cancel button to leave Project1 hidden.**

   (By the way, you and I both know that you could have closed the Project1 file without saving it. But humor me for the sake of this example.)

Figure 14-2: The Unhide dialog box can hold oodles of files.

7. **Click the Cancel button.**

   This closes the Unhide dialog box.

Arranging all files

Once in a while, it's useful to simultaneously compare and edit information in a group of files. To do that, you need to put all the unhidden files on the screen at one time. First, to make the files easier to see, temporarily hide the view bar by right-clicking in the bar and selecting the View Bar option to remove the check mark.

Using the currently unhidden files:

1. **Choose Window⇨Arrange All.**

   A three-screen display appears, as shown in Figure 14-3.

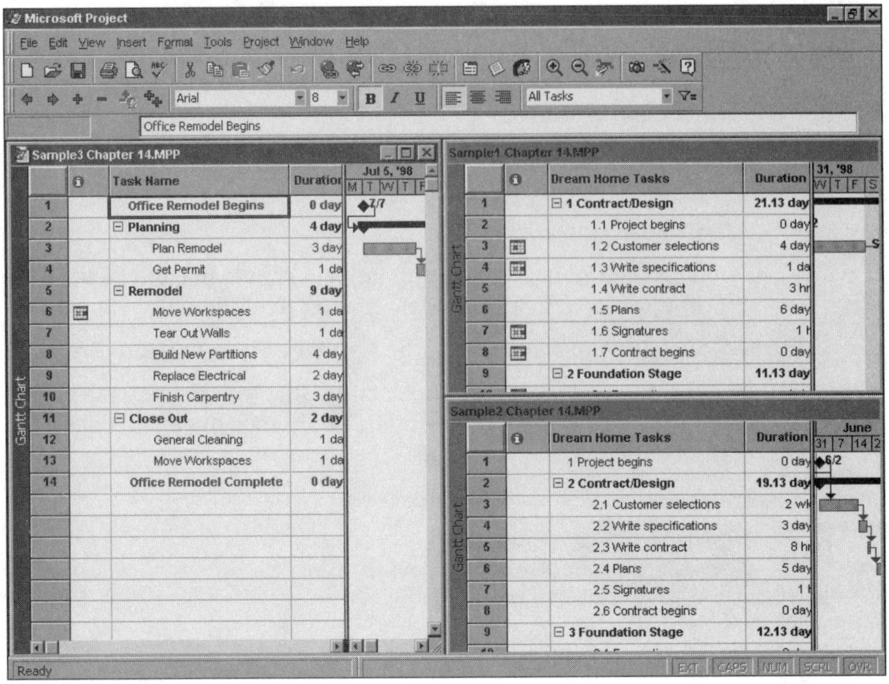

Figure 14-3: You can tell which window is active on your screen by the highlighted color of the title bar and by the thin highlighted ribbon bar on the left of the active window.

2. **Alternately click in each of the three windows.**

   Each window becomes active as you click in it.

One example of information you can assess from this multiple window display is the start date for all three projects.

There's a limit to how many project files can be displayed at one time. The resolution of the windows doesn't change, so each window is only a portion of the full-screen display.

To replace the Arrange All display with a single project display, you use the Maximize button in the active window. For example, click in the Sample2 Chapter 14 window to make it active, and then click its Maximize button. The Office Remodel project is now full screen.

Instead of using the Window menu to flip through the full-screen display of unhidden project files, press Ctrl+F6. Each time you do, the screen displays the next project file (as listed in the Window menu).

Building a new window without pane, er, pain

Another nifty standard window feature is the New Window option. With it, you can create multiple views of the same project. In addition to acting as a shortcut to various views, this gives you the opportunity to customize combination views.

To illustrate the new window option, it would be helpful to hide two of the currently unhidden project files:

1. **Press Ctrl+F6 to display the** `Sample1 Chapter 14.MPP` **project file.**
2. **Choose Window➪Hide.**
3. **Repeat Steps 1 and 2 to hide** `Sample2 Chapter 14.MPP`.

   The `Sample3 Chapter 14.MPP` project file is the active display.

With all but one of the open project files hidden, use the New Window option to create a combination view of the Office Remodel project. To do this:

1. **Choose Window➪New Window.**

   The New Window dialog box appears, as shown in Figure 14-4.

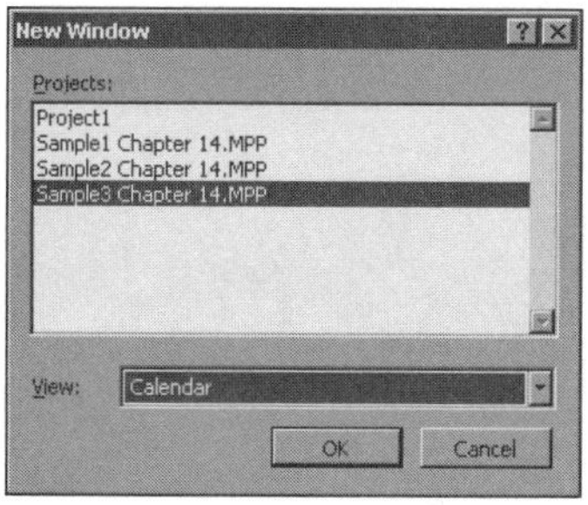

Figure 14-4: All project files (including the hidden ones) appear in the dialog box.

2. **In the View list box, select Calendar.**

   You are telling Microsoft Project that you want a new window displaying the Calendar view of the Office Remodel project. Because the Gantt Chart view of the Office Remodel project is already loaded, you'll have two active displays of the same project. What a country!

3. **Click OK.**

   The Calendar view of the Office Remodel project appears, as shown in Figure 14-5.

Now that you have two displays of the same project and because all other open project files are currently hidden, you can create that special combination view you've always wanted! Well, at least you've wanted it for the last three minutes. Simply choose Window➪Arrange All, and the combination view appears, as shown in Figure 14-6. The highlighted bar on the far left of the screen indicates which window is active. Press Ctrl+F6 to activate the other window.

Creating a workspace

You can create and save a file that remembers all the files you have opened. This can be helpful for picking up where you left off the day before or for guiding others to sets of information you've grouped for some ingenious purpose.

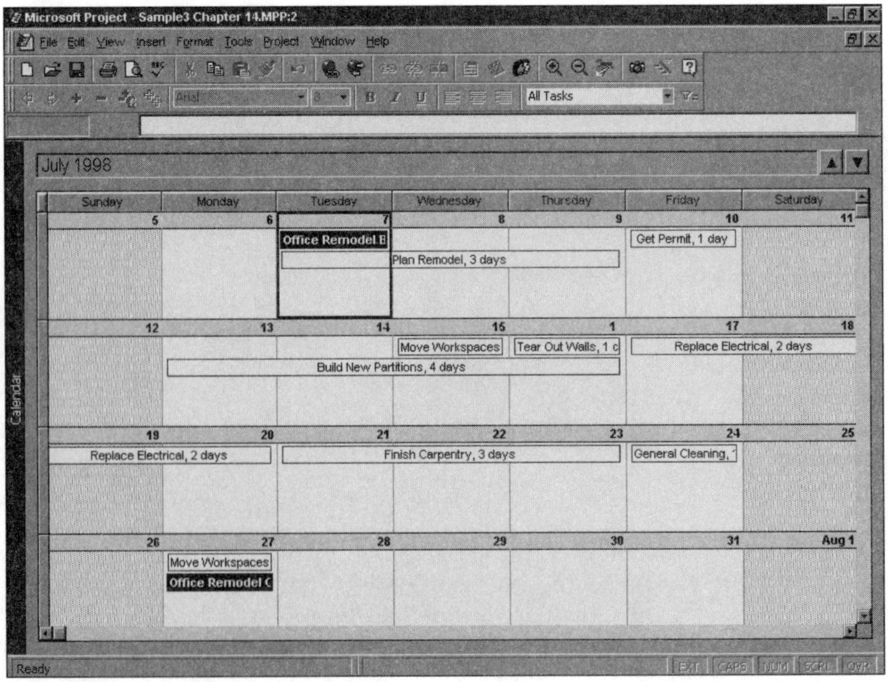

Figure 14-5: Notice that the project name ends with 2, indicating that this is the project's second window display.

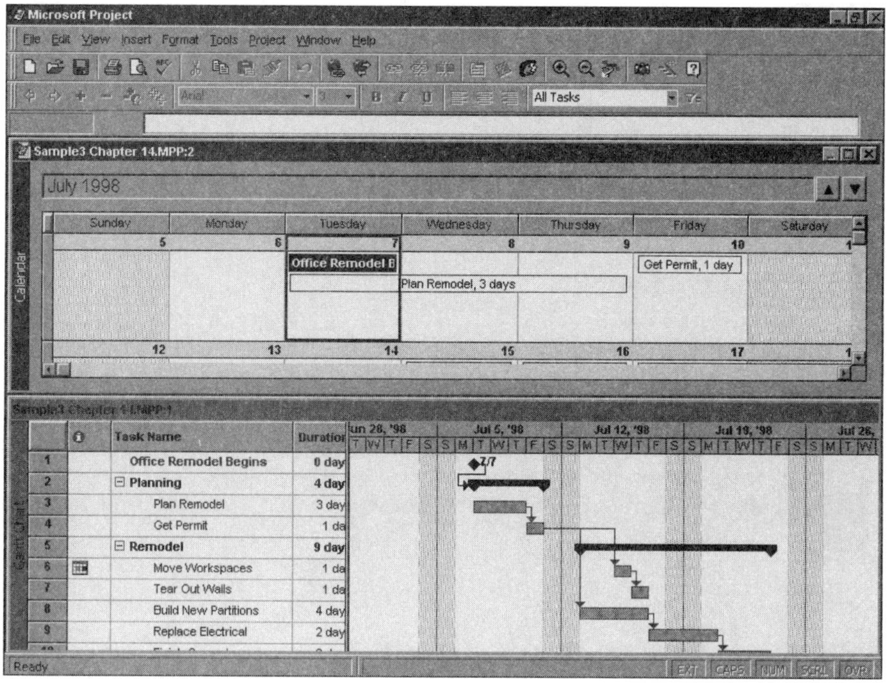

Figure 14-6: The combination view uses the standard convention that allows one window to be active at a time.

Create a workspace file of the project files you currently have open. Before you do, though, choose Window⇨Unhide to unhide the `Sample1 Chapter 14.MPP` project and the `Sample2 Chapter 14.MPP` project.

Now you're ready to create the workspace:

1. **Choose File⇨Save Workspace.**
2. **In the File name box, type a name.**

   Either use the default name, Resume, or type another one. In either case, the extension for a workspace file is mpw. See Figure 14-7.
3. **Click Save.**
4. **Click Yes in response to the question as to whether you want to save changes to `Sample3 Chapter.14MPP`. If you're asked the same question for either of the other two project files, click Yes for them, too.**

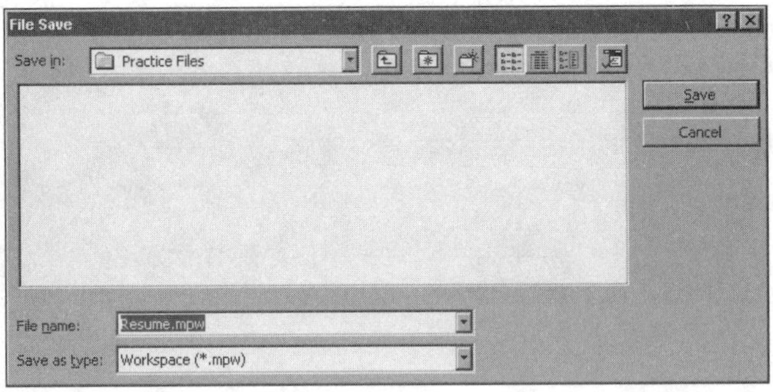

Figure 14-7: The Workspace file will be stored in the same folder as your project files unless you choose otherwise.

REMEMBER

The MPW file contains only a call to reopen the project files; it doesn't contain the project files themselves. If you make any changes to the project files individually, those changes will appear the next time you open the workspace.

Consolidating Projects

Microsoft Project offers you the opportunity to consolidate individual project files into a single window. This makes it possible for you to manage a number of projects at once, as if they were a single project.

Consolidating a project differs from multiple windows in one big way. In a consolidated project file, you can use all the information from all the projects as if they were a single project. For instance, you can use a filter for the consolidated project that filters all the project files.

For the next example, close `Sample1 Chapter 14.MPP`, `Sample2 Chapter 14.MPP`, and `Sample3 Chapter 14.MPP`. Unhide Project1 or click the New button on the standard toolbar. A project, even an unsaved blank one, must be open to access the Microsoft Project menu options. You may want to redisplay the view bar. To do so, right-click in the highlighted vertical bar on the left of the screen and select View Bar.

Now that the project files are closed, consolidate them as follows:

1. **Highlight the second task name. It's presently empty.**
2. **Choose Insert⇨Project.**

   The Insert Project dialog box appears.

3. **Hold down the Ctrl key and click Sample1 Chapter 14.MPP, Sample2 Chapter 14.MPP, and Sample3 Chapter 14.MPP.**
4. **Click the Insert button.**

   The three files are loaded into Project1, as shown in Figure 14-8.

Each file retains its specific name. Place your cursor over the indicator icon (in the *i* column) for each file. By holding the cursor over each indicator, you can determine the name of each inserted project. In contrast, the task name assigned to each inserted project is derived from its project title. A title is not a filename; it's an editable file property. You can edit a title, plus other file information, by choosing File➪Properties.

After the files are loaded, you can change their order, which affects the manner in which they are displayed in the consolidated view. For example, select the Clark House project and drag it below Office Remodel. To do so:

1. **Select the Clark House project row by clicking its ID.**
2. **Click and hold down the mouse button to drag the Clark House project row below Office Remodel.**

   A grey T-bar appears when you are at a point where you can move the task.
3. **Release the mouse button.**

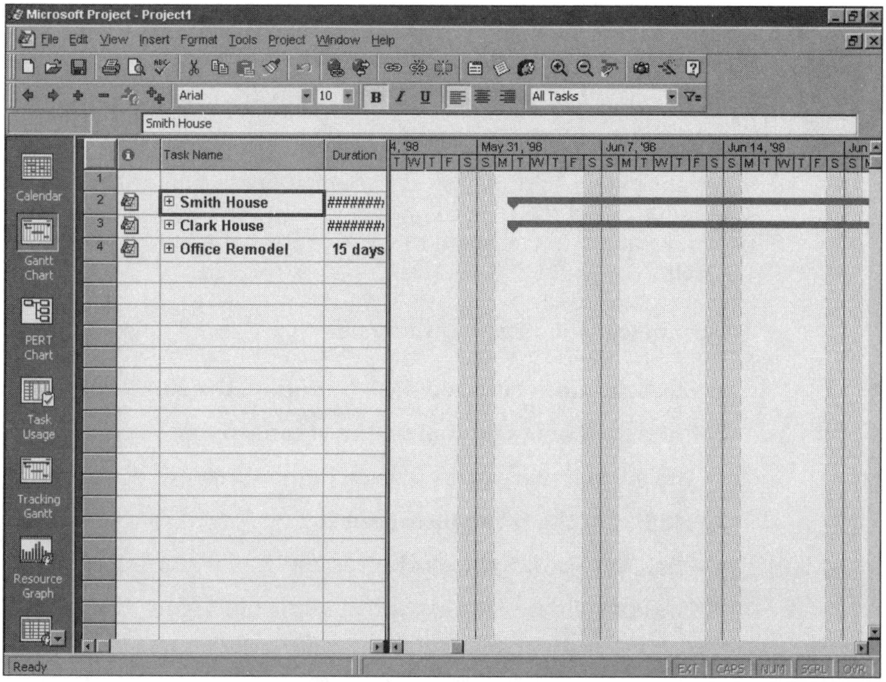

Figure 14-8: The files are listed in the order in which you loaded them.

By default, Microsoft Project allows individual file edits to a consolidated file. Any edits in the consolidated file are automatically reflected in the source file or files. However, you can protect the source files by designating them read only. To designate an inserted project file as read only, double-click the appropriate project indicator. Click the Advanced tab of the Inserted Project Information dialog box, as shown in Figure 14-9. Select the Read Only option.

Figure 14-9: The Inserted Project Information dialog box allows you to associate or disassociate the source project file from the consolidated project file.

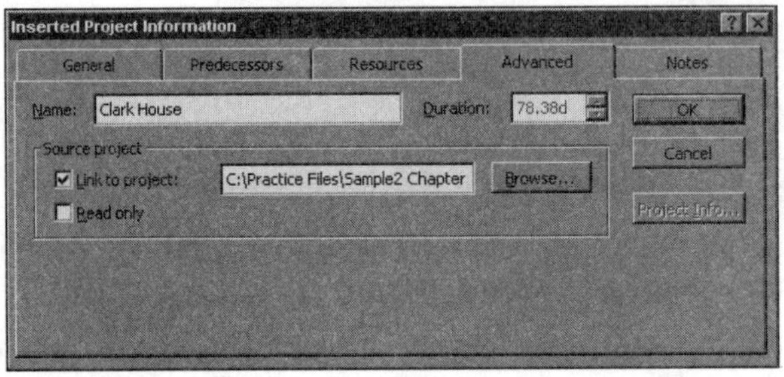

You can make some files read only and others read write. Be careful, though — you can get a big head masterminding all this consolidation stuff.

By default, Microsoft Project attaches source files to the consolidated file. If you want to edit information in the consolidated file without affecting the source file, clear the Link to project option. The Read only option dims because you no longer need to write-protect the linked source project. Click OK.

To see the consolidated view more easily:

1. **Click the Goto Selected Task button on the standard toolbar.**
2. **Click the Zoom Out tool on the standard toolbar twice.**

   The full summary tasks of each of the three projects appear.
3. **Highlight the three inserted projects.**

4. **Click the Show Subtasks button on the formatting toolbar.**

   The consolidated file expands to look like Figure 14-10.

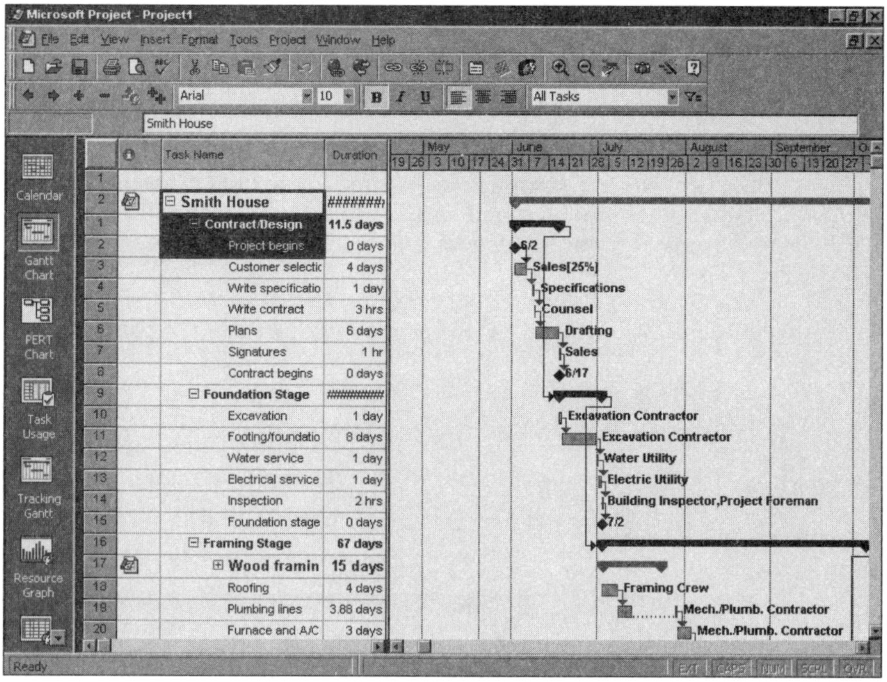

Figure 14-10: The file displays the projects, even though you haven't loaded the individual source files.

Notice that all the project tasks maintain their ID numbers in their respective tasks. As far as Microsoft Project is concerned, each of these three files is open and editable (unless you specified otherwise in the Consolidated Projects dialog box).

To save the consolidated project:

1. **Click the Save button on the standard toolbar.**
2. **Give your consolidated project a name.**
3. **Click the Save button.**
4. **If Microsoft Project asks whether you'd like to save the changes to the three projects, click Yes.**

After you're finished, please close the file but don't turn out the lights.

Using Subprojects in Master Projects

If you were to list every single task in a really big project, the size of the project could become unmanageable. Sometimes creating master projects with subprojects is a good idea.

In a master project, each subproject is listed as a single task. If you open the task, you open the subproject. This way, you can leave the details to those responsible for them. Unopened, you see a start and finish date for the subproject task in the master project. Another advantage of subprojects is that you can use them in any number of projects.

Subprojects are simply piece-of-the-pie projects. They are called *subprojects* because they're included as a single task in another project. You create a subproject in the same way you create any other project file.

For example, a number of details make up the Wood framing task in the Smith Home project. Assign a framing subproject to this task:

1. **Open** `Sample1 Chapter 14.MPP`.
2. **Scroll to the Wood framing task.**
3. **Click the + next to the Wood framing task name.**

   The subproject expands to reveal its subtasks, as shown in Figure 14-11.

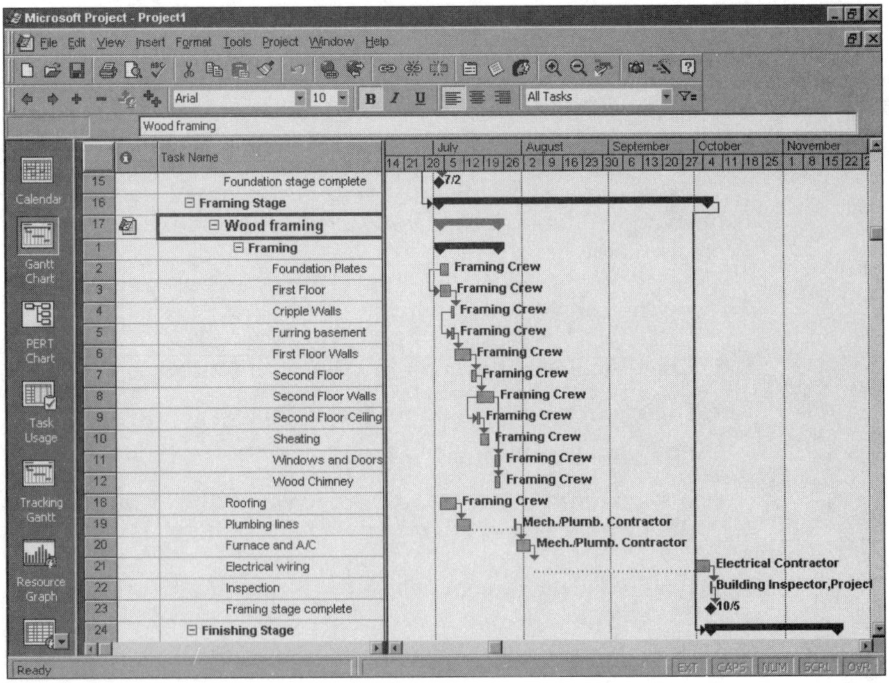

Figure 14-11: The subproject can be as complex as any other project. And it can have subprojects!

Assigning Resources to Multiple Projects

A convenient feature of Microsoft Project is its capability to assign resources from one project to other projects. This allows you to use the same resource pool for a number of projects. If you want, you can keep the projects linked by the shared resources, which makes you less likely to overallocate people and equipment.

Using the `Sample1 Chapter 14.MPP` file, assign resources to another building project. To do this:

1. **Open** `Sample2 Chapter 14.MPP`.
2. **To assign resources, choose Tools⇨Resources.**

   The Resources menu appears, as shown in Figure 14-12.

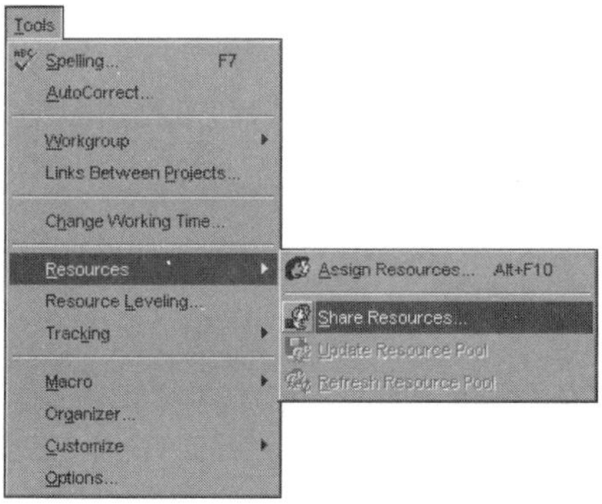

Figure 14-12: The two inactive selections are available in workgroup communications, as I discuss in Chapter 21.

3. **Select Share Resources.**

   The Share Resources dialog box appears, as shown in Figure 14-13.
4. **Select the Use Resources option.**
5. **In the From text box, select Sample1 Chapter 14.MPP.**
6. **Click OK.**

   `Sample1 Chapter 14.MPP` is now the source of the resource pool.

Now that `Sample2 Chapter 14.MPP` is a resource pool groupie of `Sample1 Chapter 14.MPP`, click the Assign Resources button on the standard toolbar. You'll see all your friends' sales and specifications. Project management is a friendly profession!

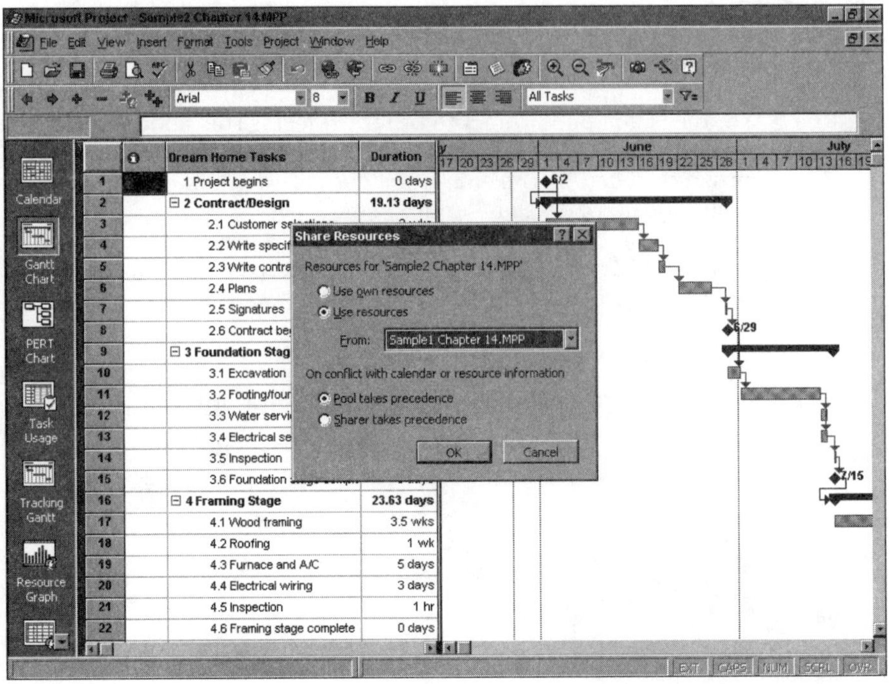

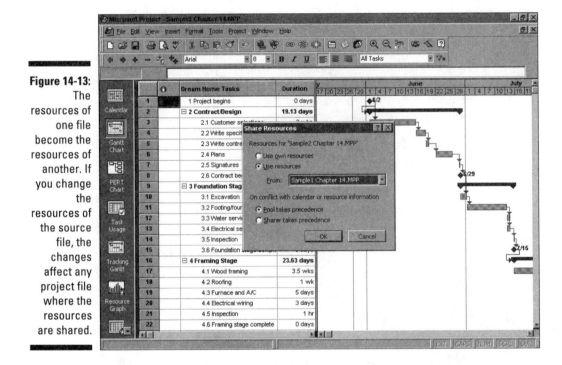

Figure 14-13: The resources of one file become the resources of another. If you change the resources of the source file, the changes affect any project file where the resources are shared.

After you have established the shared resource relationship with another project, you have created a link between the projects. For example, when you modify the resource pool in one project, the resource modification will appear in the other project. The advantage to the shared resources is that you can have more than one project using the same people and still avoid overallocation of resources.

Chapter 15

Setting and Viewing Costs

In This Chapter

- Finding work and cost discrepancies
- Analyzing cost estimate problems
- Reducing costs

Here's a wild assumption: I bet you aren't gifted at pulling money or a rabbit out of a hat (unless your project is starting a school for magicians). Even so, as a project manager, you can find money where no one else knows it exists, and you can keep the rabbits from eating the green stuff. In project management lingo, this magic is called *cost control.*

Suppose you've determined the tasks, created the links, set the durations, and assigned the costs to your project. The start date of your first project task is about to occur. In this chapter and the next, you do the final tweaking of your project to prepare for the onset of reality. To begin, you get rid of some unsightly bulges around the waist — excessive costs.

In this chapter, you use the sample project file called `Chapter 15.MPP` to make last-minute cost and work improvements to a project before its project start date. To open the sample project file:

1. **Click the Open button on the standard toolbar.**
2. **Open the Project folder on your hard drive or on the *Microsoft Project 98 For Dummies* CD-ROM.**
3. **Double-click Chapter 15.MPP.**

   The file opens in the Gantt Chart view.

Cost and Work

You should check the pulse of your project occasionally, even before it's born. One of the quickest ways to get an overall summary view of the project is by viewing project statistics. To do so:

1. **Right-click anywhere on the toolbar.**

   The toolbar menu appears.

2. **Choose Tracking toolbar.**

   The tracking toolbar appears, as shown in Figure 15-1.

3. **Click the Statistics button.**

   The Project Statistics dialog box appears, as shown in Figure 15-2.

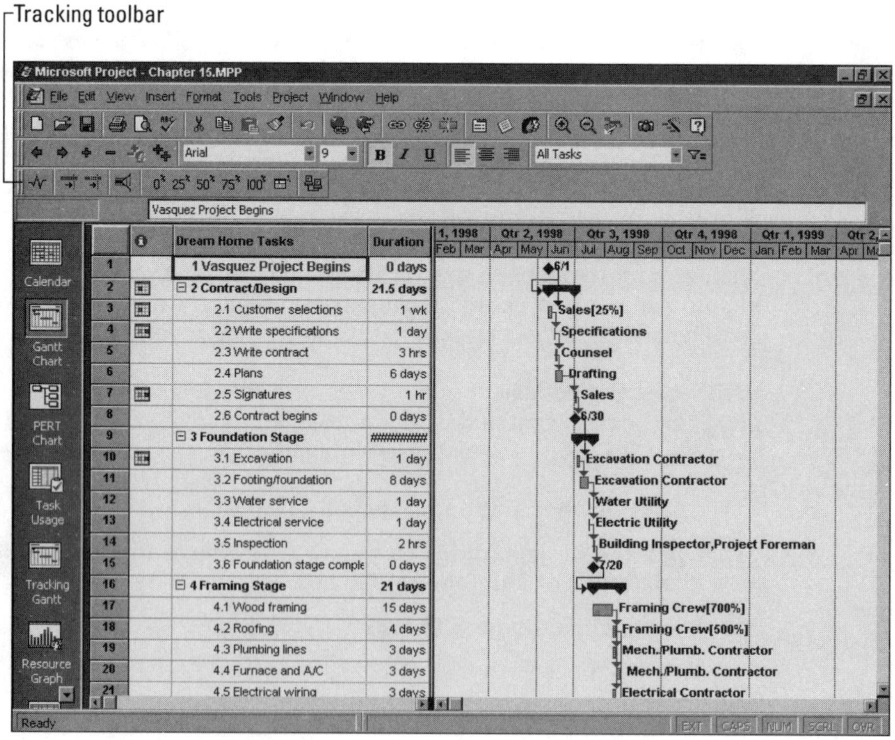

Figure 15-1: The tracking toolbar is one of 12 available toolbars.

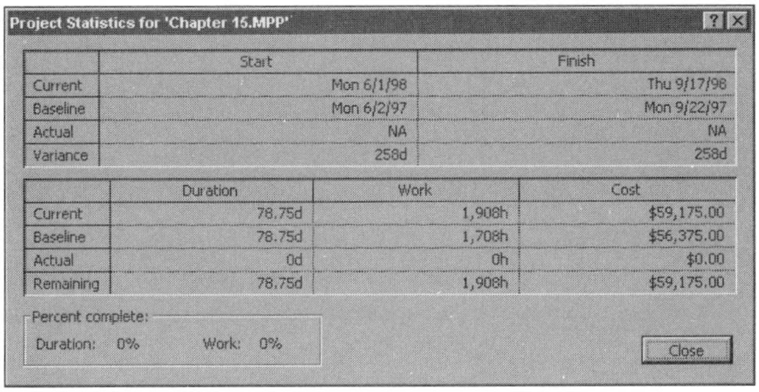

Figure 15-2: Check out the Project Statistics dialog box to see statistics about your project.

Another way to access this dialog box is by choosing Project⇨Project Information. The Project Information dialog box appears. Click Statistics.

The Project Statistics dialog box shows statistics about your project, such as the start date, the finish date, and the cost. The area in the lower left marked Percent Complete indicates that none of the project's duration has been used and none of its work has been performed. The middle section shows that the project's baseline duration was set at 78.75 days. Since the setting of the baseline, the latest estimated duration remains the same.

The Work and Cost columns are another story. The baseline estimate of work was 1,708 hours. The estimate has escalated to 1,908 hours. The baseline cost was $56,375, and the latest estimate is $59,175. This tells you that the project plan is overbudget. You need to find the culprit or culprits.

After you finish checking out the Project Statistics dialog box, click the Close button. Then close the tracking toolbar by right-clicking anywhere in it and clicking Tracking on the shortcut menu. (If a toolbar is open, clicking its name on the shortcut menu toggles it closed.)

View Detailed Work and Cost Estimates

Finding the overages of work and costs is easy in the Task Usage view. Switch to that view now:

1. **Choose Task Usage on the view bar.**

   The Task Usage view appears. The default table for this view is Usage.

2. **Choose View⇨Table: Usage⇨Work.**

   The Work table appears.

3. **Scroll down to display the Framing Stage and the Finishing Stage and their subtasks.**

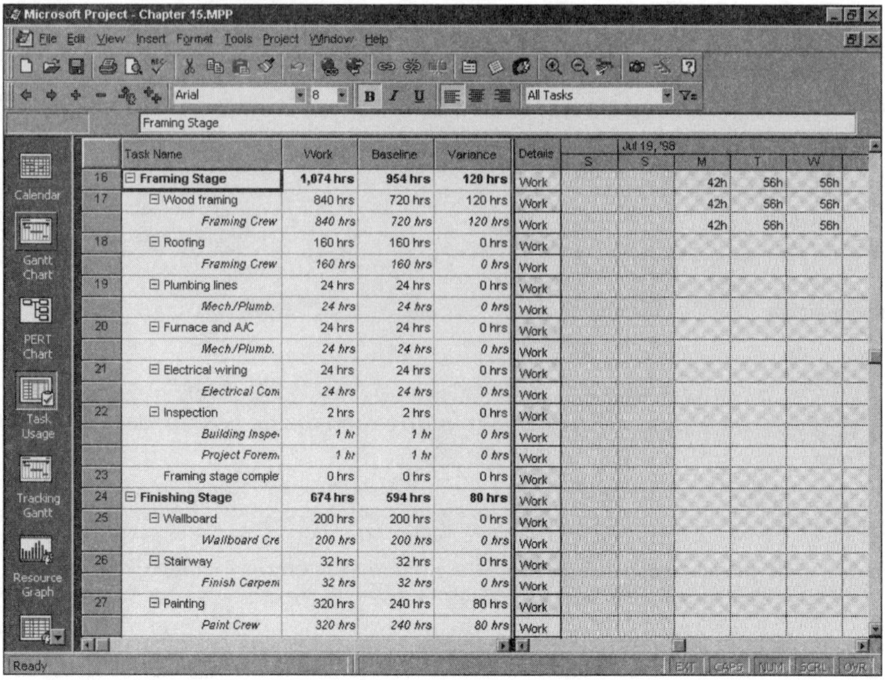

Figure 15-3: In the Task Usage view, the Work table lists all tasks, resources, baseline work assigned to them, current work assigned, and the variance between baseline and current work.

4. Drag the vertical bar separating the table and the chart to the right until the Variance column is fully exposed, as shown in Figure 15-3.

To simplify the work of viewing the Work view, use a filter. In the Filter list box on the formatting toolbar, select Work Overbudget. Now, two tasks and their summary tasks remain, as shown in Figure 15-4. If you would rather highlight the overbudgeted work, choose Project⇨Filtered for⇨More Filters. In the More Filters dialog box, choose Work Overbudget, and then click Highlight.

The Wood framing task estimate has 120 hours more labor than was originally predicted. The Painting task estimate has 80 hours more labor.

While in the Work Overbudget filter, change to the Cost Table Sheet view by choosing View⇨Table⇨Cost. This table illustrates the variance between baseline cost and total cost. The filtered Cost table appears, as shown in Figure 15-5.

The Wood framing task is estimated to cost $1,200 more than was set as the baseline. The Painting task is estimated to cost $1,600 more than its baseline.

You've found the problems. Now it's time to attempt a solution. Press F3 to return to the All Tasks filter. Then change to the Gantt view.

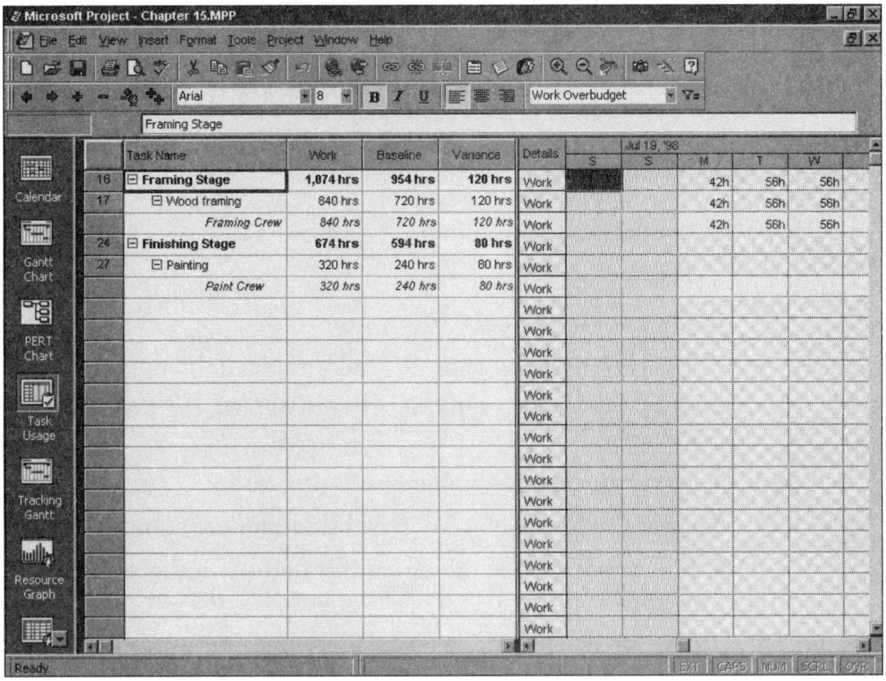

Figure 15-4: Microsoft Project filters display a subtask with its summary task.

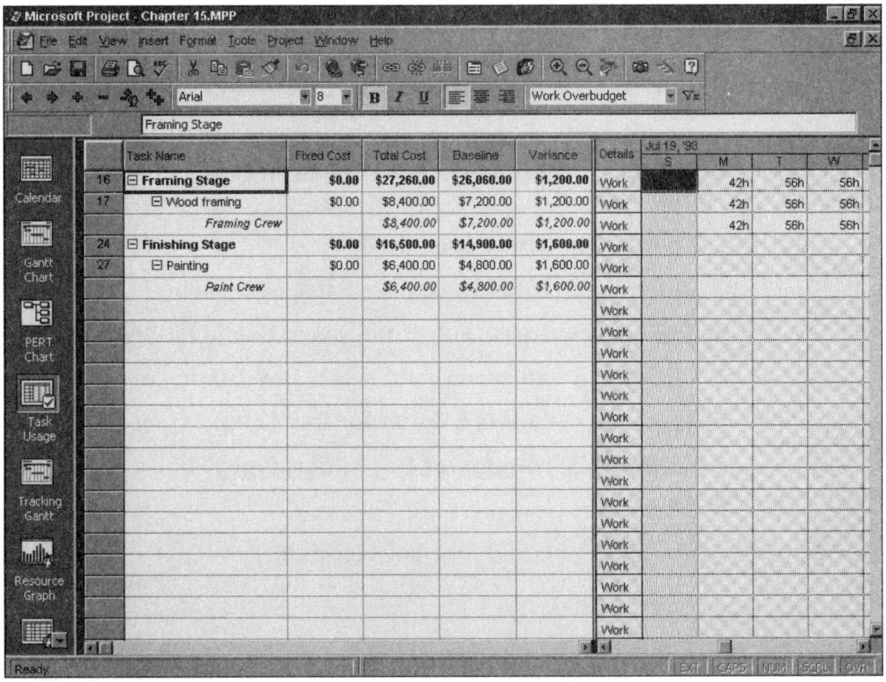

Figure 15-5: Like the filtered Work Table Sheet view, the filtered Cost Table Sheet view shows overbudget tasks and their summary tasks.

Reducing Costs

Using Microsoft Project, you can resolve cost discrepancies any number of ways. In this section, I show you one way.

Use the Task form in a split view to make the correction:

1. **In the Gantt view, choose Window⇨Split.**

   The Split view appears.

2. **Choose View⇨Table: Entry⇨Cost.**

   The Cost table replaces the Entry table in the upper window.

3. **Drag the vertical separator bar to expose the Cost table so that it includes Variance.**
4. **Scroll and select the Wood framing task.**
5. **Click the Goto Selected Task button on the standard toolbar.**
6. **If necessary, click the Zoom Out button on the standard toolbar to show the entire Wood framing task's Gantt bar.**

   The screen should look like Figure 15-6.

If the Units column in the lower window shows percentages, you can switch to decimal numbers by choosing Tools⇨Options. Select the Schedule tab. In the Show Assignment Units as: box, select Decimal.

To reduce the Wood framing task's cost, change the makeup of resources as follows:

1. **In the lower-left pane, select the units associated with the Framing Crew resource.**
2. **Change the units from 7 to** 4.
3. **In the Work column, replace 840h with** 480h.
4. **To add a resource, select the space below the Framing Crew resource.**
5. **Click the down arrow, and select Day Labor.**
6. **Type** 3 **in the Units column for Day Labor.**
7. **In the Work column for Day Labor, type** 360h.
8. **Click OK.**

   The screen should look like Figure 15-7.

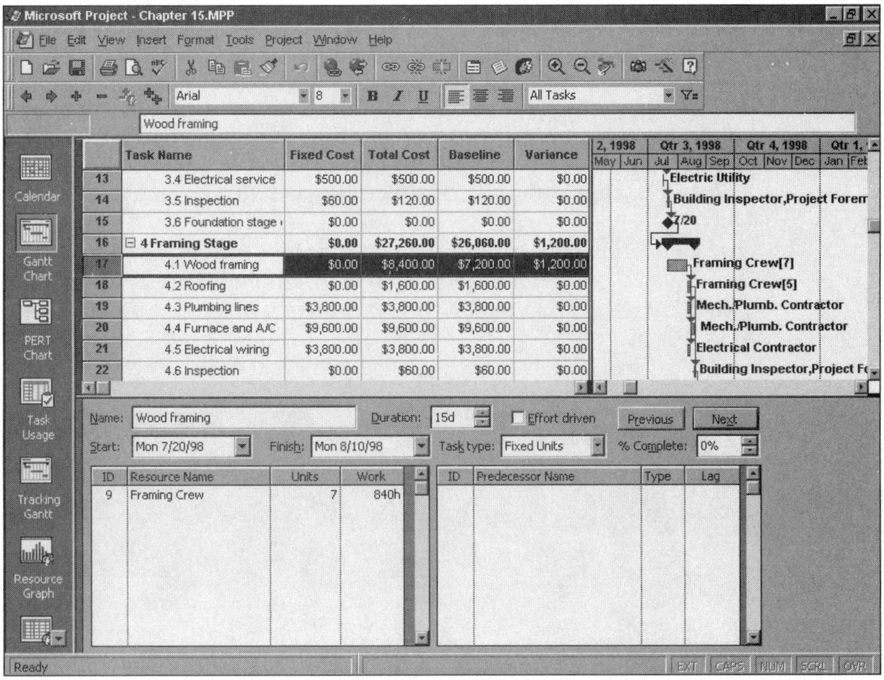

Figure 15-6: The triple view gives you a reading of cost, Gantt bar placement, and task details.

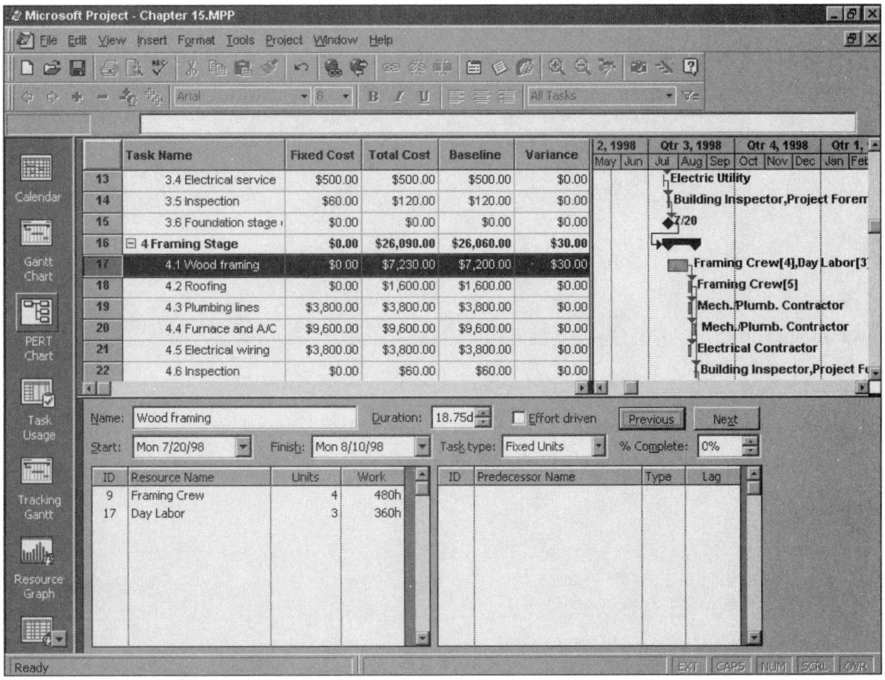

Figure 15-7: The variance for the Wood framing task is now $30.

The changes appear in the Cost table. The added resources are registered next to the Gantt bar. (If necessary, scroll the Gantt chart horizontally to expose the resource names.)

For some more practice, try correcting the Painting task yourself by assigning 2 units at 160h for the Paint Crew resource and 3 units at 240h for Day Labor. The result should look like Figure 15-8.

You can reduce costs in more ways than I've mentioned here. For example, another way to reduce costs is to reschedule work. By changing the work calendar, you can avoid paying overtime. I discuss rescheduling work in Chapter 16.

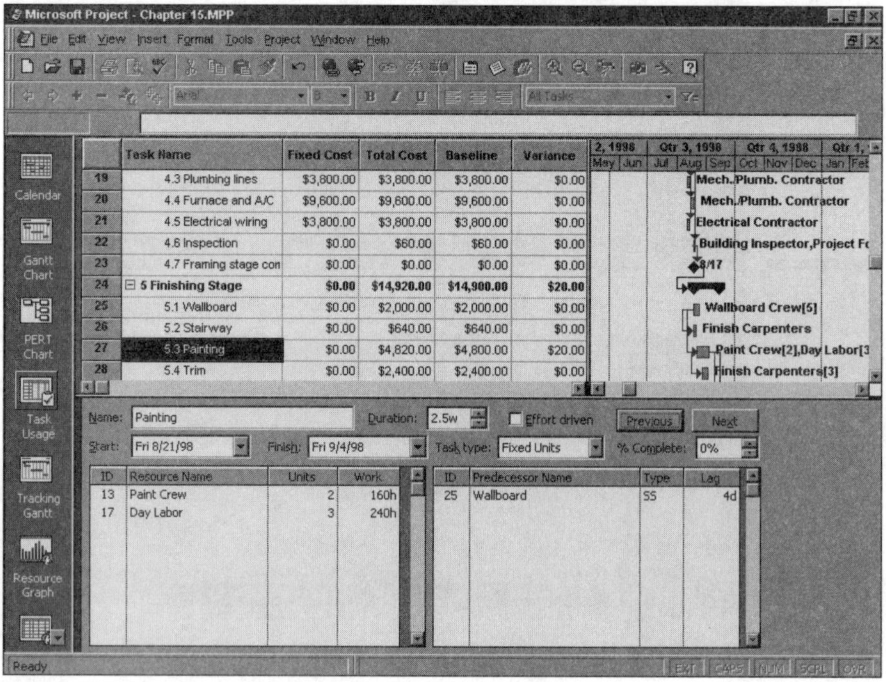

Figure 15-8: The variance for the Painting task is now $20.

Chapter 16

Optimizing Your Plan

In This Chapter

- Correcting scheduling errors
- Finding overused resources
- Crashing the critical path
- Reconciling overallocations

One of the more fascinating stages of project management is the time just before the project start date. You have all the pieces fashioned in relative order. Some things are just as you had expected, others are slightly different, and some are out in left field.

In these predawn hours before your project meets the light of day, you have the opportunity to walk around it and look up close and from a few steps back to marvel at its strengths and to search for its potential weaknesses. And you have a final chance to make improvements that may make all the difference between success and something less than success.

Don't be to bothered if everything isn't trim and perfect. By the time you reach the project's start date, it's not unusual for the plan to have a little bulge around the belt. Perhaps the schedule has become longer than originally anticipated. Maybe some resources are overused and others are underused. And it shouldn't be a surprise if the task relationships have a bug or two.

Quite often, the most challenging task of project management is remembering and using your original goals — simply doing what you said you were going to do. Ninety-nine out of a hundred times, the best course of action is the one you spent all that time planning in the first place. In this chapter, you discover the many ways Microsoft Project can help you analyze and modify your schedule to best ensure that you achieve your project's goals and objectives.

The accompanying CD-ROM has a project sample for you to use throughout this chapter. But you can use your own project if you want.

You can use a sample project file called `Chapter 16.MPP` to hone your optimizing skills. Open the sample project file from the Project folder:

1. **Click the Open button on the standard toolbar.**
2. **Open the Project folder on your hard drive or on the *Microsoft Project 98 For Dummies* CD-ROM.**
3. **Double-click Chapter 16.MPP.**

   The file should open in the Gantt Chart view.

Correcting Overallocated Resources

The term *overallocated* is very real to anyone who owns a checkbook and is associated with things such as antacids and rapid heartbeat. In project management, overallocation is also very real and can cause some big headaches, mostly yours.

One way to determine whether any of your project's tasks are causing an overallocation is by looking in a resource view. For instance, choose Resource Usage on the view bar. The Resource Usage view appears, as shown in Figure 16-1. Notice that one of the tasks, Drafting, has a yellow indicator with an exclamation point. This indicator means a resource needs leveling.

In project management, to level means just what the word implies. A resource is all bunched up in task responsibilities — to the extent that the resource has more task responsibilities than hours to do them in. Microsoft Project is suggesting that you may stretch out the tasks associated with the resource so that it can be more evenly allocated over time.

A common example of an overallocated resource is an employee who is assigned two full-time jobs at the same time. Something has to give. The employee can

- Take work home evenings and weekends (overtime or change working time or both).
- Request extra assistance (additional resources).
- Ask to be relieved of some of the duty (task reduction).
- Ask for extended deadlines (resource leveling).

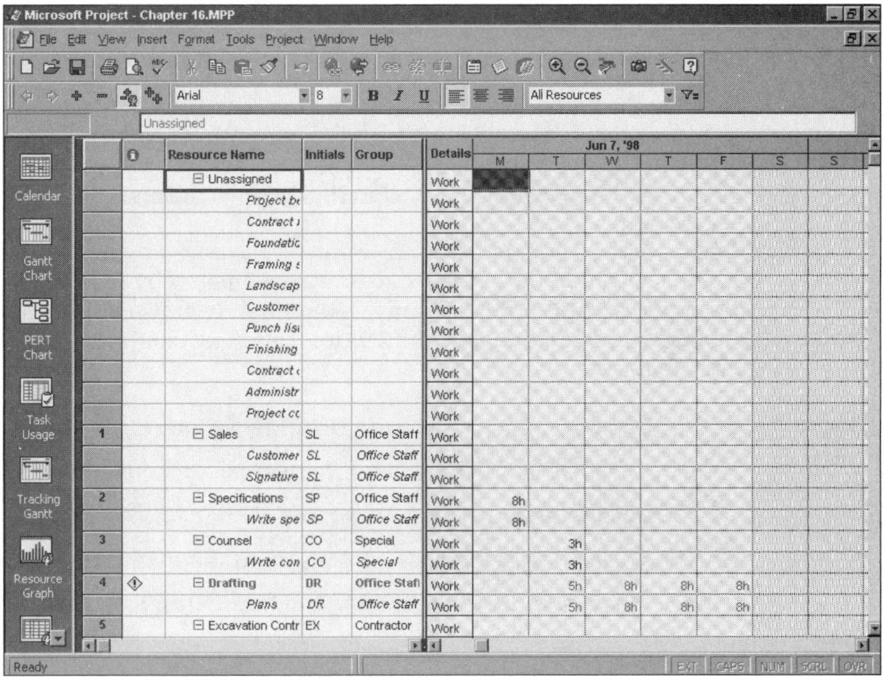

Figure 16-1: The overallocation alert often happens when you are modifying a schedule and consolidating or moving tasks.

All these are common solutions to overallocation. Only the last, requesting an extended deadline, is leveling. When Microsoft Project suggests leveling an overallocation, it's offering this solution because it can do the leveling for you automatically. (You have to work out all the other solutions.) Leveling is often the least desirable solution to an overallocation problem. You don't want deadlines extended if, for instance, your project has to be ready on a certain date.

A Resource Allocation View

You need to find out how many resources are having this problem and the severity of the problem. The best way to do your sleuth work is with a combination view.

Maybe the easiest and fastest way to get the bead on resource allocation problems is with (you guessed it) the Resource Allocation view. You can access this view with the resource management toolbar:

1. **Right-click in the toolbar area.**

   The toolbar menu appears.

2. **Choose Resource Management.**

3. **On the far left, click the Resource Allocation View button.**

   The Resource Allocation view appears, as shown in Figure 16-2. In this view, the Resource sheet is in the upper pane and a delayed Gantt chart is in the bottom pane. The delayed Gantt chart shows only the taskbars related to the task selected in the upper pane.

The Resource Allocation view is a pretty sharp way to analyze resource problems. Overallocated resources are designated by red text. Drafting isn't the only resource with problems — the framing crew and the mechanical/plumbing contractors have difficulties, too. Analyze the problems one at a time. To do so:

1. **In the upper pane, select the Drafting resource.**

   The delayed Gantt chart displays the task associated with the resource.

2. **Press F6 to activate the lower pane.**

3. **Click the Goto Selected Task button on the standard toolbar.**

   The chart and the table jump to the task dates, as shown in Figure 16-3.

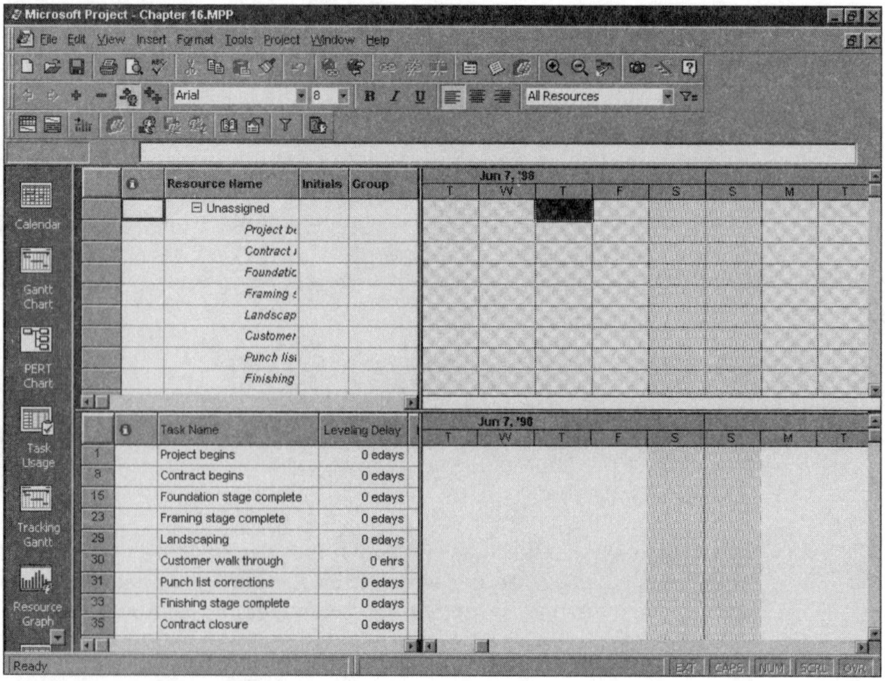

Figure 16-2: Use the Resource Allocation view to analyze resource problems.

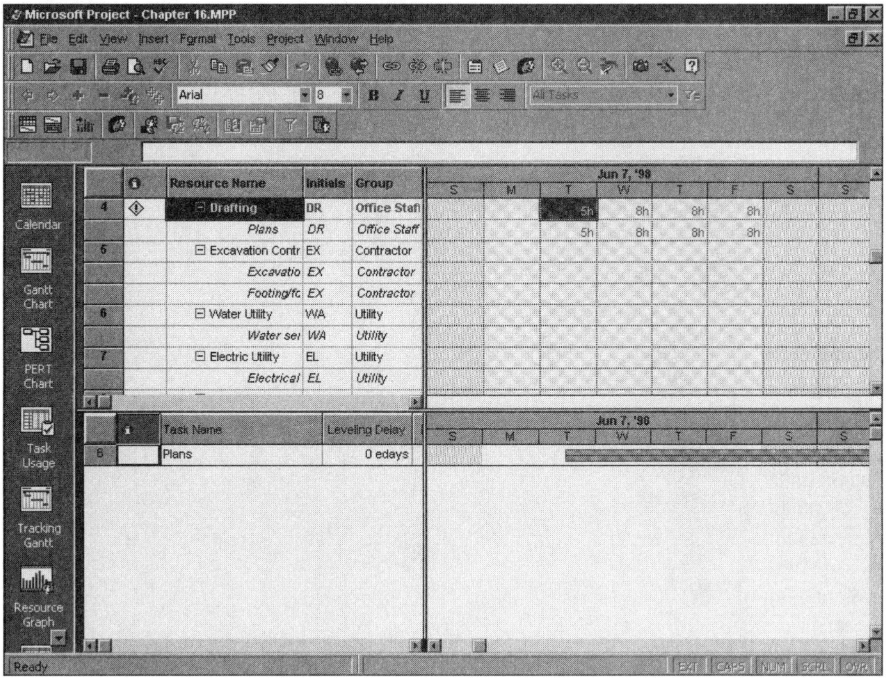

Figure 16-3: Overallocation of resources is based on the resource's calendar and units.

So what's the problem? The Resource sheet shows that the draftsman is working no more than eight hours a day. Maybe the resource information has the answer. Check it out by dragging the vertical bar to the right until it exposes the Accrue At column, as shown in Figure 16-4.

The problem is evident. The maximum units for the draftsman resource is .5. This means the draftsman is allocated a maximum of four hours per day (assuming an eight-hour day) for each of the six days of the drafting task. The original assumption was that the draftsman would be available for eight hours per day.

Before you correct this overallocation problem, check out the other two trouble resources. To do this:

1. **Drag the vertical bar back to its original position (showing the Resource Name and Initials columns).**

2. **Click the Go To Next Overallocation button in the resource management toolbar.**

   The view jumps to the Framing Crew resource. The lower pane displays the two tasks associated with the resource, as shown in Figure 16-5.

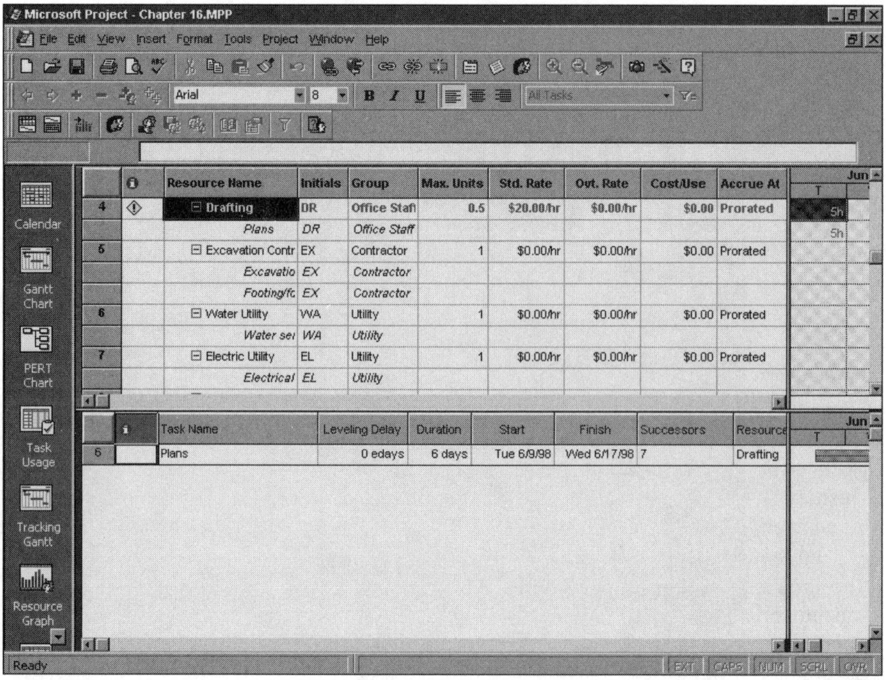

Figure 16-4: The Resource sheet holds all the information entered about each resource.

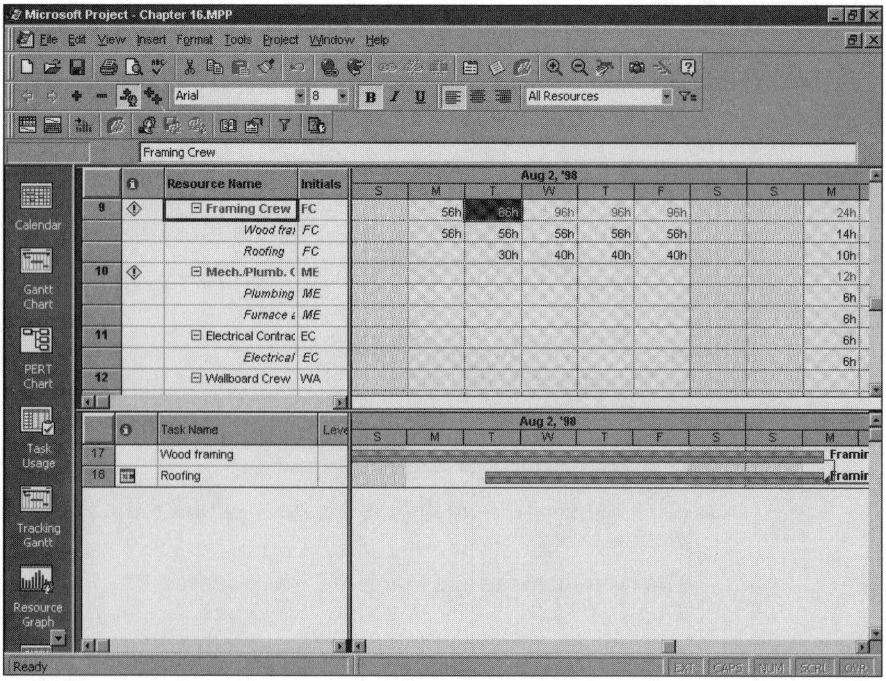

Figure 16-5: The overallocated resources shown in the upper pane align with the days in which the crew is performing two tasks.

Scroll the lower-right pane if necessary to expose the resource name and the unit assignment for the Wood framing and Roofing tasks. Notice that the framing crew is responsible for 7 units of the Wood framing task and 5 units of the Roofing task. Drag the vertical bar to the right until it exposes the Max. Units column in the upper window. The maximum units for the framing crew is 10, as shown in Figure 16-6. That's the reason for this overallocation.

While you're looking at the Resource Usage details, select Mech./Plumb. Contractor. The problem with this resource is that it's currently assigned 1 maximum unit. The contractor works for a fixed fee. It doesn't matter to you how many people the contractor uses as long as the job is accomplished according to the contract. But because only 1 unit is assigned to the resource, Microsoft Project interprets that the contractor can't perform two tasks at the same time.

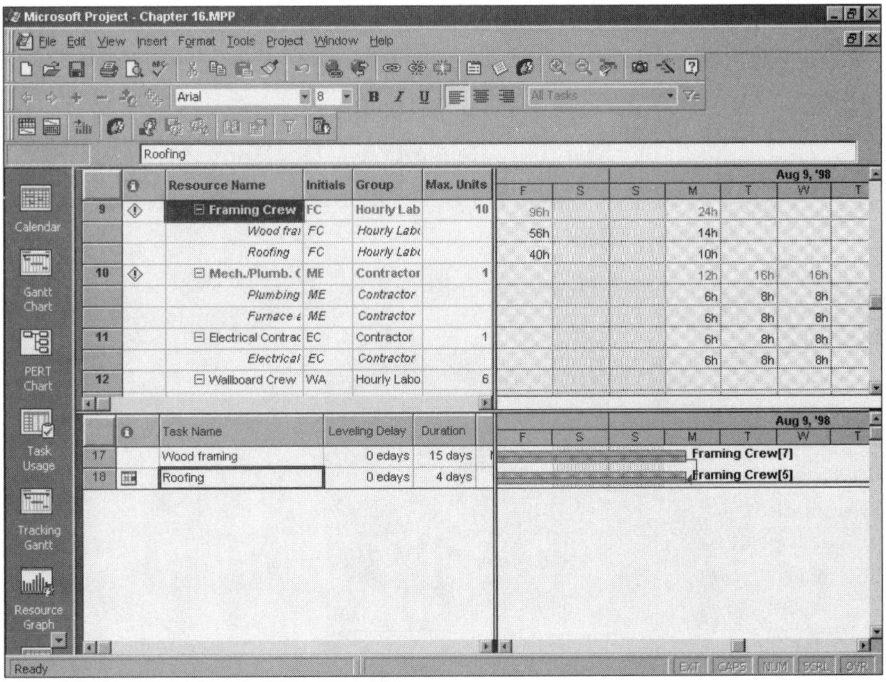

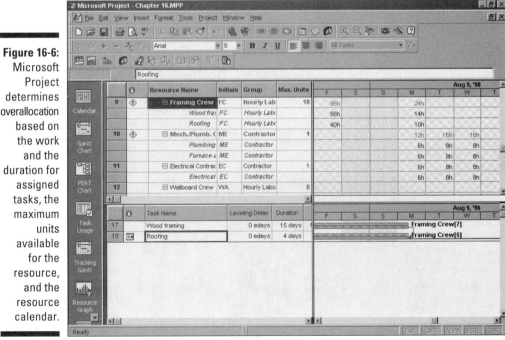

Figure 16-6: Microsoft Project determines overallocation based on the work and the duration for assigned tasks, the maximum units available for the resource, and the resource calendar.

Correcting Resource Overallocations

You can correct resource overallocations in more than one way. In this section, you use three solutions with the resource problems in this project. You extend duration for the draftsman, add units for the framing crew, and delete a task for the mechanical/plumbing contractor. Each solution is the best one for the circumstances of the resource.

The best way to perform this work is manually, rather than through automatic leveling. To do so:

1. **Choose Window⇨Remove Split.**
2. **Choose the Gantt Chart view on the view bar.**
3. **Right-click anywhere in the toolbar area and choose Resource Management.**

   The resource management toolbar closes.
4. **Choose Tools⇨Resource Leveling.**

   The Resource Leveling dialog box appears.
5. **Under Leveling calculations, select Manual.**

   See Figure 16-7. This turns off the automatic leveling option.
6. **Click OK.**
7. **Choose Window⇨Split.**

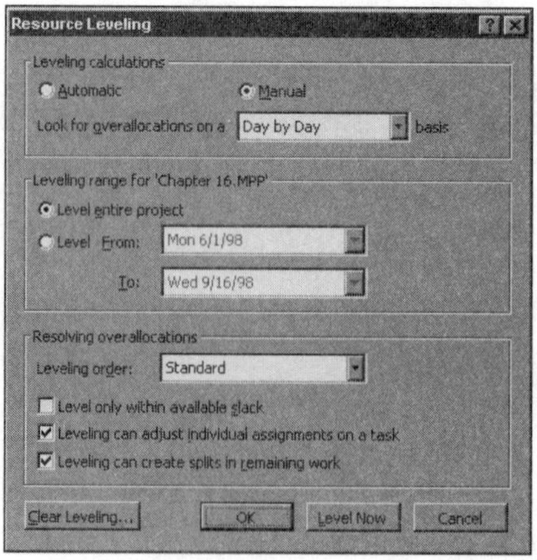

Figure 16-7: The settings in this dialog box remain intact until you change them again.

8. **In the upper pane, select the Plans task.**

   The Drafting Resource appears in the lower pane.

9. **In the Units column, change 1 to** .5, **and click OK.**

10. **Scroll the Gantt chart to expose the entire Plans taskbar and its resource designation.**

The task has leveled to 12 days, as shown in Figure 16-8. The Drafting resource limitation is maintained as 0.5 units. The solution was acceptable because adding six days to the task doesn't conflict with the successor date. And that's because the successor task is a fixed date later than the 12-day period.

You correct the Framing Crew overallocation not by leveling, but by adding resources to the Framing Crew, as follows:

1. **With any task highlighted, click the Assign Resources button on the standard toolbar.**

   The Assign Resources dialog box appears.

2. **Scroll the list and double-click the Framing Crew resource.**

   The Resource Information dialog box appears.

3. **Change Max Units Available from 10 to** 12, **as shown in Figure 16-9.**

4. **Click OK.**

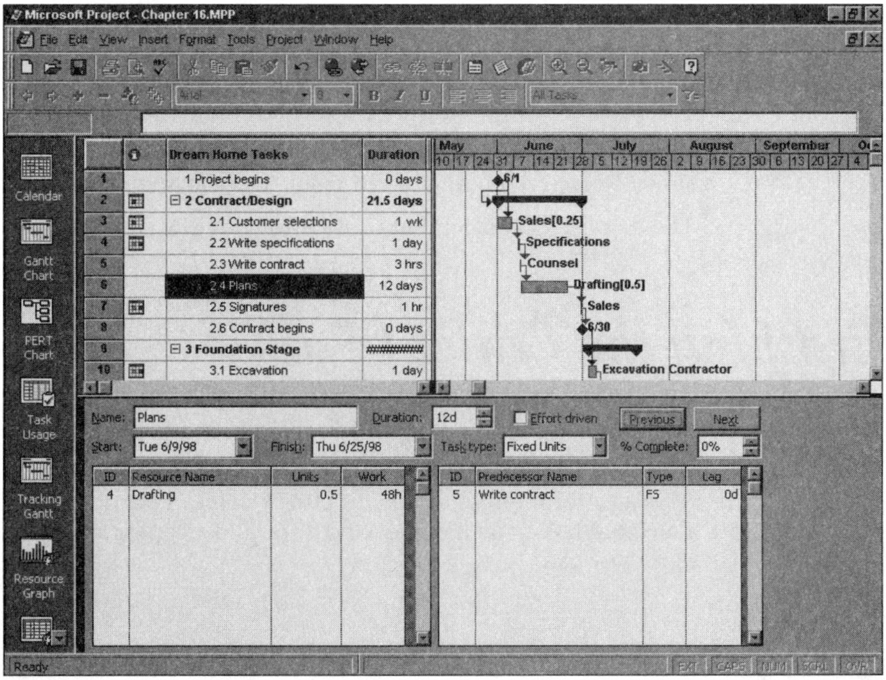

Figure 16-8: The number of hours worked by the draftsman remains the same but is extended over 12 days. The resource is leveled.

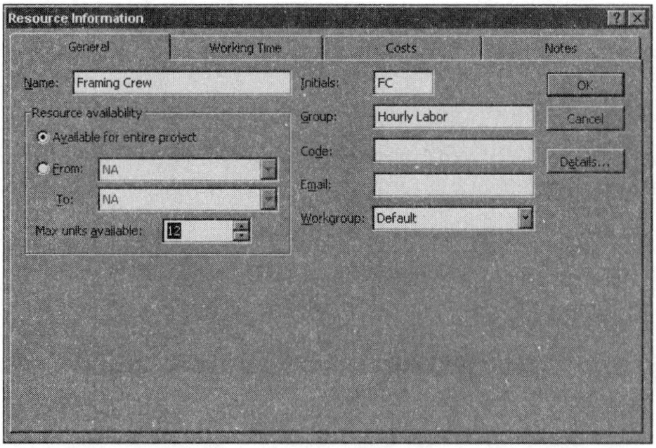

Figure 16-9: The task cost doesn't change when you increase the available units because the assigned units remain the same.

Last, you remove the Mechanical/Plumbing Contractor resource overallocation by removing one of the two identical tasks. This schedule error comes from an earlier decision to grant both the plumbing and mechanical contracts to the same contractor. You aren't changing anything by removing a task because the contractor is responsible for all the crew and related resources. To remove a task:

1. **Highlight the Furnace and A/C task.**
2. **Press the Delete key.**

   The resource overallocation is gone.
3. **Choose Window⇨Remove Split.**

   The project returns to the default Gantt Chart view.
4. **Right-click anywhere on the resource management toolbar, and select Resource Management from the shortcut menu that appears.**

   The resource management toolbar toggles closed.

Crashing the Critical Path

The term *crashing* has a few common uses, but none have anything to do with project management. One common meaning is to run into something, such as crashing a milk cart into a cow. Another meaning was spawned in the 1960s as a term for what you do after a night of partying — not running into a cow but falling on a couch or a floor and sleeping, usually at someone else's groovey *pad.*

When a project manager crashes, a higher and nobler action is happening (I hope). In project management, crashing is doing what's necessary to decrease the total project duration.

Understanding the critical path

So what's a critical path, you ask? Good question. A *critical path* is the series of tasks that determines the completion date of a project. Project management differentiates tasks that are on the critical path from those that aren't.

The critical path of the project includes only tasks that have not been performed. For that reason, the critical path becomes smaller as the project progresses.

All the tasks in the Chapter 16 project, for example, are necessary for its completion. Ignore any of them, and the customer will be quick to inform you that the project isn't complete. Even so, some Chapter 16 project tasks are part of the critical path and some aren't.

To view the current Chapter 16 critical path:

1. **Switch to the Gantt Chart view (if necessary) by choosing Gantt Chart on the view bar.**

   The screen should also be unsplit.

2. **Click the Zoom Out button on the standard toolbar until the time scale is months over weeks.**

   This will make viewing the whole project easier.

3. **Hold down the Shift key and choose Project⇨Filtered for: All Tasks⇨Critical.**

   The screen now displays the entire project with the critical path highlighted in underlined red text (see Figure 16-10).

An example of a noncritical task is the Stairway task. The stairway needs to be completed by the end of the project, but it can float around a little bit without affecting the start or completion of other tasks. To a lesser degree, the same is true of the Roofing task. Its start can be delayed a little bit as long as its finish date doesn't go past the finish date of the Plumbing Lines task.

An example of a critical task is the Excavation task. The start date and finish date of the house excavation directly affect the continuance and timing of successor tasks and, ultimately, the completion date of the project. In another way, the Wallboard task is critical in that its duration has a direct outcome on the completion date of the project. If you could find a way of decreasing the Wallboard task's duration without increasing the cost, you would be crashing the critical path.

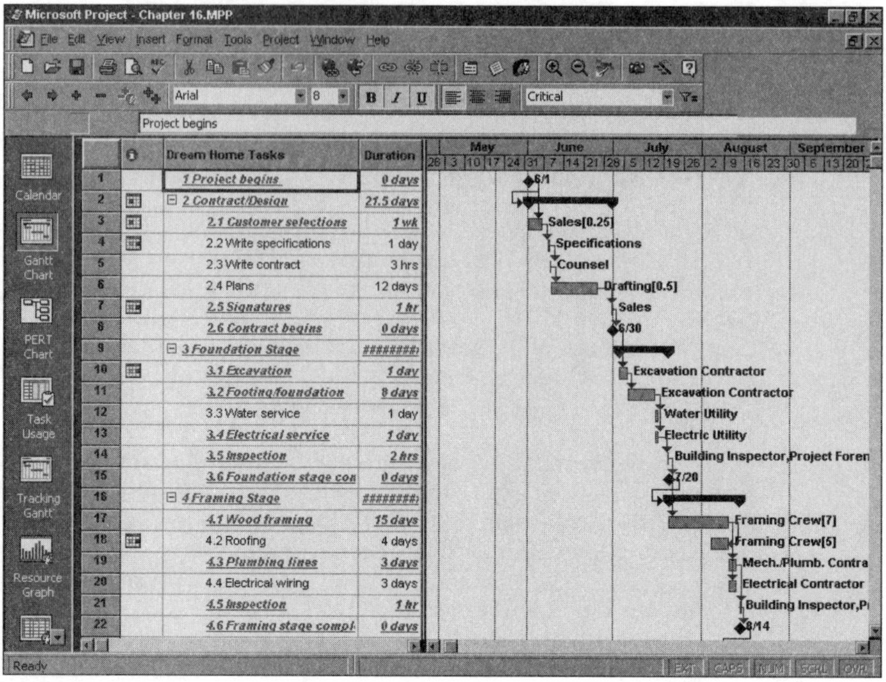

Figure 16-10: Can you spot the critical path?

Scroll the Gantt chart to expose the final task. The Project complete milestone is September 16. That's a problem. For the sake of the example, suppose your boss would like to have the house finished by September 1. Hey man, ya wanna crash at this pad? Let's go! And while we're at it, we'll cut off some extra days just in case there may be some bad weather.

One, two, three — crash!

Crashing a schedule requires some tough analysis and some pencil sharpening. Ask yourself these three questions:

- Is time being used most efficiently?
- Can resources be changed without increasing costs?
- Does the project have any unnecessary finish-to-start relationships?

Using time efficiently

Starting with time efficiency, there is a noticeable way to crash this project's critical path. You can change the construction working calendar. In the construction trades, it's common to work six days a week without incurring overtime. This is especially true in parts of the country with harsh winters. To change the construction calendar:

1. **Choose Tools➪Change Working Time.**

   The Change Working Time dialog box appears, as shown in Figure 16-11.

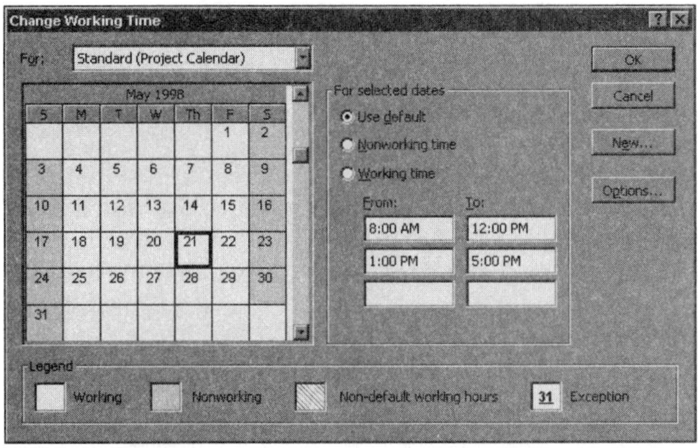

Figure 16-11: The Change Working Time dialog box is the place for editing the default calendar and resource calendars.

2. **In the For box, select the Construction Hours Calendar.**
3. **Select the heading of the Saturday column.**
4. **Under For Selected Dates, select Working Time.**

   The Working Time editing area becomes active.

5. **Change the working times from the default settings to the normal construction hours as set on the other days.**

   Times should be From 7:00 AM To 11:00 AM and From 11:30 AM To 3:30 PM. The Change Working Time dialog box should now look like Figure 16-12.

6. **Click OK.**

   The Project complete milestone has changed to September 7, as shown in Figure 16-13. You're making progress.

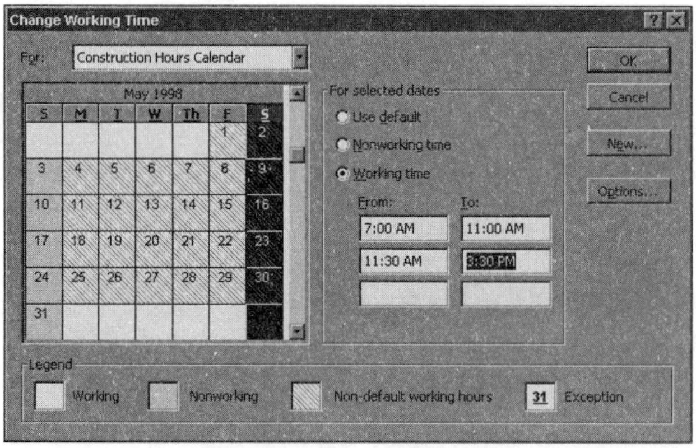

Figure 16-12: When you change one month's setting, the settings for the entire calendar change.

Changing resources

Another way to crash the plan is by changing resources. Sometimes this is the simplest and most straightforward solution to too much work and too little time. For example, in our Chapter 16 project, the Painting task doesn't have a fixed duration. Increasing resource units won't increase costs but will reduce the duration. You can further crash the critical path by adding resources to the Painting Crew, as follows:

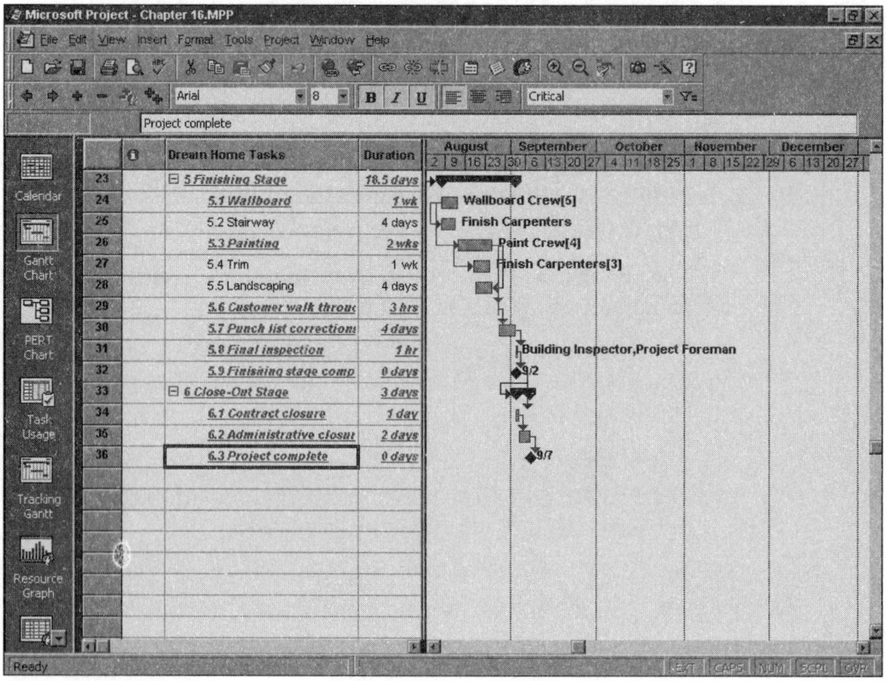

Figure 16-13: The calendar has changed for all resources that follow the construction hours calendar. As a result, there are now six working days.

1. **Select the Painting task.**

2. **Click the Assign Resources button on the standard toolbar.**

   The Assign Resources dialog box appears.

3. **Scroll and double-click the Paint Crew resource.**

   The Resource Information dialog box appears, as shown in Figure 16-14. Changes to this dialog box affect the amount of resource units available for a task.

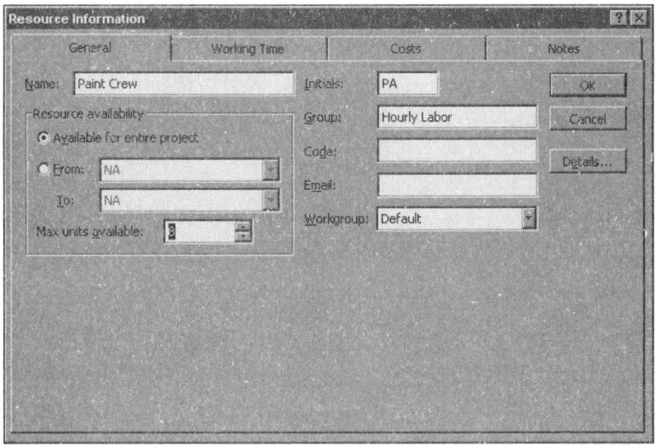

Figure 16-14: The Resource Information dialog box.

4. **Change Max Units Available to** 8, **and then click OK.**

5. **In the Resource Assignment dialog box, change the number of assigned units from 4.00 to** 8.00, **and then click Close.**

   The Gantt chart changes and shows that the Painting task has been reduced from two weeks to one week, as shown in Figure 16-15. In addition, the Project complete milestone is now September 1.

Changing task relationships

Another thing you can do to crash the critical path is to change some task relationships. Some are unnecessarily of the Finish-to-Start variety. The Plumbing lines task and the Electrical wiring tasks can be made to finish with their predecessor Wood framing task. To do so:

1. **Click the Zoom In button on the standard toolbar twice.**

   This makes working on the Gantt chart easier.

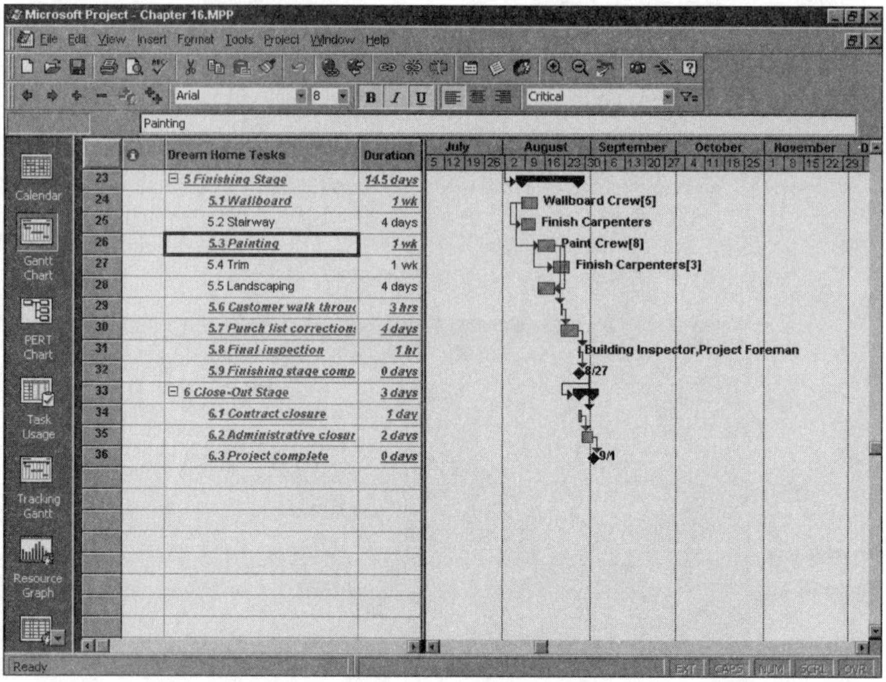

Figure 16-15: The Gantt bar for the Painting task shows the assignment of eight units.

2. **Select the Plumbing lines task.**
3. **Click the Goto Selected Task button on the standard toolbar.**
4. **On the Gantt chart, double-click the arrow that touches the Plumbing lines task.**

   The Task Dependency dialog box appears, as shown in Figure 16-16.

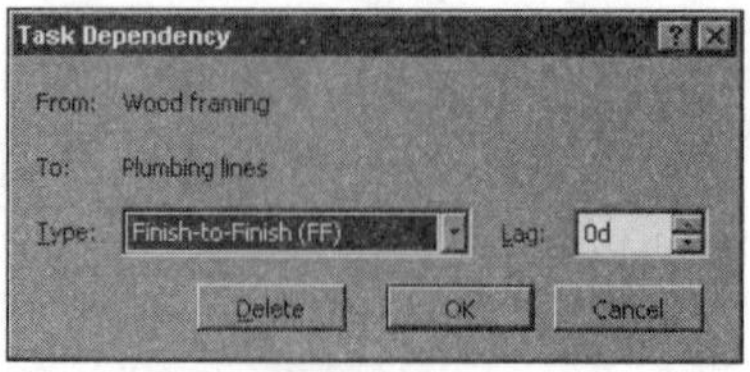

Figure 16-16: The task dependency should be from Wood framing to Plumbing lines.

5. **Change the task dependency to Finish-to-Finish (FF), and then click OK.**
6. **Repeat Steps 2 through 5 for the Electrical wiring task.**
7. **Drag the Roofing task until it has the same Finish date as the Wood framing task (8/3/98).**

   The Gantt chart now looks like Figure 16-17. If you make a mistake, choose Edit⇨Undo Drag.
8. **Scroll to the last task, select it, and click the Goto Selected Task button on the standard toolbar.**

   The Project complete milestone should say August 28. You're almost there.

Two quick changes will complete the crash. Delete the Contract closure task — it's redundant with Administrative closure. Then change Administrative closure to a one-day duration. The result should look like Figure 16-18.

Last, update the baseline. To do so:

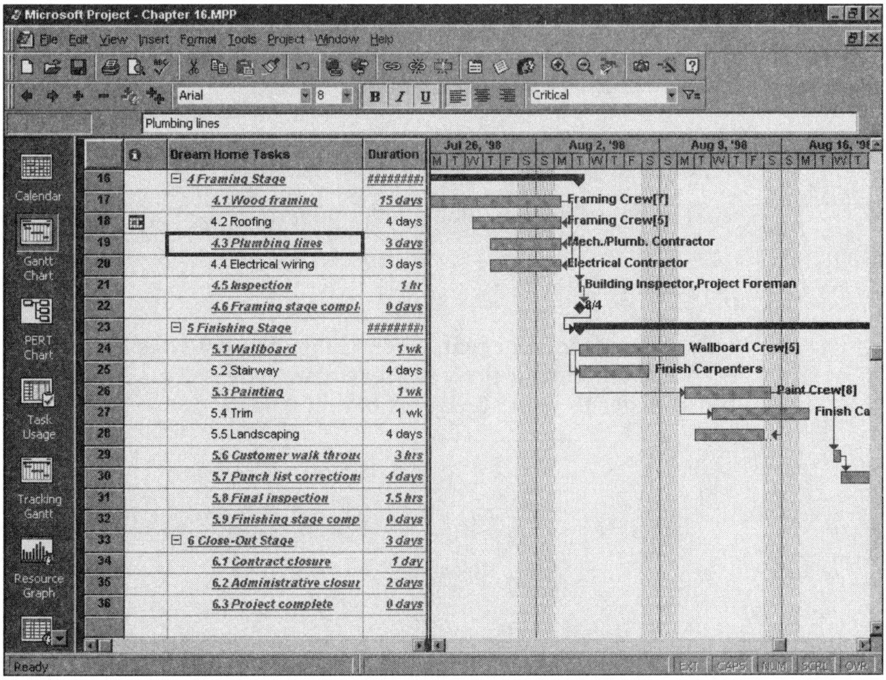

Figure 16-17: The Gantt chart offers point and click, visual tools for optimizing task relationships.

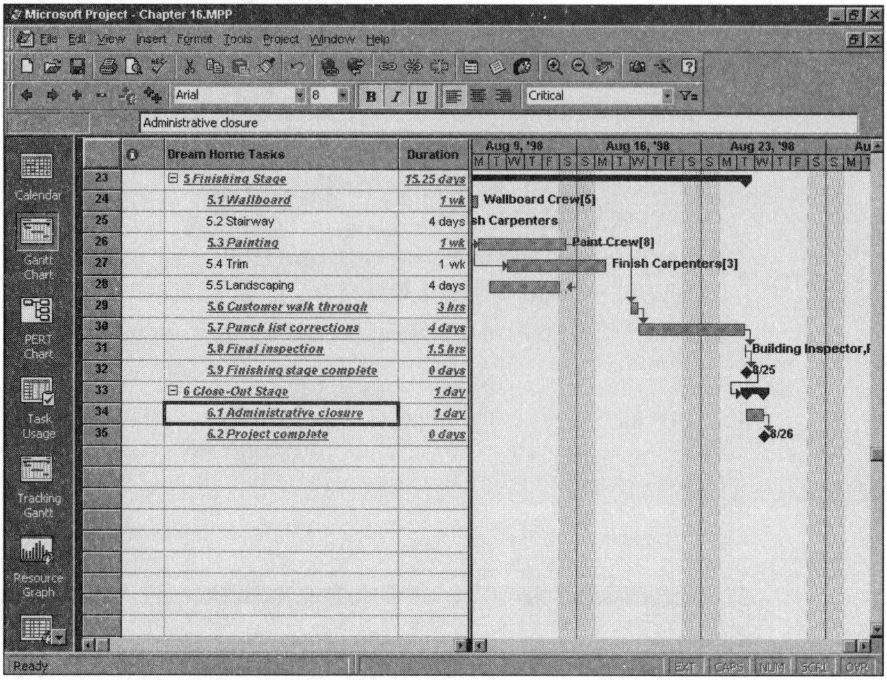

Figure 16-18: The project is within the contract time constraints.

1. **Choose Tools➪Tracking➪Save Baseline.**

   The Save Baseline dialog box appears. Make sure the Save Baseline option is selected.

2. **Click OK.**

You've optimized your plan. Everything is as ready as it can be. Take a break and relax. Come your project's start date, you can walk into the office with a little swagger to your step. This baby's going to fly!

Part V
Project Management

The 5th Wave By Rich Tennant

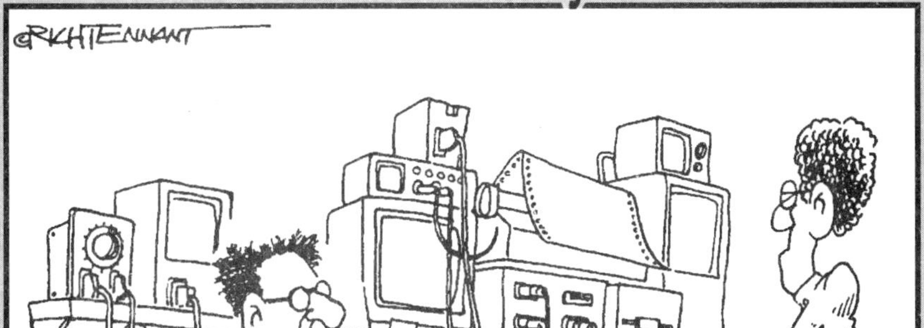

" RIGHT NOW I'M KEEPING A LOW PROFILE. LAST NIGHT, I CRANKED IT ALL UP AND BLEW OUT THREE BLOCKS OF STREETLIGHTS."

In this part . . .

It probably seems odd that this part's title is "Project Management." Isn't that what the whole book is about? Yeah. It's sort of like calling a cylindrical piece of metal with a whole lot of gizmos a *spaceship*. It's a spaceship months before it ever lifts off the ground and forever after it reenters the atmosphere. During its entire life, it is only one thing — a spaceship. Yet only a brief period of its overall life is spent in space.

In all the previous chapters, you've been building a vehicle that exists solely for one purpose — project management. In this part, you launch. You study how to track your project and how to make midcourse corrections. And you discover how to modify your project environment after it starts showing some pesky anomalies.

Chapter 17

Tracking Your Project's Progress

In This Chapter

- Understanding baseline, current, and actual information
- Tracking your project with tables
- Tracking your project with the Gantt chart
- Updating schedules and tasks

In this chapter, I assume that your project is beginning or has already begun. As you're about to see, Microsoft Project is an important asset in your project-management responsibilities. It's ready and waiting to help your project plan succeed in the cold test of reality. Although you'd like the project to go without a hitch, you know that's almost impossible. Besides, if the project had no problems, it would need only a project planner — not a project manager.

A project manager has to know what's going on to be proactive to the process of change. This requires keeping a close watch on the schedule, tasks, resources, and costs. Programs such as Microsoft Project provide a tremendous capability to analyze present circumstances against the original plan and to make adjustments to better ensure future success. The term for this is *tracking.*

Tracking has a double meaning. One meaning is *keeping track,* as in remaining informed. The other meaning is *keeping on track,* as in keeping the project going where and how it is designed to progress.

Tracking has three major components:

- **The baseline plan.** The baseline is the fully developed plan that you save before the start date of the first project task. The baseline is like a set of completed blueprints and specifications. It's your best prediction of how the project should go. You use the baseline throughout the project to maintain goals and to get things back on track.

- **Current information.** After the project begins, Microsoft Project keeps a dynamic model of the project. This model may or may not be the same as the baseline. As you see in this chapter, Microsoft Project calculates upcoming start and finish dates based on the latest information. You use current information to determine how upcoming tasks are being affected by the present and by what has already occurred.
- **Actual information.** Tasks that have already started or have finished are referred to as *actual*. As you see in this chapter, the actual start and finish dates for tasks are designated NA until they begin.

Using Microsoft Project, you can perform either minimal or detailed tracking. *Minimal tracking* refers to keeping records of the start and finish dates for each task. *Detailed tracking* is not a specific action, but a range of possibilities. You can track start and finish dates plus percentage of task completion, duration, costs, and work. You can then use the information to maneuver your tasks through complicated situations.

In this chapter, using the Mackey Home example, you track a project after it has begun. You work with baseline, current, and actual information.

Open the sample project file from the Project folder. To do so:

1. **Click the Open button on the standard toolbar.**
2. **Open the Project folder on your hard drive or on the *Microsoft Project 98 For Dummies* CD-ROM.**
3. **Double-click** `Chapter 17.MPP`**.**

   The Mackey project file should open in the Gantt Chart view.

Viewing the Baseline

You've put a lot of time and effort into creating your baseline. Wouldn't it be nice to see it? Get ready to meet your baseline:

1. **Choose View⇨More Views.**

   The More Views dialog box appears.
2. **Double-click Task Sheet.**

   The screen changes to Task Sheet view.
3. **Choose View⇨Table: Cost.**
4. **Choose More Tables.**

   The More Tables dialog box appears.

5. **Choose Baseline.**

   Baseline, meet your project manager. Project manager, this is your baseline (see Figure 17-1). All your project activity and expenses are measured in comparison to the baseline you set before the project's start date.

For the rest of your project, this information doesn't change unless you need to modify it for some reason. (For example, you may need to modify the baseline so that you can add a task to the project.)

You probably won't have a reason to use this specific table in your project, but you'll be using various parts of this information on an ongoing basis. For now, change back to the Gantt Chart view by choosing Gantt Chart on the view bar.

The Baseline in Other Tables

The baseline shows up in some of the most important places. For instance, it's in the Work table, the Cost table, and the Variance table. To see the baseline in these tables:

1. **Choose View⇨Table: Entry.**
2. **Choose Work.**

   The Work table appears.

3. **Drag the vertical bar to the right until the entire table is exposed, as shown in Figure 17-2.**

The Work table provides you with resource information about each task. The Work column is the total amount of work scheduled to be performed by all resources assigned to the task. The Variance column is a calculation of the difference between Baseline and (Current) Work. Actual is the amount of work that has been performed by all resources on the task. Remaining is the total amount of work that has yet to be performed. Percent of Work Completed (% W. Comp.) is the percentage of each task's work that has been performed.

The Cost table performs the same kind of function as the Work table except it tracks — you guessed it — cost. To see this table:

1. **Choose View⇨Table: Work.**
2. **Choose Cost.**

   The Cost table appears (see Figure 17-3).

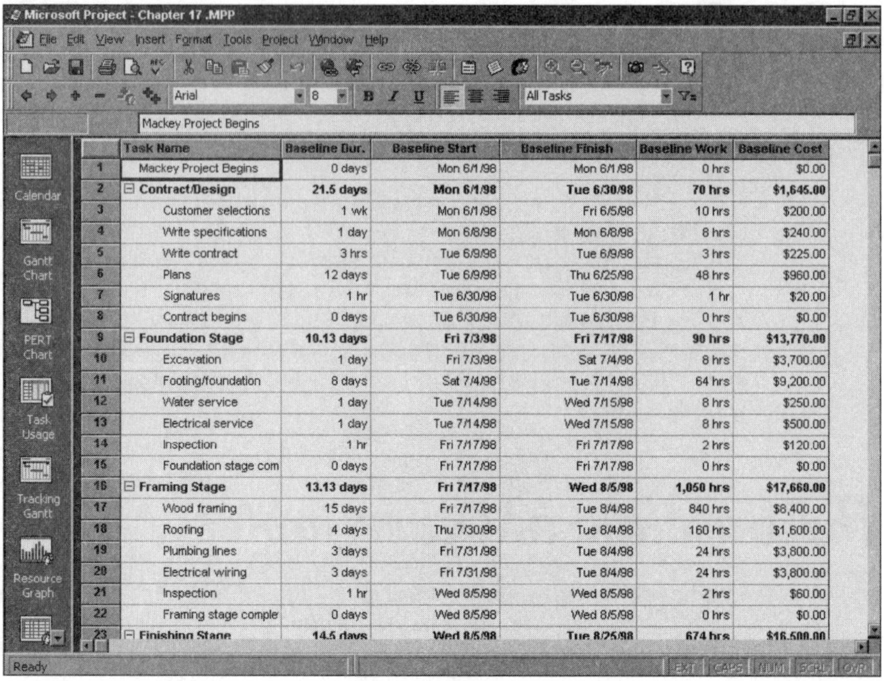

	Task Name	Baseline Dur.	Baseline Start	Baseline Finish	Baseline Work	Baseline Cost
1	Mackey Project Begins	0 days	Mon 6/1/98	Mon 6/1/98	0 hrs	$0.00
2	**Contract/Design**	**21.5 days**	**Mon 6/1/98**	**Tue 6/30/98**	**70 hrs**	**$1,645.00**
3	Customer selections	1 wk	Mon 6/1/98	Fri 6/5/98	10 hrs	$200.00
4	Write specifications	1 day	Mon 6/8/98	Mon 6/8/98	8 hrs	$240.00
5	Write contract	3 hrs	Tue 6/9/98	Tue 6/9/98	3 hrs	$225.00
6	Plans	12 days	Tue 6/9/98	Thu 6/25/98	48 hrs	$960.00
7	Signatures	1 hr	Tue 6/30/98	Tue 6/30/98	1 hr	$20.00
8	Contract begins	0 days	Tue 6/30/98	Tue 6/30/98	0 hrs	$0.00
9	**Foundation Stage**	**10.13 days**	**Fri 7/3/98**	**Fri 7/17/98**	**90 hrs**	**$13,770.00**
10	Excavation	1 day	Fri 7/3/98	Sat 7/4/98	8 hrs	$3,700.00
11	Footing/foundation	8 days	Sat 7/4/98	Tue 7/14/98	64 hrs	$9,200.00
12	Water service	1 day	Tue 7/14/98	Wed 7/15/98	8 hrs	$250.00
13	Electrical service	1 day	Tue 7/14/98	Wed 7/15/98	8 hrs	$500.00
14	Inspection	1 hr	Fri 7/17/98	Fri 7/17/98	2 hrs	$120.00
15	Foundation stage com	0 days	Fri 7/17/98	Fri 7/17/98	0 hrs	$0.00
16	**Framing Stage**	**13.13 days**	**Fri 7/17/98**	**Wed 8/5/98**	**1,050 hrs**	**$17,660.00**
17	Wood framing	15 days	Fri 7/17/98	Tue 8/4/98	840 hrs	$8,400.00
18	Roofing	4 days	Thu 7/30/98	Tue 8/4/98	160 hrs	$1,600.00
19	Plumbing lines	3 days	Fri 7/31/98	Tue 8/4/98	24 hrs	$3,800.00
20	Electrical wiring	3 days	Fri 7/31/98	Tue 8/4/98	24 hrs	$3,800.00
21	Inspection	1 hr	Wed 8/5/98	Wed 8/5/98	2 hrs	$60.00
22	Framing stage comple	0 days	Wed 8/5/98	Wed 8/5/98	0 hrs	$0.00
23	**Finishing Stage**	**14.5 days**	**Wed 8/5/98**	**Tue 8/25/98**	**674 hrs**	**$16,500.00**

Figure 17-1: The baseline is ground zero for your project. It's your best estimate of your project's duration, resource usage, and cost.

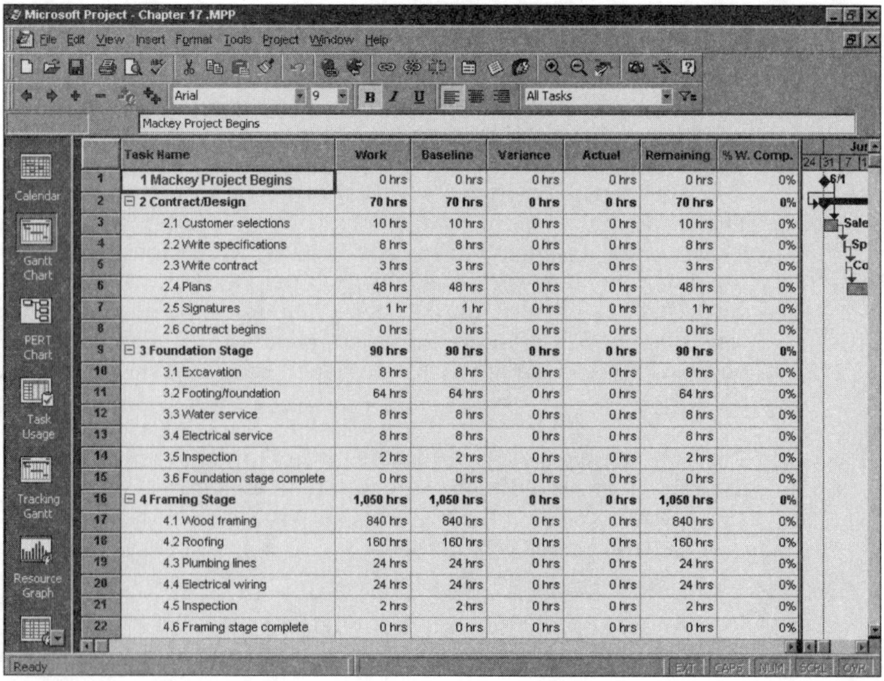

	Task Name	Work	Baseline	Variance	Actual	Remaining	% W. Comp.
1	1 Mackey Project Begins	0 hrs	0 hrs	0 hrs	0 hrs	0 hrs	0%
2	**2 Contract/Design**	**70 hrs**	**70 hrs**	**0 hrs**	**0 hrs**	**70 hrs**	**0%**
3	2.1 Customer selections	10 hrs	10 hrs	0 hrs	0 hrs	10 hrs	0%
4	2.2 Write specifications	8 hrs	8 hrs	0 hrs	0 hrs	8 hrs	0%
5	2.3 Write contract	3 hrs	3 hrs	0 hrs	0 hrs	3 hrs	0%
6	2.4 Plans	48 hrs	48 hrs	0 hrs	0 hrs	48 hrs	0%
7	2.5 Signatures	1 hr	1 hr	0 hrs	0 hrs	1 hr	0%
8	2.6 Contract begins	0 hrs	0 hrs	0 hrs	0 hrs	0 hrs	0%
9	**3 Foundation Stage**	**90 hrs**	**90 hrs**	**0 hrs**	**0 hrs**	**90 hrs**	**0%**
10	3.1 Excavation	8 hrs	8 hrs	0 hrs	0 hrs	8 hrs	0%
11	3.2 Footing/foundation	64 hrs	64 hrs	0 hrs	0 hrs	64 hrs	0%
12	3.3 Water service	8 hrs	8 hrs	0 hrs	0 hrs	8 hrs	0%
13	3.4 Electrical service	8 hrs	8 hrs	0 hrs	0 hrs	8 hrs	0%
14	3.5 Inspection	2 hrs	2 hrs	0 hrs	0 hrs	2 hrs	0%
15	3.6 Foundation stage complete	0 hrs	0 hrs	0 hrs	0 hrs	0 hrs	0%
16	**4 Framing Stage**	**1,050 hrs**	**1,050 hrs**	**0 hrs**	**0 hrs**	**1,050 hrs**	**0%**
17	4.1 Wood framing	840 hrs	840 hrs	0 hrs	0 hrs	840 hrs	0%
18	4.2 Roofing	160 hrs	160 hrs	0 hrs	0 hrs	160 hrs	0%
19	4.3 Plumbing lines	24 hrs	24 hrs	0 hrs	0 hrs	24 hrs	0%
20	4.4 Electrical wiring	24 hrs	24 hrs	0 hrs	0 hrs	24 hrs	0%
21	4.5 Inspection	2 hrs	2 hrs	0 hrs	0 hrs	2 hrs	0%
22	4.6 Framing stage complete	0 hrs	0 hrs	0 hrs	0 hrs	0 hrs	0%

Figure 17-2: The Work table is a quick and easy reference for comparing baseline, actual, variance, remaining, and percent complete information.

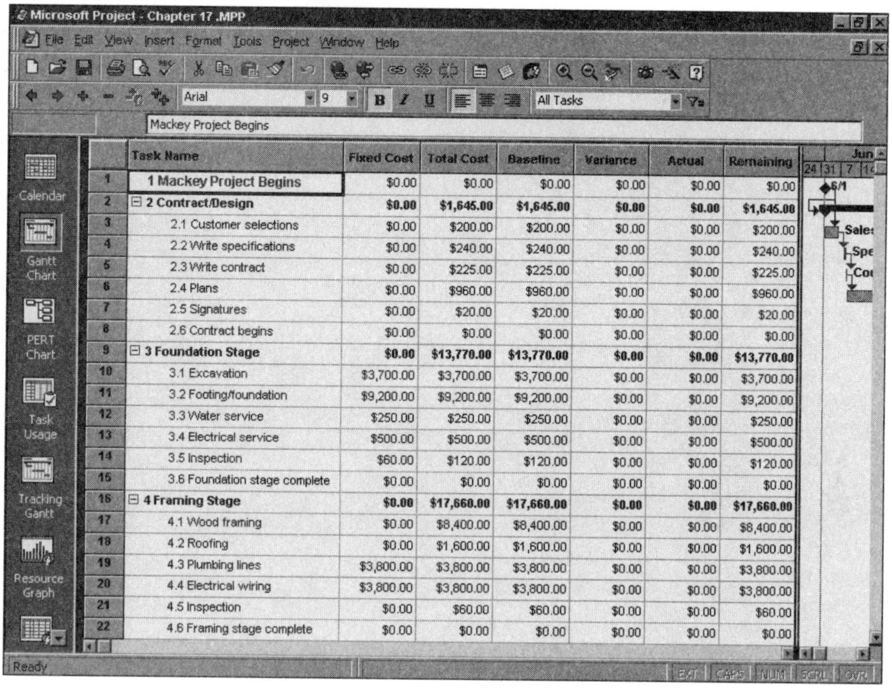

	Task Name	Fixed Cost	Total Cost	Baseline	Variance	Actual	Remaining
1	1 Mackey Project Begins	$0.00	$0.00	$0.00	$0.00	$0.00	$0.00
2	2 Contract/Design	$0.00	$1,645.00	$1,645.00	$0.00	$0.00	$1,645.00
3	2.1 Customer selections	$0.00	$200.00	$200.00	$0.00	$0.00	$200.00
4	2.2 Write specifications	$0.00	$240.00	$240.00	$0.00	$0.00	$240.00
5	2.3 Write contract	$0.00	$225.00	$225.00	$0.00	$0.00	$225.00
6	2.4 Plans	$0.00	$960.00	$960.00	$0.00	$0.00	$960.00
7	2.5 Signatures	$0.00	$20.00	$20.00	$0.00	$0.00	$20.00
8	2.6 Contract begins	$0.00	$0.00	$0.00	$0.00	$0.00	$0.00
9	3 Foundation Stage	$0.00	$13,770.00	$13,770.00	$0.00	$0.00	$13,770.00
10	3.1 Excavation	$3,700.00	$3,700.00	$3,700.00	$0.00	$0.00	$3,700.00
11	3.2 Footing/foundation	$9,200.00	$9,200.00	$9,200.00	$0.00	$0.00	$9,200.00
12	3.3 Water service	$250.00	$250.00	$250.00	$0.00	$0.00	$250.00
13	3.4 Electrical service	$500.00	$500.00	$500.00	$0.00	$0.00	$500.00
14	3.5 Inspection	$60.00	$120.00	$120.00	$0.00	$0.00	$120.00
15	3.6 Foundation stage complete	$0.00	$0.00	$0.00	$0.00	$0.00	$0.00
16	4 Framing Stage	$0.00	$17,660.00	$17,660.00	$0.00	$0.00	$17,660.00
17	4.1 Wood framing	$0.00	$8,400.00	$8,400.00	$0.00	$0.00	$8,400.00
18	4.2 Roofing	$0.00	$1,600.00	$1,600.00	$0.00	$0.00	$1,600.00
19	4.3 Plumbing lines	$3,800.00	$3,800.00	$3,800.00	$0.00	$0.00	$3,800.00
20	4.4 Electrical wiring	$3,800.00	$3,800.00	$3,800.00	$0.00	$0.00	$3,800.00
21	4.5 Inspection	$0.00	$60.00	$60.00	$0.00	$0.00	$60.00
22	4.6 Framing stage complete	$0.00	$0.00	$0.00	$0.00	$0.00	$0.00

Figure 17-3: The Cost table shows resource cost information regarding project tasks.

The Fixed Cost column contains the fixed cost for a task, such as contractor fees. Total Cost is the total projected cost for the task. The remaining columns are set up in the same way as the Work table.

The Variance table compares the difference, if any, between the project's baseline start and finish dates and the scheduled start and finish dates after the project has begun. For example:

1. **Choose View⇨Table: Cost.**
2. **Choose Variance.**

   The Variance table appears, as shown in Figure 17-4, after adjusting the columns to show the entire date.

The Variance table displays current start and finish dates. As mentioned, the term *current* refers to calculated information based on the latest changes or lack of changes to the project. The project is only beginning, so no variances exist between current dates and baseline dates.

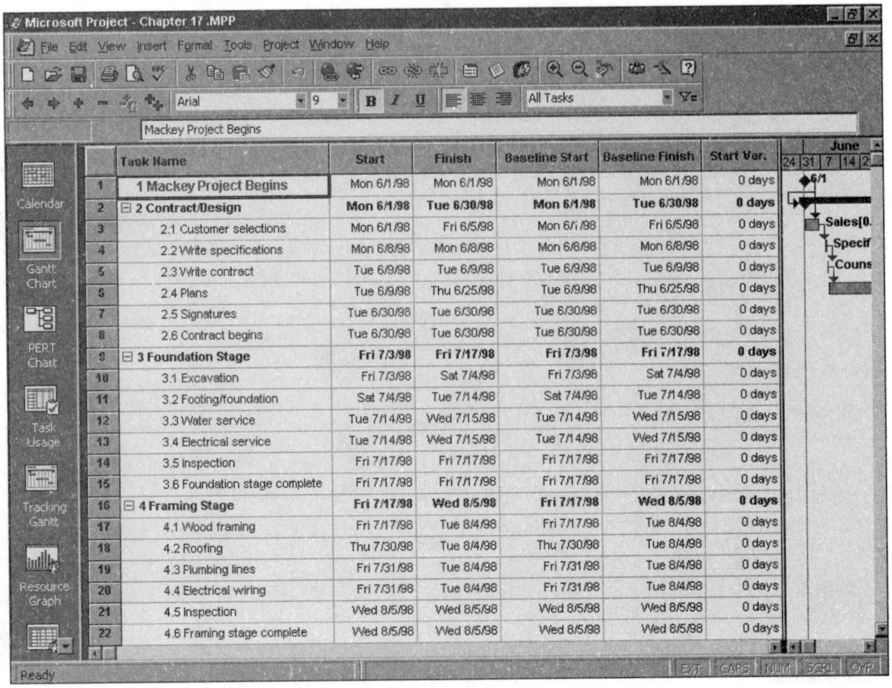

Figure 17-4: The Variance table provides columns for comparing the schedule's variance from the baseline start and finish dates of project tasks.

Tracking Project Progress

Enough of the baseline stuff already! It's time to do some project tracking:

1. **Change back to the Entry table by choosing View⇨Table: Variance.**
2. **Choose Entry.**

   The Entry table appears.
3. **Drag the vertical bar back until it is to the right of the Duration column.**
4. **If necessary, click the Zoom Out button on the standard toolbar.**

   This makes the Gantt chart easier to use.

Suppose that the project has been progressing for a number of days. Everything was going according to plan until the construction ran into a rain day. This not only delayed construction, but also affected the availability of some upcoming resource commitments.

You need to make some changes to the project. This won't affect the baseline. Instead, the baseline will tell you how the changes affect the overall project.

For this example, today is July 14, 1998. You need to inform Microsoft Project of this, as follows:

1. **Choose Project⇨Project Information.**

   The Project Information dialog box appears.

2. **In the Current Date text box, type** 7/14/98 **or select the date in the drop-down calendar box, as shown in Figure 17-5.**

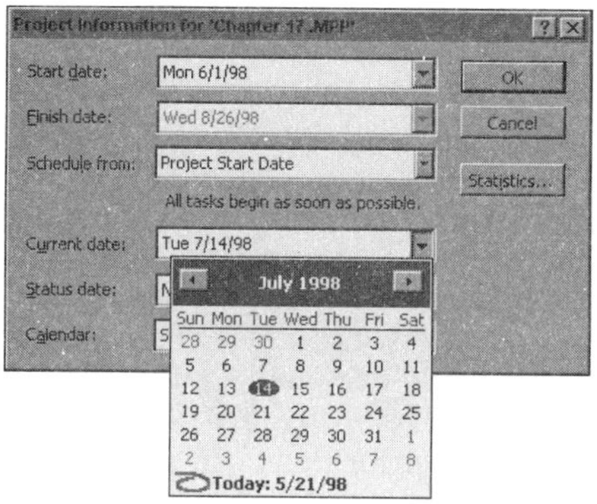

Figure 17-5: Changing the current date in the Project Information dialog box doesn't affect your computer's clock.

3. **Click OK.**
4. **Choose Edit⇨Go To.**

   The Go To dialog box appears.

5. **In the Date box, type** 7/14/98 **or use the drop-down calendar to select the date, as shown in Figure 17-6.**
6. **Click OK.**

   The chart jumps to July 14.

Microsoft Project informs you of the current date, July 14, by inserting a vertical dotted line on the Gantt chart.

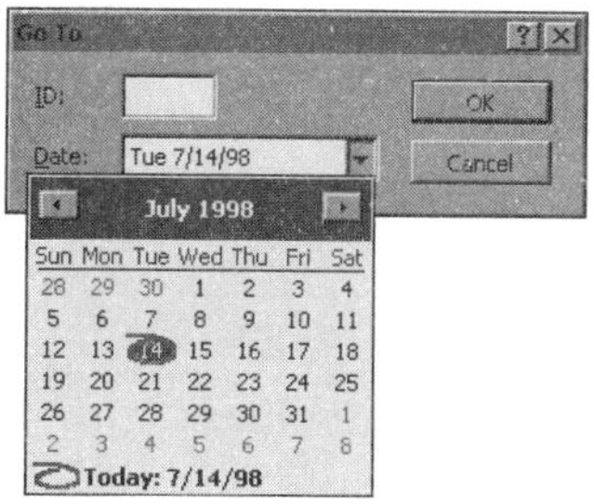

Figure 17-6: You can use the Go To dialog box to jump to an ID or a date.

Updating the schedule

As work is performed on project tasks, you feed progress information into your project file. The term for this is *updating*. Updating the schedule adds a record of work performed. Microsoft Project provides some shortcuts to aid you in this task. Some of the most common shortcuts are grouped together on the tracking toolbar:

1. **Right-click anywhere in the toolbar area.**

   The toolbar menu appears.

2. **Choose Tracking.**

   The tracking toolbar appears.

Using these tracking tools and a few others, you'll make the following updates to the project.

Tasks 1–10 were completed on time and without difficulty. Task 11 is half finished and is one day behind schedule because of mud. The ground conditions aren't affecting just the Mackey project. The Electrical service task is behind schedule and won't be performed until July 20. This affects the building inspector — the Foundation Stage inspection can't take place until electric service has been installed.

Percentage complete

Some of the friendliest tools on the tracking toolbar are the percentage complete buttons. Louis Armstrong should be singing "What a Wonderful World" in the background when you use them. For example:

1. **Select the task Project begins, ID 1.**
2. **Hold down the Shift key, and select summary task ID 2, Contract/ Design.**

3. **Click the 100% Complete button on the tracking toolbar.**

   Microsoft Project updates the selected tasks. The black bar all the way through the tasks indicates completion. By selecting a summary task and choosing one of the percentage complete buttons, Microsoft Project interprets the percentage of completion to be true of all subtasks.

4. **Select the Excavation task, and then click the 100% Complete button on the tracking toolbar.**
5. **Scroll the Gantt chart to expose tasks 1 through 10.**
6. **Click the Zoom In button on the standard toolbar.**

   The chart should look like Figure 17-7.

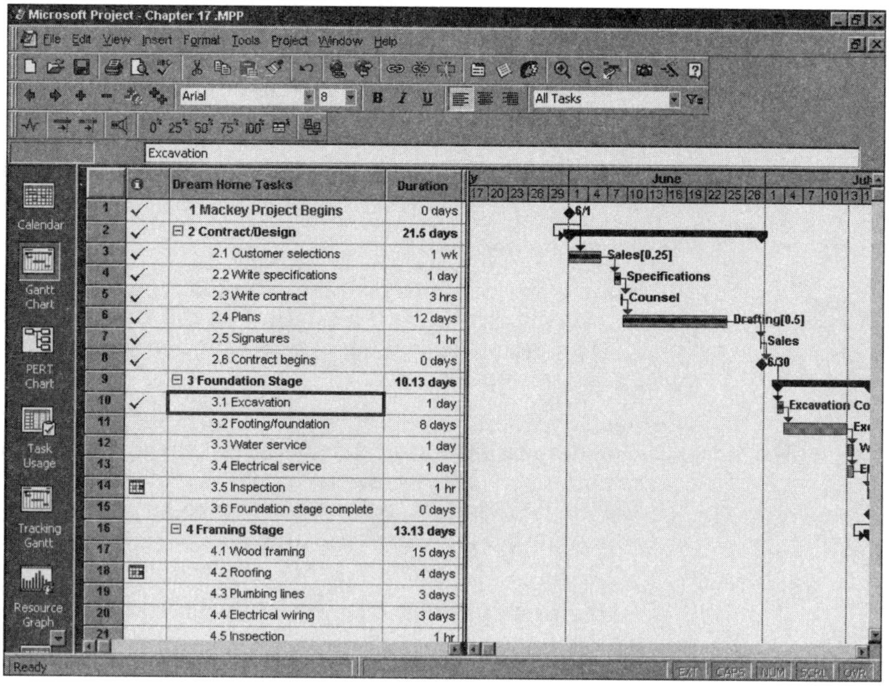

Figure 17-7: In addition to updating the Gantt Chart view, Microsoft Project has recorded the updated information to the tables. The ten tasks now have actual dates.

Update tasks

You can update specific information about tasks by using the Update Tasks button on the tracking toolbar or by double-clicking a task:

1. **Select the Footing/foundation task.**
2. **Click Goto Selected Task on the standard toolbar.**
3. **Double-click the Footing/foundation task.**
4. **Select the General tab.**

   The Task Information dialog box appears. The task is 60 percent complete and one day behind schedule.
5. **In the Percent Complete text box, type** 60.
6. **In the Duration text box, type** 9d.
7. **Click OK.**

   The Footing/foundation task reflects your changes.

Another task needs your attention. The Electrical service task can't be performed until July 20. It's currently scheduled to start on July 18. To change the task's start date:

1. **Move the cursor to the Electrical service Gantt bar.**
2. **Drag to the right until the pop-up date box says that the start date is July 20.**
3. **Release the mouse button.**

   The Planning wizard appears. It tells you that you may be creating a task relationship problem. You can turn off this option by selecting the Don't Tell Me About This Again option. I suggest you wait awhile before you choose this option.

   The Planning wizard says there's a problem because the link between tasks will not drive the start date of the later task. The wizard is saying a task relationship exists between the two tasks (the Electrical service task and the Footing/foundation task) that requires the later task to begin upon the completion of the previous task. By moving the first task's start date, everything is getting messed up.

4. **Choose the first option (see Figure 17-8), which lets Microsoft Project remove the link.**
5. **Click OK.**

   The Electrical service task is moved to July 20.

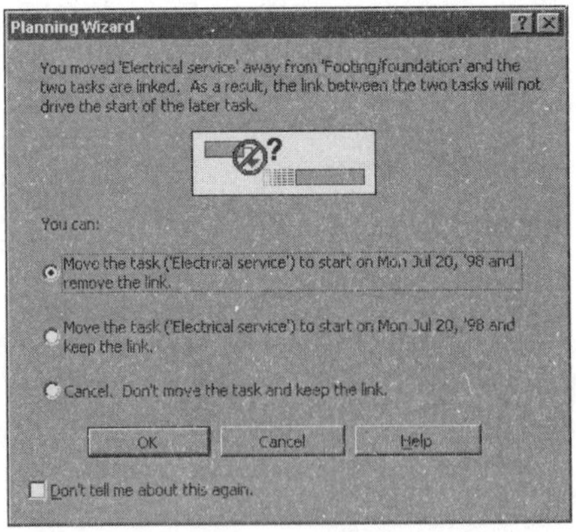

Figure 17-8: The Planning wizard appears automatically when you create a possible task relationship discrepancy.

Now you need to link the Electrical service task again. To do this:

1. **Double-click the Electrical service task.**

   The Task Information dialog box appears.

2. **Click the Predecessors tab.**
3. **In the text box below ID, type** 11.
4. **Select the green check mark, and click OK.**

   See Figure 17-9.

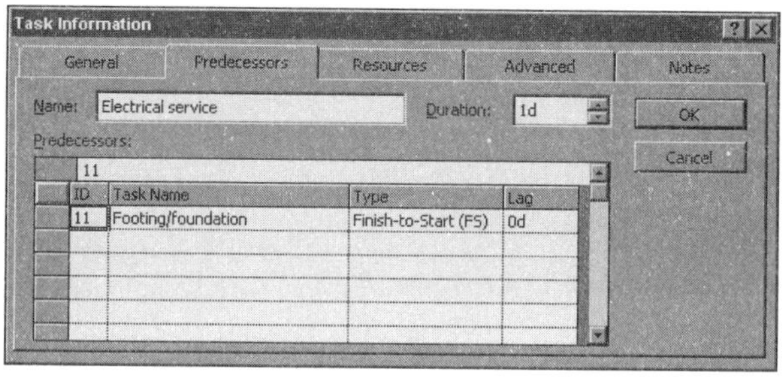

Figure 17-9: The Electrical service task is now the successor of the Footing/ foundation task.

The Inspection task has a one-day lag from its Electrical service predecessor. You need to remove the lag. To do this:

1. **Double-click the arrow point that is touching the Inspection task.**

   The Task Dependency dialog box appears.

2. **In the Lag text box, type** 0 **to replace the 1d, as shown in Figure 17-10.**
3. **Click OK.**

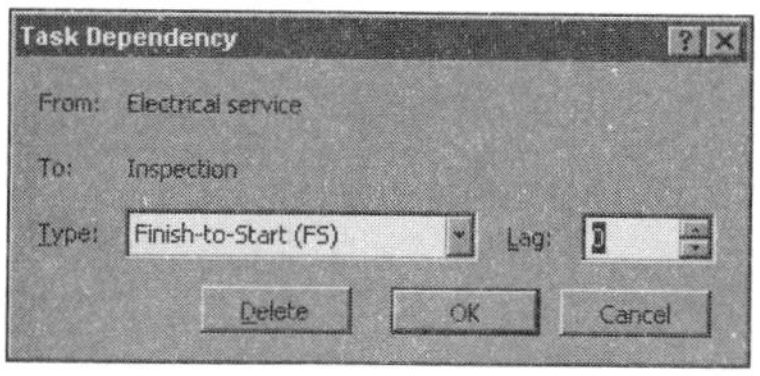

Figure 17-10: The Task Dependency dialog box.

Splitting tasks

One of the powerful ways that Microsoft Project reflects reality is its capability to split tasks. Sometimes, tasks are started and then, for some reason, put on hold for a while. You can keep track of tasks off track through *splitting.*

Suppose that the Water Service task is going to take two days with a one-day split in the middle:

1. **First, change the Water service duration to** 2d.

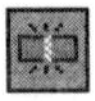

2. **Select the Split Task button on the standard toolbar.**

   The cursor changes shape to show it's ready to do some splitting, and the Split Task information box appears.

3. **Place the cursor over the Water service Gantt bar, as shown in Figure 17-11.**

4. **Click the Water service Gantt bar.**

   The task splits, as shown in Figure 17-12.

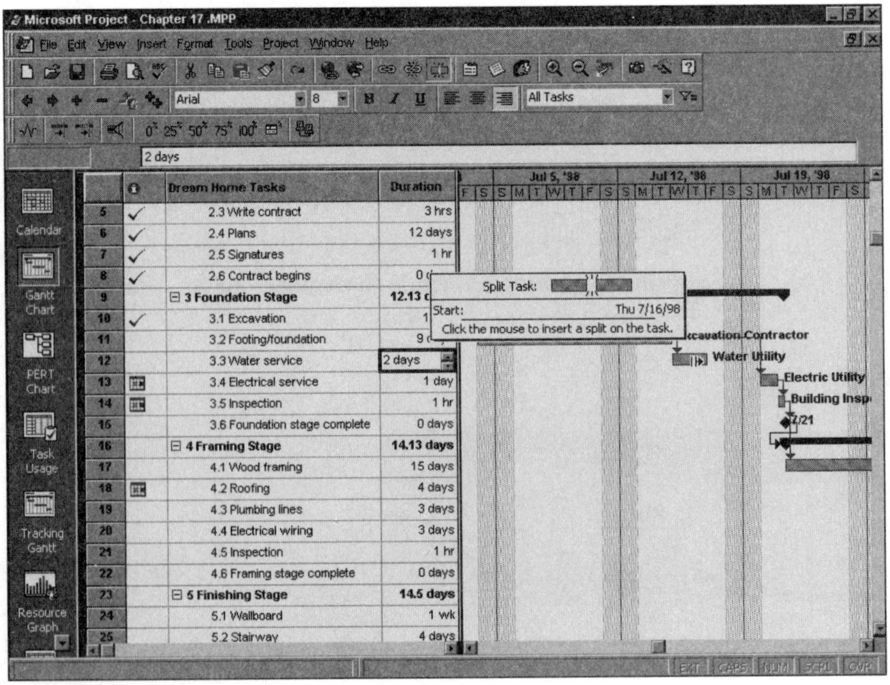

Figure 17-11: The Split Task command provides a way to separate the start and finish dates without adding duration to a task.

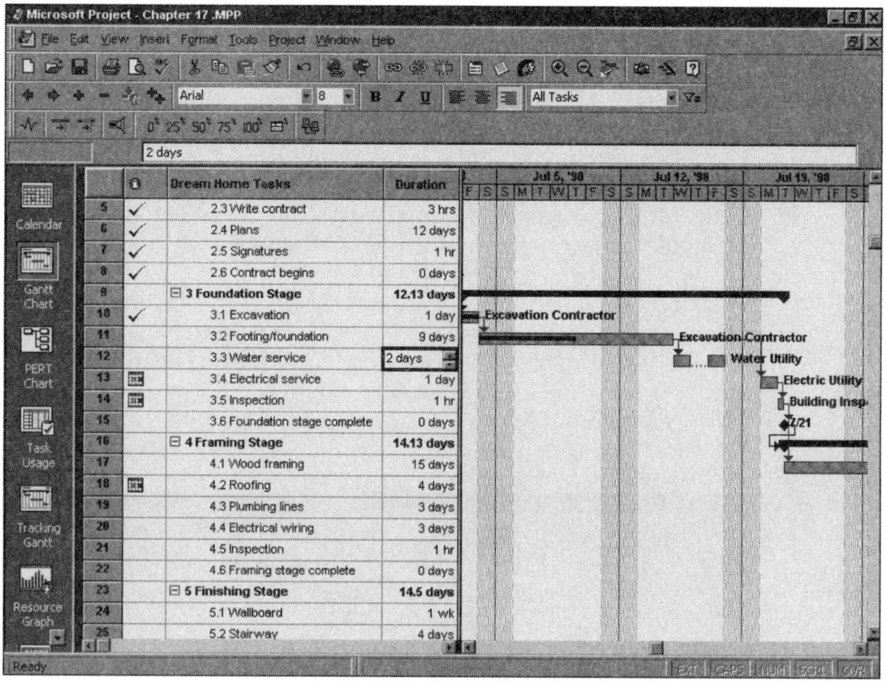

Figure 17-12: You can shorten or widen the split by clicking either part of the split task and dragging it.

The Tracking Gantt table

One visually powerful view of tracking information is the Tracking Gantt table. It's best to access the view before you read the explanation. To access the Tracking Gantt table:

1. **Choose Tracking Gantt on the view bar.**

   The More Views dialog box appears.

2. **Select the Footing/foundation task.**
3. **Click the Goto Selected Task button on the standard toolbar.**
4. **Adjust the screen to match Figure 17-13.**

A lot of visual messages are in this view, based mostly on changes of color:

- Dark gray bars are the baseline tasks.
- Dark blue bars are completed tasks or portions of tasks.
- Red bars are critical path tasks.

- Light blue bars are noncritical tasks.
- Black bars are summary tasks.
- Checkered bars are percentage of completion of summary tasks.

The difference in horizontal location between the baseline bar and its partner is an indication of the schedule status. The more distance, the further the actual date is from the baseline date. The number at the end of each colored bar is the percentage of the task that is completed.

Tracking can be a blast as well as rewarding proof of your excellent planning. But all good athletes know that backslapping is for the end of the game, not during it. Tracking is your first defense against previously unforeseeable problems. If you do it well, you'll be able to see to the horizon and — with your Microsoft Project tools — beyond.

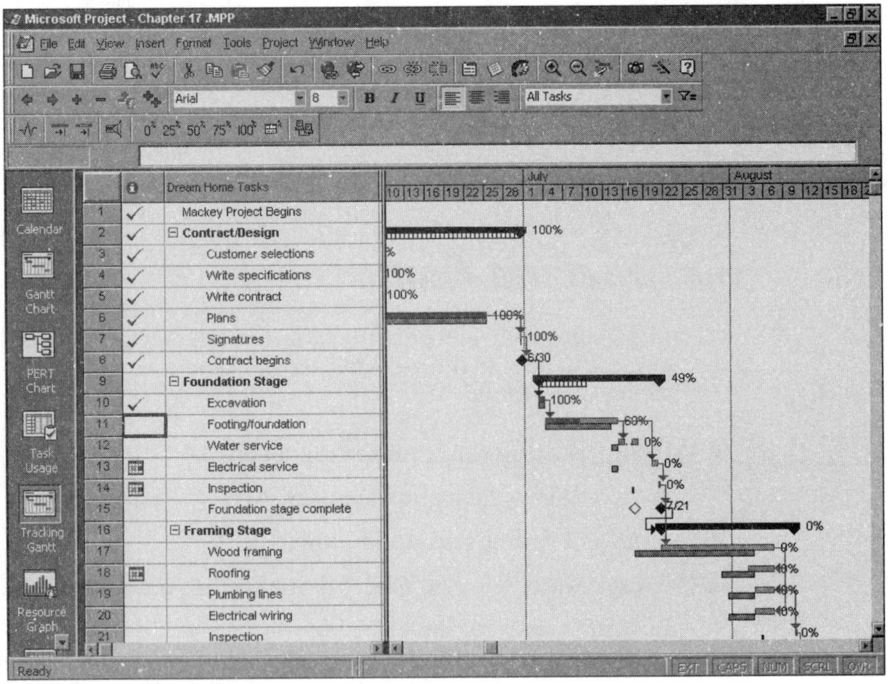

Figure 17-13: The Tracking Gantt view enables you to compare baseline dates with actual dates.

Chapter 18

Personalizing Your Project Environment

In This Chapter

- Customizing tables to see what you want
- Customizing bars to highlight Gantt chart attributes
- Adding recurring tasks for those weekly meetings
- Changing default views to fit your needs
- Customizing toolbars to group your favorite shortcuts

Telling you how to make your project environment unique is a self-contradictory task — something like my teenagers having to be themselves by conforming to their peers. Ah, life! But I've never been accused of doing only sensible things, so here is an oxymoron chapter of standard ways to personalize your work environment.

This is written in question-and-answer format because, well, I needed to personalize my writing environment for writing a chapter about personal environments. Also, the only way this subject makes sense is by using some mini case studies. But don't think that someone actually wrote and asked me these questions — I asked the questions so that you may consider the answers as samples of what can be accomplished.

In this chapter, you do a bunch of stuff to make the workspace more personal. By using the same approach in other ways, you can truly make yourself at home with Microsoft Project.

Open the workspace file called `Chapter 18.MPW` from the Project folder as follows:

1. **Click the Open button on the standard toolbar.**
2. **Open the Project folder on your hard drive or on the *Microsoft Project 98 For Dummies* CD-ROM.**
3. **Double-click Chapter 18.MPW.**

Customizing the Gantt Chart Entry Table

Question: *I want the resource names next to the task names in the Gantt chart. What do I do?*

Good idea! Why didn't I think of that? You need to do some column work to put resources next to tasks. Use the Office Remodel Project for this example. To customize columns:

1. **Choose Window⇨Sample1 Chapter 18.MPP.**

   The Office Remodel window becomes active.

2. **Select the Duration column head and right-click.**

   A shortcut menu appears.

3. **Choose Insert Column.**

   The Column Definition dialog box appears, as shown in Figure 18-1.

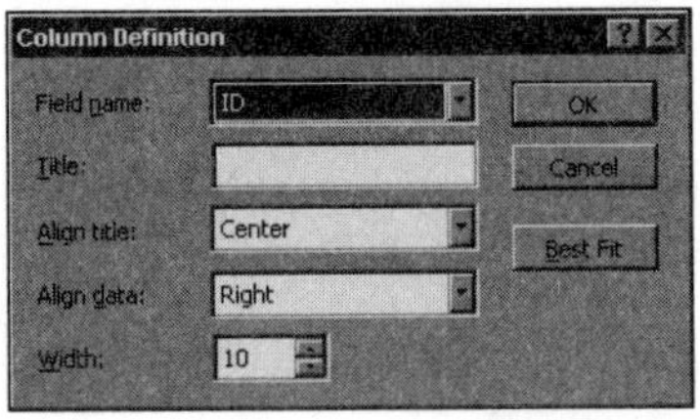

Figure 18-1: Use the Column Definition dialog box to set column field conditions.

4. **In the Field Name box, select Resource Names.**
5. **In the Title text box, type something original, such as** Reese Horses.
6. **In the Align Title box, select Left.**
7. **Rather than assign a character width, click the Best Fit button.**

   The column appears between the Task Name and Duration columns, as shown in Figure 18-2. You may have to scroll horizontally to bring the Duration column into view — but don't worry, it's there.

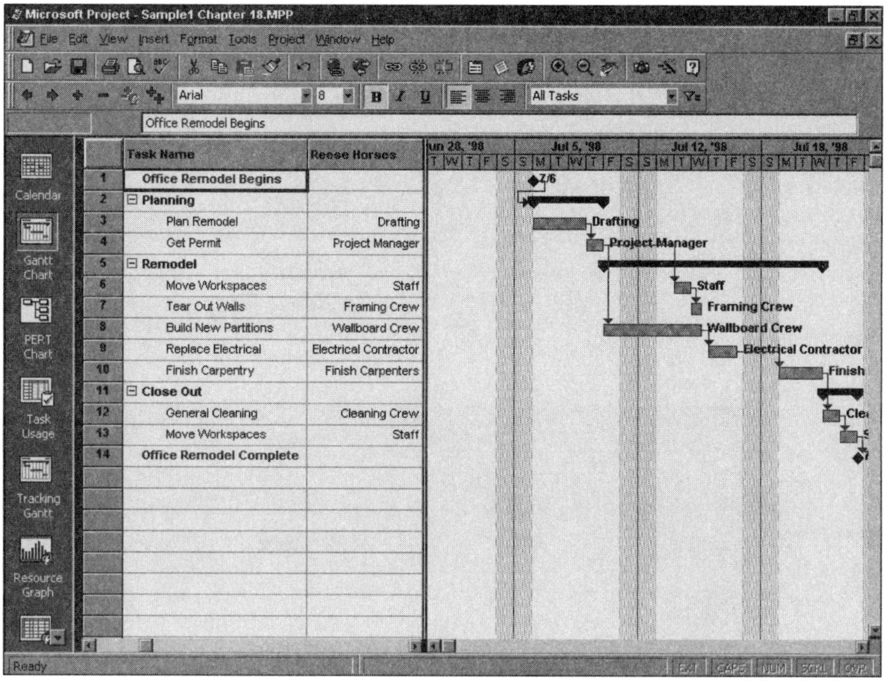

Figure 18-2: Drag and scroll to bring the information into view on the Gantt chart.

Scheduling with the Gantt Chart

Question: *I get visually confused by nonworking time. When a task duration is going across a nonworking day, I can't tell if the nonworking time applies toward the duration of a task. What can I do?*

Glad you asked. One good way to remove any doubt about tasks spanning nonworking time is to put the nonworking time on top of the tasks. You can keep using the Office Remodel project for the example. To put the nonworking time on top:

1. **Double-click the open space representing nonworking time on the Gantt chart.**

   The Timescale dialog box appears, as shown in Figure 18-3.

2. **Select the In Front of Task Bars option.**
3. **Click OK.**

   The Gantt chart now hides tasks in nonworking times, as shown in Figure 18-4.

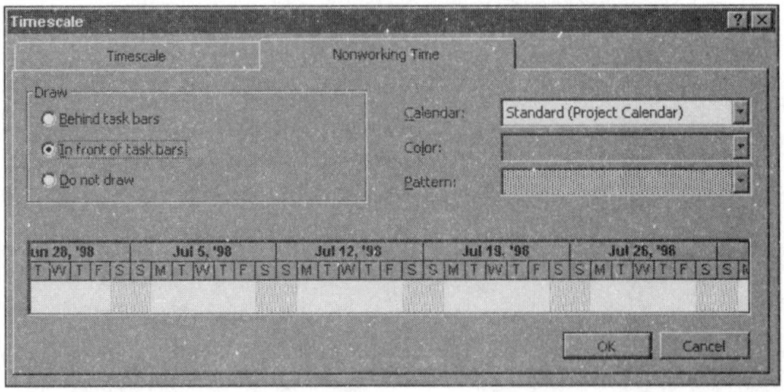

Figure 18-3: The Timescale dialog box provides options for customizing working and nonworking time.

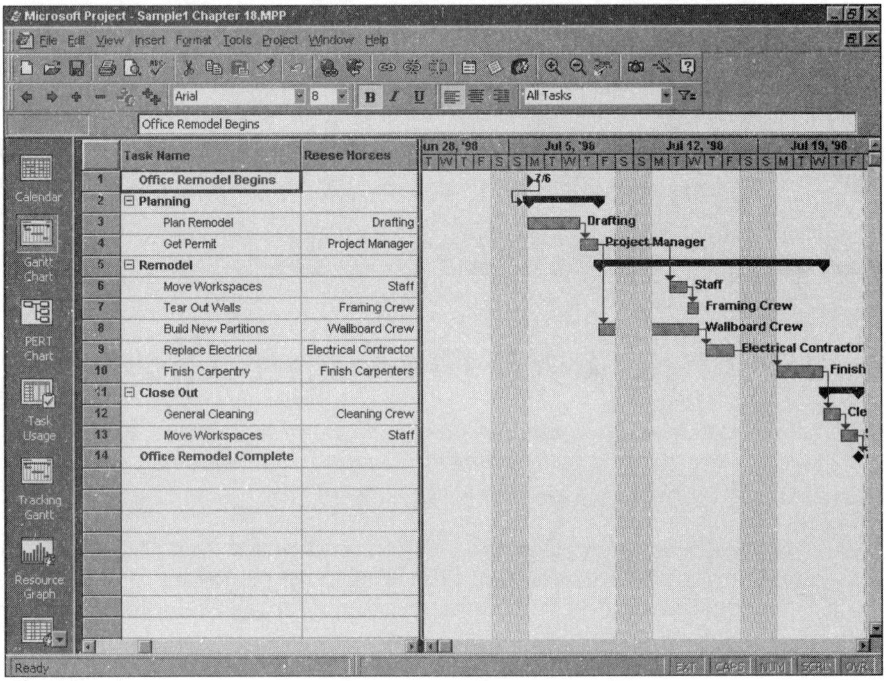

Figure 18-4: The Gantt chart durations haven't changed. The taskbars are behind the nonworking time, which more clearly represents task inactivity.

Question: *How do I change the look of bars on the Gantt chart?*

You can change the format of one bar on the Gantt chart by first double-clicking it. Or, to change the format of all the bars, double-click the chart background. Either way, double-clicking displays the Bar Styles dialog box, from which you can make your format changes. For example, in the following example, you make changes to the bars in `Sample2 Chapter 18.MPP`:

1. **Choose Window⇨2 Sample2 Chapter 18.MPP.**

   The Warren Home project is now the active window.

2. **Double-click anywhere in the working time area of the Gantt chart.**

   The Bar Styles dialog box appears, as shown in Figure 18-5. The Bars tab has options for the Start Shape, Middle Bar, and End Shape for each task category. Feel free to use your imagination to change the settings any way you want.

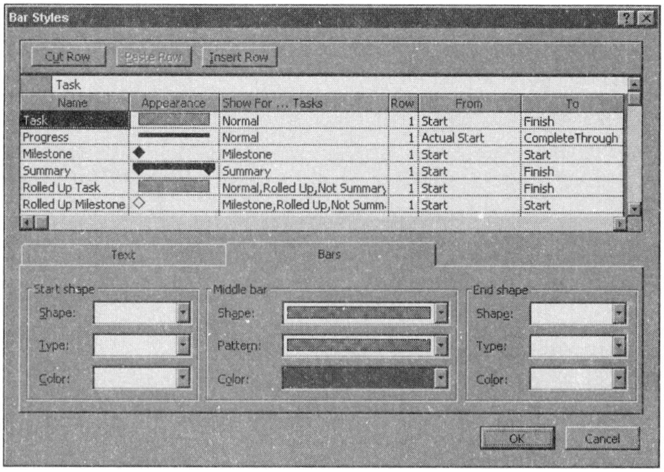

Figure 18-5: The Bar Styles dialog box shows default settings for all task categories.

Question: *I get confused aligning task names with bars. What should I do?*

This one's simple. All you need to do is add gridlines to the Gantt chart as follows:

1. **Right-click anywhere in the Gantt chart.**

   The Gantt shortcut dialog box appears.

2. **Choose Gridlines.**

3. **In the Line to Change list, select Gantt Rows.**

4. **Under Normal, choose a line type and color, as shown in Figure 18-6.**

   As an alternative, you can choose At Interval to add a second series of gridlines at row intervals of 2, 3, 4, or any number from 5 to 99 (using the Other option).

5. **Click OK.**

   The Gantt chart now has gridlines.

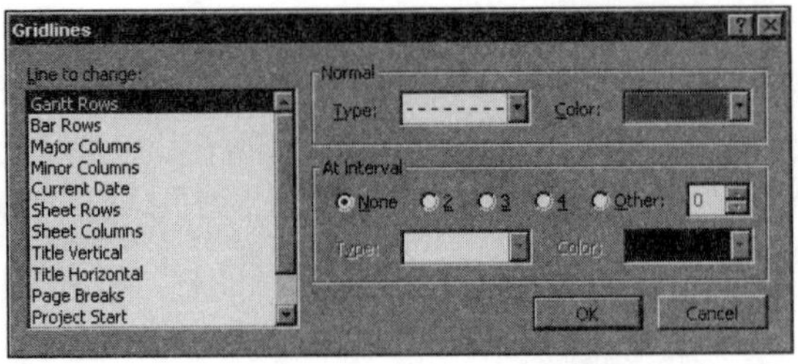

Figure 18-6: Use this dialog box to specify the pattern, color, and interval spacing of gridlines.

Recurring Tasks

Question: *I have to insert a bunch of weekly staff meetings into a project. How can I do this?*

Microsoft Project provides a shortcut for entering recurring tasks such as weekly staff meetings. Again, use the Warren Home project for an example:

1. **Choose Insert⇨Recurring Task.**

   The Recurring Task Information dialog box appears, as shown in Figure 18-7.

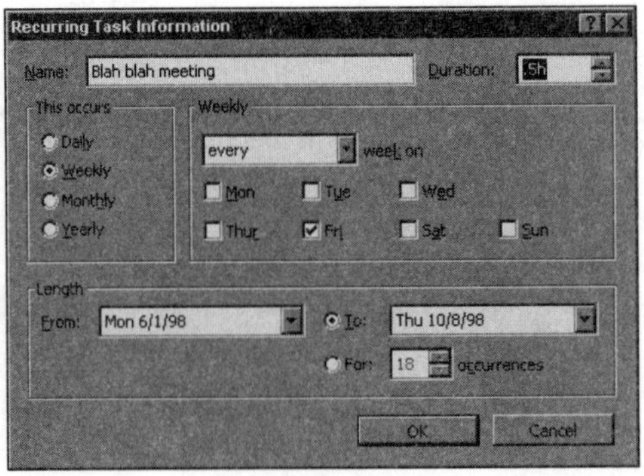

Figure 18-7: The recurring task must be a new task; you can't edit an existing one.

2. **Enter the task name, the duration, and the frequency of occurrence.**

   If you select a recurring task that falls on a nonworking day, a dialog box asks whether you want it rescheduled.

3. **Click OK.**

   The Gantt chart now displays the weekly meetings.

Personalizing Your Workspace

Question: *Enough with this Gantt chart! How do I make something else the default view?*

Yeah, the Gantt chart gets tiring after a while, doesn't it? You can change the default view as follows:

1. **Choose Tools⇨Options.**

   The Options dialog box appears.

2. **Select the View tab.**
3. **In Default View, select another view.**
4. **Click OK.**

Customizing the Toolbar

Question: *Most of the time, I use only one button from the tracking toolbar. Can I put it into the formatting toolbar?*

Microsoft Project lets you make a toolbar longer by dragging buttons onto it. To do so:

1. **Make sure that the toolbar you want to customize is visible.**

   If it isn't, right-click anywhere among the toolbars and select a toolbar from the shortcut menu.

2. **Select View⇨Toolbars⇨Customize.**

   The Customize dialog box appears.

3. **Choose the Commands tab.**
4. **In the Categories group, select the toolbar containing the button you want to move.**
5. **Drag the button from the commands group to the new toolbar.**

TIP

You can also place any button on any toolbar by right-clicking in the toolbar area and selecting Customize. Thanks for all the tough questions. Play hard with your project files. The work will follow.

Part VI

Telling the World How It's Going

"NAAAH - HE'S NOT THAT SMART. HE WON'T BACK UP HIS HARD DISK, FORGETS TO CONSISTENTLY NAME HIS FILES, AND DROOLS ALL OVER THE KEYBOARD."

In this part . . .

This is a bit much, you say. An entire part dedicated to printing? Why not just click the Print button? Yep. You can do that. If you want, skip this entire part. It's valuable only if you're interested in enhancing and customizing the look and effectiveness of your project communication. In this part, you use print preview and set margins, headers and footers, and legends. You also find out how to customize a bunch of standard reports and how to create reports from scratch.

So, before you click that Print button, you may want to give this part at least a little consideration.

Chapter 19

Previewing and Printing Views

In This Chapter

- Using Print Preview as an editing tool
- Setting margins to complement your project
- Setting headers and footers with information and graphics
- Setting legends properly for reference

Congratulations! Your project is a masterpiece. It's rich with resources, tight on the tasks, realistic about risks, and correct about costs. Only one challenge remains. You need to make the plan a basis of understanding among everyone involved in the project.

In many ways, a project plan is only as valuable as your ability to communicate it. Unfortunately, communicating isn't always easy to do. Clear and simple communication can be a moving target. The kind and quantity of information needed vary dramatically from day to day and from one group to the next. Project team members need to know schedules and resource allocations. Accountants require access to cost information. Managers must be kept abreast of work. Stakeholders want to know how things are going.

Sometimes too much information is as disastrous as too little. Other times, information is proprietary or sensitive. In some circumstances, the back of a napkin is sufficient; other circumstances require a full-blown presentation. With Microsoft Project, you can dig in, find what you're looking for, determine what and how much you'll report, customize the manner of presentation, and print the results.

If you have your own project in the works, you may want to use it rather than the sample file provided for this chapter. Otherwise, open the sample project file called `Chapter 19.MPP` from the Project folder. To do so:

1. **Click the Open button on the standard toolbar.**
2. **Open the Project folder on your hard drive or on the *Microsoft Project 98 For Dummies* CD-ROM.**
3. **Double-click Chapter 19.MPP.**

   The file should open in the Gantt Chart view.

Sending the World Your Views

Printing a view can be as simple as clicking the Print button on the standard toolbar. The value of this approach is also its deficiency. Click the button, and the computer prints the view with a bunch of default settings.

In many instances, this print option is exactly what the circumstances call for. But when you need a lot more control of the print function, a great alternative is just one button to the right on the standard toolbar. Print Preview's the name, and functionality's the game. (Sorry.)

Getting Around in Print Preview

For this example, make sure that the project is in Gantt view and set to the default timescale, as shown in Figure 19-1.

Click the Print Preview button on the standard toolbar. The Print Preview screen appears, as shown in Figure 19-2. The toolbar at the top has directional arrows that enable you to jump from page to page of your view. The number of pages in print preview is Microsoft Project's calculation of how many pages it takes to see whatever was in view when you chose the Print Preview command. If you zoom out before clicking the Print Preview button, fewer pages are printed. If you zoom in, more pages are printed.

TIP

The status bar at the bottom of the window displays the current page number, the page count, and a description of the layout.

The toolbar also has a magnifying glass and a single page button. These buttons are copycats of mouse cursor functions. As you move your cursor around the screen, the cursor turns into a magnifying glass. If you click somewhere on the screen, the information zooms to be readable and the window becomes scrollable. Click again, and it zooms back out. The same functions occur when you use the two corresponding toolbar buttons.

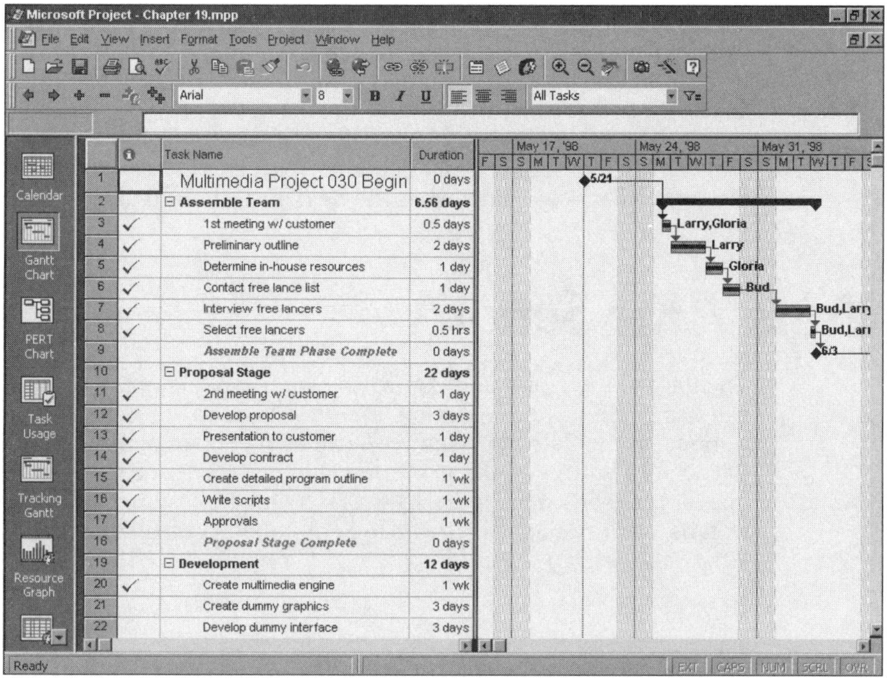

Figure 19-1: Print preview is based on whatever screen you happen to be in when you choose it. Any filters or sorts are carried into the view.

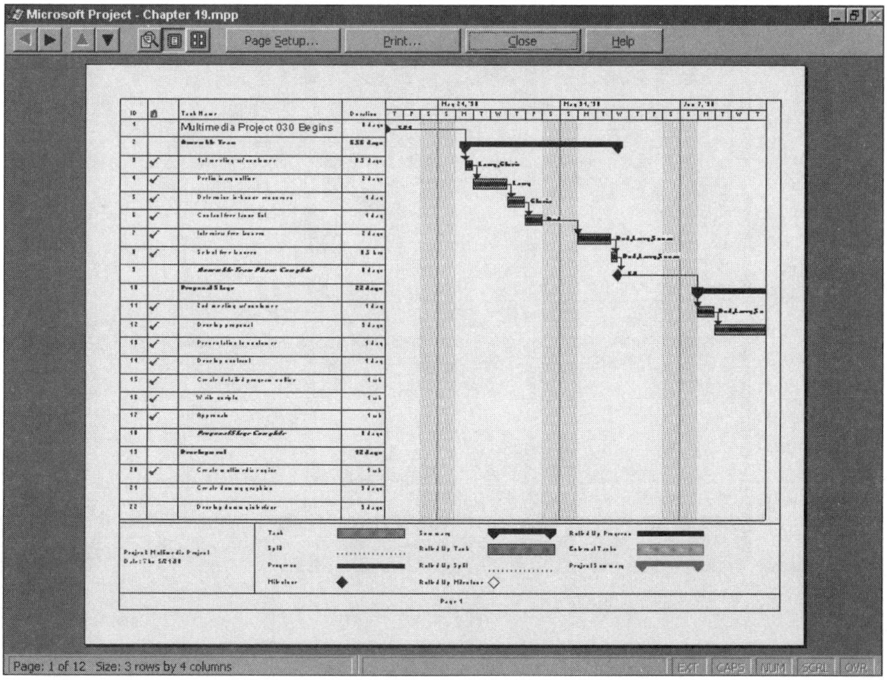

Figure 19-2: The Print Preview command displays the view as it will be printed.

Big deal, you say! Project managers are renowned for their patience, so please humor me a little longer. Click the Multiple Pages button on the toolbar. Microsoft Project displays the whole view as it will appear in print, as shown in Figure 19-3.

You can change some or all default settings and preview your work as you make the changes. That's what the next section is all about.

Using Page Setup

The Page Setup command controls certain aspects of the printed view. You can designate page orientation, margins, headers, footers, legends, and view options. In the Calendar view, you can also control units of time. Click the Page Setup button on the print preview toolbar. The Page Setup dialog box appears, as shown in Figure 19-4. The dialog box is divided into six sections, or tabs. (You can access the Page Setup dialog box also by choosing File⇨Page Setup.)

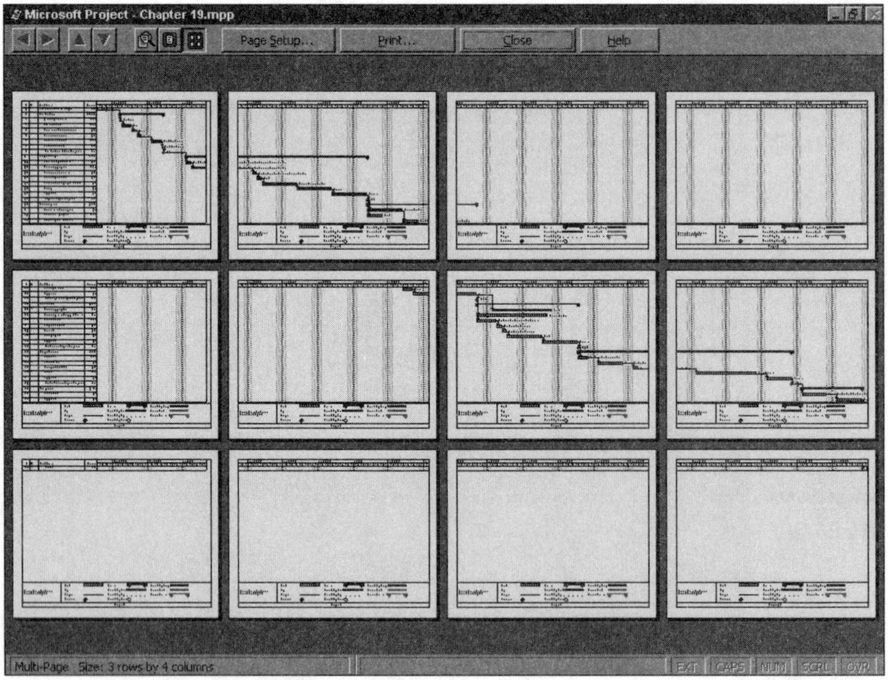

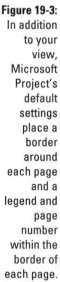

Figure 19-3: In addition to your view, Microsoft Project's default settings place a border around each page and a legend and page number within the border of each page.

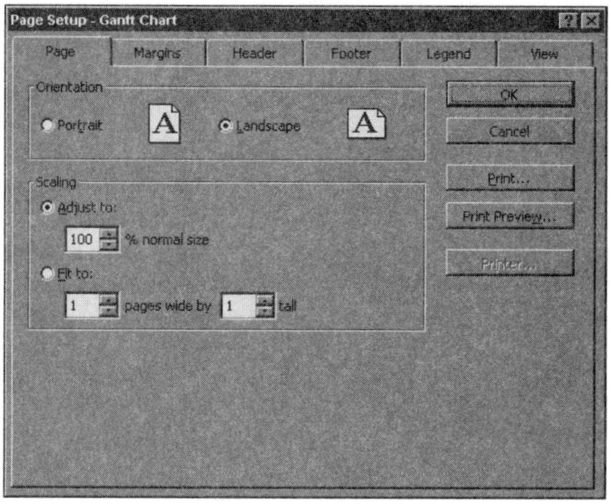

Figure 19-4: When more than one project is active, the changes to the Page Setup dialog box apply to only the file whose view is displayed.

Setting the page

The Page tab offers two sets of options. The first, Orientation, permits Portrait (vertical) and Landscape (horizontal) selections. Microsoft Project defaults to the Landscape selection. The second set of options, Scaling, enables you to size the project to a fit that best serves your printout needs.

Setting the margins

Now click the Margins tab. Two sets of options appear, as shown in Figure 19-5. If you want, in the first set of options, change the margins to see the effects of the change in the Sample box. You can further study the effect by clicking OK. The Print Preview screen adjusts to display your change. The second set of options, Borders Around, has two active selections in a Gantt view. You can turn the borders off or on around each page.

Setting headers

The Header tab offers a number of options for creating a header. For the next example, you put the project manager's name and the current date in the header on the right margin of each page:

1. **Click the Header tab.**
2. **In the Alignment area, select Right.**
3. **In the list box at the bottom of the screen, select Manager Name.**

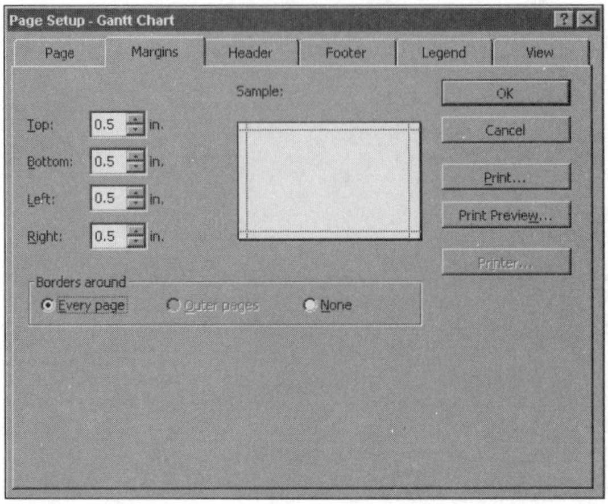

Figure 19-5: The inactive option, Outer Pages, is available in a PERT Chart view.

4. **Click the Add button next to the list box.**

   Manager Name appears in the Selection box on the Right tab. The project manager's name appears in the Sample box.

5. **Make sure that the cursor is to the right of [Manager] and press Enter.**

   The cursor in the Selection box on the Right tab drops to the next line.

6. **This time, instead of using the list box, click the Filename Code button (labeled in Figure 19-6).**

   The Filename code — &[File] — appears on the second line in the Selection box.

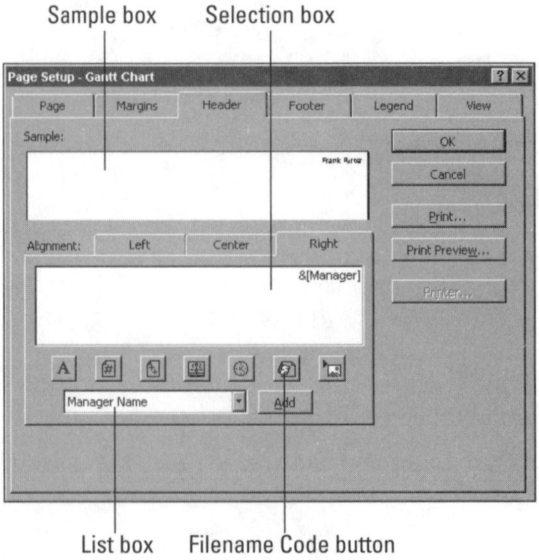

Figure 19-6: The Header tab of the Page Setup dialog box.

7. **Add text to the first line of code in the Selection box by positioning your cursor in front of the code and typing** Manager: **(be sure to include a space after the colon).**

   The dialog box should now look like Figure 19-7.

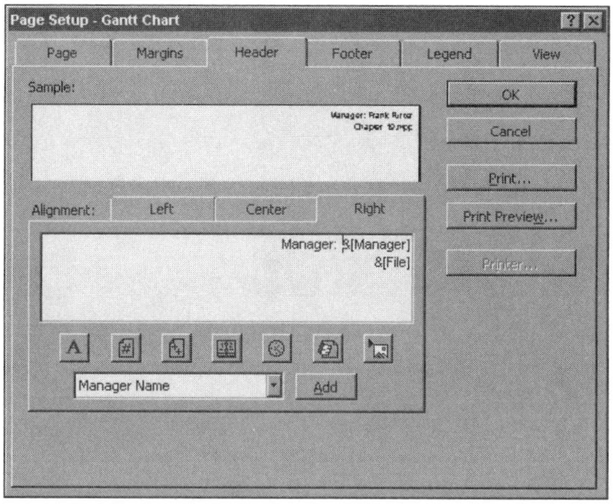

Figure 19-7: You can customize the manager name and other goodies.

One more thing before leaving the Header tab. Change the text style of the header. To do so:

1. **Highlight the first line of code.**

   Drag your cursor over the entire manager line.

2. **Click the Text Styles button (the *A*).**

   The Text Styles dialog box appears.

3. **In the Font list box, select Times New Roman.**
4. **In the Font Style list box, select Bold.**
5. **In the Font Size list box, select 16.**
6. **Click OK.**

   The Page Setup dialog box should now look like Figure 19-8.

To better see your work, click OK in the Page Setup dialog box. Then click the header once to get a close-up view, as shown in Figure 19-9.

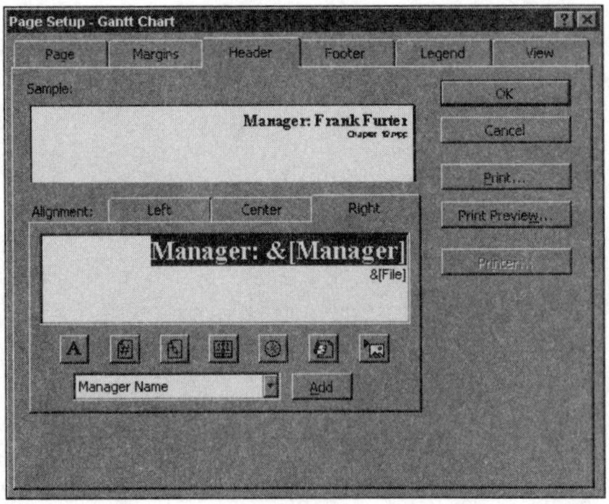

Figure 19-8: The first line is now bold. The header is limited to a maximum of three lines.

Setting footers

Click the Page Setup button to return to the Page Setup dialog box. Now click the Footer tab. The Footer tab has the same options as the Header tab. Because they're a repeat, I won't detail these options for you. But before you leave the footer, notice that Microsoft Project places a default page number in the center alignment area of the footer tab. You can remove or modify the page number if you want.

Setting the legend

You use the Legend tab to add text to the legend area of the printed view. The legend describes the meaning of the various bars and other symbols used in the Gantt chart or other charts.

Click the Legend tab in the Page Setup dialog box, and the screen shown in Figure 19-10 appears. The text options are the same in the Legend tab as they are in the Header and Footer tabs, with two additions. One additional option enables you to determine whether the legend should appear on every page, on its own page, or not at all. The other option lets you determine the width in inches for the text portion of the legend. After you have finished looking at the Page Setup features, click OK.

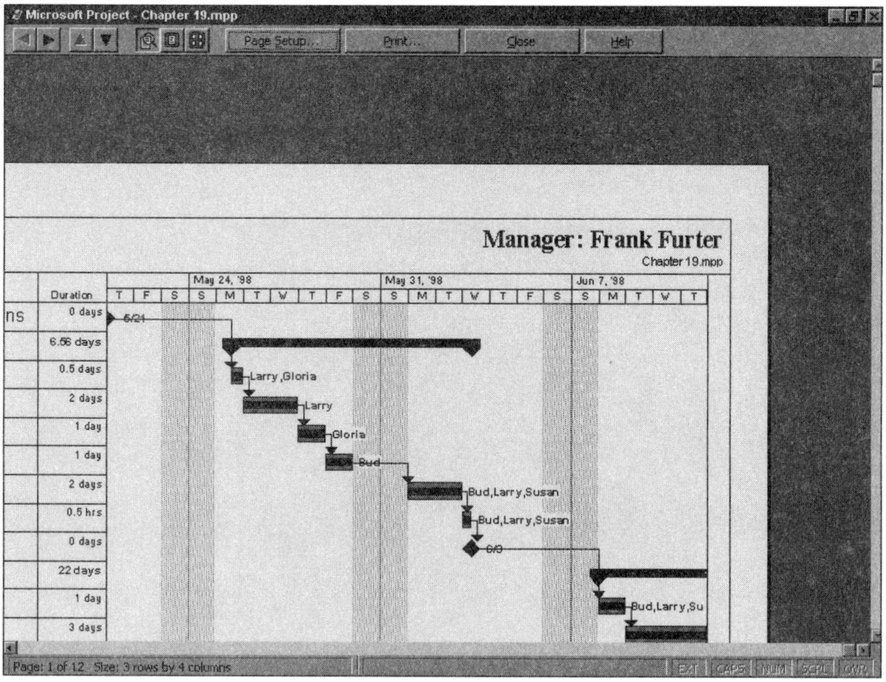

Figure 19-9: The header appears on every page of the printed view.

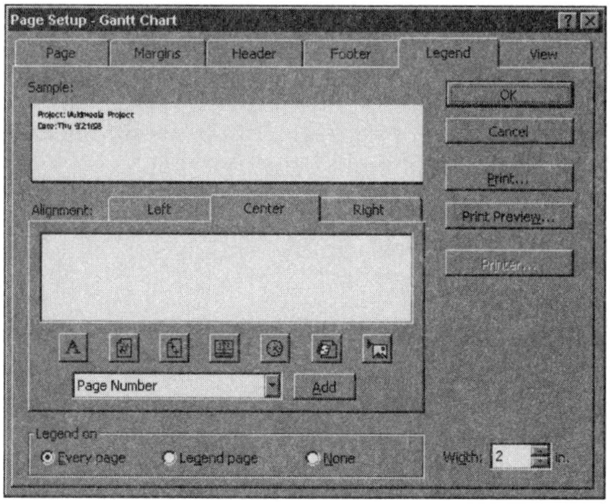

Figure 19-10: The Width option allows a text box from 0 to 5 inches in the legend portion of the page.

Printing Views

After you determine the page setup, you can move to the print options. Click the Print button in the print preview toolbar. The Print dialog box appears, as shown in Figure 19-11.

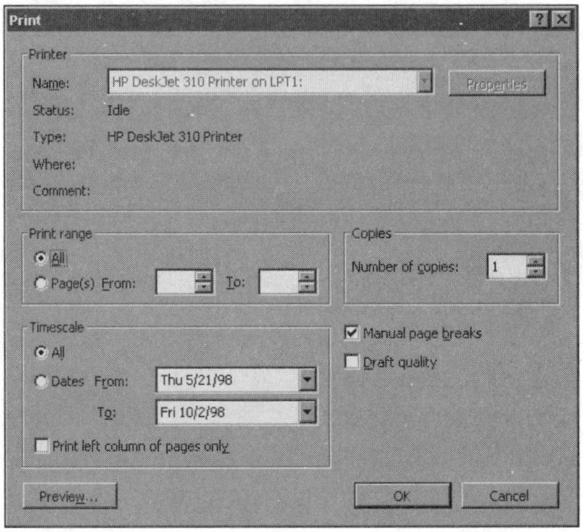

Figure 19-11: Instead of clicking the Print button, you can press Ctrl+P.

From the print preview toolbar, the Print dialog box offers four groups of options:

- **Print Range:** Select All to print all pages of the view. Select Pages From to print a range of pages as listed in Print Preview.
- **Printer:** Inactive in the dialog box shown in Figure 19-11. If you need to change your printer selection, do so by closing the Print Preview screen and choosing File⇨Print.
- **Timescale:** Select All to print all pages of the view. Select Dates to enter different start and finish dates in the From and To boxes.
- **Copies:** Type the number of copies to be printed.

When you are finished with the Print dialog box, click OK to print and then return to the Gantt Chart view.

Chapter 20

Using and Customizing Reports

In This Chapter

- Choosing from among 22 standard reports
- Customizing reports to tell the story your own way
- Creating reports for specific purposes

As much as you've come to love the Gantt Chart and PERT Chart views, you just can't take them to all the nice places. Some people will politely ask you to leave them at the door or in the car with the windows slightly rolled down. Fear not, Microsoft Project provides a solution — reports. You can take them anywhere.

Reports summarize and present specific information in an organized manner. They're designed to focus on trends or aspects of your project in a manner appropriate for the intended stakeholder or project team member.

Microsoft Project provides five kinds of reports, as listed in the next section. A sixth category, Custom, is described later in the chapter.

ON THE CD

If you have your own project in the works, you may want to use it rather than the sample file provided for this chapter. Otherwise, open the sample project file called `Chapter 20.MPP` from the Project folder as follows:

1. **Click the Open button on the standard toolbar.**
2. **Open the Project folder on your hard drive or on the *Microsoft Project 98 For Dummies* CD-ROM.**
3. **Double-click Chapter 20.MPP.**

   The file should open in the Gantt Chart view.

Using Standard Reports

Five kinds of reports are ready-made and just waiting to be printed. You can use them as they are, or you can tweak them to meet your specific needs. To access the five kinds of reports, choose View⇨Reports. The Reports dialog box appears, as shown in Figure 20-1.

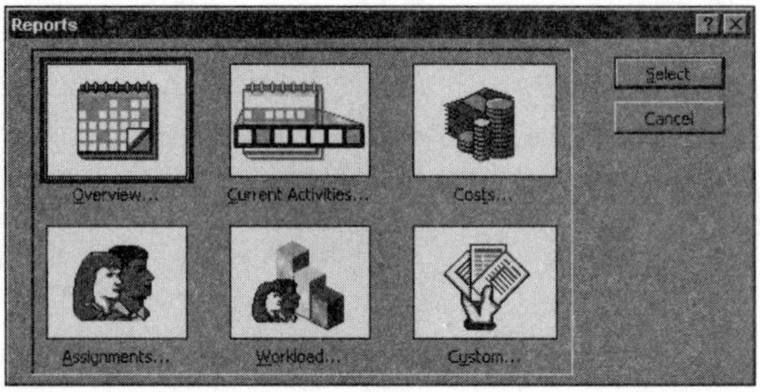

Figure 20-1: The Reports dialog box provides five categories of reports.

Following is a description of each of the reports in their categories:

Category	*Type*	*Displays*
Overview	Project Summary	The most important project information
	Top-Level Tasks	Information about top-level tasks
	Critical Tasks	Critical tasks for the project; includes summary tasks and successor tasks
	Milestones	Milestone tasks with their summary tasks
	Working Days	Working and nonworking times for resources
Current Activities	Unstarted Tasks	Tasks that haven't begun; includes predecessors and resources
	Tasks Starting Soon	Tasks that haven't started yet, given the bookend dates you specify
	Tasks in Progress	Tasks in progress and their resources' schedules

Category	*Type*	*Displays*
	Completed Tasks	Tasks completed in by-month breakdown
	Should Have Started	Tasks that should have Tasks started by a date you specify; includes summary tasks and successors
	Slipping Tasks	Tasks behind schedule; includes their summary tasks and successors
Costs	Cash Flow	Costs-per-task in one-week periods using a Crosstab report
	Budget	Budget for all tasks
	Overbudget Tasks	Overbudget tasks for the project
	Overbudget Resources	Overbudget resources for the project
	Earned Value	Earned value information for all tasks
Assignments	Who Does What	Task schedules for all resources
	Who Does What When	Tasks, their resources, and work using a Crosstab report
	To-Do List	Weekly tasks for the resource you specify
	Overallocated Resources	Overallocated resources of the entire project
Workload	Task Usage	Resources assigned to tasks, including work information and totals, using a Crosstab Report
	Resource Usage	Tasks assigned to resources, including work information and totals, using a Crosstab report

A good way to envision a crosstab report is to think of a mileage chart. In this type of chart, you find the distance between two cities by finding the box that is the intersection of the horizontal line representing one city listing and the vertical line representing the other city listing.

For the next example, double-click Overview in the Reports dialog box. The Overview Reports dialog box appears, as shown in Figure 20-2.

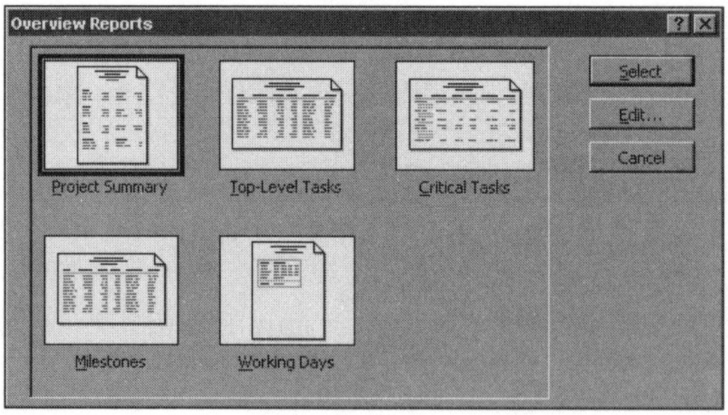

Figure 20-2: The Overview Reports dialog box doesn't offer an editing option.

Double-click the Critical Tasks report. The report is opened in Print Preview, as shown in Figure 20-3, which provides the opportunity to customize the orientation, the margins, and the header and footer.

Customizing a Report

Click the Close button in the print preview toolbar. You're back to the Reports dialog box. One special selection I haven't discussed yet is the

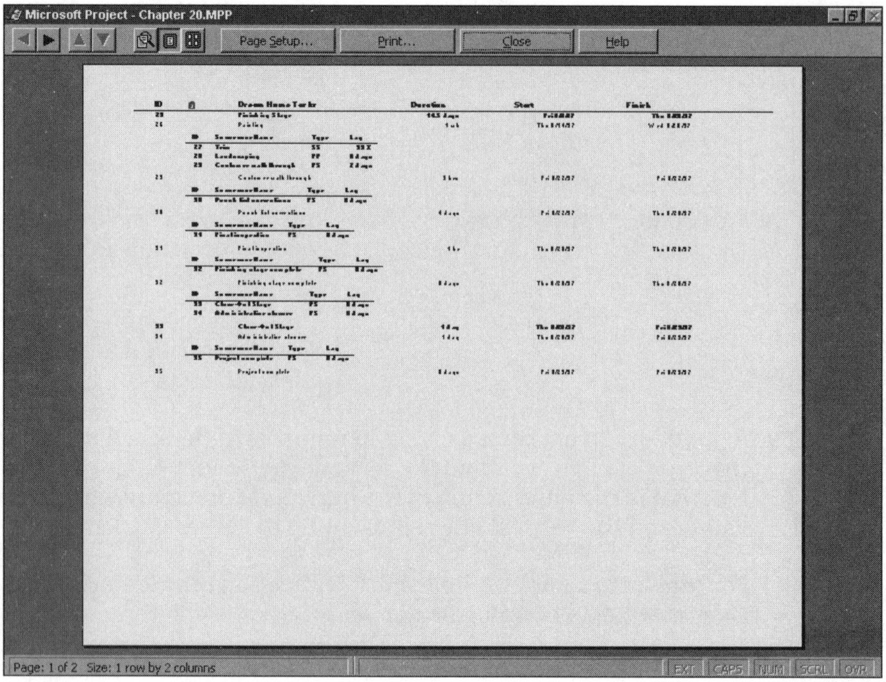

Figure 20-3: The Print Preview of reports works in the same manner as the Print Preview of chart views.

Custom reports option. By choosing this option, you are telling yourself (and soon the world) that there is no fit like a tailored one. Good isn't enough. Unless it's pleated and tucked with your own aesthetic and intellectual insight, it's just not the very best you and your public have come to expect. My! You look mahvelous.

Double-click the Custom category, and the Custom Reports dialog box appears, as shown in Figure 20-4.

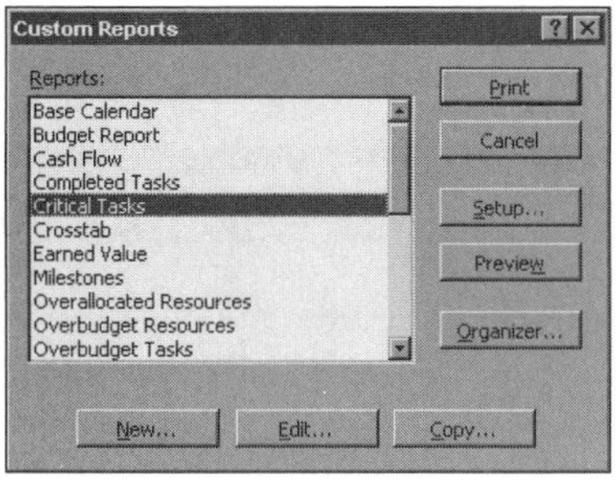

Figure 20-4: The Custom Reports dialog box offers the options of editing, copying, and creating reports.

You'll customize the Critical Tasks report so that it presents information in a highlighted format instead of an isolated format. The highlighted format shows critical tasks highlighted among all the other tasks. An isolated format displays only critical tasks. To customize the Critical Tasks report in a highlighted format:

1. **In the Reports list, highlight the Critical Tasks report.**
2. **Click the Edit button at the bottom of the Custom Reports dialog box and then click the Definition tab if it's not already selected.**

   The Task Report dialog box appears, as shown in Figure 20-5. The Task Report dialog box offers highlighted (rather than isolated) reports, gray bands to separate tasks, and the opportunity to include summary tasks.
3. **Select the Highlight option and click OK.**

   You return to the Custom Reports dialog box.
4. **Click the Preview button.**

   The revised report appears in Print Preview.
5. **Scroll to see a low-resolution-quality representation of the highlighted critical tasks, as shown in Figure 20-6.**

   The highlighted critical tasks are sufficiently readable when they are printed in the report.

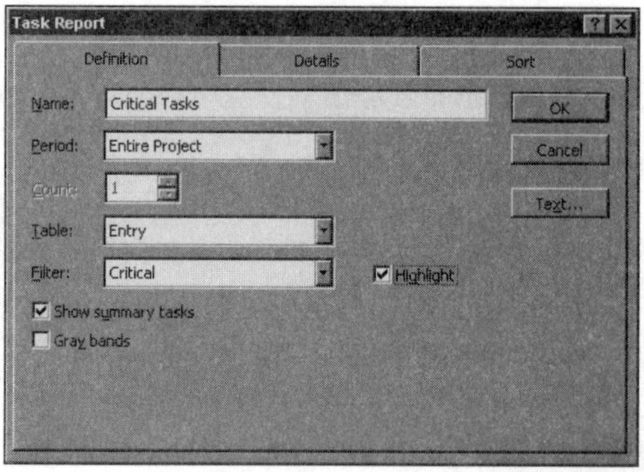

Figure 20-5: The Task Report dialog box offers highlighted reports.

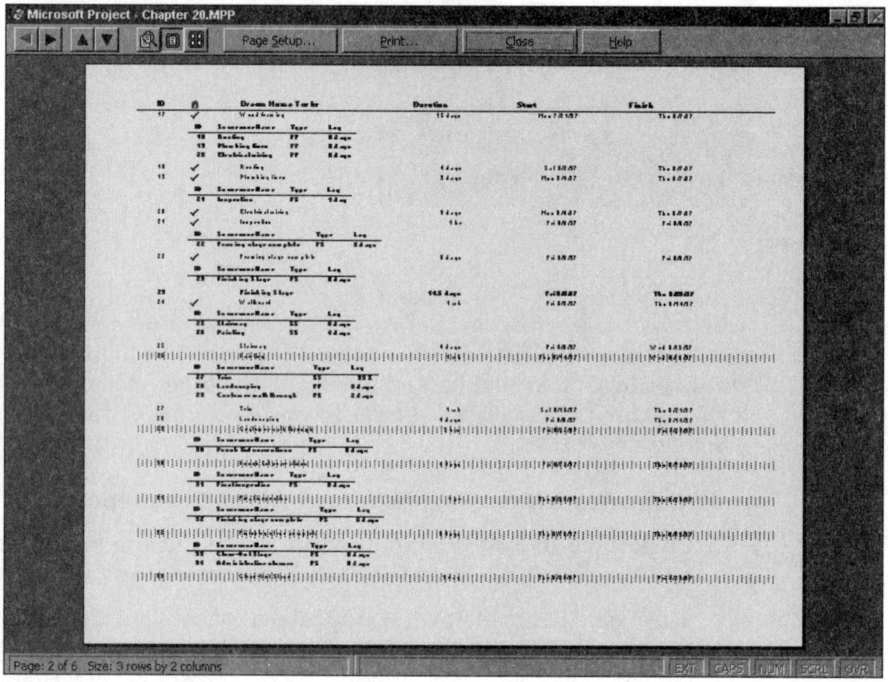

Figure 20-6: You can skip the Print Preview by choosing Print in the Custom Reports dialog box.

Creating a Report

To create a report from scratch, click the New button in the Custom Reports dialog box. The Define New Report dialog box appears. The dialog box offers you four choices:

Task	Schedule, cost, information about work, and task details
Resource	Schedule, cost, information about work, and resource details
Monthly Calendar	Graphical representations of a calendar with tasks depicted as bars, lines, or start and finish dates
Crosstab	Information about tasks and resources over a period of time

For the next example, you create a Monthly Calendar report for the resources on the Construction Hours calendar. To do so:

1. **Double-click the Monthly Calendar option.**

   The Monthly Calendar Report Definition dialog box appears, as shown in Figure 20-7.

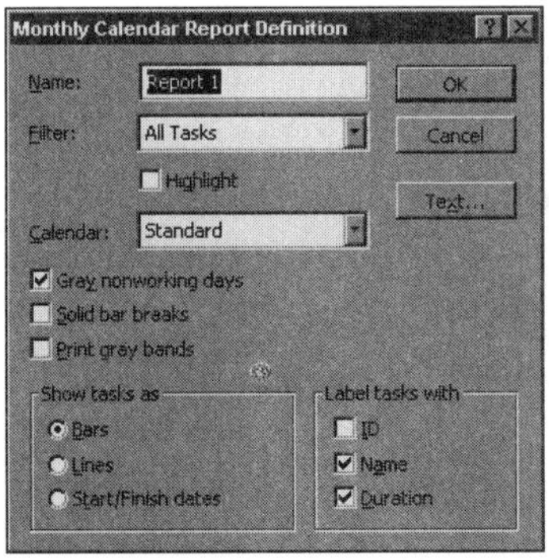

Figure 20-7: The Task, Resource, Monthly Calendar, and Crosstab Report options each have definition dialog boxes.

2. **In the Name text box, type** Construction Hours.
3. **In the Filter list box, select Incompleted Tasks.**
4. **In the Calendar list box, select Construction Hours Calendar.**
5. **Click OK.**

   You return to the Custom Reports dialog box.

6. **Click the Preview button.**

   The Monthly Calendar Report appears, as in Figure 20-8, showing all incomplete tasks assigned to resources that use the Construction Hours calendar.

Reports can be important to you as a project manager and to all the stakeholders of the project. They can also be powerful. An entire nation thought Mark Twain was dead because of some false reports. The key to success in reporting is properly presenting correct information at the appropriate time to the right people. Just do that. And be sure to report to us how it goes!

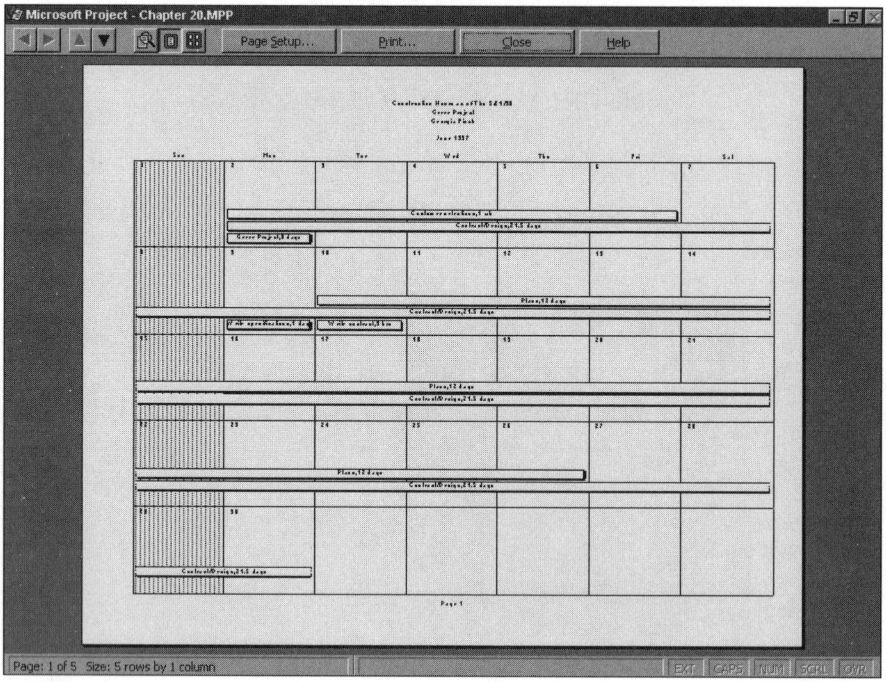

Figure 20-8: You can skip the empty calendar pages by designating the pages you want to print.

Part VII
The Part of Tens

In this part . . .

The two chapters in this part serve as an introduction to the many toolbars of Microsoft Project and an introduction to the world of project management. This part suggests ways that you can increase the efficiency of your project as well as your stature as a project manager. I hope you have a big garage for storing all these tools. And here's betting that you're pleasantly surprised about all services dedicated to making your project a success.

Chapter 21

Ten Terrific Toolbars

In This Chapter

- Finding toolbars to suit your needs
- Using toolbars as shortcuts

Toolbars are a handy way to access commands. But, just like any other accumulation of tools, toolbars can make your job easier or they can clutter up your workspace. In fact, one of the quickest ways to spot pros is their skill in knowing what's necessary for the job. The tools they want are at hand. Other tools remain stored until needed.

Microsoft Project offers 12 toolbars. Two of those, the standard and formatting toolbars, are discussed throughout this book. They're like the tape measure and the pencil — always there and available. This chapter briefly describes the other 10 toolbars, each with its own group of goodies.

Open any of the toolbars by right-clicking in the toolbar area and selecting from the toolbar shortcut menu. The toolbars that are currently in view have a check mark next to their names.

TIP

Because you're well on your way to becoming a project management pro, you can also customize any toolbar by adding tools from other toolbars. To do so, just press and hold the Alt key, move the cursor over the tool you need, press and hold your left mouse button, and drag the tool to the appropriate toolbar.

Custom Forms Toolbar

The custom forms toolbar takes you where normal forms seldom tread. A form is a type of view that gives you detailed information about a resource or a task. A typical example of a form is what you see in the Gantt Chart view if you choose Window⇨Split. In the split, the bottom window is the Task form.

The custom forms toolbar, as shown in Figure 21-1, provides shortcuts to performing work you would otherwise do with a standard form. For example, you can select a task or a resource in your project file and then select a custom form tool to modify that task or resource information.

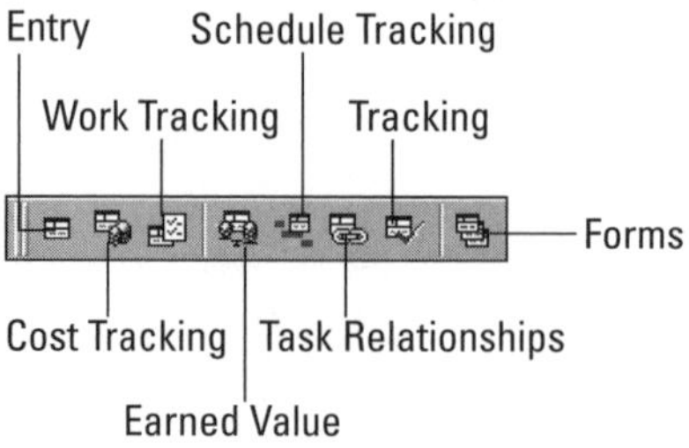

Figure 21-1: The custom forms toolbar.

Button	***What It Does***
Entry	Displays information you would find in the Entry table.
Cost Tracking	Displays a cost tracking form.
Work Tracking	Displays a work tracking form.
Earned Value	Displays an earned value form.
Schedule Tracking	Displays a schedule tracking form.
Task Relationships	Displays a form for reviewing or entering task relationships.
Tracking	Displays a tracking form.
Forms	Displays eight task and four resource forms.

Drawing Toolbar

The drawing toolbar, as shown in Figure 21-2, provides tools that you can use to spiff up your Gantt chart and make it more informative. For example, you can draw a box, add text to the box, color the box, and draw an arrow from the box to a task. You can also attach the box to a task or to a specific place on the project timeline.

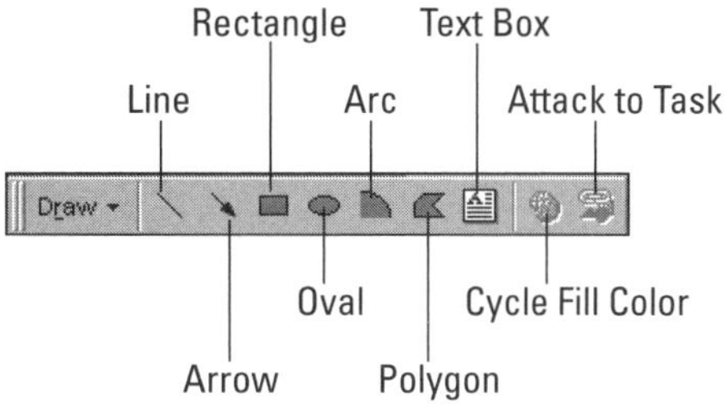

Figure 21-2: The drawing toolbar.

Button	***What It Does***
Draw	Provides a menu of layering options after you select a drawing.
Line	Creates a line as you left-click and drag.
Arrow	Creates an arrowed line as you left-click and drag.
Rectangle	Creates a rectangle as you left-click and drag.
Oval	Creates an oval as you left-click and drag.
Arc	Creates an arc as you left-click and drag. Continue to hold down the left mouse button to move the arc in any direction. After you release the button, the concave area of the arc is filled with white.
Polygon	Creates a polygon as you left-click, release, move to another spot, left-click, and so on. Complete the polygon by clicking over the original point. Adjust the polygon shaping by clicking one of the handles that surround the polygon after you select it.
Text Box	Creates a text box as you left-click and drag. Then type your text.
Cycle Fill Color	After you select a drawn object, cycles through 16 colors and a transparent option.
Attach to Task	Somewhat hampered by a misleading name, provides a number of editing functions for a drawn object, such as changing the object's size in precise increments, attaching the object to a date or a task, and selecting a custom line color, line size, and pattern.

Microsoft Project 95 Toolbar

If you're a former user of Microsoft Project 95, you've probably had little difficulty in adjusting to the features and functionality of Microsoft Project 98. But if you're homesick, the Microsoft Project 95 toolbar (as shown in Figure 21-3) may be more to your liking. If you want, use it instead of the standard toolbar. You soon notice that the two toolbars are almost identical.

Figure 21-3: The Microsoft Project 95 toolbar.

Resource Management Toolbar

Resource views and management are discussed in detail in Chapters 7, 12, 14, and 16. This section gives a brief description of each of the shortcuts on the resource management toolbar, as shown in Figure 21-4.

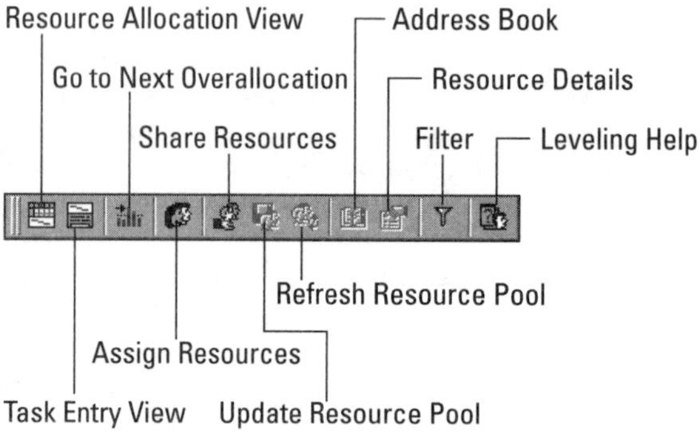

Figure 21-4: The resource management toolbar.

Button	***What It Does***
Resource Allocation View	Displays the Resource Allocation view, which is a split view that contains the Resource Usage view in the top pane and the Leveling Gantt view in the bottom pane.

Task Entry View	Displays the Task Entry view, which is a split view that contains the Gantt Chart view in the upper pane and the Task Form view in the lower pane.
Go to Next Overallocation	A handy shortcut for finding tasks with overallocated resources.
Assign Resources	Opens the Resource Assignment dialog box. (This button is identical to the Assign Resources shortcut on the standard toolbar.)
Share Resources	Opens the Share Resources dialog box, which you can use to assign resources from one project to another.
Update Resource Pool	Provides the means to share your resource pool changes and availability with other managers.
Refresh Resource Pool	Updates your resource pool with changes made to the shared pool by other managers.
Address Book	On a network, displays your e-mail system's address book if the system is MAPI-compliant. (Talk to your network administrator about this.)
Resource Details	Shows a resource's business information and e-mail address.
Filter	An interactive filter that asks you what resource you want to use as the filter. After you select the resource, the filter displays all associated tasks.
Leveling Help	A shortcut to a Help procedure that walks you through the process of leveling resources.

Tracking Toolbar

The tracking toolbar, as shown in Figure 21-5, is discussed in detail in Chapter 17. Following is a brief discussion of each toolbar shortcut.

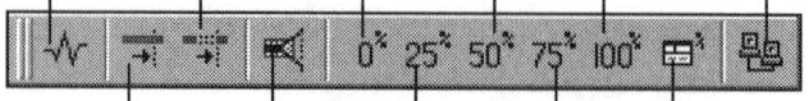

Figure 21-5: The tracking toolbar.

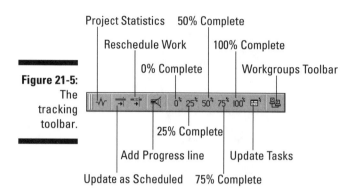

Button	***What It Does***
Project Statistics	Displays the Project Statistics dialog box, which you use to get a thumbnail description of a project's status.
Update as Scheduled	Updates the schedule of selected tasks occurring before the current date.
Reschedule Work	After you have entered a status date, reschedules selected unfinished tasks to begin or continue on the status date. Tasks that have already begun become split tasks.
Add Progress Line	Changes the cursor into a progress line tool and opens a dialog box that designates that date on which the cursor rests. After you click, a progress line is added to the Gantt chart. Peaks to the left of vertical indicate tasks behind schedule. Peaks to the right of vertical indicate tasks ahead of schedule.
0% Complete	Marks selected tasks as not begun.
25% Complete	Marks selected tasks as 25% complete.
50% Complete	Marks selected tasks as 50% complete.
75% Complete	Marks selected tasks as 75% complete.
100% Complete	Marks selected tasks as complete.

Button	*What It Does*
Update Tasks	Opens the Update Tasks dialog box for the task you have selected. Use it to register percent complete, actual or remaining duration, and actual start and finish dates.
Workgroups Toolbar	Toggles the Workgroups toolbar open or closed.

Visual Basic Toolbar

The Visual Basic toolbar, as shown in Figure 21-6, has three tools that run, record, and edit macros, respectively.

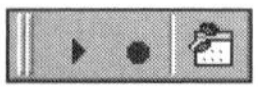

Figure 21-6: The Visual Basic toolbar.

Web Toolbar

Tools on your Web toolbar activate your Web browser to navigate on the World Wide Web or on your intranet. The Web toolbar is shown in Figure 21-7.

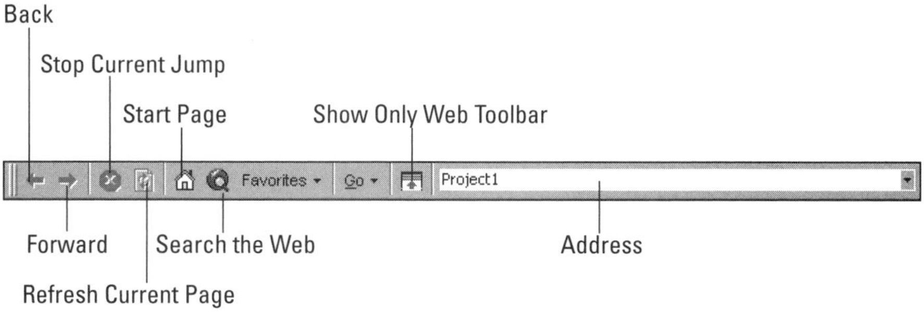

Figure 21-7: The Web toolbar.

Button	*What It Does*
Back	Moves you back a site among sites you've visited during the current session.
Forward	Moves you forward a site among sites you've visited during the current session.
Stop Current Jump	Stops your current hyperlink jump.
Refresh Current Page	Refreshes the current page.
Start Page	Opens your browser's default home page or as you set it in the browser's options.
Search the Web	Opens your browser's search page.
Favorites	Displays your list of favorite sites from your browser.
Go	Displays a shortcut menu of browser functions.
Show Only Web Toolbar	Hides (or unhides) all other visible toolbars excepting the standard and formatting toolbars.
Address	Shows your most recently visited sites.

Workgroups Toolbar

You can use Microsoft Project as a communications tool among team workgroup members. As project manager, you can communicate with team members by using e-mail, an intranet, or the World Wide Web.

If you're planning to communicate with team members via e-mail, all team members must use a 32-bit, MAPI-compliant e-mail system. For Web-based communications, workgroup members need a Web browser, a Web server, network access, a network identifier, and an Internet connection and address. See your network administrator for more information.

What follows is a brief description of each tool on the workgroups toolbar, which is shown in Figure 21-8.

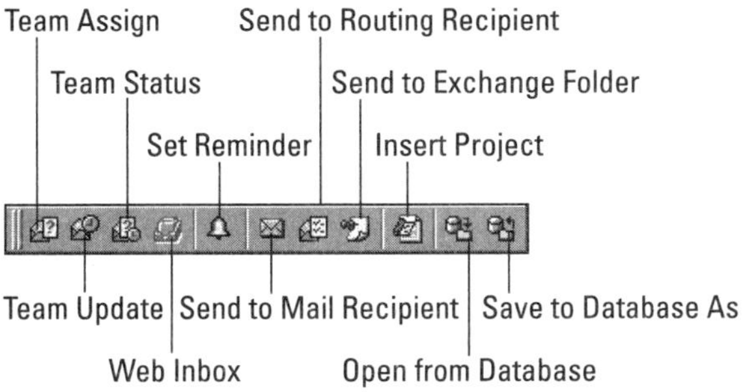

Figure 21-8: The workgroups toolbar.

Button	***What It Does***
Team Assign	Tells a team member that you want to assign him or her to a task or tasks.
Team Update	Informs a team member about changes in his or her assignments.
Team Status	Asks a team member for the current status of task responsibilities.
Web Inbox	Opens the Web Inbox, a message center in Microsoft Project for the project manager to view Web-based messages from team members.
Set Reminder	Sets reminders in Microsoft Office 97's Outlook for selected tasks.
Send to Mail Recipient	Sends e-mail to project team members.
Send to Routing Recipient	Adds or modifies the mail route slip.
Send to Exchange Folder	Sends a copy of the project file to a Microsoft Exchange-based folder.
Insert Project	Inserts another project file into your displayed file.
Open from Database	Opens a project file that was saved to a database.
Save to Database As	Saves a project file to a database file.

Analysis Toolbar

The analysis toolbar, as shown in Figure 21-9, is a simple little thing. It has three shortcuts, one of which is actually a toggle for another toolbar.

Figure 21-9: The analysis toolbar.

Button	***What It Does***
Adjust Dates	Adjusts all the dates in a project.
PERT Analysis	Toggles to open and close the PERT analysis toolbar.
Analyze Timescaled Data in Excel	Starts the Timescaled Data wizard, which takes you through five steps for exporting and graphing timescaled data from your project into Microsoft Excel.

TIP: The Adjust Dates button is one useful tool! For example, if you did a big office move a few years ago and are about to do another one, just whip out your old file, open the analysis toolbar, click the Adjust Tool, change the project start date, and whammo! You have a new up-to-date project.

PERT Analysis Toolbar

The PERT analysis toolbar, as shown in Figure 21-10, has nothing to do with the PERT view. As mentioned in Chapter 10, PERT stands for Program, Evaluation, and Review Technique. PERT analysis is a method for determining probable outcome based on three scenarios: best case, expected case, and worst case.

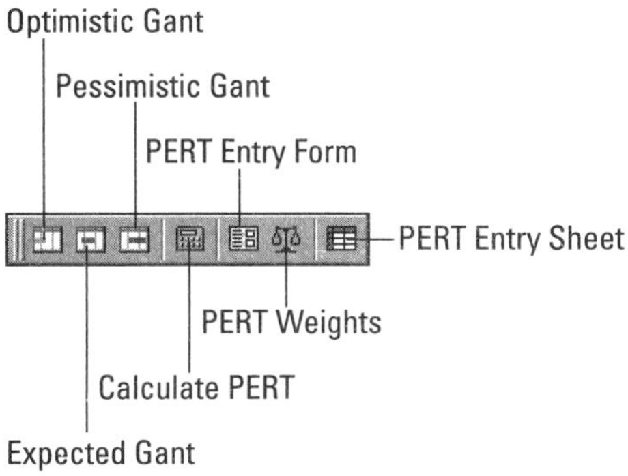

Figure 21-10: The PERT analysis toolbar.

Button	*What It Does*
Optimistic Gantt	Opens the PA_Optimistic Gantt view. Use this view to enter the best-case durations, start dates, and end dates of a project's tasks and to compare the difference between these estimates and expected and pessimistic estimates.
Expected Gantt	Opens the PA_Expected Gantt view. Use this view to enter expected durations, start dates, and end dates of a project's tasks and to compare the difference between these estimates and optimistic and pessimistic estimates.
Pessimistic Gantt	Opens the PA_Pessimistic Gantt view. Use this view to enter the worst-case durations, start dates, and end dates of a project's tasks and to compare the difference between these estimates and expected and optimistic estimates.
Calculate PERT	Runs the Calculate_PERT macro. The macro takes a weighted average of optimistic, expected, and pessimistic durations of tasks and computes their PERT durations.
PERT Entry Form	Opens a custom form that you can use to enter the optimistic, expected, and pessimistic duration of a task.
PERT Weights	Runs the Set_PERT_Weights macro, which displays a custom form that shows optimistic, expected, and pessimistic durations. A weighting factor has been entered by default for each scenario.
PERT Entry Sheet	Displays the PA_PERT Entry Sheet view. Use this sheet view to enter optimistic, expected, and pessimistic task durations.

Chapter 22

Ten Innovative Ways to Spruce Up Your Project

In This Chapter

- Breaking the mold
- Seeing the world of project management in different ways

The ten ideas in this chapter all center on you. They are assembled to help you discover new and better ways to accomplish your project-management tasks. When your responsibilities outweigh your skills and resources, you can feel very lonely. But you're not alone! A plethora of resources is available to help you with your job.

The Project Management Institute

The recent extraordinary growth of project management and the number of practitioners is due, in part, to the Project Management Institute (PMI). This nonprofit professional association provides a wealth of written materials and training opportunities. Within this organization, you can associate with fellow project managers and tap into a network of expertise in your community, industry, and special area of interest. Considering what you get by belonging, membership is cheap (about $100 per year).

You can contact PMI at Project Management Institute, 130 South State Road, Upper Darby, PA 19082. The telephone number is 610-734-3330. The fax number is 610-734-3266. Their Web site is at `www.pmi.org`.

Two of the most important resources available through PMI are the Project Management Body of Knowledge and the Project Management Professional certification, both of which I describe in this chapter.

Project Management Body of Knowledge

The basics of project management are universal. Over the years, professionals have synthesized project-management principles and practices into a standard, known as the Project Management Body of Knowledge. The 160-plus page document is available on the *Microsoft Project 98 For Dummies* CD-ROM. This document is one of the best freebies you'll ever find.

Project-Management Training

You can find a number of project-management training groups around the country. One first class group is the International Institute for Learning (IIL). The IIL provides programs around the country at convenient locations. All programs are cosponsored with a major university or college, and all attendees receive a certificate of completion from that institution. Some program modules are

- Project Scope Management
- Project Time Management
- Project Cost Management
- Project Human Resource Management
- Project Risk Management
- Project Quality Management
- Project Procurement Management
- Project Communications Management

As of this writing, the cost for the program is about $2,200. You receive a comprehensive understanding of project management and the background to prepare yourself for certification.

Master of Project Management Degree

Project-management degree programs are available at colleges and universities around the country. One that I can recommend is ITT Technical Institute's Master of Project Management (MPM) degree. The ITT objectives in the MPM program are to help students prepare for participation in project-management activities upon graduation; provide high quality graduate instruction to help students prepare for advancement and professional development in their chosen career; and foster critical thinking, communication, and teamwork. Designed for working adults, the 21-month, 56 credit-hour MPM program emphasizes the practical issues of project management in a team-oriented format.

You can contact ITT Technical Institute at 9511 Angola Court, Indianapolis, IN 46268. The telephone number is 800-937-4488. Ask to speak to Dr. Shuster. The Institute's Web site is at `www.fastweb.com`.

PMP Certification

Sooner or later, Project Management Professional (PMP) certification is a goal of all professional project managers. This may or may not be for you, but it's worth your investigation and consideration. Like other professions, such as law and accounting, project management is based on a recognized set of standards. The purpose of PMP certification is to provide recognition of your abilities as a project manager. The certification is based on a combination of testing and proven experience and service in the field of project management. To find out more about it, contact PMI. See the "Project Management Institute" section at the beginning of this chapter for contact information.

Group Involvement

For a stimulating and challenging experience, you can't beat one-on-one contact with people who share common interests. You can accomplish this in project management with a PMI shared-interest group or through involvement in a local PMI chapter. Project managers throughout the world attend monthly chapter meetings. These self-governing chapters are great for exchanging ideas and information. Check your telephone directory for a local project management society, or contact PMI at 610-734-3330 or at `www.pmi.org`.

Project-Management Newsgroups

A small number of project-management newsgroups are on the Web. One especially helpful newsgroup is the one you can access about Microsoft Project at `microsoft.com/msproject`. Select Support and then select Browse the Newsgroups.

Books and Periodicals

I don't mean to keep touting PMI, but the institute publishes an Information Source Guide that lists more than 100 books and periodicals about project management. The guide is on the *Microsoft Project 98 For Dummies* CD-ROM.

Web Search

If you have a few hours, do a Web search of project management. A large number of individuals and organizations offer services in project management. As is typical of such searches, a lot of your search will be marginal in value. However, some good sites are out there, too, such as `www.projectmanagement.com/main.htm`.

Microsoft Project

One of the least costly and most helpful study resources is the one you've been using — Microsoft Project. Microsoft Project's Help function is surprisingly helpful (ahem) in its organization and depth. One especially useful connection it offers is technical support.

At the time this book was written, Microsoft still offered limited free technical support. In the United States, no-charge support from Microsoft support engineers is available with a toll call between 6:00 a.m. and 6:00 p.m., Monday through Friday, except holidays. Call 206-635-7155. When you call, be sure to have your product ID number handy. You can find it by choosing Help⇨About Microsoft Project in the menu toolbar.

Part VIII

Appendixes

The 5th Wave
By Rich Tennant
WHY DOGS DON'T USE LAPTOPS
THERE HE GOES AGAIN. I'LL BET IF I LEANED AGAINST A TREE, I COULD DO IT.

In this part . . .

The first appendix in this part provides some basics about using data from other applications in Microsoft Project. The second appendix tells you about the contents of the *Microsoft Project 98 For Dummies* CD-ROM.

Appendix A

Working with Data from Other Applications

Microsoft Project accommodates the addition of text, spreadsheet information, graphic objects, sound, movies, and animation. Using applications resident in Windows 95 or using more elaborate applications, such as Adobe Photoshop or Premiere, you can customize your Project file to present product update discussions, customer interviews, project photos, or just about anything else you want. Microsoft Project can also send data to and receive data from databases.

Using the Clipboard

Using the clipboard to import objects may seem archaic at first, but it's actually slick. Microsoft Project uses the Windows copy-and-paste features to place data from other applications into a project.

Pasting text

You can create a list of items in a word processor and, through pasting, change the list to tasks in Microsoft Project. The value of this is somewhat questionable, but it's good to know if you've already created lists in another application, such as in a proposal.

To perform this function, open a word processor such as Microsoft Word. Create a list of items or use an existing list. Select the list and copy it to the word processor's clipboard. In Microsoft Project, select an empty task name cell, and then click the Paste button on the standard toolbar. The items in the list appear as tasks.

Pasting graphics or multimedia

You can also paste a graphic, a sound, or another kind of object. When you paste it, the object or a representation of the object appears in the Gantt chart. After it appears, you can drag the object to an appropriate spot.

Using the Paste Special command

You can take advantage of object linking and embedding (OLE) through the Paste Special command. After you've created and copied something to the clipboard — for example, text from your word processor — you can paste the clipboard contents into a project in two ways. You can designate that you want to be able to activate the text by using the word processor, or you can paste a picture of the text into your document.

To place text in the Gantt chart, for example, open a word processor such as Microsoft Word. Create text or use an existing text file. Select the text and copy it to the word processor's clipboard. In Microsoft Project, choose Edit⇨Paste Special. The Paste Special dialog box appears, providing choices for displaying the contents of the clipboard. As you select each choice, a Result message appears below the highlighted item. The Result description explains the way that selection would affect the clipboard object.

The object of the clipboard can be text, spreadsheet information, graphics, or multimedia objects. If you want, rather than displaying the object in the Gantt chart, you can choose Display as Icon. An icon appears that represents the originating application. When you place the icon in the Gantt chart, you can double-click the icon to display the object.

Inserting Objects

You can place objects in the Gantt chart not only with the clipboard but also by inserting them. To do this, choose Insert⇨Object. The Object dialog box appears. The Create New option permits you to select an application from a list and open it. After you have created the object, you return to Microsoft Project. The object is embedded in the Gantt chart. The Create from File option permits you to embed or link an existing object file. In either case, Create New or Create from File, you can display an application icon rather than the object itself.

Using Project with Databases

You can open database information into Microsoft Project or save a project file to a database format. To open a database file:

1. **Click the Open button on the standard toolbar.**

   The File Open dialog box appears.

2. **In the Files of Type list, select Microsoft Access Databases (*.mdb).**
3. **Double-click the file you want to open.**
4. **To import all the data in your project, select the Entire Project option, and then click the name of the project you want to open in the Name of the Project in the Database to Import box.**
5. **Click Open.**

To save a Microsoft Project file in a database file format:

1. **Click File⇨Save As.**
2. **In the Save as Type box, select Microsoft Access 8 Database (*mdb).**
3. **In the File Name box, type a name for the exported file.**
4. **Click Save.**

   The Export Format dialog box appears.

5. **To save all the data in your project, select the Entire Project option, and then type a name for the project in the Name to Give the Project in the Database box.**

   You can export particular fields to a database by clicking the Selective Data option and then selecting the import/export map to use for exporting.

6. **Click Save.**

   The file is saved in the Microsoft Access 8 Database format.

Appendix B
About the CD

Here's some of what you can find on the *Microsoft Project 98 For Dummies* CD-ROM:

- Sample project files for use in various chapters of the book
- Helpful resources from the Project Management Institute
- Trial version of Project KickStart to help you organize your project

System Requirements

Make sure that your computer meets the minimum system requirements listed here. If your computer doesn't match most of these requirements, you may have problems using the contents of the CD.

- A PC with a 486 or faster processor.
- Microsoft Windows 95 or later.
- At least 8MB of total RAM installed on your computer. For best performance, we recommend that Windows 95-equipped PCs have at least 16MB of RAM installed.
- At least 10MB of hard drive space available to install all the software from this CD. (You need less space if you don't install every program.)
- A CD-ROM drive — double-speed (2x) or faster.
- A monitor capable of displaying at least 256 colors or grayscale.

If you need more information on the basics, check out *PCs For Dummies,* 5th Edition, by Dan Gookin, or *Windows 95 For Dummies* by Andy Rathbone (both published by IDG Books Worldwide, Inc.).

Using the CD with Microsoft Windows 95

To use the CD, follow these steps:

1. **Insert the CD into your computer's CD-ROM drive.**

   Give your computer a moment to take a look at the CD.

2. **When the light on your CD-ROM drive goes out, double-click the My Computer icon. (It's probably in the top-left corner of your desktop.)**

   This action opens the My Computer window, which shows you all the drives attached to your computer, the Control Panel, and a few other handy things.

3. **Double-click the icon for your CD-ROM drive.**

   Another window opens, showing you all the folders and files on the CD.

4. **Double-click the file called License.txt.**

   This file contains the end-user license that you agree to by using the CD. When you finish reading the license agreement, close the program (most likely NotePad) that displayed the file.

5. **Double-click the file called Readme.txt.**

   This file contains instructions about installing the software from this CD. It may be helpful to leave this text file open while you are using the CD.

6. **Double-click the folder for the software you are interested in.**

   Be sure to read the descriptions of the programs in the next section of this appendix. (Much of this information shows up also in the Readme file.) These descriptions give you more precise information about the programs' folder names and about finding and running the installer program.

7. **Find the installation file (Setup.exe or Pkstrial.exe) and double-click that file.**

   The program's installer walks you through the process of setting up your new software.

What You'll Find

Here's a summary of the software on this CD:

- The CD contains a number of Microsoft Project files that you can use in association with chapters in this book. You'll find the files in the PROJECT folder. You can use these files from the CD; you don't need to copy them from the CD to your hard drive. The files are read-only on the CD, however, so you can't modify the files unless you save them to your computer.

If you have trouble accessing the files from the CD or would like to have them on your hard drive, I include a self-extractor to copy the files to your computer. Run the program PROJECT.EXE to move the files to C:\PROJECT on your computer. When you run PROJECT.EXE, a message box appears that tells you how much space is required by the practice files. Click OK in the message box, and the self-extractor window opens. Click the Unzip button to extract the files to the default directory, C:\PROJECT. If you want to extract the files to a different directory, just type the address you want in the Unzip to Folder text box before you click Unzip. When the files have finished extracting to your hard drive, click the Close button to shut down the self-extractor.

Smith Home Complete.MPP is a project file that approximates how your work will have progressed by the end of Chapters 5, 6, and 7.

Chapter 8.MPP is a project file that you use in Chapter 8 to discover the various Microsoft Project views.

Award Program 9.MPP is a sample file I reference in Chapter 9. You use the sample project file to find out how to tailor the Gantt chart for your own purposes.

Award.BMP is a graphic to add to the Award Program Gantt chart.

PERT Sample 10.MPP is a project file for practicing with the PERT chart.

Calendar 11.MPP is a project file you use in Chapter 11. With it, you find some of the innovative ways to use the Calendar view.

Chapter 12.MPP is a project file you use to explore the Resource view.

Chapter 13.MPP is a project file that helps you become familiar with filters.

Samples 1 through 3 Chapter 14.MPP project files show you how to work with multiple projects in Chapter 14.

Chapter 15.MPP is a project file that you use in Chapter 15 to set and view costs.

Chapter 16.MPP is a project file you use to practice finding overused resources and to try your hand at crashing a critical path.

Chapter 17.MPP is a project file to help you figure out how to track a project's progress.

Chapter 18.MPP is a project file you use in Chapter 18 to personalize your project environment.

Samples 1 and 2 Chapter 18.MPP project files are for discovering how to personalize your project's environment.

Chapter 19.MPP is a project file you use to practice with previewing and printing project views.

Chapter 20.MPP is a project file you use to find out more about Microsoft Project reports.

- Project Management Institute has provided an awesome program on the CD. This three-part program leads you step-by-step through the planning of even the most complex projects. The program also offers tools and suggestions for professional relationships that can increase your effectiveness as a project manager.

  To install the program, open the PMI folder on your CD. Double-click Setup.exe. The program adds files to your Windows/Systems folder and shortcuts to your Start menus that run the programs off the CD. Later, if you want, you can remove the program by using Add/Remove Programs in the Control Panel.

  Important: You must have the CD in your CD-ROM drive to run these programs.

- The CD also contains a trial version of Project KickStart, a program that greatly simplifies brainstorming projects as well as organizing them.

  To install Project KickStart, open the KICKSTRT folder on your CD. Double-click Pkstrial.exe. The install utility creates a folder and puts about 1.3MB of files on your hard drive. You can use the trial program for 20 days. To buy it, follow the instructions in the program. The Project KickStart program group includes an uninstall utility for removing the trial version.

If You Have Problems (Of the CD Kind)

I tried my best to compile programs that work on most computers with the minimum system requirements. Alas, your computer may differ, and some programs may not work properly for some reason.

The two likeliest problems are that you don't have enough memory (RAM) for the programs you want to use, or you have other programs running that are affecting installation or running of a program. If you get error messages such as `Not enough memory` or `Setup cannot continue`, try one or more of these methods and then try using the software again:

- **Turn off any anti-virus software you have on your computer.** Installers sometimes mimic virus activity and may make your computer incorrectly believe that it is being infected by a virus.
- **Close all running programs.** The more programs you're running, the less memory is available to other programs. Installers also typically update files and programs. So if you keep other programs running, installation may not work properly.
- **Have your local computer store add more RAM to your computer.** This is, admittedly, a drastic and somewhat expensive step. However, if you have a Windows 95 PC, adding more memory can really help the speed of your computer and allow more programs to run at the same time.

If you still have trouble with installing the items from the CD, please call the IDG Books Worldwide Customer Service phone number: 800-762-2974 (outside the U.S.: 317-596-5430).

Glossary

Accrual method: When the cost of a resource occurs. This may be at the start of a task, prorated during the task, or at the end of the task.

Actual: The facets of a task that have begun, including dates, cost, and work accomplished.

Base calendar: The primary calendar for a project.

Baseline: Also called the baseline plan or simply the plan. The final copy of all project aspects before the project start date. The baseline is used as a point of reference after the project begins.

Calendar: A list of the working time periods and nonworking time periods in a project.

Collapsed outline: The outline of tasks where all or part of the subtasks are hidden under summary tasks.

Combination view: A screen showing two views. The bottom view shows details of a highlighted feature in the upper view.

Consolidation: A combining of projects.

Constraint: A condition that limits the start or the finish of a task.

Critical path: A sequence of tasks that must finish on or ahead of schedule for a project to be completed on time.

Critical path method (CPM): A procedure for setting the start and finish dates of tasks to ensure an on-time completion of a project.

Date line: A dashed line running vertically in the Gantt chart to indicate the computer's system date or a current date set in Project⇨Project Information.

Demoting: To set a task as a subtask in a task outline structure.

Duration: The units of time of a task or group of tasks. Duration units are minutes, hours, days, and weeks.

Expanded outline: An outline view in which all subtasks are visible.

Field: A data entry point in a table.

Filter: A condition or group of conditions that acts as the basis for an information search in a project.

Fixed cost: A cost, such as a contract agreement, that remains the same independent of the duration or the number of resources used.

Fixed duration: A type of scheduling that sets a fixed length for a scheduling task. Numbers of resources have no effect on fixed duration tasks.

Gantt chart: A graphical depiction of a project. The length of Gantt bars in a Gantt chart represents duration. Lines between tasks represent task relationships.

Interactive filter: A filter that asks the user for information as the basis of a search of matching information in a project.

Lag time: A set length of time that is established between a task and its predecessor as the basis for the task to start.

Legend: Reference information on a chart explaining the relevance of graphic representations.

Leveling: A procedure of lengthening task durations to decrease demands on a resource or a group of resources.

Linked tasks: Tasks connected in some kind of relationship.

Master project: A project containing one or more subprojects.

Milestone: A task that indicates a beginning, a completion, or a significant event in a project. Milestones have a duration of 0d.

Node: The box in a PERT chart containing properties of a task.

Outline: A structured format in the Gantt Chart view containing higher-level summary tasks and lower-level subtasks.

Overallocation: The overassignment of tasks to a resource in a particular time period.

PERT chart: A network chart depicting relationships among tasks. Tasks appear as boxes, or nodes. Task relationships are illustrated by connecting lines.

Predecessor: A task that precedes another task.

Promote: In an outlined project, to move a subtask to a higher level. Promoting is performed by decreasing the indent (sometimes called *outdenting*).

Recurring task: A task that repeats at regular intervals throughout all or a portion of a project.

Report: A compilation of project information that you print.

Resource: A person or equipment that does work.

Resource calendar: A designation of working and nonworking days and hours for a specific resource or a group of resources.

Resource-driven task: A task whose duration is directly affected by the number of resources assigned to it.

Resource pool: A list of resources compiled so that they are available to all tasks.

Resource view: A view that shows resources instead of tasks.

Schedule: The current status of a plan.

Slippage: How much a task is behind its baseline start date, finish date, or both.

Subproject: A project file shown as a single task in another project file.

Subtask: A task indented under a summary task.

Successor: A task that follows another task.

Summary task: A task that comprises a summary of the duration, cost, and work of a group of subtasks.

Task: One of the planned activities of a project.

Task view: A view of a project based on task information.

Template: A Microsoft Project file format that enables you to use an existing schedule as the basis for making a new schedule.

Timescale: Units of time used to depict a project schedule. The timescale has levels of measurement — the major timescale and the minor timescale.

Variance: The difference between baseline data and current data.

View: Any one of a large number of possible presentations of project information.

Work breakdown structure (WBS): A hierarchical structure used to organize tasks for reporting schedules and tracking costs. With Microsoft Project, you can use the outline feature, use task IDs, or assign a WBS code to each task in the task detail form.

Workspace: A group of project files that can all be opened at one time. Workspace files are created by choosing File⇨Save Workspace.

Index

• C •

(continued)

• D •

(continued)

• E •

• F •

• G •

• H •

• I •

• K •

• L •

• M •

• N •

• O •

• P •

• Q •

• R •

• S •

• T •

• U •

• V •

• W •

IDG Books Worldwide, Inc., End-User License Agreement

READ THIS. You should carefully read these terms and conditions before opening the software packet(s) included with this book ("Book"). This is a license agreement ("Agreement") between you and IDG Books Worldwide, Inc. ("IDGB"). By opening the accompanying software packet(s), you acknowledge that you have read and accept the following terms and conditions. If you do not agree and do not want to be bound by such terms and conditions, promptly return the Book and the unopened software packet(s) to the place you obtained them for a full refund.

1. **License Grant.** IDGB grants to you (either an individual or entity) a nonexclusive license to use one copy of the enclosed software program(s) (collectively, the "Software") solely for your own personal or business purposes on a single computer (whether a standard computer or a workstation component of a multiuser network). The Software is in use on a computer when it is loaded into temporary memory (RAM) or installed into permanent memory (hard disk, CD-ROM, or other storage device). IDGB reserves all rights not expressly granted herein.

2. **Ownership.** IDGB is the owner of all right, title, and interest, including copyright, in and to the compilation of the Software recorded on the disk(s) or CD-ROM ("Software Media"). Copyright to the individual programs recorded on the Software Media is owned by the author or other authorized copyright owner of each program. Ownership of the Software and all proprietary rights relating thereto remain with IDGB and its licensers.

3. **Restrictions on Use and Transfer.**

   (a) You may only (i) make one copy of the Software for backup or archival purposes, or (ii) transfer the Software to a single hard disk, provided that you keep the original for backup or archival purposes. You may not (i) rent or lease the Software, (ii) copy or reproduce the Software through a LAN or other network system or through any computer subscriber system or bulletin-board system, or (iii) modify, adapt, or create derivative works based on the Software.

   (b) You may not reverse engineer, decompile, or disassemble the Software. You may transfer the Software and user documentation on a permanent basis, provided that the transferee agrees to accept the terms and conditions of this Agreement and you retain no copies. If the Software is an update or has been updated, any transfer must include the most recent update and all prior versions.

4. **Restrictions on Use of Individual Programs.** You must follow the individual requirements and restrictions detailed for each individual program in Appendix B of this Book. These limitations are also contained in the individual license agreements recorded on the Software Media. These limitations may include a requirement that after using the program for a specified period of time, the user must pay a registration fee or discontinue use. By opening the Software packet(s), you will be agreeing to abide by the licenses and restrictions for these individual programs that are detailed in Appendix B and on the Software Media. None of the material on this Software Media or listed in this Book may ever be redistributed, in original or modified form, for commercial purposes.

5. **Limited Warranty.**

   (a) IDGB warrants that the Software and Software Media are free from defects in materials and workmanship under normal use for a period of sixty (60) days from the date of purchase of this Book. If IDGB receives notification within the warranty period of defects in materials or workmanship, IDGB will replace the defective Software Media.

   (b) **IDGB AND THE AUTHOR OF THE BOOK DISCLAIM ALL OTHER WARRANTIES, EXPRESS OR IMPLIED, INCLUDING WITHOUT LIMITATION IMPLIED WARRANTIES OF MERCHANTABILITY AND FITNESS FOR A PARTICULAR PURPOSE, WITH RESPECT TO THE SOFTWARE, THE PROGRAMS, THE SOURCE CODE CONTAINED THEREIN, AND/OR THE TECHNIQUES DESCRIBED IN THIS BOOK. IDGB DOES NOT WARRANT THAT THE FUNCTIONS CONTAINED IN THE SOFTWARE WILL MEET YOUR REQUIREMENTS OR THAT THE OPERATION OF THE SOFTWARE WILL BE ERROR FREE.**

   (c) This limited warranty gives you specific legal rights, and you may have other rights that vary from jurisdiction to jurisdiction.

6. **Remedies.**

   (a) IDGB's entire liability and your exclusive remedy for defects in materials and workmanship shall be limited to replacement of the Software Media, which may be returned to IDGB with a copy of your receipt at the following address: Software Media Fulfillment Department, Attn.: *Microsoft Project 98 For Dummies,* IDG Books Worldwide, Inc., 7260 Shadeland Station, Ste. 100, Indianapolis, IN 46256, or call 800-762-2974. Please allow three to four weeks for delivery. This Limited Warranty is void if failure of the Software Media has resulted from accident, abuse, or misapplication. Any replacement Software Media will be warranted for the remainder of the original warranty period or thirty (30) days, whichever is longer.

   (b) In no event shall IDGB or the author be liable for any damages whatsoever (including without limitation damages for loss of business profits, business interruption, loss of business information, or any other pecuniary loss) arising from the use of or inability to use the Book or the Software, even if IDGB has been advised of the possibility of such damages.

   (c) Because some jurisdictions do not allow the exclusion or limitation of liability for consequential or incidental damages, the above limitation or exclusion may not apply to you.

7. **U.S. Government Restricted Rights.** Use, duplication, or disclosure of the Software by the U.S. Government is subject to restrictions stated in paragraph (c)(1)(ii) of the Rights in Technical Data and Computer Software clause of DFARS 252.227-7013, and in subparagraphs (a) through (d) of the Commercial Computer–Restricted Rights clause at FAR 52.227-19, and in similar clauses in the NASA FAR supplement, when applicable.

8. **General.** This Agreement constitutes the entire understanding of the parties and revokes and supersedes all prior agreements, oral or written, between them and may not be modified or amended except in a writing signed by both parties hereto that specifically refers to this Agreement. This Agreement shall take precedence over any other documents that may be in conflict herewith. If any one or more provisions contained in this Agreement are held by any court or tribunal to be invalid, illegal, or otherwise unenforceable, each and every other provision shall remain in full force and effect.

Installation Instructions

If you want to practice your skills in Microsoft Project without making your hands hurt, the sample files on the *Microsoft Project 98 For Dummies* CD-ROM are for you. (The CD has a few other goodies, too.) The project files on the CD are used throughout the book. Imagine mastering the ins and outs of project management without all the keystroking agony of building projects!

To install the project files or the other offerings on the CD, follow these steps:

1. **Insert the CD into your computer's CD-ROM drive.**

   Give your computer a moment to take a look at the CD.

2. **When the light on your CD-ROM drive goes out, double-click the My Computer icon. (It's probably in the top-left corner of your desktop.)**

   This action opens the My Computer window, which shows you all the drives attached to your computer, the Control Panel, and a few other handy things.

3. **Double-click the icon for your CD-ROM drive.**

   Another window opens, showing you all the folders and files on the CD.

4. **Double-click the file called License.txt.**

   This file contains the end-user license that you agree to by using the CD. When you finish reading the license agreement, close the program (most likely NotePad) that displayed the file.

5. **Double-click the file called Readme.txt.**

   This file contains instructions about installing the software from this CD. It may be helpful to leave this text file open while you are using the CD.

6. **Double-click the folder for the software you are interested in.**

   Be sure to read the descriptions of the programs in Appendix B. (Much of this information shows up also in the Readme file.) These descriptions give you more precise information about the programs' folder names and about finding and running the installer program.

7. **Find the installation file (Setup.exe or Pkstrial.exe), and double-click that file.**

   The program's installer walks you through the process of setting up your new software.

WARNING!

To run the program in the PMI folder, you need to keep the CD inside your CD-ROM drive. This is a Good Thing. Otherwise, the installed program would have required you to install a very large chunk of the program to your hard drive space, which would have kept you from installing other software.

Discover Dummies Online!

The Dummies Web Site is your fun and friendly online resource for the latest information about *...For Dummies®* books and your favorite topics. The Web site is the place to communicate with us, exchange ideas with other *...For Dummies* readers, chat with authors, and have fun!

Ten Fun and Useful Things You Can Do at www.dummies.com

1. Win free *...For Dummies* books and more!
2. Register your book and be entered in a prize drawing.
3. Meet your favorite authors through the IDG Books Author Chat Series.
4. Exchange helpful information with other *...For Dummies* readers.
5. Discover other great *...For Dummies* books you must have!
6. Purchase Dummieswear™ exclusively from our Web site.
7. Buy *...For Dummies* books online.
8. Talk to us. Make comments, ask questions, get answers!
9. Download free software.
10. Find additional useful resources from authors.

Link directly to these ten fun and useful things at **http://www.dummies.com/10useful**

For other technology titles from IDG Books Worldwide, go to **www.idgbooks.com**

Not on the Web yet? It's easy to get started with *Dummies 101®: The Internet For Windows®95* or *The Internet For Dummies®*, 4th Edition, at local retailers everywhere.

IDG BOOKS WORLDWIDE

Find other *...For Dummies* books on these topics:
Business • Career • Databases • Food & Beverage • Games • Gardening • Graphics • Hardware
Health & Fitness • Internet and the World Wide Web • Networking • Office Suites
Operating Systems • Personal Finance • Pets • Programming • Recreation • Sports
Spreadsheets • Teacher Resources • Test Prep • Word Processing

IDG BOOKS WORLDWIDE BOOK REGISTRATION

Register This Book and Win!

We want to hear from you!

Visit **http://my2cents.dummies.com** to register this book and tell us how you liked it!

- Get entered in our monthly prize giveaway.
- Give us feedback about this book — tell us what you like best, what you like least, or maybe what you'd like to ask the author and us to change!
- Let us know any other *...For Dummies*® topics that interest you.

Your feedback helps us determine what books to publish, tells us what coverage to add as we revise our books, and lets us know whether we're meeting your needs as a *...For Dummies* reader. You're our most valuable resource, and what you have to say is important to us!

Not on the Web yet? It's easy to get started with *Dummies 101*®*: The Internet For Windows*® *95* or *The Internet For Dummies*®, 4th Edition, at local retailers everywhere.

Or let us know what you think by sending us a letter at the following address:

...For Dummies Book Registration
Dummies Press
7260 Shadeland Station, Suite 100
Indianapolis, IN 46256-3945
Fax 317-596-5498

...FOR DUMMIES™ BUSINESS AND GENERAL REFERENCE BOOK SERIES FROM IDG

...FOR DUMMIES® COMPUTER BOOK SERIES FROM IDG